THE
WEST-GOING HEART
A Life of Vachel Lindsay

Books by Eleanor Ruggles

GERARD MANLEY HOPKINS
A Life

JOURNEY INTO FAITH
The Anglican Life of John Henry Newman

PRINCE OF PLAYERS
Edwin Booth

THE WEST-GOING HEART
A Life of Vachel Lindsay

ELEANOR RUGGLES

THE
WEST-GOING HEART
A Life of Vachel Lindsay

W·W·NORTON & COMPANY·INC·New York

PS
.35²³
.I⁵⁸
Z 7 6

Library of Congress Catalog Card No. 59-11337

TO THE MEMORY OF

OLIVE LINDSAY WAKEFIELD
AND OF
ELIZABETH CONNER LINDSAY

Contents

Illustrations

Between pages 240 and 241

Foreword

"One of our few great poets, a power and a glory in the land," Sinclair Lewis unhesitatingly called Vachel Lindsay after his death.

Time alone can tell what rank future generations will give to Lindsay's highly original poems, but besides his poetry he has left behind him the haunting memory and dramatic picture of a troubadour who in his youth walked the prairies of the Midwest, later the recital platforms of the nation. Whether or not his poems endure, his chanting of them was electrifying and at the time nearly unprecedented; his forceful presence before vast audiences in every state in America was unforgettable. Yet always under the platform flamboyance dwelt a man not known to the public, a dreamer of dreams and wanderer, brother in spirit to Johnny Appleseed.

Perhaps Lindsay is destined to live longest not in his poems but in the legend already forming around him as an American figure—one larger than life, with something of the rollicking western humor of Mark Twain, the gallantry of Poe, the democratic warmth of Whitman—and around his career, its early romantic vagabondage and stark ending.

Till now there has been little revealed of the illness with which he contended in his last years, but the knowledge of it cannot diminish him. Against heavy odds, he fought courageously to the end to preserve a faith in men and in himself that was essentially noble, and in his struggle will lie a part of his fame.

PART ONE

DOCTOR LINDSAY
HAS A SON

1

"My fathers," Vachel Lindsay wrote, "came from Kentucky."

> ... my great-grandfathers came
> To the west with Daniel Boone,
> And taught his babes to read,
> And heard the redbird's tune;
>
> And heard the turkey's call,
> And stilled the panther's cry,
> And rolled on the blue-grass hills,
> And looked God in the eye.

Vachel Lindsay's paternal grandfather, Nicholas Lindsay, was born in Franklin County, Kentucky, and he married Martha Ann Cave of Gallatin County in the same state.

They were married in 1842, the bride of sixteen being less than half the age of her stalwart, dominating husband, who at nearly forty was a fine-looking man. "He stood erect," his daughter Eudora told his descendants. "He never slumped down, even in his eighty-seventh year."

Martha, reportedly descended from Pocahontas, was a very loving, womanly little girl. It was her deep-abiding female and maternal qualities that had drawn her bachelor husband to her; when he first saw her she had been cosseting her corncob doll.

Nicholas' forebears were Scotsmen; to their clan belonged that fiery bard described by Scott in *Marmion*, Sir David Lindsay of the Mount. Nicholas' father, who bore the curious first name of Vachel—a name persisting in the Lindsay family—had been by trade a carpenter and in religion a Baptist of the severely Calvinistic brand sometimes called "Hardshell." Nicholas, however, though he regularly attended the Baptist Church never united with it, having been brought up in the old Baptist doctrine that the Lord in His own good time would direct him.

"He believed in God," his daughter remembered, "and in praying to Him for guidance when human wisdom seemed inadequate."

His wife, Martha, was a member of the Disciples of Christ (also known as Christians or, colloquially, Campbellites), a liberal sect initiated in America by Alexander Campbell, who early in the 1800's departed from the Baptists. "We are not the only Christians," goes the Disciples' soft answer to a perennial gibe about their name, "but we are Christians only."

Like his father, Nicholas Lindsay had been trained as a carpenter, but he had become a merchant, then after the birth of his children turned to farming. He and Martha moved from their log house to a plantation and there acquired plentiful livestock and Negro slaves. These went with the Civil War. Nicholas' fierce allegiance had been to the South, and the federal government confiscated his stock and freed his Negroes.

Yet it was his compulsive generosity, more than any other cause, that broke him financially. Equally stiff-necked and open-handed, he went security over and over for neighbors who afterward failed to pay up. There were several sons at home and they, says Eudora, "were provoked at Father."

The end of the War saw the once prosperous farmer in poverty. But the will to survive that had pushed the pioneers west over the Alleghenies still burned in him with a lively flame. Old and grown blind, yet still an erect and formidable figure of a man, he tapped his way about his neglected farmhouse with his gold-headed cane, shouting: "This needs mending! Why doesn't somebody do it?"

He could not realize there was no one left to do it, and yet at times he did realize the change, and then he imperiously exhorted his eldest son, who wished to become a doctor, to *be* a doctor, not to let himself be downed by the late disaster.

It was this son, Vachel Thomas Lindsay, born on August 31, 1843, who by the sweat of his brow helped to educate five brothers and two sisters. He taught school one winter and at other times he toiled on a neighbor's farm, digging potatoes for fifty cents a day. With part of his earnings he educated himself as well, buying the books he needed for his chosen profession and poring over them by firelight as Abraham Lincoln had done. At intervals he knocked at the door of a physician in the neighborhood who kindly heard him recite what he had learned.

Finally he had enough saved to put himself through a single term at Miami Medical College in Cincinnati. When the term was ended he journeyed home, and he and his preceptor laid their heads together over the lecture notes he had taken.

"You're better prepared for practice now than several doctors we have around here," said this good physician. "Go out and practice for a year or two, then go back to college and graduate."

Young Lindsay went north into Illinois. In Sangamon County, the county of Lincoln, he hung out his shingle at a crossroads in Cotton Hill township, about ten miles southeast of Springfield. There were three other country physicians, much older than he, already practicing in and around Cotton Hill. Lindsay, at twenty-three, resolved to battle it out with them and by the end of his second year two of his competitors had fled the field. Then "Doctor" Lindsay returned to Cincinnati and finished his medical course, this time taking his degree.

Back in Cotton Hill he built himself a modest house and made a little garden around it. He was twenty-seven and a successful man when in June 1871 he visited again the blue-grass state where he had been born to marry his long-time sweetheart, who had been his schoolmate.

To his grief, consternation and complete surprise he found

her far gone in tuberculosis and her mind failing. This did
not change his plans; on the contrary. "I hoped," as he afterward explained, "I might be able to help her and decided to
marry her at once, that I might the better care for her."

Dr. Lindsay brought his dark pretty bride, whose name was
Olive, home with him to Illinois. He was at work in his
garden one day while she sat watching, being too ill to keep
house, when he heard her piteously cry out, suddenly clear-
sighted in the midst of her distraction: "What will become of
you? I'm going to lose my mind!" He ran to her and tried to
soothe her, telling her that they would move immediately to
the boarding house out of the cruel sun, and that she would
soon be better.

But she grew rapidly far worse, and after consulting the
best physicians available Lindsay took his young wife, whose
chief fear in her mania was that he would abandon her, to
the asylum in Lexington, Kentucky. The moment when he
walked out and left her alone in such a place was the severest
trial he experienced in life, then or ever.

For a week he lingered desperately in Lexington, though
not allowed to see his wife. At the week's end, when he learned
she had refused to eat or swallow medicine since entering the
asylum, he carried her away over the alarmed protests of the
superintendent. "The look she gave me when I told her I had
come to take her home was sufficient reward for all I had
done for her up to this time."

At her father's Kentucky house, where she had lived till
her marriage, the sick girl seemed at first to recover as her
devoted husband fed her and gave her her medicine with his
own hands; but after three weeks the end came, two and a
half months after their wedding. Dr. Lindsay left Kentucky,
returned to his desolate cottage and neglected garden and resumed his work of healing among the townsfolk and farmers
of Cotton Hill.

Here he continued for four years. He had his dream, however, which had become the stronger for his wife's being taken
from him. On the Illinois prairie the hard-driven, taciturn
young doctor dreamed of the great hospitals and teachers of

Vienna. He longed for the chance of further study, and with this aim he hoarded every dollar fee paid him by the ailing farmers till in 1875 he was able to make the trip to Europe. He did not go alone, though, but in the congenial company of two young women, his younger sister Eudora and her friend the sprightly fair-haired Kate Frazee of Rush County, Indiana.

It was the end of his youth.

"For nine years—" wrote Vachel Lindsay of his father,

> For nine years near Cotton Hill
> My father practiced medicine.

The son was not writing a poem to be published. Simply, one day as he sat waiting to be served in a hotel dining room far from Illinois, far removed also from his own youth, certain lines occurred to him and he scrawled them on the back of a menu:

> For nine years near Cotton Hill
> My father practiced medicine.
> The Sangamon County farmers came
> With all the diseases known to kill.
> He gave each ill its shortest name . . .
>
> He did not put on style with them.
> I want to go and live near them,
> And see if they remember him,
> Or if his records have grown dim . . .
>
> What will they tell me of his ways,
> His passionate doctor bachelor days
> For nine years on Cotton Hill
> Fighting diseases known to kill?

When Vachel Lindsay's grandfather on his mother's side, the Reverend Ephraim Samuel Frazee, heard the news of General Lee's surrender at Appomattox, such was his holy glee that he stood for three hours before his Indiana farmhouse and rang the dinner bell with which he called his hands from the fields.

Between Ephraim Samuel Frazee and Nicholas Lindsay, the two grandfathers of Vachel Lindsay, lay the gulf dividing North from South. The War emphasized but did not create the division, for it was the difference between two ways of life.

Frazee had been born in Mayslick, Kentucky. The Frazees like the Lindsays were of Scotch and English ancestry, but in the veins of Ephraim Samuel ran an exotic current. His father, Ephraim Frazee, a physician of Mason County, Kentucky, had married Susan Doniphan, descended through five generations from the Spaniard Don Alphonse Iphan; and the name Doniphan, so prosaic as one word, so romantic when separated into two, became an heirloom to future Frazees, the reminder of a cavalier strain in their blood.

Susan Doniphan Frazee, being soon left a widow, for some years ran a little store in Germantown, Kentucky. She and her son Ephraim Samuel jointly inherited from Dr. Frazee a good-sized farm in Rush County, Indiana, to which in time they moved, crossing the Ohio River from Kentucky into Indiana, from the South to the North.

At Bethany College in Virginia, founded by Alexander Campbell and a stronghold of the Disciples or Christian Church, Ephraim Samuel Frazee, a well-built youth with bright keen eyes and craggy features, studied the Bible under President Campbell himself. In 1846 he married Frances Austen, daughter of Deacon Austen of Laurel, Indiana, whose family claimed kinship with that of the great Jane Austen, novelist.

"The proud farmer," Vachel Lindsay called his grandfather Frazee, who poured his strength and plowed his name into the acres of the new state of Indiana. He was a minister on the Lord's Day, a farmer every other day. He preached the gospel and bred short-horn cattle. He was a leader in local politics; he read the classics and also Mark Twain. He was nervous, industrious, full of enterprise, and as dominating over his household as that Kentucky grandfather who tapped with his elegant cane through the rooms of his decaying farmhouse.

On the Indiana farm the stock won prizes. There were screens for the windows, a machine to do the washing, a clothes wringer, a buggy and the latest patent harvesters. The house was of gingerbread style, with neat painted blinds, and the yard was laid out in paths and trimmed with evergreens.

Esther Catharine Frazee, eldest child of Ephraim Samuel and his wife, Frances, was born on February 20, 1848.

Catharine was twelve when on a July day at the farm in Rush County, as she was steadily picking blackberries under the midsummer sun of the prairie, she had a sunstroke that injured her sight and from which her nerves never fully recovered.

For months she was unable to use her eyes. She learned her school lessons by hearing her sisters read them to her. There were a dozen children on the farm and almost no domestic help. Time was valuable; each lesson was read through once only.

Between them, the mother and Catharine did most of the housework. Visiting kinsfolk streamed in and out, and mother and daughter often labored till near midnight ironing some two dozen men's pleated linen shirts. Frances Frazee also helped her husband with the scholarly research for his sermons, having an acute and vigorous mind, which her daughter inherited. In 1869 Catharine graduated from Glendale Female College in Ohio, graduated with the highest honors and as the class valedictorian. From the beginning to the end of her college course her marks were—perfect.

"Wish I had a girl like my Ma when she was young," wrote Vachel Lindsay. "A real lady, a brilliant intellect, but raised on a farm, and a real American."

After graduating, Catharine taught mathematics at Glendale. Later she went to Hocker College—now a part of the University of Kentucky—where she became assistant to the president. At both places she had studied painting, and at Hocker she began to teach it. She had, as her son after her, both the will to learn and the longing to communicate. She studied and she taught and she saved her money (this last an instinct not passed on to her son) till by June 1875 she had saved enough to travel abroad. So had her chum, a student and substitute teacher at Hocker, Eudora Lindsay.

Eudora's brother Dr. Lindsay had been planning to make *his* trip the next year. But he was well enough fixed so that he could advance the date by twelve months and go when the girls did.

"I found much—" writes Dr. Lindsay, reminiscing in old age about this epochal and delightful interlude, "I found much that was to be admired in my sister's friend, Miss Kate."

On shipboard he was still wearing crepe on his hat for his girl-wife, dead four years. Kate Frazee, the schoolteacher of twenty-seven, remonstrated with him. Her manner was vivacious and decided. He should remove that crepe, she said. He should be sad no longer. He had a lot to live for.

In Dresden they became engaged. They parted in Prague, for Dr. Lindsay was to spend the winter in Vienna. He rejoined the girls in Italy in the spring and all three went on together to Paris, where the doctor visited the hospitals and thoughtfully observed the brilliant if stagy technique of the French surgeons.

Kate had her trousseau made at the Bon Marché, and in London, whither they traveled next, Dr. Lindsay had the English tailors do for him what the Paris dressmakers had done for his intended. Of more significance to this pair than their trousseaux was their visit to the London Tabernacle where side by side they heard the great Baptist preacher Spurgeon and his stunning chorus of five thousand voices.

They had been gone a year; they had had their year. They sailed for home.

In July 1876, Dr. Lindsay again opened his office for practice, this time, however, in the thriving little city of Springfield, Illinois, chosen as state capital in 1837. On November 30, which was Thanksgiving Day, a snowy one, he and Esther Catharine Frazee were married at the Indiana farm—a far remove from the Coliseum and the Place de la Concorde—in a country parlor decorated with pine cones and bittersweet. The knot was tied by Dr. Burgess, the president of Butler College in Indianapolis, a Christian institution.

So the father and the mother of the poet were brought together.

"They are an amazing two, I will confess," said their son. "Pen cannot utter their dubious and interesting mixture of qualities. . . . They are my parents all right, all right."

2

In a rented cottage in Springfield on the corner of Ninth and Edwards Streets the Lindsays' first child was born, a little girl.

"Why, she looks like Ollie!" Dr. Lindsay cried involuntarily, his thoughts flying back to his first wife.

His second wife, Catharine, looked up at him and said: "Her name is Olive. I hope she will be a comfort to you."

By the birth of their second child, the Lindsays had moved west to the corner of South Fifth at Edwards, number 603. The frame house Dr. Lindsay bought on this location was designed by the architect who designed the Lincoln house and who considered this one the better of the two. It had been the property of Mrs. Clark M. Smith, the sister of Mary Todd Lincoln. Mrs. Smith paid several calls on Mrs. Lindsay to whom she related how she had many a time entertained Mr. Lincoln and Mary in the very parlor where they were sitting.

It was in the downstairs bedroom across the hall from the parlor—a bedroom where, says legend, Lincoln slept one night —that Nicholas Vachel Lindsay was born on November 10, 1879. The Illinois *State Journal*, Springfield's morning paper, noticed the birth. "Dr. Vachel Thomas Lindsay now has a son to help him in his profession. The young Nicholas Vachel arrived last night."

Nicholas Vachel later dropped the Nicholas, explaining that his middle name, by which he was always called at home, rhymed neither with satchel nor with hash-hell but was "just the same as Rachel, with V for R." There is a tradition in the Lindsay family that before the Revolution twins were born of

24

whom the boy was called Vachel to go with the girl's name
of Rachel, according to the custom of giving twins like-sound-
ing names.

After Vachel were born three daughters, Isabel, Esther, and
the baby Eudora—named for her aunt—who was still a baby
when all three little girls died within three weeks of one another of malignant scarlet fever epidemic in the city. The
whole of Springfield, even those who did not know the family,
heard of the deaths.

"I thought I should go mad," said Mrs. Lindsay to one of
her son's friends, many years afterward.

Olive and Vachel were twelve and ten respectively when a
sixth and last child was born, another daughter whom in their
uplifting of spirits the parents named Joy.

Vachel Lindsay has described his birth. Not the stork, but
the "sea-mustang"—a fabulous creature, half horse, half fish,
and driven by sea gods—delivered him to his family.

In through the window a sea-mustang brought me,
(Smashing the window sash, breaking the law).
I was tied to his back—I do not know who caught me.

Up from Biloxi, up the great Mississippi,
Through the swamps, through the thaw, through the rains that
    grew raw,
On the tenth of November (the hail storm was nippy).
Up the slow, muddy Sangamon River—
(While we heard the towns cough and we heard the farms shiver),
The high wave rolled on.

Over the raised ground of Oak Ridge Cemetery north of
Springfield, where Lincoln slumbered under his obelisk, down
through lesser streets to the straight mall of Fifth, the green
wave rolled. The mustang and the child rode its swollen crest.

We sighted and broke the high hedge of Oak Ridge,
We rolled through its tombs . . .

Swept townward: a green wave, a foam wave, a moon wave,
Up the dawn streets of Springfield . . .
Up to Edwards and Fifth street, and broke every window pane . . .
We smashed the front door. We ramped by the bed's head.
On the wall-paper pattern sea-roses bloomed red.

The baby thus by his own later account deposited into his
mother's arms was thin and preternaturally old and wise looking, and he was born with a caul, which is considered lucky.

Between four and six months he came down with "milk
poisoning," ascribed to the fact that his mother continued to
nurse him before she realized she had become pregnant again.
He was dangerously ill and for more than a year afterward
she carried him about with her on a pillow—an episode that
did something to set their relation to each other. Vachel was
in his junior year at college when he wrote home protesting
that his mother too often talked to him as if he were a "premature brilliant inspired baby."

"I never want the time to come," Mrs. Lindsay answered
her twenty-year-old son, "when I cannot associate you in my
mind with the baby I carried on a pillow and watched as his
life flickered for months."

While Olive was dark like the Lindsays, Vachel was blond
like the Frazees. He was four when, with his mother and sister
(his father stayed home), he visited in Kentucky with Grandfather Lindsay, who, stone blind and as imperious as ever, ran
his hands over Vachel's head and cried: "What does this boy
have curls for? He's four years old. Too old for curls!"

Mrs. Lindsay retired with Vachel into another room and cut
his curls off. Then she and Ollie burst into tears, but Vachel,
pleased and proud, scurried back to show his grandfather, who
said: "That's better. Boys don't have curls! Only girls have
curls."

The mother, meanwhile, selected one lock from the treasure
that lay on the floor, wrapped it tenderly in tissue paper and
labeled it "The Golden Fleece." This she preserved.

At the farm in Indiana where Vachel and Ollie visited in

summer they heard their Grandfather Frazee called respect-
fully "Brother Frazee" by his Campbellite friends. Every
Sunday they trotted after him as, wearing a stovepipe hat, a
black string tie, and with a Bible under each arm, he led the
procession to the church in Fayetteville where he regularly
preached without pay. On the way home from church a
strange old Irishwoman often walked with them. She talked so
queerly she terrified Olive, but the dandelion-headed Vachel
jabbered at her gaily till she turned off at her cottage.

He was far from shy, an affectionate and excitable little
boy who at home in Springfield raced up and down Fifth
Street wearing his Indian suit, his big kite tugging at his arm.
When their parents were away he and Ollie played their favorite game with Lucy the cook, a tall, powerful and very black
woman. With her kinky hair streaming and stuck through
with feathers, she would lead the children in single file around
and around the outside of the house, while all three chanted in
an atavistic transport: "Injun chief! Injun chief! Injun chief!"

An old kitchen stove stood on the Lindsays' front lawn and
out of the four stove holes sprang scarlet geraniums. Those
who knew the Lindsays accepted the ornament; those who
didn't know them exclaimed over it. It was unusual.

North of the house, just on the other side of narrow Edwards Street, was the Governor's Mansion, like a large white
wedding cake set far back inside its shady grounds. In contrast to the mansion's luxury and grace were the plain, wooden-
spired Congregational Church across the street from the Lindsays' front porch and the Negro tenement on the northeast
corner; Negroes formed a fifth of Springfield's population.

Within easy view from the porch of 603 were numerous
vacant lots, muddy, weedy and heaped with rubbish. But
these fell away as Olive and Vachel sat outside with their
mother and in the hot summer Sunday afternoons heard her
read aloud of Zeus and Artemis in the land of temples, groves
and mountain tops, and of the northern gods as well, Odin the
Wanderer and Thor, the god of thunder.

By her side was a little red tin box containing peanuts and striped peppermint and lemon stick candy. Brunette Olive and blond Vachel crunched and sucked, and spread the wings of their imaginations, and the midwest town grew small on the prairie beneath them.

That was on Sunday afternoons. In the mornings at the First Christian Church, of which their father was an elder, they had stood solemnly with the others in the infants' Sunday School class.

"What do you want to sing, children?" asked their young teacher.

" 'Bringing in the Sheaves.' "

When the sheaves had been brought in—"Now, children, who made you?"

"God!"

"Who was the first man?"

"Adam."

"Who was the first woman?"

"Eve."

The two little Lindsays did honor to the constant coaching of their mother, who a few doors away in the same building was clearly, learnedly and very positively teaching the adult Bible Class. One of Mrs. Lindsay's favorite verses was, "Be ye doers of the word and not hearers only."

When she was an instructor at Hocker, Kate Frazee had written and staged two miracle plays, and now as a doctor's wife in Springfield she produced these plays again during Vachel's childhood, produced them in the church itself. How she got away with this in the midst of Campbellite austerity is a marvel, even though she called her flamboyant productions by the dignified name of "colloquies," to take off the curse of staginess.

Six-year-old Vachel acted a part in one, which was about Mount Olympus. The characters, all pagan gods, ascended individually into the pulpit, where each spoke his piece. Good-looking Uncle Johnson Lindsay, being tall and having a red beard, was draped in seaweed to impersonate Neptune. Bacchus was none other than the Sunday School superintendent, over whom the authoress must have cast a spell for he clambered into the pulpit wreathed in grapes and ha-ha-ing like a proper bacchant (the church elders had something to say about him afterward). To play Venus Mrs. Lindsay selected her children's Sunday School teacher, who clasped a golden apple in one hand while to her other hand clung Vachel as Cupid.

His mother had let his curls grow again and had done them up in paper overnight. She had dressed him in a pink silk slip, to the back of which she had sewn dove's wings. Carrying a homemade bow of silver pasteboard, with a silver quiver on his shoulder filled with silver arrows, Vachel climbed up into the pulpit unabashed.

"My mother," he writes, "was a riot in those days."

He was nine when he left his mother's side long enough to travel to Colorado with his father for a visit to widowed Grandmother Lindsay, who had moved to Trinidad. With his face against the glass of the Pullman window, he watched the cavalcade of "Pike's Peak or Bust" wagons, ragged examples of the prairie schooner, which were headed for the sunset, and he looked eagerly for those that would bust, so many seemed just ready to do so.

He kept a diary, the first of many road diaries, all through this masculine adventure.

"Had fun in depot," says an early entry. "Family there that thought they were aristocratic. were very interesting acted like a couple of toads trying to be peacocks. the mother was dressed in cut glass. very interesting family indeed. their little girl about 17 was dressed in a dress of black up to her kneese fastened together with pins."

At Pueblo the broad dark doctor and his small fair-haired son visited the largest of the smelters, but as Vachel's diary records: "I was sick most of the time, and so did not interest myself very much." Again at Colorado Springs, where they missed the train and had to tramp a mile through the rain to a hotel, "Don't feel very well," the diary confides.

Much later with Olive—they were thirteen and fifteen—Vachel went from Springfield to Chicago for a day's jaunt at the World's Fair.

"I came to Chicago and was sick at stummick all day," runs his diary for this brief trip of pleasure.

Every Saturday morning after their sisters' deaths Vachel and Olive got down baskets and jars from the shelf, picked the flowers that grew around the house and lovingly arranged them. When their father came home to noon dinner he changed horses before starting out again, took the frisky Tom for his doctor's buggy and hitched steady Charlie to the carriage for his wife and children, who then drove north to Oak Ridge.

There in the Lindsay family lot, not far from Lincoln's mausoleum, was a grave made like a pretty bed, having a marble headstone with three curves to divide the names: ISABEL, ESTHER, and, in the middle, EUDORA. The mother sprinkled with a watering can, which she kept hidden behind a rosebush, the green glossy myrtle that already partly covered her children's bed and the white flowers that formed a border around it. Under her instructions Vachel and Ollie did the decorating. They still clearly remembered their sisters, and for Isabel's basket they had thoughtfully chosen blue ageratum and deep purple pansies; there were yellow calendulas for Esther, whose eyes were brown, and a bright nosegay of everything for baby Eudora.

They were very close, Vachel and Ollie, for the new baby, Joy, was so much younger as to be scarcely a contemporary. At home Vachel used to chase his big sister upstairs and down till he could catch and fling his arms around her and kiss her. But she was not the only sweet captive. A little girl friend, he told his father, had threatened to knock his nose off if he kissed her again.

"Then what will you do?" asked Dr. Lindsay.

"I guess the nose will have to go," said Vachel.

3

When he was just turned thirty-five Vachel Lindsay wrote: "I get the credit of all I ever do from my mother. The Lindsays class me as a Frazee through and through. But they are wrong."

His father, he goes on, was within his own province more of an original than his mother—Lindsay was writing while his parents still were living.

"Papa is an absolutely unconquered Ishmaelite, in his determination to do everything his own way to the last ditch. A man with a most restless energy, great self-denial—absolutely preoccupied with his family and his work, though he goes at his hard work with a great deal of fidget and slambing. 'Get it through with' is his one thought—be it visiting Nuremberg—or driving out at midnight to the sick, over a frozen road. He would much prefer to kick the barn-door open rather than push it."

Lindsay expressed himself again about his father after his father's death and when he was near the end of his own life. He was broken and ill; his inflamed imagination now brought his parent back before him as a fierce somber figure against the lurid sky of childhood, as one who had shown in the bosom of the family a "queer baffling savage streak."

"It is the thing that gave my father diabolical delight in driving at three o'clock in the morning five or twenty-five miles into the country in a pitch-black driving rain on a muddy road (the old Illinois kind) furiously whipping the frantic horse straight into the thunder and lightning."

This might be to assist into the world the grandchild of

31

some Cotton Hill farmer who had been kind to the doctor when he was young. Or the man of a family might be far gone in fearful alcoholism; without laying a hand on him, the doctor would give him such a tongue-lashing as to shame him sober on the spot. Or a dying man or woman might lie stretched out and unconscious of the entrance of the black-bearded doctor, who would lean over the bed, raise the deep emotional voice with which he chanted spirituals to his children, put forth his will and virtually summon the moribund one back to life.

Then, says his son, he would hasten home, "caked with mud, with a smashed buggy and a harness he would mend with a flat-iron and copper rivets in the interval right after family prayers among the hymn books in the sitting room—gnashing his teeth till the harness was mended."

Reluctant Vachel would be called out to help tie the broken buggy onto the spare buggy, after which the doctor "would hitch up the other horse and drive to the buggy-shop, leaving the broken one; still gnashing his teeth!"

The doctor's patients, plain folk mostly, adored him for his healing exploits. "But he could not do these things," his son declares, "without gnashing his teeth like Ashurbanipal or somebody."

Yet the doctor's fellow physicians and friends in Springfield would have read this account with surprise, for they saw Dr. Lindsay as a quite ordinary citizen, sturdy but not tall, kindly if not genial, very unassertive and self-effacing in general company, hard-working and good as gold. The masterfulness that a crisis brought out in him, his moodiness and the craving for love that only his family knew, were kept at most times below the surface.

"He was a country doctor," says Arthur Fitzgerald, a schoolmate of Vachel's. "Dr. Lindsay was not above the average, or at least not so far as his wife. But he was a fine man."

"He was a regular old country doctor," adds another family friend. "He did not have the 'best people' in his practice, though my mother did call him for us. His hands were always dirty; there was food in his beard; his clothes smelled of medicine. He was old-fashioned in his methods. But he was a sweet, fine man."

Nicholas Lindsay, Vachel's grandfather, had had nothing to do with women in all his long bachelorhood, having made up his mind, he told his girl-wife, "that my blood should never mingle with the blood of a harlot." When Vachel was of a suitable age his own father admonished him against the three great masculine evils of venereal disease, drink and tobacco, and the dire warnings sank into Vachel's mind and hardened there.

Something more directly influencing his feeling toward his father had taken place between them in Vachel's early boyhood. He and another boy, playing with matches, set fire to some barns belonging to a farmer. Fire is one of the scourges of the prairie. The powerful Dr. Lindsay flogged his white-faced little son, flogged him in a manner very different from the mother's rare whippings with a light pony whip. The punishment was something the son never forgot or entirely forgave, and possibly this was the moment of metamorphosis of the dutiful parent into the admirable but terrible figure that his father became to Vachel Lindsay.

Lindsay was forty-three when he wrote the poem *Doctor Mohawk*, which opens with the description of his birth-journey through Springfield on the back of a sea-mustang.

Then there strides onto the scene the heroic figure of a redskin chief:

"Heap-big-chief-the-Mohawk," with eye like a tommyhawk:
Naked, in war-paint, tough stock and old stock . . .

As a small boy Lindsay hoped—in his middle years began to believe and toward the end of his life categorically insisted—that he had Indian blood in his veins from an ancestor much closer than Pocahontas. There is no evidence that this was true but "Doctor Mohawk," the redskin, is his symbol of the longed-for inheritance and his portrait of his father through whom he supposed the strain to have descended:

> Plumed like an Indian, an American dragon,
> Tall as Sun-mountain, long as the Sangamon,
> With a buffalo beard.

Doctor Mohawk is Dr. Lindsay seen through the eyes of a delicate, scared boy, his mother's darling—

> I cried, and held hard to my mother's warm hand.
> And the Mohawk said:—"Red man, your first trial begins."
> And the Mohawk roared:—"Shame to you, coward and
>   mourner!" . . .
>
> I wept with my mother. I kissed and caressed her.
> Then she taught me to sing. Then she taught me to play:—
> The sibyl, the strange one, the white witch of May.

On the manuscript of this poem Lindsay has left a memorandum: "Not the facts—but the exact atmosphere of my early childhood."

Such it is to be a poet, such it is to have a poet son.

Vachel Lindsay's mother, "the sibyl, the strange one, the white witch," was regarded variously by her neighbors as a social climber, an eccentric, and a great woman, and in this last opinion almost all who saw much of her concurred. Of the two parents she was in obvious ways the more dominating. "She ruled the roost," goes the verdict of those who knew the Lindsays. Yet her husband never showed a trace of resentment, not because he was weak of will but because he cared little for appearances, was perfectly sure of his masculine role and confident in himself of filling it, at home and everywhere.

Catharine Frazee Lindsay was a small, squarely built woman, having a rawboned Celtic facial structure with high cheekbones, which her son inherited along with her light-blond hair and her light-colored, luminous, remarkable eyes. Her father, "the proud farmer," had had such eyes. It was she who was responsible for the stove on the front lawn with geraniums frothing out of the four holes. This ornament and town landmark, indicating that a vigorous individuality resided within, was what chiefly distinguished 603 South Fifth for many Springfieldians who otherwise knew only vaguely that a doctor and his family lived there.

One local opinion, still widely held, runs: "Mrs. Lindsay was very ambitious. She queened it in her own circle, which was very worthy but was *not the best social circle.* The Lindsays were not so much snubbed by Springfield 'society' as that they simply didn't exist for it. The mother, however, was always impressing her superiority on herself and her family."

And Vachel, when grown, once placed a woman friend on a low stool, sat himself down on another and reenacted a scene of his childhood when his mother, seating him on such a stool and herself close by, told him: "Vachel, there's a streak of genius in the Frazees, and YOU HAVE IT!"

"From that time on," acknowledged the adult Lindsay, "I was marked."

Outside the pattern of most Springfield housewives of correspondingly modest means, Mrs. Lindsay took elocution lessons, practiced the piano and painted pictures, at the same time that, like the others, she baked, washed, swept and sewed.

After the deaths of her three little girls her one longing was, like the Israelites of old, to fast and weep. Instead, she threw herself with fanatical ardor into every church and public opening. She not only taught the Bible Class at the First Christian Church but also organized the *Via Christi* study group, which conned the principles and achievements of Christian civilization, and this too she taught herself. She could not get enough of teaching. She was a member of the Springfield Authors' Club and, for thirty years, of The Sunnyside, a literary circle to which her old friends belonged.

"They let her lecture them two years straight—once," her son says. "By the time she was through with them she had filled them up with what I had before I was thirteen."

The house on South Fifth, he remembers further, "was

always packed with religious committees of which Mama was always chairman, and woe be to any one who proposed anything else."

Having been president of the Woman's Missionary Society of her own church, Mrs. Lindsay helped to set up the Woman's Missionary Social Union, a union of *all* Protestant missionary societies in the city, and of this as well she was the president.

She entertained constantly, a utilitarian entertaining. A few Springfield residents can remember her standing graciously to receive them just inside her parlor door, or seated at her dining room table on which, however, the refreshments laid out were hardly up to the lavish midwest standard even though Mrs. Lindsay, when she set her mind to it, was a wonderful cook. But at these large-scale serious affairs "there would be an urn of coffee and a plate of Nabiscos," recalls one of her daughter Olive's friends. "And that would be that."

Her son wrote: "My Mama is unquestionably the most powerful personality I have ever known."

After her death he revealed that he had once planned a poem, never executed, on his mother, which was to be called *Hatshepsut* after the Egyptian queen, "who seems," he writes, "to have been remarkably like her. Also Ida Tarbell's life of Mary Baker Eddy, founder of Christian Science, shows much the same kind of a person, who requires enormous long-range activities to keep from overmanaging all those nearby."

While Catharine Lindsay's son recognized the do-gooder, the clubwoman and the schoolmarm in his mother, he also perceived—with a poet's rather than a son's intuition—the mysticism deep-lodged beneath her missionary enthusiasm and Campbellite orthodoxy. She was a true visionary. As a child on the farm, her mind had been filled with the love of thunder, wind, rain, darkness, and flowers. She was given to moments of telepathy and the hearing of voices in answer to prayer— experiences that her mother and her mother's people had undergone before her.

"Springfield never knew," her son explains, "how narrowly

Mrs. Lindsay escaped being a Mrs. Besant, a Mrs. Eddy—a
Blavatsky. She had horse-sense enough never to seem to be a
mystic in public or private. Her orthodoxy was a *shell*, a suit
of armor to protect her against herself, against her almost
overwhelming instinct to be an Eddy, Blavatsky, Besant."

As he describes his father in *Doctor Mohawk*, so Lindsay
celebrates his mother in the poem *The Hearth Eternal*. He
tells of a woman on whose hearth smouldered a magic fire,
which burned on even after her death.

> her crumbling home enshrined the light.
> The neighbors peering in were half afraid.

Though beggars stole away the very walls and floors of her
dwelling, the naked hearthstone blazed supernaturally till men
deserted their separate churches to congregate before it—

> At dead of night it lights the traveller's face!

He was writing in symbolic language. By the magic fire he
meant a genius for living and a vision of the development of
the race by upward steps, culminating in Christianlike brotherhood, that was noble and prophetic. With a poet's eye he perceived in his mother a sibyl and in her home a shrine.

But most of Springfield cannot be blamed if during Mrs.
Lindsay's lifetime it saw only what it saw: an ordinary dwelling place distinguished by an iron stove on the lawn, and a
doctor's aggressive wife who ran half the neighborhood.

4

The Lindsay house always was "ugly" inside, recalls the same friend who remembers the skimpiness of the refreshments served there. "Mrs. Lindsay never bothered with handsome curtains or such fixings."

Directly ahead inside the front door were the stairs, running up straight and cruelly steep. Just at the top on the second floor was Vachel's own small room, a boy's room, which looked out across Edwards Street into the Governor's "yard," as the Lindsays called that beautiful green shady estate. Upstairs and down the woodwork was dark brown. The floors were scuffed, the rugs and the upholstery of chairs and sofas were well trodden and sat on. It was a house in which people didn't bother with fashion but lived plain and thought high.

Though Dr. Lindsay had a struggle to put bread on the table for his increasing brood, his home was filled with shelves and shelves of books from both sides of the family, with bookcases and more bookcases of the classic English and Latin authors. On the parlor walls hung reproductions of the old masters—a thousand of them, Vachel recalled, "from Michelangelo to Correggio's softest." There were stones picked up by Kate Frazee in the Forum and Coliseum, a fragment of the lava that destroyed Pompeii, a branch of delicate white coral, and on the mantel two miniatures painted on porcelain in Florence, which Dr. Lindsay and Kate had exchanged as true-love tokens.

"It might have been in the midst of England so far as its inner atmosphere went," says Olive Lindsay, "—this home of ours on a corner of a muddy street in the muddy town of Springfield, Illinois."

"In infancy," says Vachel Lindsay, "I never heard of New England. I heard of Europe every day."

The parents plied their children with tales of their memorable year abroad. With each other Dr. and Mrs. Lindsay constantly discussed not only current local but also national and world news. When Eugene Debs went to prison in Chicago, and young Emperor William dismissed old Chancellor Bismarck in Germany, the widening rings of events set in motion would sometime and somehow touch Springfield, and of this Mrs. Lindsay especially was aware. As her husband at the breakfast table read aloud an item from the *Journal*, "That person," she would comment alertly, "wants to be a new Napoleon," or "That man is trying to help us think, as Socrates did. Let us hope he will not have to drink the hemlock for his courage."

Springfield, the state capital, was Republican in the 1880's and 1890's. Dr. Lindsay was furiously a Southern Democrat, which partly explains why, as Vachel once expressed it— sitting upstairs in his room and gazing moodily across at the Governor's house—"Never yet have they had a person in that mansion with whom we as a family could be real cosy."

In 1884 he and his cousin Ruby, Uncle Johnson Lindsay's little girl, saw their fathers ride in triumph in the Democratic parade ratifying the election of Grover Cleveland for President. Long-thwarted Democrats had popped up in Springfield as if out of the ground. The two fathers on curveting horses wore wide sashes and tall silk hats, and the glaring, flaring torchlight procession behind and ahead of them went on for "millions of miles."

Ruby lived next to the Lincoln house on Eighth Street. Lincoln and his family had left this house twenty-three years before; it had since become a museum but not the careful restoration of a home that it is today. Every foot of wall space was covered with Civil War cartoons from newspapers both pro and con Lincoln, showing Lincoln the sly, the slack-jawed and uncouth, the ape-faced politician in a tailcoat and top hat; and also Lincoln the honest rail-splitter, the stanch friend to the downtrodden, the emancipator who said: "As I would not be a slave, so I would not be a master."

The custodian, Mr. Oldroyd, gave Ruby and Vachel the freedom of the place, and they gamboled in and out of the rooms through which at the same time stumped middle-aged G.A.R. veterans fighting the war over again as the controversial drawings recalled it to them.

Meanwhile, in the silver-domed State House on Capitol Avenue the Memorial Room was jammed with Northern war trophies, and at least once annually the Grand Army of the Republic swung through the streets to the magnificent Northern strains of "The Battle Hymn of the Republic" and "Marching Through Georgia."

To these same songs, which couldn't but stir them, Vachel and Ruby marched in play, though the other children in the school yard called them "rebels." Vachel's father had very early filled him with the wrathful notion that " 'way down in Kentucky, once upon a time a certain Abraham Lincoln came, with many soldiers. . . ."

Those Yankee bandits had stolen Grandfather Lindsay's horses and driven off his Negroes (which should rightfully have descended to Vachel). In a manner never specified they had somehow stolen the farm itself, burned the crops and left Papa to study medicine by the light of one candle. This at any rate was what the six-year-old son made of the oft-told tale. It was not in the Lindsay tradition to like Lincoln.

But there was also the Frazee tradition. The implacable, triumphant ding-dong of the dinner bell rung by Grandfather Frazee when he heard General Lee had surrendered, was louder—figuratively speaking—than Grandfather Lindsay's roared and impotent fulminations against the North. Thus Vachel's father's view of recent history was challenged and overborne by the mother who was "all for" Lincoln.

Vachel Lindsay was "for" Lincoln too, was for him all his life, though aware of an emotional and a blood kinship with the South. He was for Lincoln the man, even though he felt

that Mason's and Dixon's invisible line ran east and west along
Edwards Street: just on the north side stood the Republican
Governor's Mansion, just to the south the Lindsays' Demo-
cratic and rebel residence.

One of the boasts of the Frazees was that the family for
generations had been "educated people." Mrs. Lindsay used
to tell how her great-grandfather in Kentucky had taught
Daniel Boone's children to read.

It was she who taught her own children. Vachel learned
from Grimm's *Fairy Tales*. Then he and Olive shared a United
States History written in words of one syllable. On its cover
was a picture of General Washington riding a prancing horse,
with a boy carrying a red, white and blue flag before him—a
picture that survives in one of the poems of Lindsay's maturity,
Yankee Doodle, which is meant to be sung to the tune of
that name:

> Dawn this morning burned all red;
> Watching then in wonder
> There I saw our spangled flag
> Divide the clouds asunder.
> Then there followed Washington.
> Ah, he rode from glory,
> Cold and mighty as his name
> And stern as Freedom's story.

In the evenings at home Dr. Lindsay read aloud, or rather
performed, *Uncle Remus*. Vachel also remembered an everlasting series of Scott's novels rendered by both his parents
and by Olive, taking turns under the lamp. Once, however,
he had the magic clue in his hand—once he had learned his
letters—he explored the world of books on his own. At eight
he first read *Paradise Lost*, that most subtly passionate of
poems, and fell permanently in love with Milton's own love,
the goldenhaired beguiling Eve.

He was thirteen when he asked his mother one evening,
"Who was Edgar Allan Poe?" to which Mrs. Lindsay replied

in her positive way: "He was a very talented young man who died drunk on the streets of Baltimore. He wrote poetry. I think we have his poetry here." Then, crossing to the bookcase, she mounted a step to reach the top shelf where the *little* books were kept and brought down a small blue volume.

Vachel read it all through that night. The haunting *Ulalume* was his favorite of Poe's poems, perhaps of all poems, and the tragic gallant writer of it became his fascination. "Poe," he declares, "was always a kind of Egyptian to me."

"Egyptian" meant to Vachel everything there is of necromancy and weird ceremonial. His father had given him Rawlinson's *History of Ancient Egypt* in two heavy volumes packed with pictures and this treasure trove enthralled the boy, who pored over it till he had made a part of himself every detail of life in that mysterious land, from how the Egyptians embalmed their dead, explicitly described, to the functions and personalities of their beast-gods, whose names were awful as the pyramids: Ammon, Ra, Osiris, Thoth.

Another of his favorites was Stanley's *In Darkest Africa*, which inspired one of the most famous passages he ever wrote, at least this particular edition did, for its cover had as decoration a map of Africa all black on which was traced by a line of gold the course of the great river Congo—

> Then I saw the Congo, creeping through the black,
> Cutting through the jungle with a golden track.

In front of the Court House, a few blocks north, Vachel listened to the clashing supplication of the Salvation Army band, which moved him more than the symphonies of the masters. At ten he formally joined the Disciples Church and in this same year, in a vein of religious inspiration that was small and yet true and sweet, he wrote what was possibly his first poem. It was entitled *Come*.

> He that is weary come, be refreshed,
> He that is thirsty come and drink,
> "I," says the Savior, "I am he
> I am that fountain clear and free . . ."

Vigorous-minded Grandfather Frazee had once, in his book-lined farmer's living room, spoken scornfully in the fledgling Vachel's hearing of poets as "clever men, but they almost all have a screw loose somewhere," and the words had stuck in Vachel's memory, leading him to understand that if you wrote poetry you did it just for fun, on the side.

Anyhow, his gift was for art, so his mother told him. That had been her own gift. At the private school he first attended Vachel was taught drawing, and the faces of mother and son, so alike in structure and fair coloring, hung fondly over his first drawing book, called *The Aurora Drawing Book*, for on the cover was Guido Reni's picture of the horses of the dawn pulling Apollo in his chariot, with light-footed muses treading the clouds, Cupid flying ahead and Aurora strewing flowers. In an era of cubism the grown Lindsay still loved this picture.

Lindsay later almost wildly maintained that for the first sixteen years of his life his mother destined him to be an artist; that in his seventeenth year she changed and let him down. His sister Olive, however, says there is no question that both parents, imbued with respect for the professions, designed their son for a doctor from the beginning; that this was the family plan as heralded in the newspaper announcement of Vachel's birth.

While Vachel was still in grammar school his father gave him his second-best skeleton, left over from his Vienna days—his best one stood in a cabinet in his office. The bones were jumbled in a wooden box. "Learn to put these together!" commanded Doctor Mohawk.

His son tried; he did try, but he never succeeded. It was as if the pieces moved apart in the night. Their curious shapes, though, interested Vachel and he enjoyed sketching them.

Another commandment was to put up his father's horse in the barn whenever the doctor arrived home from a call—it might be after midnight. Vachel was scared to death of horses ("great terrible sneezing brutes") and could get himself through the ordeal only by chanting aloud Tennyson's poem *Maud* whose rhythm, like the roll of drums in battle, kept his courage going while he cautiously unbridled and bedded down the animal.

When his mother believed he was delivering pills for his father, as he was supposed to do, or helping out after school in his father's office on Sixth Street, where he was supposed to be, he would be either visiting the nickelodeons (he saw every one in town) or loitering about the Leland Hotel at Sixth and Capitol, especially in the cavernous room where the Negro waiters gathered around a woodpile in their shirt-sleeves to chop wood for the fires.

The blond boy, perky and persistent, harkened to, interro-gated, and drank in every alluring feature of these black-skinned, liquid-eyed, white-toothed men—their tall tales, their honey-sweet songs, their irrepressible high spirits.

Lewis Wiggins, the manager's son, complained that Vachel was a regular nuisance, he came so often.

5

As long as she could, Mrs. Lindsay dressed her only son in suits of starched white piqué, and when, still a very little boy, he entered the Stuart School, the public grammar school of Springfield, the roughs and toughs jeered at him as a mama's darling. He lived down the jeers, except in his heart of hearts.

When he was in the fifth grade, he ranked temporarily first in his class. Near the head of the class sat one of the prettiest girls in it. To occupy a desk in her neighborhood you had to be near the head yourself, so Vachel (only long afterward did he confess why) determinedly improved his marks.

That year he took part in the essay contest and won the silver medal, presented to him with full ceremony and publicity out at the teeming fair ground during State Fair Week. Next year he won the medal again. The subject assigned was "Labor and Learning," and he had satisfactorily dealt with it in the American tradition contemptuous of leisure. "A man ought not to be very much respected," Vachel wrote, "unless he has a business."

His marks were high enough for him to jump from the sixth grade into the eighth and in the fall of 1893 he entered Springfield High School.

Miss Susan Wilcox, teacher of English, noticed him among her sophomores at the beginning of his second year. Though his extreme blondness gave his whole person a lack of color (his mother made a mistake to dress him in gray, thought Miss Wilcox), two features contradicted this colorlessness:

45

his shining honest eyes and his extraordinary forehead. Almost Neanderthal ridges—Vachel called them his "horns of Moses" —had begun to develop over his scarcely visible eyebrows. Above these two prominences, which gave character to his childishly round face, his forehead rose high and thoughtful, and below them his very candid gaze returned his teacher's.

So there began between Miss Wilcox and Vachel the consciousness of an affinity that was never a sentimental "crush" but an attraction of intelligences.

Susan Wilcox, who was in her twenties, was a graduate of Wellesley College. She was a splendid teacher, a gift from the gods to Vachel in his adolescence. This being before the days of teachers' specialization, she taught him botany and zoology as well as English. The science courses he took as part of the premedical training his father insisted on, and after he had left school Miss Wilcox wryly assured him that it was only his talent for sketching the specimens that had pulled him through.

"*You* might have made a scientist of me," he suggested, to tease her, but she shook her head.

"Not in a thousand years!"

As a sophomore Vachel read Carlyle's *French Revolution* ("Greek to his classmates," says Miss Wilcox) and while reading it kept rushing up the aisle to her desk to share his thrilled response with her. They had, however, their sparring matches. When she assigned her class the subject, for an essay, of "James Russell Lowell as a Patriot," she got back more than she bargained for from Vachel.

"Conceive," wrote the boy of fifteen, "my indignation when I discovered that I was to discuss this great broadminded man as a patriot! Patriotism is a thing of tinsel and pasteboard. Patriotism in its *highest sense* can be nothing more than a love of one's fellow men, modified into a zeal and partizanship for the land of one's birth. It is as natural as life itself for an organism to prefer its own element to any other."

Possibly thus far Miss Wilcox could tolerate what she read. But at this point she found herself brought up short by the writer's sense of humor, which remained all his life a very broad, though not coarse, humor—a "barbaric yawp" to be instinctively squelched by schoolteachers and Bostonians.

"Polar bears," Vachel continued, "are not lauded to the skies because they do not prefer to live in the tropics. An oyster is as great a patriot in his way as ever man was, for 'Breathes (?) there an oyster with soul so dead' that he does not prefer salt water to tree-life?"

This paper Miss Wilcox would not even mark, saying it was "not what she wanted," so Vachel refashioned it into, by his own description, "a glorious blood-curdling, starry banner free, fourth of July oration kind of thing." Then in a two-hour spurt he did another and a serious piece on patriotism, which, like the best of his early essays, is original, yet ably organized, clear, and logical, even though the opinion it expressed was more than unorthodox—it was anathema—in a prairie town in the 1890's.

"I cannot conceive," he wrote, "of loving a body of men because they are separated from other men by insignificant boundarys. Why should the affection stop at the border?"

In 1896, when Vachel was sixteen, two things of importance happened.

During his terrific campaign tour William Jennings Bryan, Democratic candidate for President, made a stop in Springfield. He was introduced publicly by Governor Altgeld, the present occupant of the mansion next door to the Lindsays and the first Democratic governor of Illinois since the Civil War, and delivered an address to the assembled multitude, including Vachel whom, along with the others, his silver tongue charmed.

Also in 1896 Vachel's mother, as he afterward considered, "betrayed" him, an act that like his father's flogging he never quite forgave.

Ever since he was the frail baby whose curls she could wind around her finger, Mrs. Lindsay had encouraged her son's artistic talent and shared her artistic interests with him till somehow there had grown up in his mind the confidence that, when the time came to take a definite step, she would be on his side against his father, who wished to make a doctor of him. He learned now, as the hour for taking that step drew near, that she had sided with his father all along. It was one thing to continue painting and writing as avocations, while carrying on a secure profession; it was another to give yourself up for life to the uncertain practice of the arts.

After raising him to be one kind of person, his mother had turned around (or so it seemed to him later) and gone back on him by wanting him to earn his living as another. The ground had shifted under his feet. He knew not where he stood, or on whom to count.

The occasional verses that Vachel was writing were done mostly as commentaries on his pictures. He drew the picture first, then hatched a verse to explain it. It was in his senior year that he approached Miss Wilcox with a poem independent of any drawing, which he told her was his "first picture drawn in words." He had had a chilling nightmare, then got up out of bed to write about it. The title of his poem was *The Battle;* it was intensely Poesque and described how "Love fought with the withered Hag of Plague."

At this time also he wrote to little Mary Tiffany the poem *How A Little Girl Sang.* He had heard Mary sing at a high-school party; she was first in the line of what his family always called "Vachel's inspiration girls."

He was slipping verses under the front door of another older Springfield maiden and in February 1897 addressed a valentine poem to her:

> Godess! Let my duty be
> Still to worship silently
> Unseen by worshippers more blest,
> Still unknown to thee.
> Still unloved of thee.

Vachel graduated with his class on June 10. A few days before Commencement Susan Wilcox with real concern asked him about his plans for the future, and his face, scarcely less childlike and confiding than on her first sight of it, turned grave. In his father's waiting room nailed to the wall was the framed oath of Hippocrates, which was Dr. Lindsay's other Bible. His mother's often communicated desire was that her son's life should be a "fruitage" of the earnest lives, his father's and both his grandfathers', that had gone before.

"If I were an orphan, I'd be an artist," Vachel told Miss Wilcox. "But I'm not, and so I'm going to college and be a doctor."

6

At thirty-nine Lindsay looked back into his boyhood, chose therefrom one day of glory and jubilation and gave it life again. He wrote:

It was eighteen ninety-six, and I was just sixteen
And Altgeld ruled in Springfield, Illinois.

Bryan, Bryan, Bryan, Bryan is the drum-roll title of his poem about the visit paid to Springfield that day by William Jennings Bryan—

there came from the sunset Nebraska's shout of joy:
In a coat like a deacon, in a black Stetson hat . . .

The presidential campaign of 1896 was more than usually hard-fought and emotional, for it was a test of strength not only between the two major political parties but also between the western farmer and the eastern financier.

The East under the Republican banner was committed to a policy of sound currency based on the gold standard. The demand of agrarian states west of the Mississippi—states that, broadly speaking, were aligned with the Democrats—was for inflation as a means of increasing the price of the farmer's commodities and the laborer's services, this to be brought about by the free and unlimited coinage of silver.

It was East *versus* West, gold *versus* silver, the plutocrat *versus* the common man. And in Springfield, Illinois, the Lindsays of 603 South Fifth Street, perched perilously at the heart of a Republican stronghold, were for the West, for free silver, and for the common man.

This of course made doubly thrilling the day that Bryan came to Springfield—William Jennings Bryan, "Boy Bryan" (he was thirty-six) from Nebraska, who had been nominated as candidate for president by a whooping, joyous Democratic convention, which had repudiated the Cleveland administration. It was at this convention, held in Chicago in July, that Bryan—no economist but a sincere believer in his own words and an orator to whom God had given a more than usual power to sway great audiences—had made his famous "cross of gold" speech, a plea for free silver.

Since then, while the Republican candidate, Ohio's Governor William McKinley, conducted his campaign from his front porch, to which special trains brought pilgrims whose fares were paid out of campaign funds, Bryan, with his gallant wife beside him, had stumped the country. East, west, north and south, hardly a crossing was too small for his train to pause at. The brass band played "El Capitan," and Bryan shook every hand held out to him. He traveled in the end 18,000 miles, spoke to more than 5,000,000 people, and was the first presidential candidate in the history of the United States to make a coast-to-coast "whistle-stop" campaign.

The whole of Springfield had turned out to see and hear him on the day Lindsay remembered, and not Springfield alone but the tiny farm hamlets for miles around on the prairie.

When Bryan came to Springfield, and Altgeld gave him greeting,
Rochester was deserted, Divernon was deserted,
Mechanicsburg, Riverton, Chickenbristle, Cotton Hill,
Empty: for all Sangamon drove to the meeting . . .

And the town was all one spreading wing of bunting, plumes and
    sunshine,
Every rag and flag, and Bryan picture sold,
When the rigs in many a dusty line
Jammed our streets at noon,
And joined the wild parade against the power of gold.

Vachel had organized for the occasion a high-school parade in which he persuaded his friends Art Fitzgerald and Tom Dines to march.

Of that gala day of Bryan's coming, Arthur Fitzgerald recalls that most of the high-school boys were Republicans, that his own father was a Republican but that he, Art, was (he doesn't know just why) a Democrat. And Tom Dines, says Mr. Fitzgerald, was even more of a leader in the school than Vachel, and for this reason was admired by Vachel—though Tom would go out to win a friendship, which Vachel would never do.

They all marched together on that far-off afternoon of glory.

> Oh, Tom Dines, and Art Fitzgerald,
> And the gangs that they could get!
> I can hear them yelling yet.

When their own marching was over the boys watched from the sidelines, still frantically cheering. Vachel as usual had attached himself to a partner—

> The long parade rolled on. I stood by my best girl. . . .

Vachel's real best girl was a Republican, not, therefore, the girl who watched beside him. But his girl for the day was a fellow Democrat; she sufficed for poetic inspiration, and she has been immortalized:

> I stood by my best girl.
> She was a cool young citizen, with wise and laughing eyes.
> With my necktie by my ear, I was stepping on my dear,
> But she kept like a pattern, without a shaken curl.

Till at last the endless procession ended, the blaring band fell hushed, the black-coated great ones made themselves ready on their dais:

> And Bryan took the platform.
> And he was introduced.

And he lifted his hand
And cast a new spell.
Progressive silence fell
In Springfield,
In Illinois,
Around the world.
Then we heard these glacial boulders across
    the prairie rolled:
*"The people have a right to make their own
    mistakes . . .*
You shall not crucify mankind
Upon a cross of gold."

Another of Vachel's heroes was John Peter Altgeld, who
on this day of days faced assembled Springfield by the side of
Bryan.

From his bedroom window, looking out on Governor Altgeld's garden, Vachel had often seen the thoughtful, foreign-
appearing little man taking the air under the trees with a step
that was care-ridden and slightly dragging; though the public
did not know it, Altgeld was in the initial stage of locomotor
ataxia. The son of German immigrants, he was a champion of
the oppressed ranks from which he had risen. Vachel at school
talked with wild approbation to all who would listen about
the Governor's just pardoning of the three Chicago anarchists,
Fielden, Schwab and Neebe—an act that by application of
mob logic had caused him to be known as "Altgeld the
anarchist."

As Altgeld and Bryan confronted the vast crowd together
no two men could have looked more unlike; the one slight,
small and ungainly, the other tall, deep of chest and athletically
impressive. Nor were they alike in inner quality: Bryan was
a politician whose conscience was in the right place, while the
humanitarian Altgeld was of the stuff of which martyrs are
made.

But to Vachel, lost in that crowd below, Altgeld and Bryan
shoulder to shoulder on the platform stood equally for courage,
justice and brotherhood, were twin defenders of what he saw

quite simply, with the eyes of a sixteen-year-old, as the cause
of right against might.

The great day passed. There came a time of waiting.

> July, August, suspense.
> Wall Street lost to sense.
> August, September, October,
> More suspense.
> And the whole East down like a wind-smashed fence.
>
> Then Hanna to the rescue,
> Hanna of Ohio . . .

Mark Hanna, the Cleveland capitalist, was the moving
power behind the Republican candidate McKinley. It was
through his astuteness that the Republican appeal was aimed
at the propertied classes, emphasizing the "dangerous radical-
ism" of Bryan and the Democrats. Hanna—

> Rallying the roller-tops,
> Rallying the bucket-shops . . .
> Rallying the trusts against the bawling flannelmouth—

raised the largest campaign fund in the history of the country
so far. The banks contributed, the insurance companies contributed, the Standard Oil Company generously contributed.
"In God We Trust, in Bryan We Bust," was one of the gold
slogans.

Largely owing to Mark Hanna's management the Republicans, though early in the campaign they were seriously threatened, in the end did win. For months the ups and downs of
that fateful contest, the good news and the increasingly bad
(as the Democratic machine lost hope, Bryan struggled on
almost alone), every alternation and fluctuation of battle was
mirrored in Vachel's eager face. At last in November the
irrevocable word reached Springfield.

> Election night at midnight:
> Boy Bryan's defeat.

Defeat of western silver.
Defeat of the wheat.
Victory of letterfiles
And plutocrats in miles . . .
Victory of custodians,
Plymouth Rock,
And all that inbred landlord stock . . .

Defeat of the aspen groves of Colorado valleys . . .
By the Pittsburg alleys.
Defeat of alfalfa and the Mariposa lily.
Defeat of the Pacific and the long Mississippi.
Defeat of the young by the old and silly.
Defeat of tornadoes by Tubal Cain supreme.
Defeat of my boyhood, defeat of my dream.

The boy of sixteen was father to the man of thirty-nine. Lindsay recovered the dream of his boyhood. Forever defeated, it was forever reborn in him. Till the last shadowed moments of his life he believed the day must end in victory for youth against age, the bold West against the canny East, the broad against the narrow, and the great of heart against the small.

7

Mrs. Lindsay, who plotted her children's lives when she should have been sleeping, had kept Olive out of school a year so Vachel could catch up with her. Vachel was not quite eighteen and Olive just under twenty when in September 1897 they entered Hiram College together.

Vachel was dreamy, Olive vivacious. They were both full of humor, and neither one hid his light under a bushel. As Vachel put it at the end of their successful freshman year: "We are a little kin to our mother, and inspire jealousy in a few nondescripts always, I suppose."

Founded by the Disciples in 1850, Hiram is a small college in Ohio, southeast of Cleveland. James A. Garfield, the last American President to be born in a log house on the frontier, is Hiram's great man, for he was a student at Hiram in her early days and before he was thirty became the college president, wearing a heavy beard to hide the boyishness of his round Teutonic-looking face.

In 1897 Hiram was still sectarian. Recognized by her sons and daughters as the glory of their little college and her proudest, though an intangible, possession, was the "Hiram spirit," which was zealously religious, yet at the same time intellectually aspiring. It was profoundly and eagerly affirmative, engendered by the same moral atmosphere that pervaded the young Lindsays' home. The same standard of plain living and high thinking ruled at Hiram as at 603 South Fifth Street.

"Unless the American creative genius is expressed by such places as Hiram," said Vachel Lindsay years later, "it will remain unexpressed."

To the outward eye the college, when Vachel and Olive

56

entered it, was a cluster of buildings belonging to a "bad" architectural period and dominated by the original main building, an ugly and beloved landmark of dark-red brick, on the rolling rural campus of Hiram Hill. The country around made a complete change from the prairie, being hilly and wooded with oaks, elms and maples (the farmers were famous for their maple sugar), having scarlet and gold foliage in the autumn and deep snow in winter. Far off the East was visible in the hills of Pennsylvania.

"Prexy" Zollars—the Reverend Eli Vaughn Zollars—had formerly been the pastor of the Christian Church in Springfield. Counting boys and girls together, there were about three hundred students—"plenty of rubes," as Vachel wrote home on arrival, "and plenty of nice fellows."

He was rooming with another boy, while Olive had a single room in Miller Hall, one of the two girls' dormitories. Vachel was allowed upstairs for a visit with her every night after the matron had struck a warning gong and called out, "Vachel's coming up to the second floor, girls!"

His tuition, payable in advance, was $16; his books had cost a little over $5.00 and food came to $2.00 a week. "The fare," he reported, "is plain but substantial, and I guess I can keep alive on it."

Of his list of chosen studies, physics soon proved his hardest pull and the professor told him he would have to drop physics because he had had no trigonometry. He then took up trig and found it a subject with which his mind could scarcely grapple at all, even though the instructor, to help him out, worked all the examples himself. In Bible Geography, on the other hand, his imagination made the dry bones of the past live and Professor Peckham, who had a sense of the whimsical, gave him a mark of 93.

"Where is the Dead Sea, Mr. Lindsay?"

"At the hot end of the Jordan River, sir."

Vachel went out for basketball practice in the gym, where the boys had to wear long stockings held up by garters in case the girls should drop in. Every night before bed he ran twice

around campus to keep from growing soft, and for the room
he shared with his roommate Harry Harts he drew a poster
with the tonic motto

> Early to bed and early to rise
> Makes a man healthy, wealthy and wise.

Life was nothing if not social at Hiram. Though the young
people were stiff and gauche at formal functions, their get-
togethers in students' rooms were hilarious. Twenty Questions
and Up Jenkins were played and gingersnaps with red pepper
in them consumed from a small pasteboard keg.

Vachel, Harry and Paul Wakefield, son of the Professor of
Law and Political Science, crashed a sheet-and-pillow-case
party at Miller to which only girls were invited. It was just
after Halloween. The room was lit eerily by jack o'lanterns;
there was a comb orchestra and all the guests wore sheets
wrapped around them and pillow cases over their heads.

A giggling committee moved from group to group, fumbling
at the spectral figures in search of males. Vachel's hands gave
him away. The lady principal of Miller, who was an elocu-
tionist, cried dramatically: "That's a man's hand, a MAN's
hand!"

"Unmask the villain, unmask him!" she cried, and when she
had torn the pillow case off she said helplessly: "O Vachel,
who would have thought this of *you*!"

Vachel bawled with laughter.

"I am a great friend," he bragged in a letter home, "of every
girl in Hiram, have made myself dear to them all, after my
famous manner, and you ought to have heard the chorus of
welcome when the committee of man-hunters pulled my
pillow-case off my shock of hair. 'Why it's Vachel,' they said
in the same tone the surprised children in the Sunday School
cantata say, 'Why it's Santa Claus.' "

He was contributing to the college paper, writing facetious
lyrics for the *Spider Web*, the college annual, and on his own

some serious poetry. In this last his mother encouraged him. "You may be able to accomplish something in this line, at odd times, for recreation. . . ."

Yet what encouragement she gave with her right hand, she took away with her left. "Your bits of verse—" she called his poems once. "Though your bits of verse sometimes contain strong expressions, I do not see you in the future as a poet."

At home she and Dr. Lindsay read their son's poems aloud to each other—"in a flat monotone," complained Vachel, who had heard them at it. This was endurable, but what he could not endure was the free way his mother passed his poems around to all the neighbors. He wrote to her in January, when he and Olive were back at Hiram after Christmas holidays with the family, that he had left his scrapbook behind on the library table and there were several things in it she would do him a favor to let alone. "It is not right for you to read my poems to anybody, when I say I do not want it done. They are mine."

His mother answered soothingly that she had found the scrapbook but had only read a few selections from it to his father, "who works so hard that he ought to have something to feed his hopes of your manhood upon."

At fifty-four Dr. Lindsay had developed diabetes. He suffered almost constant pain from an ulcer in one eye caused by an infection long ago when a child with diphtheria coughed into his face. His whole youth and best strength had been poured out before Olive and Vachel were born. Now he was worn down by the demands of his large but unfashionable practice and nagged by the need for money, of which never, never was there quite enough. Yet as his own father stubbornly went bail for fellow townsmen who failed to pay up, so Dr. Lindsay took on and kept on many a case that he knew would never bring in a penny.

"Try every day to do your best for the sake of your father," the mother begged her children at college.

As for the driven doctor's letters, sent from his office on office paper, they were all terse, all to the same main point. "I am hustling," he wrote. "It takes much money to run us."

Vachel set himself to cut down expenses, which included striving with all his might to go without an occasional nickel's worth of candy, but it was never so tempting as when he had just eaten another of the boarding-house dinners that made him think of Tennyson's description of the face of Maud:

icily regular, splendidly null,
Dead perfection, no more.

Also, all the fellows dressed better than he, which didn't worry him a bit but he had seen that it hurt Olive sometimes.

Olive was the practical one. Her money always lasted longer; yet he pointed out to their parents that, as a male, he did have to spend more. It would be pretty conspicuous if he never did any entertaining of girls, and now it was spring and the season for what was known at Hiram as "perching"—the name originated from a special hallowed spot on campus where boards were laid across the corner of a split rail fence under an apple tree, making a perch for two.

Early in the evenings, with the sky rosy and the moon but a pale horn, the students would pair off and drift, two and two, over Hiram Hill. Sometimes the girls trooped by in a body from Miller and Bowler and sang songs to the boys, after which the boys followed the glimmering shirtwaists back through gathering dusk to the girls' dormitories to return the serenade.

Vachel wrote a note to Adeline Mugrage, a Miller Hall girl: "My dear Adeline— Do you know that I feel inspired to say some very sweet things to you tonight? But they would look rather soft and flat on paper, and perhaps you would not understand. So you don't know what you have missed."

He was perching too, but with a difference. Years afterward it was to seem to him that not till he was over thirty did he even begin to understand the passionately single-hearted ways of his girl and boy friends as he remembered them in college. At the time he had only rejoiced that there were so many fine girls around.

They were so thick around campus, he told his parents, that

though he had not yet met his ideal woman, he was sure to find someone he loved wherever he went. "When I don't happen to find a girl or so somewhere, I just let them go, and take a rest."

During the summer vacation of 1898 he wrote to Adeline from the camp near Empire, Colorado, at which his family usually spent the summers. She did not realize, he confided to her, what a peculiar inspiration his girl friends had been to him since he was eight years old.

"Believe me, child," wrote Vachel, "your trust and faith and sympathy are a decided inspiration," to which Adeline demurely replied: "You are the most thoroughly original boy I ever knew."

She had read his letter lying outdoors in the hammock, where in the hot weather she read all his letters and also the poems enclosed; Vachel was not shy about having his poems shown if he did the showing.

"To me," Adeline declared, "you are a genius. If the world never finds it out it will not make much difference to me. But whatever you may do will not surprise me."

8

Vachel had become fast friends with Paul Wakefield, a manly dark-haired boy a year ahead of him at Hiram, to whom he dedicated a poem, *The Triumph of Friendship*.

> Through the stirring storms and weather
> Let us then be friends together . . .
> Let our friendship still be trusting
> Though I seem to curse thy name.
>
> . . . whether we are side by side in dying
>   or in doing
> Or whether we are clanned as foes in all
>   the stirs of men,
> Our Friendship! Let it be immortal!

Having gone out for basketball, baseball and football, Vachel failed at them all; he was too uncoordinated for organized athletics and on the football field got a permanent scar on his chin. In his sophomore year, as part of his premedical course, he began anatomy under the college physician, Dr. Harlan Page, but his mind utterly rejected *materia medica*.

"Mr. Lindsay, will you tell us about the femur?" the long-suffering Dr. Page would ask.

Vachel would rise, teeter where he stood, tilt his head to one side and, like the White Knight, invent something.

He was trying out for the oratorical contests that were a feature of Hiram and were as enthusiastically attended as athletic meets at a less classical college. But he could never even get into, much less win, a single contest. In every attempt he made, his nerves routed him; worse still, they undid him in class and at parties. He confessed that when up against something uncongenial or someone unsympathetic he felt the panic of a bad dream.

Olive, too, suffered from her nerves. It was from their mother that they inherited the tendency. Though Mrs. Lindsay had conquered her own nerves to the extent that she was one of the best public speakers in a church renowned for oratory, she warned her children to guard against a certain "dazed condition," which often troubled her when she was overtired. Several times on the street she had known only enough to step into a store, not nearly enough to tell which way to go home. She would sit down and wait, perhaps half an hour—"no one noticing me or saying anything, until the cloud passes in a moment and I see the way to Fifth and Edwards."

Yet of one sort of stamina Vachel had plenty: the sheer physical dare-deviltry of his many college stunts was unequaled—as when one winter night in his sophomore year it reached his ears that the upstart freshmen had had the audacity to hoist their class flag on the roof of the main building.

"Vachel said to Charlie Russell, 'Russell, she's got to come down!' Mr. Russell with his ready nerve replied, 'I'm with you!'"

So Olive wrote the next day to their parents.

It was three a.m. Snow lay deep on campus and the temperature was five below zero. For three-quarters of an hour Vachel slithered back and scrambled forward on the steep slate roof above the topmost rung of the ladder till he achieved the sharp summit. Then he shinnied up the thirty feet of the flagpole.

"He held his gloves in his teeth," wrote Olive, "and in the terrible strain he chewed great holes in them. At last he gained the glorious trophy and stuffed it into his boot and climbed down. Now aren't you proud of your son's nerve? Our class all are. They say he has more nerve than anybody else in the college, and I hate to see a coward."

Undaunted by failure, Vachel began work on a new oration, this one on the subject of Altgeld, the study of whose life was proving to him what one man of ideals can accomplish as well as how the mass of men can misunderstand his deeds. No longer governor, having been defeated at the time of Bryan's defeat, Altgeld was campaigning as reform candidate for the office of mayor in Chicago, where the papers commented brutally on his failing health. In this campaign, too, he was in the end badly beaten.

"I suppose," Vachel reflected, "when he finally dies there will be no voice raised in the nation to show the world the man he was."

Vachel was doing illustrations for the *Spider Web*. His drawings, technically shaky, had a goblin humor: he drew fairies, elves and the other students looking like figures in a funhouse mirror, and a squat black bird with a sign depending from its beak, saying, "I am a bird." He did a full-page astronomical drawing to illustrate the Class Yell of his class:

> Mercury! Venus! Earth and Mars!
> Comets! Meteors! All the Stars!
> Planets! Systems! Moon and Sun!
> Class of the Spheres! 1901!

He was still writing poetry, but his concentration on his regular studies was nil and his brain "like scrambled eggs," he told his mother. Anxious about the future, he was lying awake half of every night, yet if ever he whipped his nerves into shape it ought to be now, considering the profession he was supposed to enter.

"Since I would not feel," he wrote to his father, "that I was a worthy doctor at all unless I stick to the pace you have set at hard work, I will have to get the nerves somewhere."

Everybody in his anatomy class was telling him he had no business being a physician. He had put the question to a fellow pre-med: "Price, if you were sick and I were a doctor, would you call me to treat you?"

"Frankly, Lindsay," said Price, "I don't believe I would."

During one of their confidential talks up in Olive's room Vachel burst out: "Olive, I just can't be a doctor! You know I can't." But though in his heart his decision was already made, the decision of his mind was formed more slowly.

His junior year would be his last at college, he decided.

In the course of it he scarcely went to class at all but sat in his room or in the library and read Kipling from cover to cover; he also read everything available on art, on Japan, the complete works of Ruskin and all the poetry he could find.

Once he had hungered for formal education, but that self had died in him. He was striving to make his parents aware of a nascent self, one creative and dedicated. He was no longer the downy-faced cherub, the schoolboy sweet as a peach, to whom his mother still addressed her letters. He protested to his father: "Mama makes a mistake sometimes in talking *down* to me. I am always as big or as little as you make me. If she imagined I was thirty, and wrote up to it, I might grow up to it."

He was Vachel Lindsay, who, at twenty, wanted to get over being an irresponsible kid, who—he emphasized earnestly— shaved a little, and here in college met and talked with men his own age and filled as large a place among the students as any one of them. His parents could be sure he had his shortcomings fearfully at heart. What he needed was not endless sermonizing in Mama's "Moses and the Prophets tone" but words of vigorous reassurance that would give him a grip on the sources of his power.

"I like the letters you have written this year," he told his father, "and get great strength from them."

Besides reading intensively, he had begun to keep seven notebooks, which were really diaries of the most personal sort. He had meant to devote each one to examining a separate subject: Culture, English, Pictures, Logic and Natural Laws, the Disciples, Speaking, Homiletics—but the classifications soon dissolved and spilled over from one notebook to the next as nightly he poured out his whole mind in ideas for poems and stories, prayers, philosophizings, burning hopes and inspired projects.

"This book belongs to Christ," he affirmed at the start of each diary, in which his page after page of minute script involved a labor and absorption sufficient in themselves to explain why he scamped his classes and why his concentration on prescribed studies had broken down.

"At last I am attending my choice of a college," he wrote, "it is organized within myself. I want to read all the great books and think over the great thoughts and wrestle with them as Jacob wrestled with the angel. . . . Every inch of my will up to thirty-one years goes to the evolution of myself. . . . I have a world to save, and must prepare, prepare, prepare."

He must prepare to spread the gospel of Christ through art, to consecrate art as the novel was consecrated by Tolstoy— who "after my 31st year," Vachel promised, "shall find me his literal follower."

The sooner his parents accepted that he could not be a doctor, the better. On November 27, 1899, a fortnight after he had turned twenty, he broke with the education and the life they had so long and fondly planned for him in a passionate letter ("my revolutionary letter," he called it) written from college to them both.

9

For six years, Vachel explained, he had been struggling with a classical education and for him it was no good. After this term was over he wanted to leave college and educate himself on the basis of his gifts and instinctive forces rather than by assignments imposed from outside. Nothing he claimed as his own, or would ever use as his own, had come to him from his lessons. His imagination could take hold of nothing unless he saw its use in building up his life and work—his own, his creative work.

"All I have that sticks to me has come to me in those scattered moments when I struck out under the power of the *currents within* me."

For him to continue the mental drill and discipline of class would be to chain in a tangle of educational mannerisms every faculty of his mind and baffle every creative attempt. Few people can create or have the pride of creation. Most can only acquire. The ordinary system of education is for those who want to be scholars.

"I do not care to be such a one, I cannot be such a one. My life is empty when I try to enjoy what the uncreative enjoy, it is empty when I try to find in myself the motives that they have. To hold anything, and appropriate it, I must be in the creative mood, and I am *always* in some sort of a creative mood. . . ."

He wished to become a professional illustrator or designer. He wished also to write. Some day, he prophesied, he might leave either drawing or writing behind, but for the present they must go together—art for his living, writing for his relaxation—and the time would arrive when no man in America stood above him in the one field or the other.

He pointed out that creative ability was at a low ebb in America. Writers—he had seen it even in Kipling in England —were squeezing themselves for inspiration, which, being rare, fetched a high price in the market place, so that many a well-paid contributor to the big magazines would give him, Vachel, a fortune for what he had in his head.

"You must be sure there is an ocean of the stuff that makes literature and art within me. It is long within me. I could have written you this letter when I entered high school."

He needed only the technique that comes with doing.

"No one can teach me, and nothing can discipline my mind but the pride of the artist. Nothing so well, at least. Let me try."

Vachel wrote twice again, the first time to soothe his parents. "I thought you would agree with me more. Don't be so panic stricken."

In his next letter, he told them that he had been much younger when he first made up his mind to choose the calling by which he could best preach and express Christ. "Now that I have found it must be Art, I must learn to preach my purpose into other artists."

He hoped to preach literally, to speak from the pulpit when he could. He must express, not suppress. So strong was his sense of vocation that he could wait no longer for academic chores to be over. This autumn he had got nothing from his studies, and "all the things I love—that I *could* do—whereby I could gain strength and growth and self-possession—are left undone."

His father and mother did not know how serious a need it was with him to be free from the distraction of unessential things.

"Never in all my life have I had an unfettered chance to try with all the soul within me, with my mind free, my conscience free, with no other responsibility and no other duty—to do

the only things I ever will be able to learn to do well—draw—
and write, and speak."

"My precious boy," his mother answered, "we are wrapped
up in your welfare, and only want to do whatever will be in
the end for the best in every way."

Disappointed though his father was in his hope of having
his son with him in his practice, and eventually of giving him
all he had in the way of a profession, friends and footing in
Springfield—if Vachel felt sure that he could, without any
antecedents, succeed better in some other line, the father was
willing to do everything in his power to help.

"His heart-ache," the mother wrote, "is because he fears
you are throwing away a certainty of a very useful vocation
for a very uncertain dream."

By the new year, the threshold of the new century, Vachel
had decided on a course at the Art Institute in Chicago. He
had had a flock of art-school catalogues sent to his parents,
who read them with innocent eyes. His mother had taught art
and still occasionally produced it, setting up her easel by the
dining-room window from which she had a view of the old
oak tree in the Governor's yard, yet neither she nor his father,
she reminded him, were "acquainted with one artist."

With the Lindsays, no matter how pressed, there was always
money forthcoming for education and travel. His parents
agreed that the Chicago Institute sounded reasonable and practical, and immediately Vachel's imagination burst into plans
with which he filled his seven diaries. He determined to spend
the next ten formative years of his life in three countries.

For the first five, he must master Chicago, as typical America, and make a name that would earn him his living in his
special province, which was to be "Christian cartooning." As
other topical illustrators do political cartoons, he would do
moral and religious ones. And as Christ had taken thirty years
for mental, physical and spiritual ripening, so would he.

After Chicago, he meant to live three years in France, then two in Japan, and then at thirty-one it would be time enough to begin his dedication to some Tolstoyan "scheme of suffering and self-spending." "January 1, 1911 is my consecration day. My father could set dates ten years ahead and live up to them. Let me do the same."

But his goal for the first five years was more worldly. It was simply to become, he wrote, "the biggest man of my size in Chicago."

He left Hiram in June 1900, not to return. In the college annual for this year were published the class rolls of all four classes with the name of every boy and girl followed by an apt quotation.

"Is she not more than painting can express?" was the legend after the sprightly Olive Lindsay's name, and after Vachel's, from Shakespeare's *King Henry IV*: "I am not in the roll of common men."

PART TWO

THE SEARCH FOR ALADDIN'S LAMP

❦❖

10

Though Carl Sandburg hadn't yet characterized Chicago as

Hog-butcher for the world,
Tool-maker, Stacker of Wheat,
Player with Railroads and the Nation's Freight-handler,

it was a big city in 1901 when it received Vachel Lindsay.

This was nothing to Lindsay. "Behold," he had prophesied back home before starting, writing in the notebook he called *Pictures*, "I shall be a Caesar in the world of art, conquering every sort, every language and people, and lead their kings captive before the men of Rome. (Wow!)"

When he arrived in Chicago on January 2 he was twenty-one. If at sixteen he had looked fourteen, at twenty-one he looked sixteen. His hopes were high as every morning he trudged through the snow of January and the gray slush of February and March from his room on South Paulina Street—which he shared with Fred Bogardus, a medical student from Hiram—across town to the great grim sand-colored Art Institute. South Paulina was on the west side. The walk was an hour each way.

He walked, he told his mother, with his chest "thrust well out in the Delsarte movement" against the freezing lake wind, and he reassured his father that, though his overcoat was rather shabby, his suit would do perfectly well; none of them at the Institute looked smart.

He ate his meals uptown, at a counter or in some large,

suitably cheap restaurant. Having seldom more than a dime to spend, he often breakfasted on cream puffs and lunched on lemon pie or an oyster sandwich, then on his way home bought a bag of cookies or chocolate almonds for supper.

When Fred had an evening free, the two of them went to the theater, sitting in the high balcony under the roof called "nigger heaven." They saw Richard Mansfield in *Henry V* and Bernhardt and Coquelin in *Cyrano de Bergerac*. On Sunday mornings Lindsay taught a class of boys at the nearest Disciples Church. As for the Institute—and this he liked about it—it was a huge machine that passed him along as though he were on a conveyor belt. There was not a student whose name he knew, nor did they seem to be such a valuable earnest sort of people as his Hiram friends.

In his drawing class, which was the elementary class, he drew numerous views of the human nose, then of the ear, laboriously copying from an antique cast. In his sketch class he tried a tasteful but baffling arrangement of a hat and candy box against a crumpled newspaper background. The sketch teacher, Miss Baker, spoke to him with gentle words, causing his heart to open wide. "I love Miss Baker. She is sweet and wears a blue waist and specks."

But the box, with its multitude of angles, was so difficult and his result so poor that he felt tired and rattled. He began to spend his afternoons in the Institute library, finding it a refuge, where he read book after book on the history of art. The others in his class could certainly all draw better than he, but "oh, if I can only keep up with them," he wrote home, "I can beat them entirely, entirely!"

Almost every night he was writing poetry. *A Midnight Pantheism* was the title of one piece.

"Mad with the silence of the universe," he wrote,

> And thinking all the stars will fall,
> (While the shadows gather, row on row)
> The frenzy of the lonely watcher
> Comes upon him now.

Sometimes he cut his drawing class and stayed writing in his room all day. His stuff struck him as very crude still. At Hiram he had written a long romantic poem, *The Last Song of Lucifer,* which showed the influence of *Paradise Lost,* with echoes of Longfellow's *Sandalphan* and Dryden's *Alexander's Feast.* In Chicago he was still working on it, and he sent his high-school poem *The Battle* to William Dean Howells, an editor at *Harper's.*

He was at the Institute when Howells' answer reached him and he left immediately for the day, noting in his diary: "Howells said my work was frantic, frenetic and obscure. Went home to eliminate obscurity."

His roommate, Fred, returning in the evening from the hospital, found him thus doggedly employed and they discussed Howells' verdict, Fred admitting it was "not especially encouraging." Two weeks later Elbert Hubbard, of the Roycroft Press, rejected another of Lindsay's poems, which he also began to revise the same night.

"The man who is too much in harmony with his time is a compromiser," he wrote in his *Pictures* notebook.

By the end of April he had moved to Jackson Avenue on the south side, out by the old World's Fair ground. His new room, which he occupied alone, was near Washington Park but it was far from the Institute and he had to ride the elevated both ways.

The weather was unseasonably hot. He was spending his evenings in the public library, though often lately he felt too tired to read and before moving had had a spell of what he called "almost vertigo." When his funds ran low, which happened periodically, he skipped breakfast and supper, going through the whole day on a ten-cent lunch, then, as a check from his father reached him, rushing out to refuel himself. Dr. Lindsay, who was deeply in debt and had two daughters still to provide for, sent what he could when he could and Vachel did his best to make it last.

"It is hard to go on very much less," he wrote home.

By May 16, being really broke, he couldn't eat. He couldn't draw, having no cash to buy paper. Lacking the nickel fare, he couldn't ride back to his room from the Institute, so he walked—setting out at five and arriving at seven. He borrowed from his landlord for supper. Next morning, mercifully, a check came.

At this time his mother wrote to him anxiously, after receiving his latest poem: "You *must* concentrate your mind on some one line of work soon that will be a means of support."

He would be twenty-two in the fall, she reminded him. If he meant to become a professional illustrator it was well enough for him to write poetry sometimes—"but your main thought and effort must be to choose out some one line of illustration."

"I am choosing," Lindsay wrote in the margin of her letter, which he answered by telling both his parents that he had put down in each of his seven notebooks a solemn date. He gave himself two years at the Institute and if by June 15, 1903, he hadn't finished there, he would leave anyway.

"On that fifteenth of June," he vowed, "I am going to become self-supporting as sure as I have arms and legs."

11

At noon one day during this summer of 1901 a "large alone man" wandering through the gallery of the Institute was pointed out to Lindsay as Theodore Roosevelt, who had been till recently Governor of New York and was now Vice President of the United States.

Lindsay told his family: "So I walked up to the man, and since he looked like his picture I said, 'Isn't this the Vice President?'

"He said, 'I am,' and we shook hands with mutual pleasure. Then we had a flow of mutual soulful smiles for several seconds. He wanted to know my line. I told him I was just a student learning to draw. I said, 'You don't want anybody to walk around here with you or anything like that, do you?' I was keeping step with him. We walked abreast in sooth.

"But the V.P. answered with his blandest tone that he preferred to enjoy the works in solitude.

"Then I shook him kindly by the hand and said, 'I am pleased to have met you, Governor,' and left him to the smiles of the plaster nymphs. He strode our honored galleries for an hour alone, and I am the only one who dared to beard the lion.

"I am glad I met him. I think I did him good. He left this afternoon for your country. If you see him tell him howdy for me."

Lindsay was taking the long walk back to the south side almost every other night, partly to save carfare, partly because he had much to think about. His mother was worried that he saw too few people, and his father suggested that a big city can be more lonely than the mountains.

Washington Park, which had the refreshment of trees and water, swarmed with refugees from the stifling tenements as he passed through: couples shared picnic suppers and solitary men lay asleep, their heads pillowed on the front wheels of bicycles over which their coats were thrown. On reaching his room he sat down in the dark beside the open window, deeply pondering.

"What I mean by success," he wrote to his father, "is first, self-support—secondly, a definite work in the world that no man has ever done before, which will use all my personality and force, and help a great cause."

He now had fifteen notebooks active.

"American art," he declared in one, "must be driven into great deep foundations, and in an entirely American way." He had been reading the life of William Morris, and it struck him that "the socialists want the millennium without waiting for the laws of growth to work."

"Let us," he urged his imagined audience, "be patient with the democratic house the Lord has built for us, let us strengthen its foundations and widen its windows and love it, for there is room within it for all nations and all liberty."

He called on Fred at the County Hospital, watched him assist at a major operation on a little boy, who had lost a leg and three toes in a streetcar accident, and thanked his stars for his own escape from doctoring.

At the Institute, where he had begun to draw from the nude, the teacher said his drawing was thin, and in another letter to his father, who was impatient for some word of progress, he prophesied soberly: "It will take me ten years to learn how to draw as well as I know how to write now."

He had therefore a new scheme: when the summer term was over, to join the staff of a newspaper as a reporter, save his money and study art at night. In his free time, he began to comb the city's newspaper offices, though the heat was stunning, with the temperature at 101. By early August he had personally interviewed every important managing editor and applied for any work, by day or night, to every paper in Chicago, except the foreign-language ones. "But they all refuse," he told his father, "claim to be overcrowded with help."

He applied to a big advertising agency and was turned down. He was reading a history of Greece, keeping alive on Uneeda biscuits—several times lately he had "felt funny" from bad eating—sitting in the evening in the park, studying in the public library, writing in his room, then meditating for hours with the lights out.

"I am on the bum," he wrote dispiritedly in his diary, and again to his father: "Two things are settled with me, first that I shall pay my way, and secondly I shall live and die an artist."

Lindsay went home for a brief visit in September, three days after President McKinley died as the delayed result of an assassin's bullet and Roosevelt became President. At home his parents took him to task for the vagueness of his plans. He came back to Chicago on the night train and by ten in the morning had found himself a job at Marshall Field's, in the toy department.

"*Just* such a position as I imagined would be best," he reported jubilantly to his father and mother that night. "It is manual labor, mainly."

When they answered that they wished he would make a success in some one line, he pleaded with them not to fret; he had taken the job to pay for his art education. "You are always skeptical," he reproached his mother.

For $6.00 a week he sorted boxes of dolls, wheeling them in a handcart across the huge floor and stacking them for shipment. The best thing was not having to account to his parents for his time and money, and he assured them again: "I am quite happy. I never was better satisfied with the whole world and myself."

But with the approach of Christmas, Field's toy department became chaos and the stock boys toiled from eight-thirty in the morning till midnight, at which hour Lindsay with the rest staggered out into the icy, wind-blasted street, almost too tired to stand. What price self-sufficiency? On December 5 he quit, admitting in his diary: "I guess the night work did it."

"My dear Father," he wrote, breaking the news, "I would be highly honored indeed if you would send me $5 to come home on. I quit Field's about a week ago to look around for something better after Christmas."

Out of bondage and roaming alone through the city thronged with Christmas shoppers, he now conceived a poem suggestive of the hush and reverence of desert solitude, *Star of My Heart*, his first poem of pilgrimage:

> Star of my heart, I follow from afar.
> Sweet Love on high, lead on where shepherds are,
> Where Time is not, and only dreamers are.
> Star from of old, the Magi-Kings are dead
> And a foolish Saxon seeks the manger-bed.

12

Contrary to his resolutions, Lindsay had fallen in love. At least, he thought he had; there was always an Eve in his Eden. Ruth Wheeler, who lived in Akron, had been his "perch" at Hiram—one of many, but since college one of the few to answer his long letters faithfully. Thus he kept in touch with her and, uncertain though his prospects were, his parents were pleased when he told them at Christmas of his growing attachment, for Ruth was a serious-minded, Christian girl.

How to reconcile the idea of marriage with his bachelor's dream of consecration to a great cause, he knew not. Back in Chicago in January 1902, after spending the holiday at home, he resumed his art classes, for which his father was still paying. But his certain success, he promised both his parents, was simply a matter of concentrating his will. "It is will, will, will that is needed!"

Soon the busy editors of *McClure's*, *The Bookman*, *Everybody's Magazine* and *The Century* had all, with varying degrees of courtesy, refused his poems and drawings. But the Art Institute itself was on the lookout for able young men. "I would not want it repeated," confided Vachel to his family, "but I verily believe if I fill myself *full to the top* with the real *art-spirit* I can get a place on the faculty."

"Now let's think it over," he urged.

A tremendous exhibition by Chicago illustrators had opened and "I wish you could see it. In ten years I can beat such a gang as they are!" he boasted to his father.

His private doubts were for his diary. For his own eyes he

wrote: "I mustn't think for a minute that I am going to be a failure. I must be both an artistic and a financial success. Every man of my station in a civilized land should. Those who love him have no right to be happy if he is not a success."

Yet at the Institute few took him seriously. His hopeful attempts at friendship were rebuffed. In a desperation of mental solitude he sent the Chicago clergyman Herbert Lockwood Willett, editor of the *Christian Century*, an ardent letter from his very soul, imploring help out of one of the confusions that beset him—his search for a belief. He recalled later: "I wanted to know *someone*, no matter who, whose brains and position I could respect, with whom I could thrash out the questions that were shaking me to pieces."

Dr. Willett's scholarly, condescending reply ("A colossal egotist—" was one phrase) brought no comfort and Lindsay cast inward, writing in his diary: "I have faith in many religions for many other men but I have not enough religion of my own. God, give me a place where the spirit can rest and grow, give me a real rock of ages cleft for me, give me a labor of love that shall not be in vain."

So far, he had little to show for his time in Chicago. He had come seeking freedom to create, but the Institute, where his chief instructor was Frederick Richardson, taught art as it might teach arithmetic. For months now he had plodded on, copying pyramids of blocks, plaster casts of parts of the body, then the human face and last of all the divine but treacherous human form. Richardson's aim was for his pupils to reproduce literally what their eyes saw, whereas Lindsay's aim for himself was always to "start art with a *vision*, with a beautiful idealization of the thing you see."

Vision he had. In his very first class, though, he had discovered he couldn't draw a flowing line, nor could he sketch or handle masses. Since then his technique had barely strengthened, but he had read much and pondered—noticing how in his reading an idea that was nearer to literature than art carried him along more powerfully—and his best output lay between the covers of his well-filled diary-notebooks, in one of which, begun in September, 1902, he inquired thoughtfully what ought to be "the attitude of a good Democrat and American" toward the old European masters of art.

Then he answered: "Our young Republic must inherit the masters, but scarcely their disciples."

A good American, continued Lindsay, should study the art work of his native country, seeking out in American artists what they have got from the masters directly—"the biggest and most vital elements, the eternal stuff of art"—yet, other than this, concentrating on the distinct American quality.

"Find the absolutely native American painters," he laid down. "Study, study, study them, and on this choose to live and die. It will be your own field, your own, for no one else has attempted such a synthesis. One little thing done from the spirit of the soil is worth a thousand great things done abroad."

All along, too, he had been writing poetry and in January 1903 he made another entry: "It certainly does not pay to be anything but one's self, giving it the highest, most complete artistic expression. Write as we will, there is only one set of people that an earnest soul can vitally move—those are souls that are forever akin.

"The way to strike home most thoroughly and permanently to the largest number is just to be thoroughly true to one's highest—never fearing it will be too exclusive, too personal, too exceptional, too aristocratic, to be understood."

Lindsay thought that sometime he would like to set aside three months just to hear from the beginning the family history of his Grandmother Frazee as only she could tell it, "with the wisdom thrown in." Especially was he interested in American pioneer days; he wanted the origin of the Midwest settlement traced up through his grandmother and mother.

He was reading Keats and Landor, whose rich language gave him the idea of developing an idiom just as romantic but on a wholly American basis. There were plenty of ringing American allusions to take the place of knight-at-arms and dales of Arcady, and he began to list them:

> "Liberty and Union
> Log cabins
> Honest Old Abe
> The Little Giant
> Texas Rangers
> Prairie Schooners
> Indian named rivers

"The forests and prairies our grandfathers found, wild flowers, Grandma's old house. In general, the tradition of Lincoln in Springfield, of one's childhood running around the yard in Springfield, one's dreams of Kentucky."

He had set down the first two lines of a poem to be called *The Land of Lincoln*—

> This is the land of Lincoln,
> Sons of the land, be true!

and though the poem never went further, he proposed to read Lincoln's addresses and Webster's orations for classic American phrases and to eliminate from his writing, even as figures of speech, "these kings, knights, princesses, etcetera."

It was harder than ever to buy art supplies this spring because he was painting in oils, using bigger canvases. In March, innocently taking with him some studies he had done of the nude, he paid a visit home. He was forced to quit the house almost on his knees and from Chicago to compose a letter of abject apology: "My dear Papa, I am very very sorry."

Dr. Lindsay—as a medical man ignorant of no squalor and perversity under the fair face of the prairie—as a father believed that for Vachel to draw from the nude was an act of infidelity to Ruth. "Please," his son entreated, "do not deduce from my drawings made with so much prayerful earnest effort and resolution and loyalty to my lady anything less than these. I am not going to the bad. There is where you do your only son a great wrong.

"Viewed theoretically, I do not like the nude much better than you. I am going to neglect it all I possibly can. I am going to study hard on draperies and conceal my ignorance all I can by them. It may cheer you to know that I received *my first commendation* from Richardson this afternoon on a composition in which the figures were very heavily draped."

Long ago he had named June 15, 1903, as the day when he would become self-supporting. The time was almost up but he had postponed the decisive date indefinitely. He wrote to tell them at home they were no longer to imagine he had dreams of being on the Institute faculty—"I have other dreams now."

His latest was to go to New York in October to study painting with William Merritt Chase and Chase's associate, the revolutionary Robert Henri. By early summer he had his parents' reluctant consent—reluctant because it meant that at twenty-three he would still be dependent on them. Nevertheless, the money would be found.

Meantime, he went back to Springfield. While the rest of the family was in Colorado, he stayed behind in the house, watering the grass and seeing that the cat was fed. Mornings and afternoons he devoted to drawing and writing; he was conscious of the promise of better things coming in his work. Susan Wilcox, to whom he still took his poems, advised him to bring out their natural music, to be less preachy and "never to suppress his appetite for magic."

The long summer evenings were for sociability. He called on the girls as they held court on lawns or in porch swings, while the phonographs sang appropriate selections. Back at the echoing house, he dragged his mattress downstairs and slept in the hall inside the front door, which he left open for coolness, with the screen door hooked.

He sent Ruth half a dozen American Beauties. She was to work all summer in a hot YWCA office, he to live on will power and love letters and manage somehow to send her another half a dozen roses before summer ended—or, if he could, a dozen—which would be to court her "not as *you* would like to be courted," he explained in a letter to his mother, "but in the way *she* loves. You see I am fereful of being scolded and I can't bear to be scolded on such a sensitive place. Now *please* don't let Olive know."

13

Lindsay stopped in Akron on his way to New York and he and Ruth became engaged. That is, "she considers herself engaged," he wrote home.

At the New York School of Art on West Fifty-seventh Street, where he was now enrolled, the teaching was modern, the method intimate. The classes were picked and the quality of the students' work ten times superior to that of the Chicago Institute, though the school was much smaller. There were no gentle little Miss Bakers wearing blue waists and spectacles. The gods who inspired were masculine. They were William Chase, irascible and dandified, having always a white carnation in his buttonhole, and Robert Henri (pronounced *Hen*-rye), who was Chase's right hand, a lean dark tall man of thirty-eight with punchinello features and a rasping voice in which he scoffed at art for art's sake, urging his pupils to look all about them at the great violent city and paint what they liked in it.

"Chase is a much broader man than Henri, in life and art," was Lindsay's student verdict. "But Henri is electrical, intense, fascinating."

Lindsay collared Henri right away for a criticism of his drawings and "he praised them a-plenty" (thus Lindsay to his family). Chase also talked strongly to him, telling him he ought to aim high. "I feel," he wrote home, "I am holding my end up."

Right away, too, he had felt the difference in atmosphere over Chicago. In a fragment written later, a casual jotting down of lines, he reminisced of the days

87

When Henri made it springtime weather
There on Fifty-seventh Street,
When Chase was still alive and fleet,
When he stood on his tiptoes to glower,
And praised great Whistler by the hour.

But Henri was the dashing one,
The hero of young students then . . .

On Sundays Lindsay divided most of his time between
doings at the Disciples Church and the Metropolitan Museum
of Art. But he also strayed into the Church of St. Paul the
Apostle at Columbus Circle, presided over by the Paulist
fathers, then went again. The same hint of invisible forces
communicated by Egyptian sculptures in the Museum he
sensed in the mystery of the Host and the glory of the Mass.
It came to him that the whole history of art is the history of
temples and priesthoods and he made up his mind to understand *every* church.

Studying with him under Henri on weekday mornings were
Rockwell Kent, George Luks and George Bellows. In the afternoons he brushed his clothes, looked his sweetest, and taking
his muse bravely by the hand led her up and down the streets
of a city bigger even than Chicago, whose historic buildings
were older than any in the West and whose new ones like
the Flatiron brought to his mind the towers of Babylon, while
he called on picture dealers and magazine editors.

At the office of *The Critic*, the assistant editor was Ridgely
Torrence, reputed one of the coming younger poets. Torrence
at once expressed enthusiasm for Lindsay's poems and drawings, but the stumbling block to acceptance seemed to be the
Critic's editress-in-chief, the acidulous Miss Jeannette Gilder.
Then in January Lindsay wrote home the glorious news that
not only had "the wicked Gorgon" (Miss Gilder) accepted
some of his poetry, she had taken his drawings to show her
brother, Richard Watson Gilder, editor of *The Century*—
"who used in describing them the dreadful phrase 'young
genius.' "

"Your son has arrived at last!" he exulted, and on the envelope of his letter his thankful mother noted: "Vachel's first
real success. Preserve!"

But her thankfulness was premature, for the weeks went by
and nothing happened except that through Torrence Lindsay
met Zona Gale, a gifted newspaper woman, who praised his
verse, and that he submitted to the *Century* a huge folder of
his pictures and had them all turned down. "I am a terribly
poor painter," he confided in another letter home, "but I hope
some day to paint better than I can draw. That will be none
too well."

Of his dozens of poems submitted, *The Queen of Bubbles*
and one other finally appeared in the *Critic*. Three years later
all the rest were returned. The *Century* would have none of
him, ever.

It was a disappointment that never ceased to rankle; indeed,
it festered in him. "Take the Richard Watson Gilder story—"
he wrote in 1929, passing furious final judgment on an editor
whom most young poets had found sympathetic and accessible,
"after sending me endless flatteries via Zona Gale and her set,
Ridgely Torrence and his gang, I was kicked down the coal-
hole for fair!"

But he was still optimistic when in June 1904 he went home
for Olive's marriage to his friend Paul Wakefield, just graduated from Rush Medical College. There had been some words
between him and his mother over his homecoming, he first
insisting he much preferred to stay in New York all summer
and seek paying work.

"A manufactured excuse," Mrs. Lindsay called this.

"My dear mother," retorted her son, "are you the only
person who can possibly have a high motive when there is a
difference of opinion? I am here in New York because it is
my *duty*."

The wedding ceremony was at Springfield's First Christian
Church. Diminutive, dark Olive in her white veil made an
exquisite bride. Vachel in a cutaway was the best man. The

five bridesmaids, carrying on their shoulders down the aisle a fragrant chain woven of sweet peas and smilax, included fifteen-year-old Joy, and Ruth had come from Akron to be maid of honor.

For a wedding present Vachel had given Olive two of his poems. In the matter of his poetry she had stood by him like his second self—"always understanding," said her brother, just as his father, though without understanding, had stood by him financially.

Lindsay stayed on at home after the wedding and during the summer he began to have some curious experiences. He called them "visions." He never lost his head over these visions or tried to explain them as other than the projections of a strongly visual imagination, but it should be understood that—like William Blake—he actually saw them.

"It is plausible, I think," he wrote afterward, "that for one who had so long co-ordinated drawings and poems for drawings, his religious experiences should paint themselves before him in the air. Being taught by that admirable practical but unimaginative master William M. Chase never to draw a thing till I saw it on the blank paper before me, it was only the terrible power and blaze of the pictures that came that made them unusual."

The first time, which was at night, he beheld with his bodily eyes, so clearly that he could have painted them, the prophets of the Old Testament pass in gorgeous garb through his bedroom. The second time, by day, he saw the prophets march gravely before the tall elm tree in the front yard.

He believed his visions were not infallible but to be interpreted however he chose; they were a part of his artistic capital. Yet they had been sent, like all strong convictions. It was late, late at night in the awed aftermath of the first of them that he wrote his mystical poem *A Prayer in the Jungles of Heaven*.

For the next six months, which he spent in Springfield, he lived in a fever of imagining as he constructed in his mind the cosmic system he called his "universe," drawing on paper an elaborate map of his imaginary realm, then writing about it intensively in poems and stories that on his return to New York he brought together in his first book—never published—called *Where Is Aladdin's Lamp.* The title was from the poem by James Russell Lowell:

> When I was a beggarly boy
> And lived in a cellar damp,
> I had not a friend nor a toy
> But I had Aladdin's Lamp.
>
> When I could not sleep for the cold
> I had fire enough in my brain,
> And builded, with roofs of gold,
> My beautiful castles in Spain!

Fire enough Lindsay had, indeed. In prose and verse he tells the adventures of three striving young heroes, aspects of himself, known as the Painter, the Evangelist and the Counselor. Sensitive to the invisible, they search through the wild universe of his creating for Aladdin's Lamp, guided in their quest by "the gleam"—as in Tennyson's poem *Merlin and The Gleam*—which is that magic or unknown quantity in spiritual life proposed by the seers, like Blake and Poe, and denied by the scientists, like Edison and the Wright brothers.

Lindsay uses visual symbols in *Where Is Aladdin's Lamp* and his "Map of the Universe" that recur in some of his most famous poems. In these early tales blooms the Amaranth, his emblem of eternal beauty, and winged censers in the air pour down purifying incense over the roofs of Springfield. He writes also of the crucifixion of the angels who sided with Lucifer, first of the great poet-vagabonds, against God, and of the profane love of the Archangel Michael—he of "the great purple wings"—for a beautiful witch who lives in Lake Michigan.

He tells how the prophets, led by Isaiah, descend at night from heaven in a cloud of silvery flying boats, how they disembark and go about with jars of purple wine—the blood of the angels crucified for beauty—pouring and repouring it till every jar holds a drop from every other.

"This is the communion wine of the universe," writes Lindsay. "When it is mingled a little Christ enters into it a little; when it shall be mingled completely, Christ shall enter into it in the fullness of His power. . . ."

Thus was the simple communion ceremony that he grew up with in the Disciples Church transfigured and the pouring out of angels' blood become his symbol of the union of faiths, of a dream of the Church Universal, "which, however it may change its form, you have given me so that it can never leave me," he once told his mother.

When he returned to New York after Christmas, it was not as an art student. He had reached an understanding with his parents, which was that his subsidized year was over and he would find a job immediately. "Tomorrow I start out," he promised them, writing on New Year's Day 1905.

Though he was no longer Henri's pupil, he sought out the painter in his studio. *Where Is Aladdin's Lamp* was finished. Lindsay had illustrated it, copied it in his own writing with many misspellings, bound it between yellow pasteboard covers on which the title was hand-lettered and embellished in India ink, and in the preface thrown down his gauge to editors: "This book was written, invented, illustrated, designed, decorated and bound by me!"

He laid the weird-looking manuscript before Henri who—after commenting that the faces in the drawings were doll-like and the figures lacked action—abruptly advised him to show the book to some publishers, starting with the big men at the top. "You'll find as many fools there as anywhere else," said Henri.

"Mr. Henri," Lindsay told his parents, "is a terribly frank man."

At the office of Harper's the art editor fussed over him like a proud uncle, telling him he was sure to succeed, even if Harper's was too conservative for his stuff. At Scribner's the business manager read through the poem about the Archangel Michael and the lovely witch and then said "he was sorry, his house didn't handle that line of goods."

Lindsay stopped in at the *Century* to see Mr. Gilder (he hadn't yet lost faith in the Gilders), who almost bought, but in the end did not buy, a large and fanciful poster he had made. Over at the *Critic* office Miss Gilder, still cordially disposed, gave him a letter to the American business manager for John Lane, which raised his hopes sky-high, till he discovered that that individual was out of town.

On January 21 he reported home that he had been "hustling and hunting" for three weeks, and three days later, to his father: "I will have to ask you to keep me for another month, I hope no longer."

He had rented a room in a boarding house on West Fifty-sixth Street, where the other young men were kindred spirits: Willard Wheeler from Springfield (no relation to Ruth), Jack Jones, who knew the sculptor Gutzon Borglum, and George Mather Richards, an art student under Chase. "I am associating with three fellows who are Christian gentlemen," he told his mother. "We are plenty conservative in our behavior in all matters in which you have any right to be anxious."

They strode four abreast down Broadway, their arms linked and swinging, and Vachel, his blond hair blown back, chanting at the top of his lungs, "The hounds of spring are on winter's traces!"

Still jobless, he went again to Henri's studio and this time asked the painter if he thought that he, Vachel, ought to concentrate on writing for a while and put drawing second. His authentic inspirations for poems, which came to him in flashes, were born without any reference to pictures and he never intended to illustrate his *best* verse. Then he jumped to his feet and recited for Henri and for Mrs. Henri, whom her husband called in from the luncheon table, a very long, strange and musical poem from his book, *The Tree of Laughing Bells*.

During the year that Lindsay studied with him, Henri had

noticed how his imagination far outstripped his execution in drawing and painting. Now, no sooner had the boy left off reciting, than Henri spoke out forcefully, urging him to make the shift.

For Lindsay it was a turning point.

For Henri—"one of my great memories," he wrote to his former pupil in 1926, "is the day long ago when you came to my studio and read to me *The Tree of Laughing Bells*. As I have followed you in all the great work you have done, I have a kind of pride about that moment because I had said to myself then, 'This fellow is a poet—he is a singer of songs.' "

14

A few days after his talk with Henri, Lindsay ordered printed one hundred copies each of two of his poems, his friend George Richards helping him with the money.

Next he took a plunge. Inspired partly by the stories told of President Roosevelt—who, when up against stubborn opposition, was said to bypass the entrenched powers and go with his case straight to the people—and also by the example of the troubadours of old, he put on his overcoat, stuffed the pocket with printed leaflets of one of his poems, *We Who Are Playing Tonight*, which was about children in the Chicago slums and was illustrated with a grotesque drawing, walked briskly down the steps of his brownstone boarding house and headed for Tenth Avenue.

It was eleven at night on March 23, 1905.

Keeping to the west side of the avenue, he proceeded—slowly now—downtown, peering into shop windows of which only about one in ten was still lighted. He was in search of "kindly faces, honest faces." He went first into a bakery and tried to give a copy of his poem to the big sleepy shock-haired baker, who listened dumb and bewildered, then with a touch of irritated independence thrust the paper back, saying he had no use for it.

Lindsay took the hint. At the next shop he said nothing about giving but told the proprietor he would "sell him that" for two cents. The man (his name, for posterity, was Charlie Suess, at 881 Tenth Avenue) smiled and answered, as he picked out the money from the till: "Newspapers cost only one cent," to which Lindsay gamely rejoined: "You can see me, the author. That's why I charge the other cent, and I made that myself."

"It looks like it," said Mr. Suess, laughing.

At the Klondyke Fish Market the stringy, sympathetic little boss uttered not a word as, quick as a wink, he bought the proffered work of art, his manner intimating: "Poor devil, you're trying to earn your living and I wouldn't hold you back from it, knowing how it goes."

The next place was a candy shop. But as Lindsay noted afterward, "the whole tour, the candy shops turned me down. They deal out sweets for the flesh, not the spirit."

In a Chinese laundry five Chinamen were ironing the night away as he marched up to the long linen-swathed table.

"Good evening, gentlemen!"

Five flatirons swung hypnotically.

"I have here a beautiful and unworthy little poem for your exalted and celestial eyes."

Not a yellow face changed.

"Awake, O slumbering China! Here is a message for you."

It was no use. At last the messenger capitulated, saying, "Goodnight, gentlemen," to which the five Chinese with instant and extravagant politeness replied: "Goodnight!
Goodnight!
Goodnight!
Goodnight!
Goodnight!"

At Forty-second Street Lindsay turned east and trudged a lonely block to Ninth Avenue, passing a few prowling drunks and several of what he called "bad women." On Ninth, after only three sales ("Every cent counts with us," said one shop owner), he challenged himself: "Now for Broadway!"

Three men were lounging and kidding in a Broadway drug store. When he walked in and offered his poem, one of them shuffled away fast, the second gazed bleakly at the back wall, while the third stared straight through Lindsay, who began to read his poem aloud, causing the staring one such fearful embarrassment that the poet took pity on him and departed.

"Poor confused things!" was his verdict. "Maybe they had a notion that poetry is only found in books."

"Did you ever do any drawing?" he jauntily asked the young boy clerk in the next store. "Here is a little idea of mine. I sell them for two cents."

"This is a hell of a time of night to bring around those things," said the boy finally, as he sauntered behind the till and threw out the coins.

"Now let there be here recorded," Lindsay wrote next day in his diary, "my conclusions from one evening, one hour of peddling poetry. I am so rejoiced over it and so uplifted I am going to do it many times. It sets the heart trembling with happiness. The people like poetry as well as the scholars, or better."

He had made thirteen cents, but he was not after money. Not even the refusals had much power to hurt him, and the glances of understanding, smiles of brotherhood and words of sympathy that had come his way flowed through him with a spreading warmth. What he was really seeking was love.

"Those that bought under all disguises could not conceal from me that they had hearts full of dreams, and some of those that refused were dreamers too shy to confess it to themselves. Oh, they are my friends, and I have loved all those that bought my work and some that did not."

He went out again, taking with him his second poem, *The Cup of Paint*, which he had had printed on red paper, then cut each sheet in the shape of a cup and pasted the red cups onto stiff black paper. He had written the poem after his first and only visit to a burlesque house in Chicago; its meaning was that every actor, unless he is a real artist, is no more than a "drinker of paint."

This time he tried the east side. His principal duel of personalities was with an ogre in a cigar store. "I made this picture for you," he began.

"I didn't ask you to make it for me."

"Don't you like it pretty well?"

"No."

"I want to give it to you."

"I don't want it. Don't care for it at all."

"Ah," says Lindsay's diary, "he was business, business, business. . . ."

On April 8 he went out for the last time, to Hell's Kitchen on Eleventh Avenue south of Sixty-third, but it was Saturday night; shopmen and customers were preoccupied. There was no use trying to talk to people in a store with a customer. The empty shops were the kindly ones. It struck him that men who are susceptible to poetry are likely to be those with little gift for business, whom the throng passes by.

He did not again try peddling. He had other things to think about. A week earlier he had written to Ruth a long and long meditated letter asking that their informal engagement be terminated, and then one to his parents saying that if there were blame in the matter he would take it.

15

Lindsay's mother answered him sympathetically, and in a third letter he laid before her his case for breaking his engagement—the outside of it, at least. The inside was pretty hard to explain.

If he had an income and could marry Ruth the next day, he would. It was the strain of waiting, waiting, with no end in sight that was too much. There was no mental companionship between them to bridge the separation. He had far freer, more spirited communication with Olive and Paul, or Susan Wilcox, or Henri and Richards.

He and Ruth had both tried hard, but all the time they were engaged she was undergoing a struggle between her heart and her home training. "The Wheeler ideals," said Lindsay, "are three: orthodox religion, style and money."

After his very first visit to the Wheelers when he was still in college, he had mercilessly compared them with his own vigorous and unconventional people. "To perfectly satisfy the Wheeler family," he told his mother now, "I must abstain from all ideas that are new, all points of view not fully expounded in the *Ladies' Home Journal*. I must confine my restless mind to saying my prayers, dressing my manly form in style and making money. *Nothing* based on deep reading, personal observation, or a study of the real masters on any line is understandable. These three, prayers, money and style, are the whole gauntlet of human endeavor."

By the standards of the Wheelers of this world, if the poems he worked so hard over were printed in the papers *then* they must be all right. "The appearance is the thing. The soul and the dreaming and the life that go behind these things is absurd. It never entered the Wheeler imagination. Now—Ruth is a modified Wheeler. She makes all kinds of effort to follow and enjoy these things, but with several states between us, with nothing but Wheelers around her, how can we live together in spirit?"

Since ending their relationship, he had felt very lonely but lightened of strain. He could plan ahead without panic, without trying to make an income for two every day and therefore making nothing.

"When we see the uncertainty from day to day it behooves us to look forward to the certainty of the ultimate goal," he reminded his mother. "I think that everything points to permanent success."

But after four years of struggle to establish himself he had begun to realize that, after all, success with him would never be a money success. "Once I have a bare living, I want to bend my soul to really *being something* to my time, to *count* for something and not be a mere scratcher for money."

To his mother a year earlier he had confided: "There are hours when I feel I am a man with a message. . . ."

He had not known, and he did not yet know, what his message was to be, only that for the present he must give his thoughts time to grow. His creative work came first of all. He must allow no false standard of duty to keep him from it. His first divine call was as "a maker of beautiful things," after which and only then would he have a second call, to preach— to speak directly to his age and nation and religious brotherhood and the Midwest.

Now he ended with an appeal: "I am sorely in need of real intercourse with your mind, but it is a real exchange I want. Set aside your tendency to write me orations. Get into the mood in which you used to make your pictures or write your best verses when you were a girl of seventeen."

He and his mother could be sweethearts again if she would go back to seventeen. He was offering her his real heart. It did not open every day and he begged her to accept it.

16

Free of his engagement, Lindsay felt a spurt of creative power and he projected a poem on Edgar Allan Poe in hell, writing in his diary that "morally Poe is to be damned. He knows it, we know it. We admit that and pass it by. . . . But in your heart of hearts" (he was speaking now to Poe) "a demon whispers consolation and all the other demons gather to comfort, saying 'You are the magician.' "

He also conceived the idea of writing American songs in city rhythms and a brass band style and, again in his diary, planned a host of poems on the "eternal splendid antithesis" between the roar of modern machinery and the whisper of the supernatural. He would pit the old world of prophet-wizards against the modern one of science.

"Rouse, ye demons," he exhorted the spirits invisible. "Suffer yourselves to be no longer driven into the corner! Come forth, beautiful witches, and challenge the electric light, tear it from the pole, dash it down, leave the city in darkness. . . . Lead the souls of the buffaloes against Chicago. Lead them roaming across the continent, till they shall outroar the city—and beat it down."

This was the genesis of his later poem *The Ghosts of the Buffaloes*, in which the poet wakes at midnight to find the city gone and his house become a hut of logs on the prairie, across whose rim gallops the spectral herd:

> Buffaloes, buffaloes, thousands abreast,
> A scourge and amazement, they swept to the west.

Yet still the terrible dependency of his position drove him almost crazy. He still dashed from pillar to post importuning this man and that, getting nowhere. He could not be a successful "drummer"; he could not. He had not the art of blandishment. He believed it was even wrong to cringe and plead with editors and publishers to accept what they could not understand. "Better than this is to heave coal. Better than this is to dig ditches."

Nor would he lower the quality of his product to meet the requirements of this or that class. "One is slandering the race when he does anything but his best work. Your true democrat is Poe as much as Longfellow."

Notwithstanding Henri's advice to concentrate on writing, his creative impulse was still divided, though he knew the time had come when he must centralize: he had long been aware that he had too many points of interest, that he should choose one, stick to it and hammer away till something happened. "I am absolutely demoralized unless I can concentrate. I have tried everything and done nothing since January first."

He was sitting in his hall bedroom at three in the morning of May 16, 1905, while he thus dejectedly took stock. "God help us all to be brave," he wrote.

At this dark moment newspaper work seemed the thing again. He began to plan how for a start he would bombard the papers with timely articles on the sights of modern Babylon, of which his notebooks teemed with details. When day came, the plan still seemed good and he wrote to his father, thanking him for his years of loyalty and begging him to stand by just a little longer till the new idea could be given a trial.

On May 29 he wrote again. "Will you please send me $25. I groan as I ask for it, and I don't want it unless you can spare it. It will not always be this way. When I once make my own way, I will be a new man."

That evening after writing home, he left his room and took the subway to Brooklyn Bridge, where he paced to and fro along the almost deserted walk for foot passengers. The sky was a beautiful deep brown, the water of the river black-purple. The city of Babylon lay asleep under a scattering of lights. Below him were the railway tracks and the cars careered by at intervals, leaving in the wake of each thundering passage a silence so sensitive he could hear his heart beat.

The next night he sat again in his room. "At half-past one this morning," he wrote, "my heart is hungry with desire to lay hold of, and live and die with the vision that possesses me. I see God in the greatness of His cold high beauty."

Suddenly he knew why monks spend their lives in prayer, with what motive Michelangelo carved the great statues of Night and Morning. "Oh my God," he continued, "give me this thing to hold to—let my rock of ages be granted to me— if I can only have this vision for a moment every day I can do all things that I have been sent to do."

It might be that this moment's intuition of "the Beauty that no man can name" would never return. The very words he was setting down to record it might soon read cold and dead to him. He prayed that this would not be so, but that the principle of eternal beauty in all things (the element in the poetry of Keats that stands higher than the bloom and ripeness) would abide with him, to give his spirit strength and calm his trivial passions.

"I have seen my God face to face," Lindsay wrote. "How can I blaspheme Him ever? Why am I made to forget what I lose, to lose the dream I worship, to be stupid, to be shameful, to be hot with fool fire, to be paralyzed by the struggle for life, to be daunted by the stupidity of men?

"God make me strong—help me to look you always in the face and see your stern eyes on my soul. Then if I am weak, I can wait for strength, then if I am wounded, I can be healed, then if I am still selfish, I can at least be worth something to men—serving my God, I can serve them."

17

If he had no job by October, he would come home, Lindsay promised his parents. He had no job by August, but he had a new plan of endeavor for the writing, printing, illustrating with his own wood blocks and hand-binding of little books, each one of which should be a work of art. The series could start with children's fairy tales and later volumes contain his poems, which he would be perfectly content to have go before the world thus—"I have the egotism to consider my poems valuable and I have perfect faith they will take their rank in time."

He had joined with George Richards and several other men to form a bachelor club in a house they rented in the West Eighties. They had engaged a cook and a small boy to help, and that cook and that boy were the last straw to Dr. Lindsay, to whom it appeared that his son, a feckless dreamer at almost twenty-six, was living in luxury with a retinue of servants.

He said as much. He said a good deal more (Vachel had just proposed his booklets) so that with hurt and anger the son retorted: "The gist of the matter is, you are about as impatient for me to be off your hands as I am to get off."

But the members of the club hung together and one of them, a youth named Nicholls, spoke a word in time for Lindsay to his own father, who ran a factory in New York. In October 1905 Lindsay was hired by the Nicholls Gas Tubing Works to load armfuls of rubber tubing into the freight elevator and hoist barrels of it onto trucks. He wore overalls, ate a sandwich lunch and discovered for himself the social experience sung by Whitman—if you work shoulder to shoulder with a good man (at Nicholls' it was Frank, the shipping clerk) though having no other thing in common with him but decency and kindness, you love him.

With his nerves calmer than in years and his dreams no longer haunted by the money nightmare, it was in a changed and happier mood that he turned again to them at home, pleading "Now let's be good to each other."

Olive, who was expecting her first baby, and Paul were to sail within the month for China, where Paul had been appointed a medical missionary, and their going would make a gap that Vachel longed to fill. He was the son; it was for him to be more of a son, to help carry his share of the burden.

Then there was talk that Joy might be sent east to Smith College and, if it were possible, he would like to pay a part of her tuition, he told his parents. "It is no more than right that I should. Remember that you have a son who wants to be a comfort to you. Don't leave me out, I am not leaving you out. If we cannot think alike, we must agree to disagree and love each other anyhow.

"I want to be true to all of you, and this in spite of the fact I cannot think the way any of you do. It must just be trusting and loving all the way round."

It was at night when the factory let out that he did his real living, as on Tuesdays from eight to ten when after a lively supper at the club ("Where we have grace before meals, and generally," Lindsay added, "many graceful remarks during meals") he went to the YMCA. There he led a class in art— "a bunch of about twenty fellows around a table with their elbows on it, asking me all the questions they please."

Every Friday at the same hours he personally conducted the same twenty, which included several loyal club members and a few students he had known at Chase's, through the picture galleries of the Metropolitan. Before the Nicholls Works hired him, he had approached the secretary at one of the Y houses and begged for something to do. "What can you do?" the man inquired.

He could organize and teach a class in art appreciation, said Lindsay, and the secretary, Mr. Powlinson, told him to go ahead. At first he was paid nothing, but soon he landed a new course of five lectures on art, at $10 apiece. Since the lectures took time to prepare and the ten dollars equaled his weekly wage, he gave up the tubing works.

Now every teaching day he awoke happy; the sun streamed down through the skylight onto his pillow. In the classroom at night he sat at the head of the long, attentive table: it was a great experience. "I may kindle a fire yet within that little room!"

But when his classes at the Y should be over beyond the possibility of any further stringing out, he would be willing to go back to Springfield. He needed to earn his salt while he developed on the side his system of book making and cover designing. As he got a little income in his pocket, besides contributing to Joy's tuition he hoped to help Olive and Paul. So "if you could find me some sort of a position, or suggest one," he conceded to his ever-doubting parents, "I might take it, some day."

18

Ever since the months he spent at home after Olive's wedding, Lindsay had been having "visions." Sometimes he used the word to mean pictures that for all their vividness remained within the chamber of his brain —he saw them not with outward eyes; at other times he meant real apparitions.

In December 1905 he volunteered to distribute 2,000 tickets for a YMCA meeting among shops and restaurants from Forty-second Street to Central Park, and as he tramped the city, visions came to him so many and wonderful that their account filled two notebooks. He set one book aside for "magic" or "spiritual adventures that approach the unseen," while the other was for actuality, or "all other things but magic."

Into this second book went his encounter one day at noon, in a cheap lunchroom on Sixth Avenue, with a young girl whose exotic, eastern-looking face had gone straight to his imagination. On entering, she had bowed to the YMCA worker with him, who whispered behind his hand that she was a manicurist, only eighteen, working her way, but keeping pure.

But to Lindsay she was Cleopatra.

"Only eighteen—" he wrote that night, "her eyes were thirty years old, her manners ten thousand years old. I will keep far from you, but Oh, Queen of Egypt, I give thanks to Isis and Osiris that I have seen you! Shame upon the city that will not throne you! If I were Antony, with a kingdom to waste, I would spill it into the ocean for you grandly, grandly. Let the YMCA pray for your soul. But you pray always for Antony, and in vain. Good night."

In his other notebook he was setting forth at the end of each day of passing out tickets what he called "adventures as seen from the eyes of the spirit, all spiritual adventures based upon this mere YMCA task," acknowledging that "there are books on the evidence of religion, but this book is on the evidences of magic in our daily life, when we are caught up into the unseen not so much that we may be saints of heaven, but rather kings of Chaos; that we may create new worlds that will praise us, rather than praise the Power that made us."

"Giving all reverence to the Father," he continued, "our chief joy in this book is that we also are possessed of children."

He was speaking as an artist, a creator. New York was an enchanted city: as he walked the streets, the stone and flesh, machine and material reality were touched by his gaze as by a wizard's wand till "sometimes," he declared, "the walls of the squalid stores open and our souls go into new wonderful passageways. Sometimes the stones beneath our feet turn to jasper. Sometimes the women passing by have their faces flushed with a radiance beyond mortality.

"Let us not shut our eyes to these things."

"Saturday night, December 23," Lindsay wrote. "MacClain, the Scotchman, and I saw three processions down Broadway tonight, as we walked from eight to ten." (The Scotchman was a real person, one of the members of the club.)

"The first procession was led by that king with the purple blood whose name is a grief and a wonder to the ages. He was in a chariot that was all purple wings. He was driving foaming dragons bound to the chariot by bonds unseen; he hissed over their heads a whip of snarling fire."

Behind him marched his armored legions.

"The clank of their tarnished trappings made the roar of the elevated like a still small voice, and their shields of tempered flame made the lights of Broadway like dusty sunflowers at noon."

Then the dazed poet beheld the skyscrapers on either side of Broadway topple, pushed down to the ground by an invisible power. He heard the walls of the buildings scream, like beasts wounded. The legions shouted till the whole city lay in rubble around them, and still they marched on. Suddenly they sank into the earth.

Then the thing happened, "which must happen always," wrote Lindsay, "with those who wait and open their hearts."

The sky became filled with the boats of the prophets sailing earthward like giant feathers. The prophets disembarked; they poured out their purple wine. The great city rose again, and it was the city of the Millennium. A light shone through its anointed walls; the people who trod its streets, though again they were merely human, had a fire behind their eyes.

In the Church of the Paulist fathers, Lindsay had burned more than one candle before the crowned image of Mary, Star of the Sea, whom he accepted as an ideal of motherhood that had grown in the bosoms of all his ancestors "back from the day when Isis, the first Madonna, nourished the sun god, Horus."

"My silver woman," he called the little statue in the niche.

A few days before Christmas, as he walked past Central Park behind the Museum of Natural History, he saw—saw actually —Mary, the Mother of God, hovering in the air before him, smiling, with her golden hair unbound, her hands open and moving as if to shake down to him an armload of flowers, a figure twenty cubits from the ground and twenty cubits tall.

It was a picture cast by the longing of his soul, that he knew. "Nevertheless," he exulted, "I saw her and I loved her."

He had also at this time clear manifestations—these before the eye within—of the bride of his dreams, his ideal maiden. Awake in bed, he contemplated her; asleep, he dreamed of her. He was conscious of desires in himself that he prayed might be "without sin." "Teach us, O Lord," he besought, "the goodness of passion."

And to this rosy daughter not of heaven but of earth, whose body beneath her petal-drapery was radiant with the blood of maidenhood, he promised one day to sing the Song of Songs, to find in her all grace and to her be true forever. He called her Psyche—or Eve—or Lady Romance.

19

Lindsay might dream about his ideal bride, but he had problems enough without taking her to himself. He warned his parents that poems and pictures were as near to grandchildren as they could expect from him for a long, long time. His work alone counted, and the opportunity to do his work must be protected.

This was his state of mind when in March 1906 he suddenly turned his back on the city and sought the open road. He was to go on three walking trips in the next half-dozen years, and each time the space and freedom and the easy contacts with simple men shook things into place in his mind, soothed his nerves and freshened his imagination so that while he was stimulated to produce poems the fever in his brain subsided.

His first hike came about quite naturally, though later his memory blew it up into a solemn pilgrimage and symbol of protest. His parents and Joy were to sail for Europe in June and his father, generously in the circumstances, invited him to go too. But Vachel declined, saying that he must pay his own way abroad. Besides, he wanted first to see his own country.

On March 3, instead of returning to Springfield as his parents expected, he put a letter in his pocket, some leaflets in his knapsack and with a New York friend, Edward Broderick, boarded a boat for Florida. From Jacksonville they planned to walk back north.

"To whom it may concern—" read Lindsay's letter, written for him by Mr. Powlinson of the Y, "the bearer, Mr. Nicholas V. Lindsay, proposes to make a pedestrian tour of parts of the

Southland. Any courtesies extended to him through the Young Men's Christian Association will be thoroughly appreciated." This was his passport. The leaflets were the coin of his realm. He meant to exchange them for bread and shelter along the road; they were copies of *The Tree of Laughing Bells*, which he had had printed (begging fifty dollars for the purpose from Grandmother Frazee) and bound in red covers decorated with bells drawn in purple. He also took with him a blank notebook. It soon flowed over; he filled three altogether.

Going south, he and Broderick stopped off in Charleston, where Lindsay sought out the ancient slave market. Abraham Lincoln had walked through those stalls, which in his day had not been empty.

Below Jacksonville they disembarked again, then hit the road west. The moon was shining through the orange groves and the bell of Rollins College chiming as they walked into Winter Park, a luxurious little college town with twice as many shops as Hiram. Lindsay led the way into a combination grocery and confectionery, noisy with students, where he and Broderick, conspicuous in their old clothes and heavy boots, supped on lemonade, root beer, sardines and Van Camp's canned beans eaten out of the cans with soda spoons.

Broderick, who back in New York was a writer of advertising copy, blushed all the while they ate, but Lindsay was used to this sort of thing.

They slept at a boarding house, and next day Lindsay made himself known to the president of Rollins and asked if he might lecture to the students. On being told yes, he sauntered up and down Main Street, issuing invitations. Nineteen students turned up that evening at Knowles Hall and he read Poe's poems to them. Afterward Broderick, his cheeks flaming again, passed around the hat, taking in almost $3.00.

Next morning they pushed on to Orlando, where Lindsay got permission to lecture in the YMCA hall. As before, he stumped Main Street but this time drew a meager bag: three drifting old men; a traveling salesman, likewise unengaged for

the evening; two old women and one young girl, her presence
unaccountable but in whose face he delighted as he talked, for
it was "beautiful."

Broderick, blushing rather less by this time, collected eighty-
five cents.

On Sunday, March 11, Lindsay set out to walk to Tampa
through the Florida midland. He was without Broderick, who
was taking the train. His imagination began to throb as all
around him he saw live oaks dripping with Spanish moss, tiny
balloon-throated green lizards, snakes that moved without
sound, great turtles hoisting themselves up from the palmetto
swamp, brown and white mocking birds, flocks of lanky blue
cranes and scarlet cardinals.

Ideas for poems came crowding and he paused to jot them
down: "What the red-clay lady said. What the white-sand
lady said. What the turpentine-tree lady said. What the
orange-and-tangerine-and-grape lady said. . . ."

At ten at night on Tuesday he swung into Tampa to find
the town on the boom, with the streets lit up and the roller-
skating rink and band-concert hall going full blast, but no
Broderick. In the morning arrived a letter to say Broderick had
left the train at Lakewood because he wasn't feeling well and
guessed he would rest there a day or two.

Lindsay knocked around Tampa looking for work. Having
no money left, he brought out *The Tree of Laughing Bells*
and began to employ what he called his "Ancient Mariner
eye" as he offered the poem to strangers in return for cash or a
meal. A traveling man from Alabama accepted three copies
and stood Lindsay breakfast and lunch (the drummers were
always generous), and that afternoon he was hired by a man
named Eckland to paint signs in a paint shop. The job didn't
start till next morning.

"It is to me a matter of much speculation," he wrote in his
notebook, "as to whether I can paint signs and how I will
enjoy it."

That night a dealer in farm products gave him supper and

slipped him the price of a bed. On Thursday Mr. Eckland swept with a contemptuous look his first painted sign and fired him. On Friday morning Lindsay managed to beat down the resistance of a suspicious fellow, who said he was a lawyer and seemed to think he was being buncoed, and to unload one copy of his poem, thus earning a nickel to buy breakfast rolls.

At last came Broderick.

It was he who paid both fares as they continued by train and boat to Jacksonville, where Broderick decided he had had enough and caught the steamer for New York—"called by industrial tyranny," mourned his poet friend.

Left alone, Lindsay went to church.

It was again a Sunday, and after church he, too, started for the North, walking along the slender footpath that led out of town beside the railroad ties, a path worn by generations of the unquelled. He felt that he was taking another plunge.

In his pocket he had a sack of peanuts bought with his last five cents and while he strode on his way he mentally rehearsed a soft-spoken challenge to be delivered at hopeful thresholds. "I am the peddler of dreams," it began. "I am the sole active member of the ancient brotherhood of the troubadours."

Two memorable months later he walked into the house of his Aunt Eudora, his father's sister in Kentucky. He had hitched a few train and wagon rides but had gone on foot the rest of the way from Jacksonville to Grassy Springs, some 600 miles.

In those weeks of wandering, he had knocked at many doors and from some he had been turned away and at others, often the lowliest, bid to enter. The formula for hospitality among the wilderness folk ran: "If what we have is good enough—" and their reason for making welcome the traveler was a simple one: "A stranger needs takin' care of."

20

The first to take care of Lindsay was a Florida cracker who lived in a pine forest a few miles beyond Jacksonville and couldn't refuse a stranger because he had once been stranded himself and had slept out in the rain for three nights when no one, nobody, would give him shelter.

After they had eaten the evening meal this man, his shy wife—who at table stood to serve the others—and Lindsay, the wayfarer, sat all three before the glorious focus of the poor abode, a leaping fire of pine knots. There Lindsay, trembling all over with the ecstasy of the moment and amazement at such kindness, sang for his supper with a little poem he had written about crickets and another about fireflies, and then recited *The Tree of Laughing Bells.*

Never did he forget the gentle pair. Neither one could read, yet "they laughed and sighed at just the right places," he remembered. "They ate and drank with me in the land of the heart's desire."

Next to show him hospitality was a country minister in the log village of Crawford, a patriarch with six sons, who for one night made the stranger his seventh son. In this house the broad hearthstone was the altar at which family prayers were offered; the young mother, a lean American madonna, nursed her baby, and the old father, seated but erect, raised a clarion voice and sang, "The Son of God goes forth to War."

Lindsay passed through the great swamp called the Okefenokee and crossed a trestle bridge over the Suwannee. He had been tramping alone for three days and for the first time his spirits sagged. When he limped into Fargo, Georgia, he was ready to quit and wire to his father for train fare home, or anyway to Macon, only the telegraph office in the town wouldn't take a money order.

Then a railroad inspector scrutinized his YMCA passport and let him ride as far as Valdosta in the caboose of a freight. A redhot stove roared on the pitching floor inside and one handsome sweating Negro was polishing lanterns as black and shiny as his face, while "there was a gold filling in the teeth and ivory white to the eye of the black brother bending over him," Lindsay noted with instantly revived delight. "It was a study in lacquers and gold and ivory!"

Soon he took to the road once more and he went his way on foot, rejoicing. On April 7, after many adventures, he entered Atlanta and chose this Saturday night to try what he romantically called "sleeping under the stars."

After writing letters in a half-darkened hotel lobby till one a.m., he walked over to the post office from which, before he was ready to leave, he was ignominiously ejected by a loitering man with a rough voice—"I preserved my dignity this much— I went out slowly."

He tried to peddle his poem in several all-night drug stores and was rebuffed. It began to rain and he ran back to the post office where this time unmolested he wrote more letters till the rain let up and then for an hour, between four and five, he slept curled on the post-office steps, though no stars shone. On waking, he went to Mass, dozed a little on his knees among the maid servants, yet got some comfort from the eternally unchanging ritual and the cool pure look of the high altar.

He spent the next night in a dingily Protestant atmosphere in the Salvation Army barracks, in whose front hall, using a pencil on the wallpaper, some hand had scribbled: "Why do you sware? Would you like to be swareing when Jesus comes?"

In Atlanta, Lindsay drummed up an audience for a lecture on the Pre-Raphaelites, for which he was paid $10. He rode out of the city on a streetcar headed north. After a while he got out and walked, looking from side to side and whistling.

"Healing and Herb Medsern—Sold by Agent," read a sign on an unpainted post before an unpainted house.

"Hello, white folks, you're feelin' good, ain't ye?" said a Negro who passed him.

He decided to keep walking all the way to Washington and in his enthusiasm began to lay plans for a book of walking poems. There were poems to be written on the stories of their lives that silent men will divulge to the listening stranger; there was a poem on the highly individual old men he had met, one on the enticement of lighted farmhouse windows approached just at dusk, and one on faded old guideposts.

It was the end of April when he came to the Falls of Tallulah in northern Georgia. The afternoon was bright and sparkling. Clambering down the sun-warmed rocks, holding on by roots and shrubs, he threw off his clothes, edged out under the booming, silver-flashing cascade and lay back against the incline, his feet braced dangerously in a notch.

A wild and wonderful shower bath smote his shoulders. In the heady solitude he laughed and shouted aloud. Never had he come so near to the pure joy of living! Surely, there was a nymph behind that crystal curtain or below in the creaming depths—"whiter than a cloud or a lily," he exulted, "whiter than snow or a feather—my queen woman is there. . . ."

In Tennessee a few days later he was entertained for the night in the smoky hut of a jovial little moonshiner, who jabbed playfully with his pipe at Lindsay as they lolled in male glory beside the hearth—while the grim wife champed her snuff-stick in the background—and chuckled: "You're just a run-away boy, that's what you are!"

The exquisite views, appearing and disappearing, as he wound on foot among the mountains of the Blue Ridge swelled Lindsay's heart. He determined that if he could not beat the economic system there below, he would die protesting. He would count that day lost in which he failed to give away some of the work of his hands.

Yet there were not always ready takers. Beyond Asheville, North Carolina, he bawled *The Tree of Laughing Bells* into the ear of a deaf, surly householder who then refused to accept the poem in return for lodging. He demanded thirty cents, and the poet had to substitute his shirt and collar.

At this, another garment fell away from Lindsay: his philosophy. Suddenly he could think of nothing except that he was far from home, with no money. Even $5.00 in his pocket, he admitted, would give him all the fight in the world, and he resolved to include in his projected book two or three poems addressed to the world's business men: "I must say, 'Brothers, though I have rebelled, I must acknowledge sometimes that there are few things more honest than a trade.' "

Indeed, at this moment, to be penniless seemed to him almost dishonorable because, he reflected disconsolately, when a traveler is both broke and worn out his soul cannot "emanate enough spiritual glory" to make fair exchange for his night's board.

He decided not to walk to Washington but to cry quits when he had reached Kentucky. Doubling back into Tennessee, he passed through the Cumberland Gap and arrived at the spot where a stone marks the conjunction of Tennessee, Kentucky and Virginia.

There he stepped over the invisible line into the state from which his fathers came and hastened north over Big Hill by the old Daniel Boone trail, now a pike of white limestone— harkening at tables along his way to talk of illegitimate loves, of stabbing and shooting in that passionate neighborhood—till after a time he reached the home of his father's sister, near Grassy Springs.

Eudora Lindsay South, a statuesque and motherly woman, was much revered in this region of Kentucky. She and her husband kept a school called Excelsior Institute, so named in her days of youth and hope when she was back from climbing mountains in Europe. Vachel once said that all his Lindsay relatives wanted was "one big hot kiss and one big hug," and when his Aunt Dora read rebellion and despair in his face and exhaustion in his attitude as he appeared unannounced on her doorstep, she took him in her arms without question and gave him both.

He remained at his aunt's house for a month, a healing interlude. "I will never forget the easy, dreaming Kentucky and the droning bees in the blue grass and the walks with Aunt Eudora and Cousin Eudora."

It was to his young cousin, Aunt Dora's namesake, in tribute for being so good to him, that he addressed his delicate little poem *The Flower of Mending*. As for his aunt, all his later nostalgia for Kentucky and sense of belonging there originated in his heart-to-heart talks with her when at the end of each busy schoolday they paced together up and down the white-colonnaded porch.

He knew that, with the exception of a few rare dreamers, the people along his way endured his poems and took him in out of kindness. What he craved from his depths was to be recognized publicly as a poet, he told the sympathetic Aunt Dora. She gave him his chance on Commencement Day when Vachel, following after the sweet girl graduates (though not, as he liked to remember, in his vagabond clothes but in a neat brown suit borrowed from one of his boy cousins) ascended the flower-decked platform of Aunt Dora's little country school and recited *The Tree of Laughing Bells*. He asked no better debut.

"I will never forget the queer feeling of being the family disgrace somewhat straightened out when I stood up to recite to the school in my beggar's raiment. I must be grateful forever to my kind aunt for taking the fury out of my heart. My father and mother were certainly at this time intensely hostile to everything I did, said, wrote, thought or drew. Things were in a state where it was infinitely easier to beg from door to door than to go home. . . ."

So said Lindsay in 1927, but his memories then must be

somewhat suspect, for in his last years he interpreted the past through the perturbed imagination of the present.

Early in June 1906 he did perforce go home, where his father, at Aunt Dora's tactful intervention, renewed the invitation to a trip abroad. This time Vachel accepted. With his parents and Joy, he left Springfield for New York and on June 23 they sailed all four for Liverpool.

21

In Europe, as in his own land, there were two Vachel Lindsays. By day there was the son on leading strings, member of a family quartet. But after night fell there was the dreamer and it was he who asked, then answered in the privacy of his hotel room and the secrecy of his diary-kingdom: "What do you poor little people mean when you say 'Go get experience'? I tell you I was Solomon, the son of David, king in Jerusalem, and the Queen of Sheba came walking to me upon the crystal floor.

"Do you say 'Go forth and do battle'? I tell you I was Tamerlaine, I have been Attila.

"I met Dante in his wanderings, and young Milton came to me; and I was the aged Galileo, and we spoke of the stars together."

Dr. and Mrs. Lindsay, Vachel and Joy saw England first, then hastened on to Holland, thence to Germany, Belgium, France and back to England. Vachel ever afterward remembered his parents as "abetting each other like twin bulldogs" the whole time. The adolescent Joy took it amiss that they traveled in the very thriftiest way, never going into the dining car like other people but eating in their seats out of a lunch basket.

For the inner Vachel, his visits to the Louvre were the high point. In the Venus of Milo he saw beauty absolute, beauty eternal that lifts up the soul beyond delight—"and I have felt it," he mused, "in the pathway of bronzes alternating with golden sarcophagi, marble, yellow with time. I have felt it in this avenue that leads upstairs to the Winged Victory. . . ."

Yet he couldn't help thinking how much more he would have got from the trip if he had been alone. His free roaming through the American South now seemed to him the beginning of wisdom. If he had come abroad on his own, how many more ghosts of history would have appeared to him, as by those rural waysides!

"I almost saw one at the tomb of Napoleon, though my father was there and an impatient commandant ordering us out and a restless group of sightseers. But to have done it right I should have come to Europe alone. There are a thousand gracious nerve filaments that only expand themselves and unroll in solitude."

Though most civilized people, Lindsay granted, must live on art visible rather than art invisible, *he* had seen all his life so many "dragons, demons and angels" right where he was that he needed not London or Paris.

Distance only made it easier to meditate on America, where nothing was fixed and "all, all," he reminded himself, "is yet possible." He was planning another book, one of art criticism that should go beyond Ruskin in linking art with religious principles. It could be his message to the whole American people and after it was finished he would make a great world journey, a pilgrimage undertaken that he might bend the knee in all the religious capitals. Following the dreams of men, searching for Aladdin's lamp, he would go to Jerusalem, Constantinople, Saint Petersburg, Mecca, Kamakura, Calcutta, Benares, Lhasa.

The day was July 26, 1906, when he entered the new ultimatum in his diary: "Five years from this date I shall be upon my way!"

Later he was to recognize that, though he knew it not at the time, he was this summer—after conflict in his flesh and soul between Hellenism and Hebraism, Apollo and Christ—

bidding his goodby to art as a single aim and beauty as a single desire.

Possibly he was again having visions. His past visions were much in his mind. "Every artist sees pictures in the air. The only differences are—mine seem to bear a religious, a ritualistic, a prophetic import."

Artists who have given their hearts wholly to beauty, to whom the things of every day come as revelations to be written or painted, "they too, like us, have visions in the night more glorious than Mohammed's, but they are not troubled with the religious fire that ate his blood and mine."

In the great synagogue of Amsterdam he had been almost overpoweringly tempted to "bow to and kiss the law after the Jewish manner." Cologne Cathedral thrilled him; so in Antwerp did the sight of men and women sinking to their knees as a priest passed along the streets bearing the Host to the dying. "Tomorrow the Louvre," he wrote on his first night in Paris, "but tonight my heart is searching the Taj Mahal and the temple of Nikko."

On the practical side, his book when written ought to land him at least an assistant professorship, and "I would prefer," he wrote, "to be a professor in Columbia by the time I start around the world."

Lindsay admitted that the interpretation of his visions was often beyond him. His task as an artist was to present them in such a way that they retained their structural beauty and yet were all things to all men, so that every poet, dreamer and God-seeker could find in them his individual desire.

On September 4, as the ship neared New York harbor on the last night of the homeward crossing, Lindsay in the stateroom he shared with his father dreamed a dream, which next morning lingered in his mind with such glittering distinctness that he spoke of it always afterward as one of his visions.

"Last night," he wrote, "I saw Immanuel singing in the New Heaven . . . in a bright grassy place . . . singing almost alone . . . singing wonderfully, as became a son of David. He was almost as simple a shepherd as David, and his robe was Angelico red. His lips scarcely sang at all, it was his harp that sang. And some one listening behind me said, 'It is *Immanuel.*' "

This was not the pale Galilean but the joyful Christ of the Millennium, whom Greek Apollo does not outshine in comeliness. Lindsay later wove a meaning into what he had seen— explaining that after Christ sets up the moral order He sings a requiem for all beauty destroyed by the Day of Judgment— but at the time, when he awoke dazzled and with fast-beating heart, he only exclaimed aloud: "I have found my God."

Out of his dream he wrote one of the most beautiful of his religious poems. Too often the beauty-lovers are plain pagans, the God-lovers blind to beauty. "This poem," said Lindsay, "represents their reconciliation in my own humble special case. It stands for the moment of transfiguration, when the Gospel became fire in my mind."

I Heard Immanuel Singing was begun in New York on November 10, 1906, his twenty-seventh birthday, and finished on Christmas Day. Though he had conceived of the Christ that is coming as a God of beauty and laughter, his poem has still the pensiveness, plaintive melody and artless rhythm of one of the old gospel hymns and it is written (so he directs) to be in part spoken, in part sung, and all "very softly."

> I heard Immanuel singing
> Within his own good lands,
> I saw him bend above his harp.
> I watched his wandering hands
> Lost amid the harp-strings;
> Sweet, sweet I heard him play.
> His wounds were altogether healed.
> Old things had passed away.
>
> All things were new, but music.
> The blood of David ran
> Within the Son of David,
> Our God, the Son of Man.
> He was ruddy like a shepherd.
> His bold young face, how fair.

Apollo of the silver bow
Had not such flowing hair . . .

When this his hour of sorrow
For flowers and Arts of men
Has passed in ghostly music,
I asked my wild heart then—
What will he sing tomorrow,
What wonder, all his own
Alone, set free, rejoicing
With a green hill for his throne?

What will he sing tomorrow,
What wonder all his own
Alone, set free, rejoicing,
With a green hill for his throne?

22

Again this fall Lindsay led his culture-hungry little crowd through the Metropolitan Museum, standing up before the art works to describe them confidently in "my own fresh sketchy way." Again he lectured at the Y, and in January 1907 he opened there a series of "fireside talks" on the poetry of Sidney Lanier. Before each talk began, a fire was lighted in the living room; the lamps were turned out and a violinist played soft melodies. Then as the night classes were dismissed and fifty to a hundred men came pouring downstairs, they heard the cajoling violin; some few ventured into the shadowy room, gazed at the eye of the fire and were caught.

"The purpose," he explained to his parents, "is to send them home with sweet-flavored thoughts, so they will not be tempted before they get to their little hall bedrooms."

By the spring he was also lecturing at four settlement houses and yet his New York days, he knew, were numbered. "If I can only quit here feeling I have made good in some fashion," he wrote to his father, adding, "it *is* making good to hold the interest of such men as I have."

Such men were streetcar conductors, policemen, clerks, carpenters, bricklayers and pearl-button burners. If his pay was a pittance, he was making those listen who never had listened before to discussion of Praxiteles, Leonardo and Burne-Jones. In the exchanges he had a teacher's reward. "My soul growing," he noted in his diary, "because of teaching my art class and the few visible results upon the work of a few students. . . ."

This was in a brand-new diary, one that was to be given over to his "first serious effort to find out what is true, what is right, and how to move the innermost souls of men in matters of the whole life, rather than of art alone."

Keats could cry that "beauty is truth, truth beauty," but "beauty is *not* truth"—Lindsay's diary continues—"for I *know* beauty already. It is truth for a certain all-aesthetic type of nature, I have no doubt. But I have a profound ethical nature that has grown wild these ten years, neglected in the beauty search."

He saw now that his art desires had reached their full ripeness in the vision of the singing Immanuel. Since that time his restless aestheticism had found rest and he had changed the direction of his search. One thing he knew he sought—sought on his knees—was a Christ whom he could worship with unfaltering faith and trust, and such a figure is hard to find. The historical Christ meant little to him and the radiant Immanuel of the Millennium, who had been his inspiration in his art life, was no longer enough, had begun indeed to seem to him but an artist's dream.

Then he looked into the faces of his students, to whom he had given something of his mind and heart and from whom he felt already a little of the divine return. Here was a result in which to anchor new hope: it was borne in on him that there exists a Christ who is not a figment of the fancy, or a poetic phase, or an illusion.

"It is the *Christ* that *is in them*," he wrote. "Now a real worship can be given to this Christ. In dreaming of a religious revival that will stir all hearts deeply, yet stir up no dogmatism, it is possible I have found it here. It is the Religion of Humanity and varies with humanity."

He thought back to the writing of *Star of My Heart*.

That poem was the expression of his aloneness, as *I Heard Immanuel Singing* the expression of his dream of beauty. Now his interchange with his young men was teaching him that not only is beauty not enough but also that he was not alone, that "the souls of the rest make a blaze in the heart one can seldom kindle alone."

"Oh, to have fire, fire, fire, perpetually in my heart that I may give it freely to all who come!"

This was his plea.

He knew that he had written enough of the purely subjective, abstract and aesthetic. If he would surrender himself for the present to his fellow men and to the machinery of society around him, then when at last he took time to dream and write again the discipline of the human contact would show in the fiber of his writing.

He was sunk in reflections like these, immured like his brothers of the Y in his little hall bedroom, when suddenly his hand moved as though another hand closed over it and he wrote:

> If you were a pebble I could crush you and drink you.
> If you were a fire I would burn like dead leaves.
> If we were two lion cubs I would devour you.
> If you were a gleaner, my bones were your sheaves . . .

His diary is studded with such entries, made when his passion and chastity—for his life was one of strict continence—burned at white heat. If a real woman inspired these lines, it would have been enough for him to meet her casually or to catch sight of her only once, like the beautiful manicurist with the face of an Egyptian queen. He gave a title, *The Foolishness of Desire*, to the unbidden fragment and wrote the day—March 4, 1907—of its inception, then commented that the lines, coming while he was in the midst of setting down other notes, gave him much to think about concerning the two sides of man, or rather three sides, "the beast, the father, the worshipper."

Sternly he bade himself to "rein the beast," to worship and prepare for being "the worthy father." There were moments at least when it seemed to him that he wished to fill a strong and normal man's place in the world, to multiply his kind and defend and provide for them, to be "a real shelter for some faithful woman."

This though he was still dependent even for himself, and in other mood could prophesy that he would never love any woman enough to hold her heart constant toward him.

Lindsay's great book of art criticism, which was to make him a professor at Columbia, was not yet even begun (it was never written) but he applied to Hiram, asking if he might receive his bachelor's degree on the basis of studying done on his own since quitting college prematurely. His *alma mater* sent back the frosty little reply that no degree could be awarded him unless he put in "further resident work."

"Never mind, Hiram shall give me a degree yet, for I shall always get what I want in this world—but money." So he consoled himself, and when in October he sent Robert Henri a line of greeting, just to keep in touch, Henri's answer was warm.

"You are one whose doings are always interesting to me," wrote Henri, "one of the searchers."

This winter Lindsay and his artist chums, in return for free meals, decorated with mural paintings the walls of their favorite restaurant, The Pig and Goose, on West Fifty-ninth Street. In the classroom he plunged his students into a new course, which he called "Dominating Personalities of History." He was writing and reading to his class a poem on a kindred subject: the superhuman quality in men who have won the admiration of the race, whether dreamers like Pharaoh Amenophis IV, conquerors like Alexander and Julius Caesar, saints like the fiery Paul and the weeping Francis, or artists like Titian and the mighty Michelangelo

> who hewed the stone
> And Night and Day revealed, whose arm alone
> Could draw the face of God, the titan high
> Whose genius smote like lightning from the sky—
> And shall he mold like dead leaves in the grave?
> Nay, he is in us! Let us dare and dare.
> God help us to be brave.

"God help us to be brave" was the refrain ending each stanza. Lindsay used it as his working title for this faulty, remarkable poem, later published as *Litany of the Heroes*. He scraped together money to have the poem printed and he also had printed, for the first time, *The Last Song of Lucifer*. Among his friends and the fellows at the Y, "I am beginning to have a tiny public," he told his parents.

So sped the winter, but in the spring his classes came again to a standstill. His students in Dominating Personalities (who called him "Professor," degree or no degree) gave him a farewell dinner and an album in which their signatures propped up verses, as

> "It is the spirit of unrest
> That bids us climb and do our best."
>
> Mr. Lindsay, this is the
> spirit your course has given me.

Still he fluttered on in New York for three weeks more, trying vainly to get his fingers into something that would keep him there, till he bethought him that so far his only sure remuneration from writing had come from some articles about his southern hike, which *The Outlook* had accepted. It was then that he decided to go home—for a short time only—and to go on foot, seeking grist for future articles.

His father, who had to borrow to do it, sent him $25. Lindsay used part of the money to pay for the train ride with which this hike ended, even though he afterward remembered —and bragged, without intent to deceive—that he had only a few cents in his purse when on April 28, 1908, he set out to walk to Springfield. But he had lined his pockets with pilgrim's scrip in the form of *God Help Us to Be Brave* and *The Last Song of Lucifer* and on his second hike took with him a necessity of pedestrian travel he had badly missed the first time, carbolic soap.

He carried, too, an automobile guidebook, in which many people were more interested than in his poems.

23

His first night out Lindsay spent at the Salvation Army hostel in Newark, and of this adventure his road diary tells: "Paid my fifteen cents and received bed on third floor. Bed no. 134 (I think), lower tier. Men asleep on upper tiers on each side, none just above. Man on the right half drunk but crossed himself and said 'God keep me tonight' before he slept.

"Forty-four beds in the room. Most of the men slept naked, some in underwear. Kept running to wash-room. A goodly number snored. More snorted and spat spat spat on the floor. About three, half drunk, talked till midnight. Finally the fat one rolled off his bed, falling about eight feet, naked, and almost breaking his head. That shut them up. He boasted he had had fifty beers yesterday. The sheets were filthy. Mine had blood on them. The pillow cases were well oiled. The place was on the whole better than the one in Atlanta."

Next morning the captain in charge refused to let Lindsay into the washroom for the shower bath to which he was entitled, explaining goodnaturedly that a lot of men were already in there scrubbing up, "and you wouldn't like it."

The "gentleman adventurer," Lindsay called himself on this second hike.

At the end of his second day he strolled into Morristown, New Jersey, supposed to be the wealthiest little burg of its size in the United States. Finding no Salvation Army headquarters, he wandered over to the Presbyterian Mission where in the shiny mission chapel, down which the aisle ran like a chasm, he and the other guests—after chopping kindling for two hours to pay for their beds—were seated all together.

On the other side of the aisle was a handful of sightseers. A clergyman stood up and read from the Beatitudes, which so swamped Lindsay with emotion that he scarcely noticed the callowness of the sermon that followed. When another clergyman rose and urged all who repented of sin to raise their hands, Lindsay in a glow raised his hand.

"Where did you come from?" the first of the two asked him afterward with dry curiosity, and Lindsay answered humbly in the words of Scripture: " 'From going to and fro in the earth and walking up and down in it.' "

A few minutes later he was partnered with a bum just off a box car, and hustled upstairs into the bathroom. A trusty directed both men to strip and hang their things on a rack lowered through a trapdoor after which the rack was hauled aloft to the floor above, where the clothes of new arrivals were fumigated.

"Git in the tub," the trusty ordered the unclothed bum, tossing him a repulsive washrag.

When the bum had finished and risen from the turbid waters ("like Venus from the foam," reflected the unclothed gentleman adventurer) he was given an old stiff-bosomed dress shirt for a nightgown. He pulled it on over his head and, emerging, asked: "Ain't I a peach?"

Lindsay, who came next and into whose softened heart hate was stealing, made a nuisance of himself by refusing to use the bum's washrag and a towel that was "a fallen sister of the washrag" and then to wear the soiled pajamas held out.

"You're awful particular, aren't you?" jibed the trusty. "If I had my way, you wouldn't of been let in."

Lindsay demanded to know why, when his underwear, which was clean, had to be fumigated, he should be forced into sleeping wear that was "dirty as the conversation of a drunk Negro." He got no answer, but was packed off to a dormitory bed that again was "dirty, dirty," where he instantly shuffled out of the vile pajamas and lay awake in the noisome dark, surrounded by heavy breathers and raging against the two clergymen, the Scribe and the Pharisee.

Their hypocrisy had made a fool of him. Inwardly he bade them to cut short their canting sermons and inspect the towels and sheets. "Blessed are the meek, for they shall examine the washing," he mused.

He went on his way. Generally speaking, it seemed to him as it had on his first hike that, leaving out the charitable organizations, about as many people took him in as do any one thing in society. About one in three goes to church or the circus, or buys ten-cent magazines or has a taste for horse-radish—"and just so many will take care of the stranger for meals or lodging whether they suspect him or not, whether they think they ought to or not."

So with the Pennsylvania-Dutch farmers he was beginning to meet, most of whom were too stolid to get much out of his poems but were plainly good citizens.

On the far side of the Poconos he descended to Wilkes-Barre by one of the new and seemingly interminable automobile highways, which, being in a pilgrim mood, he named Giant Despair. Beyond the smoke-hung city lay the coal country. Toward evening, after trudging seventeen miles over a desolate no-man's land of slag heaps, he walked into one end of a double row of company houses, wooden cottages just alike, set off by themselves in cindery front yards on the wild and dreary outskirts of the mining town of Shickshinny.

At the last house in the row he was taken in by one of the settlement's few American-born miners (most were Polish or Bohemian), who expressed himself as "awful glad to see a white man," and whose wife slipped on a blouse of torn lace and caroled that she "loved" poetry.

"I just keep cheerful, I don't keep house," she told her guest.

Turning from the blackened waste outside, Lindsay pulled up to the lamplit kitchen table with the friendly couple and their two handsome dirt-streaked little boys, and with them devoured savory steak and onions, mashed potatoes, gravy, bread and butter. All along the road he had been innocently surprised that though none of his hard-worked benefactors was enjoying as easy an average of life as he, yet none was more tired at night or ate more.

After supper they went in single file into the unused parlor where the mother arranged the rest of the family on chairs, and Lindsay, as he had done many times since leaving New York, prepared to entertain his hosts. He did not forget that these were mining folk. There is a dynamite, he explained first, that is not the nitro-glycerine exploded underground but the earth-rocking power of the soul. There is a detonation that the world calls "fame."

Then he chanted *God Help Us to Be Brave*, rolling it out with a preacher's unction but laying less emphasis than usual on the saints and artists and more on the wise lawgivers, like Confucius:

> Lord, show us safe, august, established ways,
> Fill us with yesterdays,

and the intrepid warriors, like Julius Caesar:

> Would I might rouse the valor and the pride,
> The eagle soul with which he soared and died!

The serious black eyes of the two little boys remained fixed on him. "It is a good book!" exclaimed both the parents as one when he had finished.

The mother promised Lindsay to have each of her sons choose a hero to live by as soon as he was old enough to understand his choice. Then she put away the copy of the poem he gave her in the kitchen-table drawer with her few treasures.

Lindsay crossed from Pennsylvania into Ohio and on May 18 reached Hiram, where Joy had ended up a student after all. Unlike last time, he could hardly wait to get home, for he had a pile of projects in his head and was crazy to be at them. He took the train the rest of the way.

PART THREE

A RUSHING
OF WINGS

24

His home town greeted Lindsay with covert smiles. It seemed obvious he was home to stay because he had nowhere else to go. Still, all Springfieldians are in a sense cousins and he was welcomed back, said Vachel, as one of them—"a slightly boresome but harmless cousin."

This summer of 1908 his parents and Joy went to England but Olive and Paul were in the house, having come from China with their baby son to be in Springfield for the birth of a second child. Young Dr. Paul, in the place it had been hoped Vachel would occupy, was looking after his father-in-law's practice.

Vachel fell to work redecorating the old-fashioned Sixth Street office, which was a wilderness of dusty books and medicine bottles. Working outdoors under a big maple tree in the backyard at 603 and using ordinary house paint, he painted a large extraordinary picture, better than six feet wide and five feet high, illustrating his poem *The Tree of Laughing Bells*. This he had carried over to Sixth Street and hung in the absent doctor's anteroom, where waiting farmers and their wives could contemplate it. It showed a tree bending in wild obeisance before the winds of Chaos, a tree from whose turbulent branches red bells swung.

He next had a hope of decorating the dingy corridors of the Springfield State House. He put it to his neighbor Mary Humphrey—whose father was Judge Humphrey, a power in the town—that if she could help him bring this about, there would be a twenty per cent commission in it for her.

The hope was never realized, but often this summer he called on Mary, a handsome self-assured young woman. "Since Mary Humphrey came back from Europe," he told Olive, "there isn't any Europe left. I think I'll try Asia."

Still it was convenient to go to Europe merely by climbing the steps of the Humphrey porch. "O Mary," he exclaimed one night, "what great things we could do together for Springfield!"

But the capable Mary Humphrey had other plans, and didn't want to do great things for Springfield and didn't want to do them with him. As they sat side by side on the porch ("She makes any chair her throne," said Vachel) he seized her hand and began to stroke and fondle it.

"Vachel was great for taking your hand in his and flipping it back and forth," Miss Humphrey recalls, "but that was about as far as he got."

In the heavy days of August a race riot broke out in Springfield during which two Negroes were strung up, one of them on a post in the schoolyard. Vachel and Olive at the dining-room window heard the terrible mob cry and they watched the rioters rush roaring down the street, then swarm in a terrifying shortcut across the Governor's well-kept lawn. "City of Abraham Lincoln hanging innocent Negroes," their mother far away in London read in the *Times*.

Years later Lindsay was to say to Stephen Graham, an Englishman, that he had come to believe the only way to end lynching would be to thrust yourself into the thick of such a mob and make the men slay you instead of the Negro. "When they realized what they had done, their hearts would be touched, their consciences shocked."

At the time there had seemed nothing he could do except to bombard the daily paper with letters of protest. But he was driven to think seriously about his Negro fellow citizens, some of whom lived right on the other side of Fifth Street. Besides Negroes, Springfield had Irish, Germans, Jews, Italians, Greeks, Poles and a few Chinese, and the more he reflected, the more he was stricken by the contrast between their mean lives and lowly occupations and their proud racial and national inheritances.

For behold in America the tribal chief of ebony-skinned warriors become the humble wielder of a whisk broom in a Pullman car! Behold the descendant of the poet-Irish a cop swinging a night-stick, his bardic wisdom dwindled to parody in the jokes of Mr. Dooley! Behold the Italian—he whose ancestors breathed the air of Dante's Florence—a pushcart peddler of fruit, and the Jew with his bent for religion traves-tied on the vaudeville stage as a money-getter!

"The first requisition is to have a big heart for alien men," Lindsay laid down.

He was speaking at the local YMCA, where he delivered a series of free lectures on the subject of the races pouring in from abroad that were making America a melting pot and giving Springfield a composite citizenship. And though all cities in the land are much alike, "why not," he asked, "make Springfield different?"

Why not develop, instead of submerging, the genius peculiar to the race of the naturalized citizen? "The Italians can teach us how to make Springfield rare as little Florence and still a business city, the Greeks can remind us that little Athens proved moral aspirations not inconsistent with a noble city life for her boys."

When Lindsay took his assorted students to the Metro-politan Museum they used to gather in the central rotunda, then move from one to another of the small plaster models of the Temple of Karnak, the Parthenon, the Pantheon, Notre Dame and the Arch of Triumph, while in running commentary he compared the classic architecture with United States sky-scrapers like the Flatiron and *Times* buildings. And from his own comparison—proving what men had done and could do—was born his ideal of a future Springfield: he had been dream-ing ever since of a city, then of an America, where industry and commerce should be set in second place and civic beauty stand next to civic godliness.

His homecoming had been easy because he felt he had something real to accomplish. On leaving New York, he promised his friends he was going home to spread his gospel of beauty; there was enough talent right in his own corner to make of it a brilliant little community.

"Let this, our city, be our luxury," he wrote at this time in *On the Building of Springfield*, a poem that he paid out of his pocket to have printed.

Let not our town be large, remembering
That little Athens was the Muses' home,
That Oxford rules the heart of London still,
That Florence gave the Renaissance to Rome ...

Let every citizen be rich toward God.
Let Christ the beggar teach divinity.
Let no man rule who holds his money dear.
Let this, our city, be our luxury.

We should build parks that students from afar
Would choose to starve in, rather than go home,
Fair little squares, with Phidian ornament,
Food for the spirit, milk and honeycomb.

New Year's Day 1909 found Lindsay still in his father's house. Nothing had opened for him in New York. After years of study and search, when it cost his father much to maintain him, he had made no mark in any profession and could give his family no good reason for going back. From now on Dr. Lindsay kept him on a short rein financially—so Vachel considered; the town's opinion was that both parents spoiled their son.

He began to ally himself with civic causes. The Anti-Saloon League of Illinois was a pet project of his mother's, and as one of its field workers he strode in through swinging doors and straight up to the brass rail, where he lambasted the evils of drink, talking hard and loud against the inevitable heave-ho. "Vachel is no coward," testified his brother-in-law, Paul.

Every Sunday, wearing a black-tailed coat, black cravat and high starched collar, he was sent into a different section of the state to speak in favor of the hoped-for prohibition law. He was paid ten dollars for every speech, but what he gained and valued most was an intimate knowledge of the little farming towns set apart from one another on the wide plain.

These were "dry towns," "Bible towns." In Carlinville, Maroa, Liberty and dozens more, a leading father of the township—of the type of the old Roman farmer-patriot—would meet him at the station, where a small crowd was gathered to watch the Sunday train go through, and drive him to the church—often one of the foursquare white-frame churches that might have been lifted bodily from a village green in New England and the sight of which communicated to him a breath of spirit-power: he felt the air tantalizing with spiritual suggestion.

And once or twice, as he was in the very act of speaking from the lofty pulpit, looking down into the rows of rustic, Sabbath-stilled faces, the scene was transfigured. "The whole place," he writes, "was turned to a nowhere of ivory and gold and that bright army of perfectly carved countenances became Greek before my eyes (though mine was a mighty Puritan cause)."

Even while he thundered the dour invectives of the Hebrew prophets, the wooden aisles became classic colonnades and there rang in his imagination Swinburne's lines, describing

> The bountiful infinite West, the happy
>   memorial places
> Full of the stately repose and the lordly
>   delight of the dead,
> Where the fortunate islands are lit with the
>   light of ineffable faces
> And the sound of a sea without wind is about
>   them, and sunset is red.

In February the centenary of the birth of Lincoln was celebrated in Springfield. Orations were delivered by William Jennings Bryan and Senator Dolliver of Iowa, while one of the city's own native orators made a quieter speech, which was not widely publicized.

Lindsay's talk was to the coal miners of the outlying district of Ridgely whom he addressed in the Ridgely Reading Room on February 11, reminding them in the name of the Great Emancipator that the blood shed by the mob of the past August was on all their hands till they made amends to the memory of the two lynched Negroes and to their race.

"Until we have completely set the Negro free," insisted Lindsay, "we are disloyal to Lincoln, and worse."

Unfailingly did the idea of Lincoln kindle Lindsay, as it had done Walt Whitman. The most moving of the stanzas of his poem *God Help Us to Be Brave* is his invocation to the Lincoln spirit:

That which is gendered in the wilderness
From lonely prairies and God's tenderness.

In his address to the miners of Ridgely he was aroused less to eulogy than to thoughtful prophecy. What is freedom?

"No working man is free," said Lindsay, "till he has all the knowledge that any man can have, till he has all the leisure that any man can have, till he uses that leisure to exercise and develop his highest faculties, surrounded by all the health-giving comforts that any man can have. Not till he is a completely ripened man, in justice, benevolence, breadth of view, depth of knowledge, is he wholly free. The workmen of the world are beginning to know this."

Thus spoke the local doctor's visionary son, inspired in the day of President Taft by the social reformer Altgeld as well as the moral reformer Lincoln.

He spoke also to the congregation of the First Christian Church during one of the regular Sunday morning services at which the doctor himself, as a church elder, often recited the prayer. Dr. Lindsay wrote out his prayers beforehand on scraps of brown wrapping paper; they impressed all who heard them by their intense religious feeling.

The son's talk was on "the necessity for reverence," for the

religious awe that deepens aesthetic delight, the contrite heart
preserved in the midst of sensuous pleasure. He repeated to his
congregation the lines of Lanier, who saw God revealed in
nature in the Glynn marshes:

> As the marsh hen secretly builds on the watery sod
> Behold I will build me a nest on the greatness of God.
> I will fly in the greatness of God as the marsh hen
>   flies
> In the freedom that fills all the space twixt the
>   marsh and the skies.

Then the fever of the seer began to burn in him. He went
on to tell his hearers of the America of his dream: a land fair
to look on, splendid to enjoy, and of the new era when will
be crowned king the Christ of the first chapter of Revelation
with face that shineth as the sun and eyes of flame.

Yet behind the flame are the eyes of the craftsman of Naz-
areth. And who knows but that in the end all man-created
splendors will be sheared away? "Who knows," asked Lindsay,
"but that the only beauty left be the world that God saw was
good in the beginning, and simple homes holding contrite, reverent humanity?"

The neighbors and friends who heard him speak in public
at this time say that his delivery was crude. In this field, too,
he was slow to find himself. The earnestness was there; it had
been there from the beginning, but the springs of the elo-
quence by which he was later to command great audiences
were still submerged.

25

"I loafed around Springfield as the town dolt," said Lindsay afterward of the years 1908 to 1912. Certainly, his fame never quite erased the picture his town formed of him at this period.

Yet he did himself something less than justice: these were years of incubation. Upstairs in his bedroom he sat writing. Outside the house he lectured and preached. Grown men were too busy to pay much attention; he led study groups of half-grown boys at which they chewed the cud of culture and drank cocoa. When he earned any money, as from his Anti-Saloon League speeches, he spent every penny to have what he had written put into print.

In 1909 he had printed at a local union shop and distributed with his own hand five remarkable leaflets. The first, issued on July 19, he called *War Bulletin Number One.*

"Why a War Bulletin?" He put the question at the head of his first column.

After thirteen months at home he had worked himself into angry defiance—not of Springfield, nor of America, but of sterile provincialism and the squat spider Mammon. He was in revolt against Main Street, for the place existed in 1909, though anonymously. He was in revolt against Babylon.

He had been reading *Sartor Resartus* in which the tough, sensitive, apprehensive Thomas Carlyle—who like most mortals walked through life trembling—all at once asked himself: "What *art* thou afraid of? Hast thou not a heart? Canst thou not suffer whatsoever it be, and as a child of Freedom, though outcast, trample Tophet itself under thy feet?"

An hour later Lindsay began on the Introduction to his

first War Bulletin, which was to be his initial bold step out of frustration and blow struck at compromise.

As he explained: "I have spent a great part of my few years fighting a soul battle for absolute liberty, for freedom from obligation, ease of conscience, independence from commercialism. I think I am farther from slavery than most men. But I have not complete freedom of speech. In my daily round of work I find myself taking counsel to please the stupid, the bigoted, the conservative, the impatient, the cheap. A good part of the time I can please these people, having a great deal in common with all of them—but—*the things that go into the War Bulletin please me only.*

"*To the Devil with you, average reader. To Gehenna with your stupidity, your bigotry, your conservatism, your cheapness and your impatience!*

"*In each new Bulletin the war shall go faster and further. War! War! War!*"

After this Introduction came a story, a parable called *The Golden-Faced People*, laid in the next millennium when the United States has been conquered by the Chinese and the white people are emancipated by a noble Chinaman named Lin Kon. Lindsay was considering the plight of Negroes in America from the Negro position.

War Bulletin Number One cost only a nickel, but nobody bought it. He ended by giving it away and all future Bulletins were free—"free as bread and butter in a hospitable house," said their editor, who could be seen on the street corner passing them out.

In August appeared *War Bulletin Number Two* with a satirical attack on the "conventional Christianity" of that Presbyterian mission in Morristown where Lindsay, yearning for comfort to his soul, had been fobbed off with a smug sermon. Then in *War Bulletin Number Three* on August 30 he exposed before the whole of Springfield his most personal religious views.

When friends of the Lindsay family read the first Bulletin, the image called forth in their minds by the son's challenge

was that of the father on his daily round, his years not few—
of the faithful doctor, who never in his life sought freedom
from obligation. But it was Vachel's statement of his religious
creed in the third Bulletin that really finished him in conservative local opinion.

"The Creed of a Beggar," he called it (a sad blow this, to
Frazee and Lindsay pride) and he wrote: "I believe in God,
the Creeping Fire. I have met him. He has scorched the walls
of my arteries. . . . I believe in Christ the Socialist, for I
have seen the Sermon on the Mount many times illustrated
by my hosts on the road. . . . I believe in that perilous mad-
dening flower, the Holy Ghost, the most dangerous bloom in
the Universe, I have eaten of it. . . .

"I believe in the Unitarians, in all the Evangelical Protestants,
especially the Disciples of Christ, in the Mass, the Eucharist,
the Virgin Mary.

"I take for my brother the Lord Buddha remembering with
happy tears the hours when he was my master. I take for my
friend the founder of Christian Science. I can not accept her
teachings, but I can rejoice in the peculiar presence I have
found in her churches. In a special sense I take Saint Francis
for my master, and pray that I may attain to his divine
immolation.

"I believe that Beggary is the noblest occupation of man."

What he did *not* believe, Lindsay concluded, was in the in-
fallibility of any one book, teacher, church. "Heaven is no
goal for me! The kingdom of God on earth is vastly more
significant."

Next he made his "confession," beginning: "Let me declare
that I love money. I am just as deferential as you, good reader,
to people of wealth."

In warfare against this wretched but universal tendency, he
exhorted all who would to break into the great metropolitan
business offices with him, slam the desk lids shut, cut the telephone wires and pitch the keys of skyscrapers into the river.

Let there be no violence, only if the kings of oil, grain and
cattle, swollen with covetousness, do not quit their spiders'
dens of their own accord—then, said Lindsay, let a few of us

go forth "carrying neither purse nor scrip, ragged with the beggar's pride. . . .

"Let us be casting out the devils of money-lust in those we meet. . . . If any man has a dollar in his pocket let him throw it away, lest it transform him into spiritual garbage."

And he begged: "Waste not your precious youth in industry. America is too rich already. She lacks most those things that come to idle men. . . . Oh, farmers, so jealous for your grain, give all your time to fields of cloud and air!

"The man with a house painted and fields in order is in danger of hell fire. It means he has not taken all his time to worship the Christ of Beauty. He has not gathered his children by the fireside to carve something lovely that has not the damning touch of machinery upon it, to look into some wonderful new doctrine or old tradition, to tell an antique story or sing a homely song."

Lindsay also spoke frankly to his readers of his visions, those blazing pictures in the air that once had come to him in cataracts, though since his return home they came no more.

War Bulletin Number Three ended with a story, *The Boats of the Prophets*, in which a proud, hungry young composer, who "would not bow the knee to Baal," stands alone one night on Brooklyn Bridge and witnesses the descent from heaven of the prophets in their winged boats. He sees the bearded old men, in rough garments, with faces of love and power, begin to pour down from the ships the wine of the universe whose fragrance fills the air, whose effluence rolls up from the streets of New York and Brooklyn in a purple mist.

The young composer "breathed the mists," wrote Lindsay. "The fury and glory of ancient Prophecy entered into him. The perfume was the Word of God in his breast. He said, without knowing why, 'Here am I, Lord, send me.' "

"My religion has not so very much to do with my behavior," Lindsay confided later, "but it has a lot to do with my life and

I cannot be friends with any one as I like till I understand something of their religion."

It was thus doing as he would be done by that he had tried to tell his friends in Springfield he had faith in the supremacy of spiritual values and his imagination responded to the best in all beliefs, though for himself he chose Christianity.

This was the meaning of *War Bulletin Number Three*. But what his extravagant language provoked from most who read it was a wave of mockery and from others a permanent distrust. "Ridiculous Rachel," some people began to call him. Even "the friends of my heart gave scorn," he wrote in his diary in a fragment born of his hurt.

> I cared not to please the crowd,
> I hoped to please my friends.
> The hate poured in at the doors and windows—

When he could write calmly on the subject, he declared that at the time he had gone no farther on that path. "I see no particular benefit in going down an alley of swords. Whenever I see Hate in the way, I go no farther. Then it's back to John Keats and the Grecian Urn."

In September Lindsay brought out under the title *The Tramp's Excuse* a collection of his poems, which he had had printed and oddly bound in what looked like a stenographic notebook. He called this his fourth War Bulletin, and in permanent importance it topped all the others.

War Bulletin Number Five, issued around Thanksgiving, was another leaflet, with a hilarious story, "How the Ice Man Danced."

His last Thanksgiving in New York he and four artist friends had spent the evening in an Italian barroom, where the others drank claret and Lindsay sarsaparilla. The riotous crowd from the Italian quarter that flowed around them had been in costume—the men dressed as women, the women as men—and one very drunk fellow the applauding artists called "the ice man," because of his brawn and chapped hands. He was wearing "a big blue dress and a scarf."

Then as the hurdy-gurdy ground wild and free, "the ice man," wrote Lindsay, "lifted his skirts. He kicked sawdust all over the cat. He danced and drank at once. He jumped into the air. He sprawled. He saved his face by 'doing the split.' Italy and America cheered. He slid to his feet stiff-legged, going down the same way. He did it half a dozen times. . . ."

Lindsay's humor had run away with him, but the original solemn purpose of his story had been to show how drink degrades. This fall in Springfield he was considering renting a room out at Ridgely and living there, for so long as the Ridgely miners drank he ought to be among them, preaching to them.

"I ought to preach till I drop," he reminded himself, which went against his earlier reminder that the making of beautiful things must come first with him.

But he was not happy. He believed the reason was that his monstrous desire for attention and artistic outlet was eating him up. Ever since his return home, he had tried to fill his need by joining with the local zealots: prohibitionists, socialists, single-taxers and YMCA men. And had he been satisfied really and only to serve them, to remain a private in the army of social service (which had too many generals), he would have found contentment, he was sure—"then every day would have had little bits of happiness in it."

He was writing in his diary on Sunday afternoon, November 21. It was a new diary—significantly, his father's only present to him for the milestone of his thirtieth birthday. "Vanity and ambition and self-service are the sources of all my misery," he continued. "My steadiest principle, the hatred of money, is negative. I need a positive unselfish principle."

What had he to show for his thirty years?

Forlornly, he resolved that the rule governing his future writing should be to avoid publicity and personal prestige, and endeavor only to help society. "Let pictures and verse have a social use, or nothing," he ordered himself, which was very well except that his muse declined to be fenced in.

The next thing he knew, he was drafting *The Wizard in the Street*, a poem about Poe—allegiance to whom made him turn on the complacent average citizen in passionate defense of the mystery seeker, the beauty server:

Useful are you. There stands the useless one
Who builds the Haunted Palace in the sun.

26

It was in an attempt to turn the other cheek (remembering the slap given his third War Bulletin) that Lindsay next printed and distributed free *The Sangamon County Peace Advocate*, in which he tolerantly proposed "a Christmas truce."

He had been at home for eighteen months.

> In this, the City of my Discontent,
> Sometimes there comes a whisper from the grass,
> "Romance, Romance—is here. No Hindu town
> Is quite so strange. No Citadel of Brass
> By Sinbad found, held half such love and hate."

So he testified in a new and lovely poem, *Springfield Magical*.

His Springfield cousins came across him in the busiest section of the city pressing on hurried Christmas shoppers copies of his *Peace Advocate*, which contained this poem and others. He had not moved out to Ridgely after all, but remained where he was.

Casting afar his lines of communication, he felt an occasional responsive twitch as odd and isolated persons wrote to him. "Dearest my friend Mr. Lindsay!" began one Paul Reps, an immigrant machine-shop worker from Russia, living in St. Louis, "I understand *very noble* you work printing 'War Bullitin' 'Peace Advocate' and giving it to people. You are good, and because you are great, you do not care if some people should call you 'a fool' for you know very well that great men was called 'a fool,' prosecuted and condemned."

Winter's end saw the bringing forth by Lindsay of *The Spring Harbinger*, a diminutive paper-covered booklet of comic drawings with limericks to match. Its purpose was to "take a swat at Folly," and he had drawn the picture of his muse, her hair in flying pigtails, doing just that, while tears sprang from Folly's eyes.

Most of the jokes involved big fearsome women confronting little placating men (whose pixie faces were portraits of the artist), and there were two gabbling village women:

> "I know you,"
> Said vague Mrs. Brown.
> "Your ways are the talk of the town."
> "Why, what have I done,
> My dear honey-bun?"
> "Never mind,"
> Said vague Mrs. Brown.

He had been mailing his private printings to everyone he knew—personally and by reputation—in Chicago and New York, asking those already on his list for the names of others who might care to have his sort of goods. The answers had begun to be encouraging, both in number and still more in kind, as when, replying from Vermont, the young poet Witter Bynner proposed Ezra Pound, William Marion Reedy and Arthur Davison Ficke, and from New York, Anna Hempstead Branch suggested Jessie Rittenhouse and Fannie Stearns Davis.

Neither Bynner nor Miss Branch had met Lindsay, but "I like your wild music," Miss Branch, herself a poet, told him, "and am always pleased when it blows in at my window as if from an Aeolian harp."

The summer of 1910, working as author, editor and publisher in the office of his small hot bedroom, he produced *The Village Magazine*, which he offered to all his prospects, old and new, at $1.00 a copy. He had had 700 copies printed of his first and only issue; they represented his last cent. "Childe Roland's last blast upon the Ram's horn," he called it.

The text was illuminated with little pen-and-ink pictures of acorns and sprays of berries and flowers; there were ardent poems from *The Tramp's Excuse*, clumsy but funny cartoons from *The Spring Harbinger* and four crusading editorials dedicated to the midwestern farming village. Alone in the empty house at the time of composing them—for his family was in Colorado—"Write to me, sir, I am as lonely as Hell and Brimstone," he begged Witter Bynner.

In one editorial, "For the Art Student Who has Returned to the Village," he held up the city man, a slick dummy in a Hart, Schaffner and Marx suit: "What a task then has the conscientious Art-Democrat to find the individual, delicate, immortal soul of this creature!"

But when we return to the crossroads that gave us birth— "there," said Lindsay, "we meet the real citizen, three generations before he is ironed out into a mechanical toy. *His crudity* is plain, but his delicacy is apparent also.

"If you have any cherished beauty-enterprise, undertake it where you are. *You will find no better place in all America.*"

The tendency everywhere was toward subordination of the towns to the great cities and of the cities to Washington; a phrase much in men's mouths was "the New Nationalism." As a balance, Lindsay was meditating "the New Localism," which was his hope for a deep-rooted rich provincialism that would do more in the end to protect States' Rights and save the American soul from being sucked into a central maelstrom than John C. Calhoun could do, though he rose from the dead.

Having had his ideas of God and sainthood laughed down, he had retreated to John Keats: beauty is truth, truth beauty. He was trying also to establish a significance and discover a purpose in his prolonged stay at home. Everyone to whom he sent *The Village Magazine* was supposed to do his bit toward improving his own place.

"Prepare to serve your town!" he bade them all. "No matter where you go, come back, prepared to serve your town. Go to Rome, Munich, Benares, Nikko or Kamakura, if you must, for Beauty's sake, but bring back all your inspiration to help us here."

When the new localism should be the way of America, each township would strive to work its own vein, each region boast suburbs unique and lovely, each village fly the banner of its civic coat of arms. There would be civic flowers, crafts and mannerisms of workmanship to proclaim the town's grace wherever its trade went.

"Fair streets are better than silver," Lindsay wrote, "green parks are better than gold."

"Bad public taste is mob-law, good public taste is democracy."

"Ugliness is a kind of misgovernment."

But—"I have not so clear a faith as you have in the power of civic beauty to produce civic righteousness," objected Arthur Davison Ficke, whose name had been on Witter Bynner's list. "*Can* you please both the village and yourself at one and the same moment?"

Ficke was addressing Lindsay from his own midwestern village of Davenport in darkest Iowa. He was an extraordinarily handsome young man; it was to him that Edna St. Vincent Millay cried in her passionate heyday:

> And you as well must die, belovèd dust
> And all your beauty stand you in no stead . . .

Ficke had studied law and been admitted to the bar. He wrote poetry and with a far more exquisite sense of style than Lindsay. Yet if his muse stumbled less than Lindsay's, she also had less faith; she dared less. Ficke had aspired to be a poet whose work should mean all things to all men and catch the minds of—in his own words—"the inattentive and crude majority." But that was once.

"Closer association with practical affairs disheartens me," he admitted to Lindsay now. "The vision fades as I look into the faces of one after another of the beings who people my external world. What do they care for poetry?

"As well call to the galley-slave in the midst of his labor

to meditate on the splendor of the stars: as well try to divert with sweet music the hunter intent upon the trace of his prey. These men cannot, will not listen, though Milton and Shelley should speak to them—do speak to them.

"I feel that no artist will do well to try to adapt his work to the tastes of those who reject what Milton and Shelley put before them. . . .

"But good luck to you."

And, in a postscript: "What would the real Shropshire yokel think of Housman?"

Of the beings who peopled Lindsay's external world only about thirty, and almost none of them church folk, attended his "Ruskin Revival," held at the YMCA in November and December 1910, for the benefit of the new Christian Church building. He had bought himself a shelf-long set of Ruskin and prepared with care his course of five lectures, based on the principles of *The Stones of Venice*. The price for the course was one dollar, with a copy of *The Village Magazine* thrown in.

"Come with the civic fire in your soul!" he urged beforehand, when he hoped all Springfield would be present.

Then to his scanty audience he spoke fervently of cleaning up town politics and building up town pride, of the talented children of Springfield and of using their gifts toward the glory of the city. He boldly proposed that the ample prairie landscape shape the architecture of future Springfield houses. He pleaded with his indifferent townsmen to take the same possessive interest in their City Hall as in the Capitol at Washington.

27

There was a world beyond Springfield.

Floyd Dell, associate literary editor of the Chicago *Evening Post*, had had passed on to him a copy of that strange little book *The Tramp's Excuse*. Lindsay had sent his earlier War Bulletins to the *Post* and received a number of sympathetic responses from supposedly hardboiled newspaper men. As one of them wrote, almost wistfully, after making a quick survey of the vistas thrown open by *War Bulletin Number Three:* "I thought I had long ago sealed up all the avenues by which a mystical appeal could reach me, but I am not so sure now. I think you have somehow got inside."

When Dell, who was only twenty-two and did not know Lindsay, read *The Tramp's Excuse* he thought the poems in it extraordinary. It was probably he who reviewed the book for the *Post* on October 29, 1909, writing warmly, in one of the first serious appraisals ever given Lindsay's poetry, that "Nicholas Vachel Lindsay is something of an artist; after a fashion, a socialist; more certainly, a religious mystic; and for present purposes it must be added that he is indubitably a poet!"

These poems had all a message. The socialist in Lindsay spoke in poems like *On the Building of Springfield* (especially commended by the *Post* for its "throbbing, glowing idealism") and *Why I Voted the Socialist Ticket.*

Why had he voted the socialist ticket? "I am unjust," he acknowledged,

> but I can strive for justice.
> My life's unkind, but I can vote for kindness.

I, the unloving, say life should be lovely.
I, that am blind, cry out against my blindness.

Many of the poems had been the outcome of his visions and
all were written before ridicule and distrust blighted his seeking after an august, protean Creator.

O great heart of God,
Once vague and lost to me,
Why do I throb with your throb tonight,
In this land, eternity?

The lines are from *A Prayer in the Jungles of Heaven*, later
published as *Heart of God*. Also in the book were *Star of My
Heart, I Heard Immanuel Singing,* and the amazing *Hymn to
the Sun:*

Christ the dew in the clod,
    Christ the sap of the trees,
Christ the light in the waterfall,
    Christ the soul of the sun,
Innermost blood of the sun,
    Grant I may touch the fringes
Of the outermost robe of the sun;

    Let me store your rays till my ribs
Carry the breath of lightning,
    Till my lips speak the fullness of thunder
To waken world-weary men:
    Till my whisper engenders lions
Out of the desert weeds.

Lindsay had illustrated *The Tramp's Excuse* with his drawings, of which the principal one was his "Map of the Universe," now first appearing in print. He explained it to his
readers in a special note, explained it with the same devoted
earnestness with which he addressed the Ridgely miners and
preached at the First Christian Church.

Near the top of his Map rise three jagged shapes, which are, says Lindsay, the three thrones of the Trinity hewn from three ancient mountains and still giving out white light, though fallen into ruin. Above them swim the boats of the prophets, who prophesy the new universe and eat of the flower of the Holy Ghost, which is the Amaranth; whoever eats of it becomes filled with the love of eternal beauty.

Below the abandoned thrones lie the Jungles of Heaven, whence souls are fled and where Lindsay in imagination often roamed, sometimes with the woman of his dreams. They are a waste-land—once a city, now a place of moss-hung palaces, streets silent but for the wind, rotted harps, broken crowns and swords of rusted gold.

Bounding them is a granite wall that drops sheerly down to the little globe of earth. The "great-leaved, heavy-fruited" vine of the Apple-Amaranth grows like Jack's beanstalk on this wall, a ladder between heaven and earth.

Missionaries of the universe are the angels, superb bright beings who ceaselessly adventure forth to the outermost stars, there to be crucified "on millions of crosses, on millions of suns and stars and planets," leaving heaven behind them—a jungle.

"It was by a leaping of the flame from the Harp of the great singer Lucifer," writes Lindsay, "that the angels fell in love with suffering and went forth to the stars to be forsaken of God. Thus was Lucifer King of the Universe the moment before he was cursed with eternal silence and sealed in his tomb."

> just for a breath he conquered and reigned,
> For one quick pulse of time he stood;
> By flame was crowned where God had been
> Himself the Word sublime—

On Lindsay's Map the flame leaping from the harp of Lucifer rises upward in a great curve from the engulfment of hell and past heaven to the three throne-mountains, while far below—below hell itself—over the tomb of the silenced singer flows the River of Hate.

When the blood of the martyred angels has been shed, it enters the wine jars carried earthward on their ships by the prophets. Then as the old men pour the wine from one jar into another it is diffused into a purple mist, which in the eyes of dwellers on earth is the gleam, the mysterious glory of which saints and poets are aware. The gleam becomes sound: it is the still small voice, the voice of love, that whispers in the human heart.

Some day this angelic wine shall be poured down in a purple flood and the kingdom of hell redeemed by it.

Near the center of the Map under the granite parapet of heaven floats the soul of a butterfly, which is called Beauty— the soul of the earth redeemed. Far to the south beyond the edge of hell lurks like a dragon-monster of old the soul of a giant spider, whose name is Mammon.

East of the universe rises the Palace of Eve, with its towering Doric pillars, archaic and immemorial—"whence come the perfect brides," says Lindsay.

To the west grows and blows musically in the winds of Chaos the Tree of Laughing Bells, one wine-red bell from whose tossing branches "will quench all memory, all hope, all borrowed sorrow."

Somewhere deep in the Jungles of Heaven lies hidden Aladdin's Lamp, by whose magic the new universe can be created. "The Genii of the Lamp can be commanded to carry the Laughing Bells to every soul, and thus redeem them all. The angels and prophets declare that the New Universe comes by the power of the Wine of God, that is the blood of the crucified angels."

And in this universe, after the Millennium, then shall Immanuel sing.

Lindsay's Map may not be ignored, for its symbols, like the Amaranth, the Jungles of Heaven and the little boats that are sometimes empty and sometimes manned by prophets or angels, appear repeatedly in his poems, as in the final stanza of *The Congo:*

There, where the wild ghost-gods had wailed
A million boats of the angels sailed.

Fantastic though his symbols are and intermingled with elements of fairy tale, they are religious symbols and, if much
of his cosmology is unintelligible, the thread of his meaning can
be traced. Through the shedding of blood—through noble
living and self-sacrificial dying—men's souls will be delivered
from darkness and their way of life from materialism.

Aladdin's Lamp is a visible sign of the artist's imagination,
a magical holy talisman, without which there is no spiritual
redeeming.

In the blood shed by the angels for beauty's sake rages the
hot conflict between desires mortal and immortal that Lindsay
knew well. As for great Lucifer—he is the singer, the magician, the divine malcontent whose aspirations soar to heaven,
even though the turbid waters of hate have stilled his song.

Lindsay had sent *War Bulletin Number One* to Robert
Henri, who in 1908 had organized an exhibition of the paintings of his best pupils, including Luks and Bellows, that was
laughed at by the public for its revolutionary realism, which
portrayed slums, gutters and elevated railways, and inspired
the critics to speak derisively of "The Ash Can School."

This earlier pupil was equally a non-conformist. Henri now
told him so, writing that he was sure many would think Lindsay "quite crazy, some partly so, and others clairvoyant."

"The sum of your actions will prove which you are," said
Henri. "I shall not criticize you. You have an energy and you
are doing things in the effort of stating yourself that appear
perhaps disconcerting at times."

To Frederick Richardson, his chief at the Chicago Art Institute, Lindsay had sent *The Tramp's Excuse*. "Frankly," replied
Richardson, "many of your poems seem to me so unbalanced,
so diseased, so egotistical that I can find no sympathy in them.
Your drawing, as I have always said, is all of this—it is bad."

From Cambridge, Massachusetts, the psychologist and philosopher William James acknowledged receipt of *The Tramp's Excuse* and *War Bulletin Number Three*. Lindsay had read James' *The Varieties of Religious Experience*, pondering it in the light of his visions, and James was touched that this unknown youth should turn for "comradeship" to an academic personage like himself.

Only it was, he said, "too late, too late!"

He was writing in October 1909, ten months before his death. "I am sick, dried up, have no strength to read aught but the barely needful for my own tasks, have grown, moreover, positively to *hate* poetry in these last years. I can only stand old poems learned by heart in my childhood and adolescence. How then should I shoot the rapids and ride the whirlwind and tramp the wilderness with you?"

James was not at all sure that he understood the "Map of the Universe." "I *do* think Bulletin No. 3 anarchistic; I *do* think it incoherent; but I do think it may represent an excellent personal religion. Don't enter the Catholic *priesthood*, whatever you do! Your semi-automatic inspirations are very interesting, in conjunction with your free attitude toward them. . . .

"Go in peace and God be with you, brilliant being that you are, and leave me to my decrepitude."

In New York, George Mather Richards gave *The Tramp's Excuse* to an acquaintance who, after reading it, laid aside his habitual shyness and wrote to the poet, naming himself "Marsden Hartley, likewise a visionary, who finds companionship in thoughts such as yours."

Hartley was a painter. He was thirty-two, and no more than Lindsay had he yet found himself in his art. He was a man of cumulative, unfacile emotions—"not given to effusion usually," he confessed in his letter, "so that in speaking to you I speak directly out of the heart. I somehow think nothing sounds to us more beautiful than the words of appreciation from an occasional one who divines the meaning of the soul as put forth in poems and designs like yours."

Hartley had met Lindsay in New York but they had never come to know each other and the painter's only memory of the poet was of a face "filled with blond light, glowing with its own splendors."

"To you," he wrote, "I could be little else than a grey shadow, of which there are millions in the world of the visionary. But these things matter little. Let it be my happy business now to say I like your poems and designs in *The Tramp's Excuse*—like them exceedingly. I get real cosmic thrills from your lines.

"I do not say, as they who only criticize would say, that these poems are metrically not as strong as the art poets make them—I say that they are great because the soul speaks in them and not the mind only."

With Lindsay, Hartley thought of W. H. Davies of England, another poet and vagabond. Yet he believed Lindsay was nearer temperamentally to Blake than to Davies. "You have something a little more celestial in your vision, a kind of religious ecstasy, which carries work beyond that which sees merely divine beauty in Nature."

Hartley was soon to leave the city for the wilds of his native state of Maine. There, working and roaming in the silent places among his mountains, far from the railroad, he would keep Lindsay's poems with him; they would be welcome guests. Who knew but what one day he might stop a wanderer on those mountain roads and ask his name, "and you will tell me that you are the tramp who sang 'such willing music in my listening ears' in among the noises of tired and still untiring New York."

28

Olive and Paul had sailed again for China.

"Vachel writing, *writing* all the time," Mrs. Lindsay told Olive in a letter, and she added, "I wish most deeply it might not prove to be 'the bag of gold at the end of the rainbow.' "

Since an audience he must have, Vachel at intervals clattered downstairs to ask Joy and her chums: "Would you girls care to hear a new poem?"

Supper every night was at six. Afterward he emerged from the house to prowl—to seek unannounced whom he might devour. He wrote to Olive: "I go to the Logans once a week. I don't agree with them on any important question on earth except that a pleasant evening is a pleasant evening."

There were two Logan sisters still at home. "If Mrs. Logan would only marry off one of the girls, I might court the other a bit, but I find them both too charming. . . ."

Instead, he spread his "Map of the Universe" on their living-room floor and knelt to interpret it to them. He should have his suits pressed more often, said golden-haired Elsie, the younger sister.

"N.V.L. goes forth—" he described his evening rounds. "He goes forth, calling on the girls for the men will have nothing to do with anyone who is silly enough to write poetry, and if one of the men calls at the same time they view him as they might Wu Ting-Fang, and the girls get a little resentful of his presence, and wish he would call some other night."

Truly, since Paul had gone there seemed to be no men of his own age in town to hitch to, though occasionally some contemporary would stop him on the street and josh him "like the town drunk." When there were no calls to pay, he drifted over to the lobby of the Leland, where he read the papers, then went to Stuart's ice cream parlor for a dish of ice cream, then by himself to the movies. The films were short and elemental. Sometimes he saw three or four in a night, going from theater to theater till as he staggered out into the air for the last time he felt sick; the whole world turned on a reel and the enormous jerking images continued to whirl past his eyes.

Often then he strolled up Sixth Street to Adams. Against the background of the unlighted County Court House the Salvation Army band, a dedicated cluster, could be heard a block away shouting salvation into the Illinois dusk, pounding it on the kettledrum and blaring it on the trumpet as the men and women in their shabby uniforms sang:

> Have you been to Jesus for the cleansing power?
> Are you washed in the blood of the Lamb?

Then they knelt in a row on the Court House grass and prayed aloud, Lindsay with them. After their departure in military formation carrying their instruments, he walked slowly around the darkening square, from Adams Street to Washington—and again around it, alone, alone. It was about nine p.m.

No one really saw him at all, said Lindsay once, who hadn't seen him then.

Sometimes he took Susan Wilcox to the show with him, paying for her if he had the money. When he first came home, he had read to her *Where Is Aladdin's Lamp*, whose originality and beauty she, like Henri, at once recognized. Not so his mother who, shocked by the book's religious unorthodoxy, responded cruelly and without any understanding, he told Miss Wilcox. In his diary he referred to "the blown-out lamp" and he began to drop dark hints that he had "burned" the book. This was not true, for it was found after his death, but an unknown hand, probably his own, had roughly mutilated it, tearing away whole pages.

Susan Wilcox (she was "Susan" to him now) was a reader of the *Atlantic Monthly;* they quarreled a little about that. She also subscribed to a socialist publication and they studied it together, with mixed emotions, on Sunday nights at her place.

Another of his havens was the house of the George Lees on South Fourth Street, where Susan went, too, and Rabbi Tedecshe and Duncan McDonald, secretary to the United Mine Workers of Illinois, and the Frank Bodes, who were liberal Democrats, and Maydie Lee's brother, Willis Spaulding, commissioner of public property, whose re-election to City Hall was fought every time by the conservatives.

Mr. and Mrs. Lee entertained for the radical lobby that annually came from away to lay siege to the State House. Maydie Lee was the real power in the branch of the Woman's Trade Union League in Springfield. They all moved around, said Lindsay, from socialist meetings to trade union meetings to woman's suffrage meetings. They had all stood stanchly by his War Bulletins (except Number Three) and they were the only people in town who wanted anything to do with him.

Dr. Lindsay's medical practice now brought in little, and every available room in the old house was rented by his wife in an effort to make ends join. Often at night the parents lay sleepless, and they talked of their son and his lack of prospects but the dark did not give answer.

"Vachel's self-centered life, indifference to the church, aloofness from our family life and impractical ways make me *very anxious,*" his mother confessed to Olive.

Said the downright Joy simply: "I feel so sorry for Vachel. He ought to have some good sensible girl to look after him," and Olive, the sister of his heart, wrote: "My dear Brother, I think you need someone especially to love you."

It was in the summer of 1910 that Lindsay met Octavia Roberts, who was beautiful, literary and a little older than he. She had lived for some years away from Springfield and had

had two short stories published, which in her home town made her an author. On her return she was told at once that another author had come back before her and was agog to meet her.

Nobody moved to introduce them, but one very hot night her telephone rang. "This is Nicholas Vachel Lindsay," said a man's loud clear voice. "I desire to make your acquaintance."

Fifteen minutes later Vachel was on the Robertses' front porch, where he and Octavia sat talking for an hour in the pitch dark. "If we were to meet again, I shouldn't know you," he said as he rose to go. "Would you mind stepping into the house so I can see your face?"

Octavia's friends had been careful to warn her that Vachel was an "odd stick," but he seemed to her like any young man till they stood together in the lighted hall. Then she felt a difference. He laid one hand on her shoulder and with the other gently raised her chin. Studying his face, she was reminded both of a wild-eyed faun and of an itinerant evangelist, while the concentrated, blazing look he bent on her "might have sufficed Orpheus," she writes.

Not only was it intolerable to Dr. Lindsay to have an idle son, it was the judgment of the other Springfield doctors that that hulking boy was simply sapping the weary old man, his father.

"They say—" cried Vachel, overheard in the sanctum of the Lees' living room, "these They that discuss me, these great overwhelming invisible They—THEY say 'Why don't Vachel Lindsay go to work?' "

Then he burst into disconcerting laughter.

Yet the pressure of a disapproval he pretended to despise drove him early in 1911 to look for a job. Willis Spaulding found a place for him as day laborer out at the city waterworks, where a new boiler was being installed, but after two weeks of getting up at five, wheeling barrows of bricks and lugging sacks of cement among men who never seemed to tire, he quit. He was lame, worn out and ready to guarantee boiler building as a "sure cure for poets."

29

It was a dull time, a desperate time and yet, as Lindsay wrote in his diary,

> Not often, but once in a while
> At the end of a dull dull time,
> There comes a rushing of wings
> And strange words and strange rhyme.

He owed $150 on his printing expenses, for which he was dunned over the telephone till his parents paid the debt, his mother contributing from her room rent. "Vachel took the money as a baby takes its bottle," she told Olive.

This spring of 1911 the nation—Springfield in particular—was aroused by a political scandal involving Republican senator William Lorimer of Illinois. Lorimer in 1896 had been instrumental in selecting John R. Tanner as candidate for governor and it was Tanner who had defeated Altgeld in the Republican sweep that was the defeat of Lindsay's boyhood.

Broken in health and prospects, Altgeld died on March 12, 1902, when the public repented of its neglect sufficiently to eulogize him in the press, to turn out in droves for his funeral and even, in humble individual cases, to shed tears. Lindsay and Paul Wakefield, both students in Chicago, had gone together to view his body, standing in line with thousands of others.

Nine years had since passed over Altgeld's grave. The firebrand issues of his governorship were ashes. With Taft in the White House and Charles Deneen, Republican successor to Tanner in the Governor's Mansion, with woman's suffrage and prohibition superseding Haymarket, the Pullman strike and free silver in the public consciousness, who was there to remember Altgeld, much less to commemorate him?

Yet if one heart in Springfield remained faithful to the past, it was Lindsay's. On the Frazee side they had the sense of the future but he, Vachel—he confided to his father, who detested such unbosomings—had also a passion, which he believed was a Lindsay characteristic, for being loyal to things as they were and cherishing every one of his "old thoughts and purposes, along the main purpose" till he could use it creatively.

Of the dreams and adventures of his childhood and boyhood he never lost a crumb. The genesis of his major poems is traceable in his early prose and letters, his notebooks, scrapbooks and diaries begun as a boy. Thus the year 1896, which had seen Altgeld's star wane, saw Vachel, then sixteen, cut out all the important newspaper and magazine references to the Governor he could lay his hands on and paste them in a special scrapbook with Altgeld's picture on the cover, while three years later his Hiram oration on Altgeld went into the book.

Altgeld by that time was known to be ill, and Lindsay's speech begins: "If any man today would give his genius and his life for political purity, let him first count well the cost. He will be giving his life for his enemies."

It took nine years from Altgeld's death for the inspiration of his memory to come to flower in Lindsay. It was in the spring of 1911 that Lindsay, prompted by the name of Lorimer in the news and by the anniversary in March of Altgeld's passing, wrote his poem *The Eagle That Is Forgotten* dedicated to John P. Altgeld, which, appearing in the Illinois *State Register*, attracted more attention than anything he had done and was reprinted in papers throughout the Midwest.

One of the last items inserted in his scrapbook was a letter from Mrs. Emma Ford Altgeld, who still recalled him as her young neighbor next door and asked to be remembered to his mother. "I thank you so much," she wrote, "for your appreciation of the work my dear husband tried to do—and for the

beautiful way you express it. There is grandeur in the poem."
Of Altgeld, Lindsay had written:

Sleep softly . . . eagle forgotten . . . under the stone.
Time has its way with you there, and the clay has its own . . .

Sleep on, O brave-hearted, O wise man, that kindled the flame—
To live in mankind is far more than to live in a name.

Himself, he crept behind his dreams like a snail in the wake
of a chariot, Lindsay told Witter Bynner. He wished he were
a centipede and could write with his feet.

Since his coming home he had had published in *The Outlook*
the "Letters of a Literary Tramp," describing his southern
hike; in *The Independent* his poem *Why I Voted the Socialist
Ticket* and a prohibition poem, *King Arthur's Men Have
Come Again;* and in *Collier's* a prose sketch, *The Factor in the
Village.*

But for every poem or story accepted, dozens were turned
down. By 1911 he was peddling his manuscripts furiously and
collecting rejection slips. Since he kept about fifteen pieces
on the road at all times, there was the possibility any day, hour
or moment that one was being chosen; dug in at his desk in
the morning, he reminded himself of this. Next morning he
reminded himself again.

And then in March 1911 *Current Literature* amazingly devoted a two-page editorial to that obscure offering *The Village
Magazine*—of which "no mere words can convey the quaint-
ness," exclaimed the editor, and he called on readers everywhere to pay heed to Nicholas Vachel Lindsay, an Illinois art
evangelist and authentic western poet.

It was Witter Bynner who had directed the staff's attention
to Lindsay. The unexpected editorial stirred a widening ripple
of interest. Upton Sinclair, impressed by the note of social
passion in the quotations given from Lindsay's work, asked
his secretary to get hold of *The Village Magazine;* several
great university libraries, among them that of Harvard, requested copies.

In Chicago, Hamlin Garland read the editorial. Garland, just over fifty, was an established novelist of the West. When he understood what Lindsay was saying, he was struck by how this young unknown had gone him one better in pleading with Americans to look for and discover inspiration in their native land second but in their home towns first of all.

He sent $2.00 for two copies of *The Village Magazine*. On its prompt arrival, his sympathy with Lindsay's arguments was confirmed; he honored him for advancing them, and yet what really made the thrill of discovery run cold down his spine was the poetry, especially *The Wizard in the Street*, Lindsay's vindication of Poe the artist—of the brotherhood of Lucifer—to the man in the street:

> Useful are you. There stands the useless one
> Who builds the Haunted Palace in the sun.
> Good tailors, can you dress a doll for me
> With silks that whisper of the sounding sea? . . .
>
> Which one of you can spread a spotted cloak
> And raise an unaccounted incense smoke
> Until within the twilight of the day
> Stands dark Ligeia in her disarray,
> Witchcraft and desperate passion in her breath
> And battling will, that conquers even death?

The miracle to Hamlin Garland was that such an expression should come out of Springfield. He knew Springfield. "Your poems, your prose," he wrote back to Lindsay, "gave me joy. But in order to 'smash your thumb' let me say that you must be very careful not to write anything casually, and you must not permit the ethics of your message to at any time dominate your art."

He invited Lindsay to come to Chicago, expenses paid, and speak to them at the Cliff Dwellers, a club of regional writers, artists and professional men that Garland had helped to found. When the poet turned up at this invitation, which he accepted immediately, Garland had another surprise. Nicholas Vachel

Lindsay was from Springfield, all right. The prairie was in his voice; he hailed his host as "Brother Garland."

In the small, well-appointed club dining room in the Orchestra Hall building overlooking Lake Michigan, Lindsay got to his feet during luncheon and said some words on the "new localism" to the members, among whom his loud, insistent way of speaking raised smiles. Afterward he and Garland went across the street to the Art Institute, where Garland had arranged for him to address the students. Here there was more space; in his old haunts he felt at home and his idealism met response, yet it was not till the evening at Garland's house that he quite satisfied the high hopes raised.

Then alone with his host and two others—Lorado Taft, the sculptor, and Henry Fuller, the novelist—he recited several of his poems, ending with the one on Poe, and then indeed he cast the spell of genius over the three awed men of talent.

His crudity was plain, but in this quiet hour his delicacy was apparent also. It even seemed to Garland that the young poet was not fully aware of his endowment or his accomplishment—rather that he sang like the bards of old, who when they swept their harps became entranced and inspired.

Soon Lindsay was notified in Springfield that he had been elected a non-resident member of the Cliff Dwellers and that his dues for the year were to be remitted.

He wrote to Olive of the honor, along with more homely items: "Stuart's ice cream is still pretty good. Papa has bought a new hoze-nozzle, and Mama wants our front porch painted. Papa has given me the paint to paint the side fence and maybe I will, and I have been made a member of the Cliff Dwellers Club."

But for the present he kept away. For one thing, he couldn't afford the fare to Chicago; for another, though nearly paralyzed with gratitude to Garland, he had been chagrined on the day of his introduction at mingling on falsely equal terms with men of formidable achievement—he who had nothing to offer as calling cards but a few private pamphlets.

Brother Garland, in the meantime, having in April passed through Springfield had called at 603 South Fifth where in the role of Vachel's patron he met the bearded taciturn Papa, who sat listening almost without a word, and the schoolteacherish yet oddly fascinating Mama, who talked about her missionary daughter carrying out in China "the purposes from which she herself had been prevented."

"Your son," said Garland to them, "is a genius. Be patient with him a little longer."

30

On Lindsay's bedroom dresser were pictures Olive had sent from China of the Kamakura Buddha and, from a piece of Gandara sculpture, of Buddha after the forty-day fast. Both of them were great consolers, he told his sister, for spiritually he had at last attained Nirvana or something like it. Since if religion should lead to anything it should lead to peace, he had decided after the abuse and ridicule that greeted *War Bulletin Number Three* to cling fast to peace.

He had set religion aside as a main consideration and, where once he had begged to have fire perpetually in his heart, he now thanked God for the tranquility that filled his whole soul. After *War Bulletin Number Three* even the Disciples had come to stand to him for hatred.

He was on extra good terms with his parents—"we haven't had a good old cat-killing time for ages." But about all the religion he had at present was gratitude for inner serenity, he went on. He was unburdening himself to Olive at one-thirty in the morning, when Springfield slept and only his light gleamed.

By day Lindsay heaped up in both hands the peace that was his temporary accomplishment, and he held it out to the brown-haired, blue-eyed, queenly Octavia Roberts in the visible forms of a red rose and a poem he had written to her. He called the poem *With a Rose, to Brunhilde.*

Brunhilde, with the young Norn soul
That has no peace, and grim as those
That spun the thread of life, give heed:
Peace is concealed in every rose.
And in these petals peace I bring:
A jewel clearer than the dew:
A perfume subtler than the breath
Of Spring with which it circles you.

Thus the poet to his lady. The brother to his sister wrote only that he and Octavia were becoming "pretty thick. Mama is beginning to get sentimental. Papa is merely silent."

Octavia had asked him to call again, with the result that he came much too often. "She is one of the most attractive women I ever met and evidently has Vachel bewitched," Mrs. Lindsay in her turn told Olive.

Octavia herself hardly knew what to make of a beau who drank no wine and didn't dance, and at one of the first parties they went to she shipped him as soon as they arrived. Riding back beside her on the streetcar, he spoke tentatively: "Octavia —you know—I'm sensitive."

"Darling daughter of Babylon," he addressed her in another poem,

Leading Belshazzar's chattering court,

by which he meant the Springfield country club.

She was diverted by his tramping stories, though the idea of an able-bodied male offering bits of verse for bread to put into his mouth seemed to her grotesque. In his genius she had little confidence. As for taking seriously as a suitor a man of thirty-two who begged a nickel from his father to go to the movies—this, for Octavia, was impossible. Yet Vachel as the months went by protested that he wished to be taken seriously, till at last she told him his love-making sounded like something out of a book read so often the pages are blurred.

He was bitterly hurt. Where now was his independence of religion? "I think on Heaven," he wrote piteously,

for in that air so clear
We two may meet, confused and parted here.

The lines are from the first of two *Easter Stanzas*, which at Easter 1912 he slipped under the door of her who

scorned my graceless years and trophies few.

To Octavia the reproachful poems seemed to blow up her relation with him into something much bigger and more dramatic than she had ever willingly allowed it to be. She found them simply irritating; after reading them she could understand why Fanny Brawne, whom posterity calls cruel, had treated John Keats the way she did.

Though he felt estranged from the Disciples, Lindsay had contributed $115—an accumulation of his "little dabs" from writing and speaking—to their new church building. At Christmas 1911 he gave his father $65, of which the doctor gave him $10 back. Ever since then he hadn't had a cent, his mother told Olive, except what came out of the family pocketbook.

It was about eight weeks after Easter that he cut the knot of his frustrations by seeking the road for the third time. Lucky neither in love nor in work, disappointed and disappointing, he walked west out of Springfield. He was bound for California and he meant to be gone at least a year, to hike from Los Angeles north to Seattle, then back across the country. His parents, having no alternative, let him go.

"Vachel is getting ready to make another of his foolish tramps," his father wrote to Olive.

"Vachel seems to me to be passing through a period of preparation," wrote his mother, who in spite of their temperamental clashes had faith in her son. "I believe he will come up sometime, in some way, somewhere, but the waiting is very discouraging."

The waiting was nearly over.

Lindsay had recently written a number of short poetical prose articles he called "canticles" and sent them to the *American Magazine*, from whose editor he hadn't heard a word. But Octavia had done work for the *American*, and "this morning," Vachel's mother continued—she was writing to Olive on April 4—"Octavia phoned that she had a letter from the *American* saying they had received some remarkable articles from Nicholas Vachel Lindsay; that he was of her town: would *she* investigate him and write up a sketch of him for their department 'Interesting People.'"

This was not only encouraging, it was absurdly funny.

"Nicholas Vachel Lindsay written up in the *American* by Octavia Roberts! (If the article ever appears, several people will sit up and take notice!) Besides, if they accept the 'canticles' they will pay Vachel quite a sum—for him—and Papa, who is half beside himself because he lacks $300 of paying his taxes, will get some of it, and every little helps."

Next the *American* accepted two poems by Lindsay: for June, *The Knight in Disguise*, which was about O. Henry, and for September, *The Proud Farmer*, in which he celebrated his grandfather Frazee. The editor also agreed to consider publishing the letters he planned to write from the road to his mother and Octavia.

Too close to these omens to read them, Lindsay himself was in a mood to dramatize his sense of failure, which had lasted for four years. He recalled the log houses of the Blue Ridge, the rings of faces lit by the fire from the hearth while he chanted, and it seemed to him that the only times he had lived had been on his wanderings.

"I can remember," he wrote afterward of his days at home this chafing restless spring, "the desperate need to throw off everything and the desperate struggle to do it. . . ." The night before he left he called on Octavia, handed her his worn little purse and bade her keep it till he came back, for it held all his wealth, one dime.

This time he took with him two new leaflets, the first headed "The Gospel of Beauty"—a gospel, he explained, that did not say No to any established creed.

After all, he was drifting back into religion. Philosophic serenity was not enough: he was a believer. "I come to you penniless and afoot," his proclamation began. "I am starting a new religious idea. . . . Let the denomination to which you now belong be called in your heart 'The Church of Beauty' or 'The Church of the Open Sky.' The Church of Beauty has two sides: the love of beauty and the love of God."

His second leaflet, *Rhymes to be Traded for Bread*, contained poems. The unpaid printing costs amounted to $42.50 and he left behind him another little bill for $15, telling both his creditors, "Mother will stand good."

He also carried with him a large scrapbook of pictures, for which he had made a cover of black oilcloth to save it from the weather. He had worked over his scrapbook all spring, choosing every picture in it to illustrate one side or the other of his Church of Beauty.

First was a photograph of Rudolf Marschall's sculpture of Jesus as the good shepherd leading his flock. Then came pictures of the interior of Brantwood, Ruskin's house in the English Lake district, and of the statue by Lorado Taft of Chief Black Hawk on the shore of the Rock River near Oregon, Illinois; then a bust of Poe and two etchings of Whistler (rebels who in their revolt from democracy served it well); then an ancient Egyptian temple, the Parthenon, the Pantheon, the Greek Orthodox church of Saint Sophia in Constantinople, the Taj Mahal, the leaning tower of Pisa, Notre Dame, Saint Peter's, and Trinity Church in New York.

The last pages were given over to four of Lindsay's special saints: Saint Francis, Saint Lincoln, Saint Tolstoy and Buddha. There were pictures of Lincoln's house and law office in Springfield and Tolstoy's estate of Yasnaya Polyana. There was a photograph, taken during Bryan's visit to Russia, of Bryan and Tolstoy side by side, dressed Russian-style in fur

caps, boots and fur-trimmed overcoats. Beside another picture
of Tolstoy, as a young man, Lindsay had pasted his own poem
Look You, I'll Go Pray.

All this he meant to interpret to the farmers and merchants
along his route, to open their imaginations to the loveliness—
first—of things visible. He took with him, too, a pocket diary
and a spare notebook for new poems. So he set forth, on May
29, 1912.

George Lee, representative of all his friends, walked out on
the road with him, then shook hands and stood looking after
him as Lindsay, with his tramp's bundle on a stick over his
shoulder, cut rapidly across country and went striding off
down the railroad tracks.

31

His spirits were already rising when a few miles out of Springfield he came on Automobile Number 28058 of Illinois abandoned by the roadside. He passed the lonely hulk, mud-streaked and spider-infested, at a steady pace till it was a speck far behind, but the sight of it he took as a good sign, having himself discarded mechanical chariots and all they stood for. When later, on the plains of Kansas, he met several west-going Conestoga wagons, this was another good sign.

His walking speed averaged a mile every quarter-hour. On May 30 he sent back a postcard from Valley City to the Illinois *State Register*, which passed the word on, in a not unfriendly line of large type: NICHOLAS LINDSAY WILL ENTER MISSOURI TODAY, IS BEING WELL RECEIVED ALONG THE ROAD.

It was on the evening of June 1 that he crossed the Mississippi, pearl-colored in the fading light, after reciting his poems in many a hospitable Illinois farmhouse and at least acquiescent village general store. Three days into Missouri, as he was tramping through the country below Hannibal, he heard the elfin voice of a bird he could not identify. "Shivaree! Shivaree!" sang the bird.

He made marks in his diary to indicate the soaring and sinking of the notes. The next night when he was taking shelter in the cabin of a kindly Negro, the old man told him the wild meadow bird he talked about, so sweet of song, was called the Rachel Jane.

Lindsay displayed the treasures of his oilcloth-covered scrapbook to this good old Negro and his wife, who hung fondly over the pictures of Lincoln's house and law office and couldn't get enough of the fact that their guest was from Lincoln's town.

"Goin' west harvestin'?" the Negro asked.

"No," firmly answered Lindsay.

He had been giving the same answer to the same question since he started out. He found the best excuse he could make for his walk was to say he meant to put it into rhyme: people accepted the idea of a traveling rhymer.

After a week of sleeping in his suit and using his derby hat to pick berries into, he began to look like somebody whom stay-at-homes *expected* to work, and those householders who fed him now began to require some stint in payment: he was to split kindling, or cut grass with the scythe, or hoe corn. Then would come dinner, hearty and tasty, and afterward the whole family would ease its chairs back.

Lindsay would rise and, as the commencement of his gospel message, peal forth *The Proud Farmer*, his poem about his Indiana grandfather who, notwithstanding that he tilled the soil, had lined his walls with books and preached to his neighbors.

He recited *The Illinois Village*, which applied just as well to a village in Missouri, and *On the Building of Springfield*, which needed a little explaining first. Then sitting down again, looking from one face to another, he handed around the stolid table his scrapbook with its pictured masterpieces.

On the road beyond Clarksburg he drafted some compensatory lines to the innkeeper's softhearted wife in the town behind him, who refused to let him work for his bed and board.

> Tenderly pitiful lady . . .
>
> Your welcome so gracious and high
> Is more precious to me than the whisper of song,
> More precious to me for this hour than my dream.
> I am truly, most truly the beggar I seem . . .
>
> And little you know as I knock at your door
> I knock at the door of the world.

His walk so far had been fertile with hints for poems. Before Clarksburg he had passed under a green hill with three trees on top like the place in his dream where he had heard Immanuel singing. Now bound for Tipton, walking the railroad ties, he kept pausing to write down the names of field flowers that paraded beside him: bluebells, larkspur, Indian paint, sunflowers and brown-eyed Susans, a prolific pink and white blossom called by the farmers "sheep's tea," white poppies, and roses of every hue known to the rose.

"Goin' west harvestin'?"

"I have harvested already, ten thousand flowers an hour," said Lindsay.

But there were days when glory fled. In a country hotel where he recited, one guest marched out in the middle. Next morning the voice of another guest floated through his open bedroom transom: "That was a hot entertainment that young bum gave us."

And then a second voice: "He oughta go to work, the dirty lazy loafer."

The farther Lindsay went into western Missouri, the more moments were there when he felt burdened and embarrassed by his own do-nothingness. To left and right, before and behind, all humanity except himself seemed to be up to its elbows in the lusty soil. His lurking fear had been that if he tried harvesting it would be just like his failure at the waterworks, and yet each time he shook his head in answer to the recurring question he found himself a little less eager to counter with his trilogy of poems.

One night near the Kansas border, after he had shared the supper of a farmer and his wife, whom he had come on just at the close of day in their field and who were so cheerful and hard-working that he felt "deathly ashamed" to take their bread, his courage turned in him. When the farmer asked the usual question he answered, "Yes."

On June 14 he entered Kansas. With his back to the sunrise, he walked straight across that vast hot windy state, stopping three times to harvest.

32

Ten miles out of Emporia, Lindsay hit the Santa Fé Trail, highway to the West, where a mud road, an auto trail, ran parallel to the railroad tracks, where—with klaxon horns hooting, curtains flapping, pennants flying and tents and blankets lashed on the rear—the touring cars whizzed past from earliest dawn till the country night came down. Then traffic slackened, and in the softly rustling fields was lifted the clear voice of the Rachel Jane.

Often during the next days Lindsay, in his shabby suit and derby hat, his ordinarily pale face bright red with sunburn, sat him down by the side of the road and hugged his knees and watched and listened, at intervals pulling out of his pocket and working over with busy pencil the tiny notebook in which he wrote his thoughts.

Like him, the careering cars were heading west:

> They are hunting the goals that they understand:
> San Francisco and the brown sea-sand.
> My goal is the mystery the beggars win.
> I am caught in the web the night-winds spin.

So he was to celebrate his experience in his poem *The Santa Fé Trail*, but the time for poetic celebration was not yet. Kansas was in the first flush of the harvest season. He had made his decision and on June 24, near Newton just inside the wheat belt, he was hired to shock wheat by a Mennonite family, the devout and unworldly Longneckers.

The twelve-hour day in the fields was a challenge to any man. Following the swath cut by the reaper, which was driven by old Longnecker's son and pulled by a team of four mules, Lindsay and his partner, a Mennonite apprentice still in his teens, bound the sheaves of ripe grain with twine and built them into shocks against the powerful, almost perpetual wind.

The boy, singing as he worked "The day-star hath risen," handled two of the cumbersome sheaves to one of Lindsay's. His movements were straight out of the old illustrations to Scripture; he stepped ahead, lithe and brisk, while Lindsay toiled behind under the terrible sun that beat down on his unaccustomed head, on which he wore a borrowed hat, and sucked up the sweat from his face.

After every circuit of the immense field they all three paused by a gap in the thorn hedge to drink long draughts from a big crock of water. Lindsay wasted water by dribbling it over his head. Like one of Coleridge's mariners, he held up his burning cheeks to catch any breath of cool air. His heart was light, though, and he ventured to tell the others a little joke about the ten educated hens he had met on the way to Emporia waddling Indian file and swearing. He had addressed the last hen: "Why are you swearing, sister?"

"These Emporia people are going to give a Sunday-school picnic," replied the hen. "Meantime, all us hens have to lay deviled eggs."

Young Longnecker jumped up from the grass.

"We do not laugh at jokes about swearing," he said and he clambered up onto the reaper, while Lindsay's boy-partner stalked out from the protecting shade into the yellow glare and began once more to heap up sheaves.

The sun was at his fiercest at half-past two; they stood him off as did Samson the lion. This was the hour when Lindsay's brain and sight whirled, his nerve all but failed him and the spiny wheat straws caught inside his heavy gloves became fiery sword-points.

Still he felt a faint saving sweat under his shirt. Just ahead of him sang the agile lad, and taking courage, Lindsay began to sing, too, every glory-raising hymn he could think of. When

a little after four o'clock the boy left for the barn two miles
away to do the evening milking, he followed in the path of
the reaper by himself, all but alone in the great field, still singing, and, after the long-repeated rhythms of the day, striding
and bending like a dancer.

> Oh, I have walked in Kansas
> Through many a harvest field,
> And piled the sheaves of glory there
> And down the wild rows reeled.

Again the poetic celebration came later. At the time, his
day's work over, he was too tired to do more than fall into
bed in the spare room of the farmhouse, while his ears rang
with the prayers of thanksgiving lifted at the otherwise silent
table by the patriarchal Longnecker, and his imagination
glowed with the parables of the New Testament—of the
sower who went forth to sow and the planting of the good
seed and the tares.

At the end of the week Lindsay had $7.87 in his pocket.
Before leaving home he had laid down some rules based on his
previous hikes: to keep away from cities, go the whole way
on foot and have no truck with money. Yet he couldn't well
refuse to take his earned wage; anyhow he had stretched his
rules before now by accepting lifts—in railroad and hand-cars,
farm wagons and the despised automobile. Even though he held
the motor car "a carnal institution," to be steered clear of by the
genuinely spiritual, there were stretches of road along which
he, for one, got fed up with being spiritual.

On July 1 he walked from the Mennonite farm on into
Newton, where he bought a Buffalo Bill hat and a pair of
dazzling yellow trousers that made him look "much more like
somebody." In the public library of a town a few miles farther
west he wrote a letter to his parents, who were soon to leave
for Colorado. Octavia had been invited by his mother (at his
request) to join them; it was already settled that when he

passed through Colorado he would stop at the family camp and see them all.

He recited for his supper at houses between Newton and Ellinwood, usually leaving his gospel leaflet behind without comment. On July 5 he arrived at Great Bend, a town deep within the wheat country, where his glittering blue eyes under his new sombrero observed the crowd moving slowly up and down the main street: migrant harvesters and desperate farmers accosting strangers in their search for hands.

Here he again hired out for harvest work. His boss was a man named Frank Weaver, under whose supervision he shocked wheat and pitched alfalfa hay. At night his bed was in the barn loft; he lay with his hands behind his head and, with the wind in his face and the sweet smell of hay in his nostrils, gave himself up to dreamy contemplation through the wide-open loft door of the everlasting wheat, the spinning windmills and the rising moon.

Though by day the sky was a bright Kansas blue and the sun descended on the prairie like the stroke of a golden hammer, there was darkness and death at the Weaver place. Both Frank and his brother Forrest, who worked with him, had a certain hard attractiveness—"but their cruelty," pronounced Lindsay in his diary, "was bottomless."

On Sunday, July 7, he was in the sitting room writing letters when he heard a fearful row out beyond the barn. Frank and Forrest were exciting themselves by disciplining Dick, a frisky broncho colt, whom they had tied up and were beating over the head—one with a double-tree, the other with a pitchfork handle—while Forrest plied himself with swigs of whisky so that he could be as mean as Frank.

Lindsay heard the roars, oaths, thuds of the bar and stick, whinnies of pain and tattoo of hoofs all the long afternoon till at six o'clock Frank's fat and patient wife May ran over to the barn and protested, reminding the men it was Sunday and warning them they wouldn't be blest and would lose a day's harvest.

On Monday morning the little broncho Dick was hitched to the reaper along with three large mules. He went dancing out to the field, looking devilish, defiantly objecting to keeping his head on a line with the others and hauling the great load almost by himself. That night he came dancing home. On Tuesday he went out again dancing for battle, but returned at night dragging and panting.

On Wednesday, just past the hottest hour, Lindsay was working in the field with Forrest. About three o'clock the pony, who till then had been feebly dancing, went mad. He strained against his halter. His eyes were distended. Blood oozed from his mouth. His hide—a mass of wounds from Sunday's torture—was clustered thick as fly paper with thirstily sucking flies.

Lindsay, who had never quite overcome his childhood terror of horses, put fear behind him and between them he and Forrest managed to pull the lunging animal away from the mules and restrain him by two halter ropes while Frank, the more savage brother, was sent for. Frank, cursing, tried to lead Dick back to the barn, but when they reached the pasture of long uncut prairie grass the pony sank down into it and kicked the air convulsively with all four feet. Then his heart broke and he died.

"If God gives me grace," Lindsay pledged, alone with his diary, "some day I shall write his memorial—THE BRONCHO THAT WOULD NOT BE BROKEN."

Less than twenty-four hours later he himself collapsed.

Like the broncho, he had up to now danced out into the field each morning, but just before noon on Thursday, realizing that he must either take a day off or quit altogether—since he could scarcely any longer raise even one sheaf from the ground—he told Frank, who fell into a fury, raged that he hated a quitter and taunted Lindsay with losing his nerve.

"That isn't my brand of nerve," retorted Lindsay.

He accepted his wages, which came to $12.50, presented both the startled brothers with copies of his gospel and his rhymes, and then he left that place. He understood now why he had been directed there: so that the broncho Dick—whose name, said Lindsay, ought to be Leonidas, and who was "in all the wide farm-place the person most human"—should have one mourner.

In Great Bend he bought himself two flashy cravats to go with his sombrero and corduroys and paid cash for a room overnight at the Saddlerock Hotel. Standing up in the hot post office he wrote a letter enclosing ten dollars to his parents and next morning, with empty pockets and by the grace of Saint Francis "unharnessed," began to walk west again.

It made him tense with dread to think of resuming his battle with the sun when on July 15 near the town of Wright he undertook his third harvest. This time, though, he lasted through. Harvesting oats and barley as well as wheat, he spent hours on the high deck of a header-barge from where he could survey the level floor-land for miles. His new employer was Louis Lix, a German Catholic, a man unconditionally on the square with his workers and as God-fearing as the Mennonite Longnecker. Lindsay, having made a point of attending meeting with the Mennonites, now went to Mass along with the Lix family.

In the rest periods in the field or as the horse-drawn barges pulled for the barn in the evening, Lix's hired stacker, who during the winter was a Baptist preacher, sang drearily pornographic cowboy ballads—to counteract which, Lindsay one noontime lifted up his own voice and under the blazing sky declaimed from Swinburne's *Atalanta*:

> When the hounds of spring are on winter's traces,
>   The mother of months in meadow or plain
> Fills the shadows and windy places
>   With lisp of leaves and ripple of rain.

This hit the spot with the far from insensitive stacker, who called for an encore. Early next day, ready for work, he began right off:

When the hounds of spring are on winter's traces,
The mother of months . . .

"Damn it, what's the rest of it? I've been trying to say that piece all night!"

By the end of the week Lindsay's hands were so tough he could leave off his gloves, and mortally afraid though he had been the whole time that he would jab some man working on the ground below him in the eye with his pitchfork, he had not. On July 22 he sent his latest wages home, keeping back enough for a splurge dinner with sherbet and finger bowls at the station restaurant in Dodge City. Then he spent the afternoon in the Dodge City public library, reading Thoreau.

"What old people say you cannot do," the thirty-year-old Thoreau had written, "you try, and find that you can. Old deeds for old people, and new deeds for new. . . . I have yet to hear the first syllable of valuable or even earnest advice from my seniors. . . .

"Here is life, an experiment to a great extent untried by me; but it does not avail me that they have tried it."

Once again Lindsay started west, walking alongside the Santa Fé trail, which after a day or two turned northwest from the railroad track. The sun was hot, the wind strong. Neither tree, beast nor farm was to be seen, not even a grain elevator, nothing but the wide road and the shadows of the telegraph poles.

In Garden City he bought the August *American* and beyond the town dropped his eyes from the skyline long enough to turn to "Interesting People" and read the article about himself by Octavia, who when she wrote it was oppressively conscious that the mother of her subject just lived around the corner: it was not for her to make the son of Catharine Frazee sound like a real hobo.

"A quaint young man, a young artist-poet . . . who might

have stepped out of a novel of Locke's or Hewlett's," she described Vachel.

He crossed over into Colorado and the character of the country changed; he began to descry small mesas on the horizon. Just west of Granada a band of gypsies in five wagons rattled past him, spied his sombrero, saffron-colored corduroys, tie like an oriflamme and the bundle on his shoulder; then one wagon after another flung him a brotherly hail: "What ya sellin', boy?"

As the landscape was radically changing, so was his state of mind. His sense of guilt was driven under; though farmers all along his road solicited him, he did not again hire out for more than a half-day's work at a time.

"Labor by the week is noble and exhilarating and illuminating," he resolved, writing in his diary, "but by the year, twelve hours a day too hard. But my special job is to celebrate the exhilaration. The other fellow can take the long hours."

He, Lindsay, felt he simply must get his legs under a table and unburden himself of his flocking ideas: for an illustrated "Golden Book of Springfield"—like *The Village Magazine* but "four times as impressive"—and for a companion volume, the "Golden Book of the United States," and for poems "about every corner of the United States . . . rhymes on Florida moss, Georgia violin, a New Jersey orchard in the spring, New Jersey hills in the morning, a California orange grove, a Washington apple orchard. . . ."

The high altitude elated him. A notion began to simmer in his brain of finding the natural meter for some of these poems in famous gospel hymns and song hits and old ballads. Robert Burns had shaped his poems thus, though Lindsay didn't at the time think of it, and General William Booth, founder of the Salvation Army, unwilling to let the devil have all the good tunes, had turned worldly melodies like "Robin Adair" into settings for some of his best soul-rousers.

Nor was the idea altogether new with Lindsay, who when he wrote *I Heard Immanuel Singing* had had at the back of his mind an exalted musical strain similar to the first eight lines of "The Holy City."

On July 31 he reached Orchard Park and there at a country hotel he spellbound the proprietor's five small children by reciting, with action, some verses written long before, which were all of them about the moon: how the hyena, baying at the sky, thought the moon was a golden skull; the shepherd dog said it was a candle; Grandpa Mouse believed the moon was the fearsome queen of the owls who kept legions of owlets in a jar under her arm. . . .

Back in Springfield the same whimsical series had fallen flat. His success with the children so delighted him that he vowed not to stop till he had brought his moon verses up to a hundred, and in the next few days, seated by the road and on deserted station platforms, he did write several new ones besides the draft of a more ambitious poem, *Aladdin and the Jinn*.

As he passed through Colorado Springs, the views were magnificent; he remembered from his childhood how he and his father swept through this region as sightseers. He was close to the family camp now and anxious to get there. In spite of increasing weariness and a sore heel, he made Denver on August 5, and forty-eight hours later on a sparkling bright afternoon began laboring up the steep slope of Mount Clinton, a mile west of the tiny railroad station at Empire.

The first person he saw on the camp outskirts was his father going about the errands in old clothes and dark glasses. Lindsay then hastened on into Camp Olive, which consisted of three shabby tents flying little American flags, pitched in a wooded canyon with snow-streaked mountains rising all around. But when he came in sight of the womenfolk he saluted them with a casual flourish of the hand as though he had just happened to stroll in. He had been on the road for seventy days.

33

Octavia was there when he arrived.

For a girl no longer quite young and accustomed to the comforts of a modern summer cottage, it was roughing it to live in tents, sleep at night directly under blankets on a straw mattress with a hot stone at her feet and break ice in the water pitcher every morning. Yet the lovely prospect made up for all. Only the mosquitoes were vile, though the hardy Lindsays never seemed to notice them. Meals were eaten outdoors under the trees, within earshot of a clamoring waterfall, at a table decorated with wild flowers and set with white granite plates and cups, and Mrs. Lindsay, who knew all the tricks of high-altitude cooking, whipped up wild-strawberry shortcake and broiled fresh-caught trout from the nearby mountain-fed stream.

The three girls in the party—Octavia, Joy and Irma, who was a friend of Joy's—shared one of the tents, from which each day Mrs. Lindsay would rout them out into the splendor of the early morning with a "Young ladies, young ladies, arise, arise!"

Then came Vachel, to occupy the third tent.

He was footsore (he thought possibly something had bitten him; his father had twice to lance his foot) and he admittedly craved to take it easy in surroundings that seemed to him luxurious. He and Octavia washed the camp dishes together. Part way down the valley, across a rustic bridge, was the ranch house where they went to fetch milk and, not quite so far down, a swing—a board hung by ropes—in which he pushed her so that she soared far out over the drop below.

Here in the mountains he was no longer the odd figure of the town. She was the outsider; everything he did seemed right and natural. Yet "sometimes," she recalls, "even on the lonely mountain trails he made the miners stare, for in response to the usual country greeting of a short nod, he would remove his broad felt hat in a sweeping gesture, bending his body in a deep obeisance and calling out in a ringing voice: 'I wish you well.'"

One day they walked far up a mountain and came to a hut, almost a hovel, where a woman was frying doughnuts for two or three men. They went inside—it was a terrible, smoky, dirty little place—and both ate some doughnuts, Lindsay with immense relish; then as they left he said dreamily to Octavia: "How I wish that were you and me, and that were *our* little house!"

"Perhaps you wish it," thought Octavia to herself, "but I don't."

Lindsay's inspiration quickened. He made a list of possible songs to use as poetic patterns:

> *Sweet Alice, Ben Bolt*
> *Nellie Was a Lady*
> *Alexander's Ragtime Band*
> *Put on Your Old Grey Bonnet*
> *Clementine*

and to the familiar tune of *Gaily the Troubadour* he now wrote his poem *The Flute of the Lonely*.

After supper the neighbors from the ranch house usually strolled across the bridge and the entire group sat around the glowing cookstove in the main tent, where Dr. and Mrs. Lindsay slept. One night when rain drummed against the canvas walls Vachel read to them his earlier poem *The Wedding of the Rose and the Lotus*, written to commemorate the

Panama Canal, which was still a-building. Rose and lotus were the emblems of Occident and Orient, their marriage of an intermingling—

> The genius of the lotus
> Shall heal earth's too-much fret.
> The rose, in blinding glory,
> Shall waken Asia yet.

As he chanted the delicate lines over the rain outside, they sounded wonderfully musical.

Sometimes the family together walked or drove for miles, exploring Mount Clinton and Mount Flora. High on one of the slopes Vachel ran ahead to belabor the others with scooped-up snowballs; in the depths of a ravine he cupped his hands around his mouth and shouted—the echo shouting after him: "Hurrah-ah for Debs!"

This year was Eugene Debs' fourth time of running for President on the Socialist ticket.

Another day a storm overtook them. Darkness fell, thunder pealed and as they tried to make their way down the mountain, the steep descent was lit up by a livid glare. Lindsay, in his element, let out his voice and roared against the thunderclaps:

> Give me that old-time religion,
> I want that old-time religion.
> An old-time religion,
> It's good enough for me!

On August 18 Octavia left for Denver on her way home. Before her going, she and Vachel climbed the heights alone and as they sat resting halfway up he spoke to her thoughtfully of his idea of using the gospel hymns as rhythmic models. Then he sang till the rocks rang the tremendous evangelical interrogation—one of the battle songs of the Salvation Army, in which an aroused audience participates—"Are You Washed in the Blood of the Lamb?"

This was an ear-opener for Octavia, who as an Episcopalian

had been accustomed to the decorous renderings of choirboys in surplices, punctuated by sibilant responses from a subdued congregation.

Three days after she left, the news was flashed around the world that General William Booth, the Salvation Army's blind and white-haired commander-in-chief, had died in London at eighty-three.

Lindsay remained with the others at Camp Olive till August 22, when the party broke up. Down in Denver he went to the movies while his family shopped, then he saw them onto the east-bound train—promising to meet them at the camp the next summer and go home with them—and he allowed his father to pay for him overnight at the hotel, renew his wardrobe and bestow on him $1.00. So says his diary, though years later he used to insist that when his father offered him money at their leavetaking he flatly declined it—"God, how I hated money those days. I would almost spit at the mention of it!"

Never before had he felt so loving toward his parents, or so reluctant to say goodby. He was left standing alone on the railroad platform. That night he spent his dollar in entertainment and the next day went out of the city by himself and on foot. A reaction had set in from his fortnight of almost perfect happiness.

Notwithstanding that the September *American,* just on the newsstands, contained two contributions by him—his proclamation of his gospel of beauty and his poem *The Proud Farmer*—he felt "terribly low in spirits," he acknowledged to his pocket confidant, as he prepared to trudge back to Colorado Springs and from there on to California.

34

Lindsay had not walked very far when it came over him that the fun had gone out of his hike. Locusts and wild honey were all right only if there was enough honey. The adventure begun so enthusiastically had become a bore.

Too much the same kind of thing was happening. At a farm ten miles south of Denver he stopped and thinned beets and weeded onions, but his brain boiled with writing projects and he began to feel so homesick that about twice in every twenty-four hours he was in danger of turning in his tracks and heading home.

In Trinidad he sought temporary refuge with some friends of his family named Day, in whose spare bedroom he brought forth fifty more moon poems. Here he had a blow: the editor of the *American* notified him it had been decided not to print his hiking letters. He did what he could to help Mrs. Day around the house (conscious, he told his diary, of "a slight feeling of being an imposition"), and in the local library he reread Ruskin. From here he wrote to his father asking for $5.00, out of which when it came he had his shoes half-soled, then bought stamps, postcards and a box of candy for his hostess.

When he left Trinidad on September 8 he was teeming with sun poems, as yet unwritten. In Raton, over the border in New Mexico, the realization loomed up that he had 1138 miles still to go before Los Angeles, where his Uncle Johnson Lindsay and Cousin Ruby now lived, and where he could sit down again and write himself out.

The landscape around him was a wide plain encircled by mesas. The sky was dramatic with tremendous clouds. But the road seemed to be getting rougher and the half-breed men along it tougher, while in the sparse towns the houses were filthier. He plodded through French and Springer, finally into Wagon Mound, some forty miles above Las Vegas, where it rained, he got soaked to the skin, could find no work anywhere, and the bed offered him was crawling with bugs.

Octavia Roberts recalls that Lindsay always refused to talk about his trek south from Trinidad, turning white and looking distraught whenever it was mentioned. She speculates that in that desolate country something ugly may have happened: he may have passed a night in the company of vagrants who made him, or one another, unholy advances, opening his eyes to a hidden aspect of evil. A year or two earlier (Mary Humphrey tells this story) when Lindsay in Springfield was calling on a girl whose front porch swarmed with boys, all much younger than he, he had innocently described to the appalled and comprehending group how a man he came across on his first hike had done this very curious thing . . . what did they think it meant?

His poem *I Went Down Into the Desert* refers enigmatically to his tramp through the wilds of northern New Mexico. He had gone down, he says, to meet John the Baptist:

> I spied foul fiends instead.

He had gone down to meet his God:

> And I met the devil in red.

Yet Lindsay's devil may have been no other than his own lack of hardihood. When he reached Wagon Mound his morale was at rock bottom.

It was here, on Thursday morning, September 12, that he ignominiously threw up the whole issue of begging and preaching, walked fast into the telegraph office and wired to his father for money for train fare (including "eats") to Los

Angeles. When during his hours of waiting the telegraph clerk twitted him with losing his nerve, he gave the same retort he had given Frank Weaver: "That isn't my brand of nerve."

In his diary he reasoned it out.

A full thousand miles more of a country that was mainly desert lay between him and the west coast. To cross this stretch on foot would be "merely a stunt," he argued, "like walking on one's hands for a wager. I am not out to do a stunt, and I allow myself to lose my nerve whenever I please, knowing I shall get it again in good time. My business is writing and preaching the Gospel of Beauty each day as I see fit, and not doing the thing that bores me, merely to be consistent."

All of which was true, as any sensible man would have assured him. Yet when that evening a draft for $40 via the Albuquerque Bank reached him from his father and he boarded the Santa Fé railroad (going Pullman, like a sensible man) he felt worse defeated and scourged by self-contempt than in years.

It was thus miserably brooding over his failure to see the thing through that he crossed the Arizona desert and on Sunday morning arrived in Los Angeles. Afterward he used to say that on this, his third and most ambitious hike, made without a dime in his pocket, "the good God had taken care of him till he got to California."

The good God had had a deeply furrowed brow, smelled of medicines and worn a grizzled beard.

Lindsay spent over a month in California.

Conceivably he didn't learn of the death of General Booth till he got off the train in Los Angeles, by which time the news was almost four weeks old. But it was in this city, soon after his arrival, that his imagination burst into hot flame, kindled by the image in life as well as in death of the godly old man, who died blind yet

> still by faith he trod,
> Eyes still dazzled by the ways of God,

and kindled too by his own defeat, for if in New Mexico he had met the devil, in California he wanted the General to get even for him.

All one frenzied night he walked in Los Angeles' Sixth Street park, up and down under the palm trees, his head wagging, his hands working, and there, in one surging effort— to the remembered beat of the revivalist hymn and music of drum, banjo, flute, tambourine and dedicated voices—he shaped his poem *General William Booth Enters into Heaven.*

> Booth led boldly with his big bass drum—
> *Are you washed in the blood of the Lamb?*
> The saints smiled gravely, and they said: "He's come."
> *Are you washed in the blood of the Lamb?*

By morning, after his hours and miles of walking, Lindsay's poem was "miles long." But his excitement persisted: he re-tired to his Uncle Johnson's house, where he spent a week cutting and polishing the piece—rewriting it, he claimed, just about a hundred times—spurred on to heroic enterprise by a sense that now General Booth was doing his tramping and preaching for him, that each time the General hit the drum it was *one in the eye for the devil.*

At week's end he set out on foot northward from the City of the Angels, but before half a day had gone he felt he couldn't take another step. Back he fled to the hospitality of his astonished uncle, in whose front room he spent two weeks more, this time deep in the writing of seven new prose "Procla-mations of the Advent of the Church of Beauty."

Then he started north again, going by train to San Fran-cisco. In Oakland, on the other side of the bay, he was be-friended by Professor Olan James, a member of the English Department at Mills College, who made him his guest and lent him a presentable pair of trousers.

Now again he was fearfully depressed—"awful within and without," he recalled later, "suffering terribly, persecuted by my family for being a poet and artist. . . ."

Along with his inspiration, the feeling of accomplishment

had petered out, leaving him in a state of mind to jump into the bay, "the deepest part." Again he was "ashamed to go home, hating to go home."

Before Wagon Mound he had ached with homesickness. But at Wagon Mound, as he always considered, life had challenged him and to his eternal discredit he had failed the challenge.

He stayed with the Jameses for several weeks and then he did go home. "Home is the place," another American poet has written,

> where, when you have to go there,
> They have to take you in.

He returned by train, in spite of his original resolve, which in Oakland he temporarily renewed, to walk back, to finish this curtailed trip "with *some* kind of honor, dignity and self-respect"—and again it was Dr. Lindsay, most faithful of Philistines, who sent him the money for the fare.

On the whole, said his mother to Olive afterward, his hike cost his father a good deal more than if he had gone by train the whole way.

But though Lindsay ever and always remembered that desperate interval on the coast as his zero hour, the tide of his life had turned. When he came back to Springfield in October after less than five months away—came back on the eve of his thirty-third birthday, "licked, down and out and wanting to die"—he was on the eve of fame.

PART FOUR

GENERAL BOOTH
LEADS BOLDLY

35

In the summer of 1912, while Lindsay tramped the roads and searched the skyline, Miss Harriet Monroe was poring over the periodicals in the Chicago Public Library, making her own search, which was for good poetry.

Her eye lit on Lindsay's name in the *American*, in whose care she wrote to him. He answered her first from the road, then in October he sent her from Springfield a large envelope bursting with two dozen moon verses, most of them written when he was a guest of the Days in Trinidad, Colorado. He also sent her his Los Angeles poem *General William Booth Enters into Heaven*. The poem on General Booth was his first contribution to appear in Miss Monroe's new magazine *Poetry*.

Harriet Monroe seemed a mild little woman, but she had the force of destiny within her. Though never herself a first-rate poet, she was a woman of first-rate vision and under her prim surface anything but mild. "One of the hardest fighters on American soil," Lindsay called her when he came to know her.

At fifty-two, having behind her a trail of gallant failures with her own poems and plays, she was founding in Chicago a magazine—one of the very first of the "little magazines"—to be given over to the best contemporary poetry she could find. Her action was backed not only by ten months of intrepid financial canvassing among Chicago businessmen but also by her intimate understanding of the poet's need for a public to speak to. There was no ready outlet in America for a poet's art; there was little room for his development and scant encouragement to his groping.

The giant popular periodicals of the stamp of *McClure's* and *Collier's* bought verse by the line as filler. In the solemn literary publications that were the goal of young aspirants the path of poetry was worn into a rut in which had walked for years Richard Henry Stoddard, Edmund Clarence Stedman, Thomas Bailey Aldrich, Joaquin Miller, Richard Watson Gilder, and more lately, Bliss Carman, Ella Wheeler Wilcox and Louise Imogen Guiney.

Since his passionate statements met but cool response, it was no wonder if a new poet's incentive slackened and his voice turned querulous. Out in Iowa Arthur Ficke sat down and lamented because the mass of men passed poetry by. Lindsay in Illinois was an example of another sort. Believing it was up to the poets to go forth themselves and "lay hold of the people"—one hundred million Americans were perishing while the poets sang on an island to one another—he had fought obstinately for a hearing.

If the poet were to go on and his art were to grow, he must be heard. The inspired Harriet chose as the motto for her undertaking the line by Whitman: "To have great poets there must be great audiences too."

The first issue of *Poetry, A Magazine of Verse* was dated October 1912 and actually published on September 23. In this and the two next issues were two sonnets by Arthur Ficke; two poems by Ezra Pound, born in Idaho but at twenty-seven a resident of bohemian London; a highly wrought poem with a title in Greek by a very young Englishman, Richard Aldington, who belonged to a group of experimenters calling themselves *imagistes*; five lyrics by William Butler Yeats; a ballad by John Reed, which was dedicated to Lincoln Steffens; and, to wind up the December number, some beautifully cadenced translations from his own work by the Bengali poet Rabindranath Tagore.

Yeats and Tagore had established reputations. Pound and Ficke were known only slightly, and Reed and Aldington were

altogether unknown, even to the fragment of the public that
was liberal and literary.

The fourth number of *Poetry* in January 1913 led off with
General William Booth Enters into Heaven. This was a poem
that had little in common with any of the contributions before
it—from the melodious, archaic plaint raised by Aldington
over "cold lips that sing no more . . ." to Pound's sardonic
name-calling (in *To Whistler, American*) of the fellow coun-
trymen on whom he turned his back as "a mass of dolts."
Lindsay had submitted two different versions of his poem
to Harriet Monroe. Only the second contained his "musical
directions," written as headings, in which he proposed imaginary accompaniment to each verse by bass drum, banjo or
sweet flute music. Himself, he thought the musical effects
were the least part of the poem, but when he left it up to
Harriet she chose the second version.

Yet it was not the technical innovations she had in mind
when she later called the publication of *General Booth* "a
great event in the art."

To her it was significant historically that the poem appeared
in the next number after Tagore's serene, philosophical and
mystical writings. As Tagore stood for the East, Lindsay
stood for the West. His poem was different. It was fresh. It
was triumphant. At the end of a long poetic apprenticeship
he brought a vitality, moral fervor and religious exultation
into what his discerning editress believed was "an authentic
strain of the lyric message of this newer world."

> Booth led boldly with his big bass drum—
> *Are you washed in the blood of the Lamb?*

Lindsay's poem was more than a tribute to the Salvation
Army, more than the portrait of a leader or the picture of a
familiar scene. It was a universal affirmation of the goodness
of man and the humanness of Christ. "Whoever tries to make
a cynic of me is wasting his breath," he was to cry during the

desperate days of his final struggle. "I *believe* in the human race. . . ."

And when with bang and blare of drum and trumpet and with hallelujahing, the procession he describes, made up of the derelicts of the earth, is led by the great general—a soul just passed over—around and around the mighty courthouse square of heaven, the merciful judge who is Christ Himself steps from out the courthouse door and stretches His hands in blessing above them.

In a flash their limbs are straightened, their blighted faces shine, their forms are clothed in apostolic garments, while the bystanders, who are the heavenly host, raise a shout of joy:

> Oh, shout Salvation! it was good to see
> Kings and princes by the Lamb set free.

Once steadfast and high-hearted, Lindsay had danced down the harvest rows; once by the desert's edge he had looked within himself and been humbled. Both moods are in his poem. Christ comes with robe and crown for Booth, and as the tall old soldier—he of the eagle countenance—stands in reverence to receive them his blind eyes are opened:

> He saw King Jesus—they were face to face,
> And he knelt a-weeping in that holy place.
> *Are you washed in the blood of the Lamb?*

It was with this appearance that the sword of fame touched Lindsay's shoulder.

"Perhaps the most remarkable poem of a decade," the *Review of Reviews* called *General Booth*. "This poem, at once so glorious, so touching and poignant in its conception and expression, can scarcely be read by one to whom the methods of martial religion make an appeal, without bringing tears to the eyes."

William Dean Howells, who had dismissed Lindsay's early verse as "frantic, frenetic and obscure," now, writing for the

Editor's Easy Chair of *Harper's*, admitted not to shedding tears but to experiencing a leap of the heart when he read this "fine brave poem."

Lindsay confided to Harriet Monroe that, because of where and how the poem was written, its success was a very personal matter with him. With its acceptance by her, and with the acceptance by *Farm and Fireside* of his seven "Proclamations," also written in Los Angeles, he was beginning to get over that "licked feeling."

In April he took the train to Chicago, where in the office of *Poetry*, the former drawing room of a remodeled mansion at 543 Cass Street, he met his editor, whose quiet style he liked and whom he found to be a woman "plain spoken as the Old Testament, with an awful wallop, for all she looks such a shy little thing."

Earlier visitors, dropping in at *Poetry's* headquarters to sit for an hour before the marble fireplace in a wicker armchair already called "the poet's chair," had been Arthur Ficke, Witter Bynner, Alfred Noyes from England, and from India Tagore, who materialized majestically in a gray Bengali robe and with a sweeping patriarchal beard.

Again Lindsay's appearance directly followed Tagore's, this time in person. He swung into the little office as if from straight off the prairie, carrying his chin at a humorous angle and wearing his fair hair rampant. "From Lincoln's own country a poet of Lincoln's own breed," was Harriet Monroe's description. "Mr. Lindsay is the real thing."

36

These were great days in Chicago, days that Lindsay only ten years later—but the war had intervened and the world been changed—would have "given anything to recapture." As editors, Harriet Monroe and by 1914 Margaret Anderson, who founded in the city another trail-blazing journal of the arts, *The Little Review*, were attracting to them midwestern writers of achievement and powerful promise.

After Lindsay came Sherwood Anderson, Theodore Dreiser, Carl Sandburg, Maxwell Bodenheim and Edgar Lee Masters. Before long there were more visitors from afar as Tagore was followed by Yeats and James Stephens, Rupert Brooke and John Masefield, so that Harriet, in challenge to New York, could call Chicago "the Athens of America" and Vachel, in 1923, could remind her wistfully of that splendid, now lost relation—"the concentration and intellectual and personal devotion we had when adventure in *Poetry* magazine was supreme adventure, and I first came from Springfield to thee...."

In July 1913 twelve of his moon verses were published in *Poetry*. The same issue had two poems by Amy Lowell, a New Englander. In August appeared Joyce Kilmer's *Trees*, which was the most widely quoted poem the magazine ever printed and for which young Kilmer contentedly accepted $6.00. To be paid at all was enough for most poets. Lindsay had been grateful for $22 for *General Booth* and $100 for the moon verses, assuring Harriet he was in no hurry for pay; it was an audience he wanted.

Suddenly he had an audience. Suddenly his stuff was in print: his poem on O. Henry in the anthology *The Lyric Year* (which included also Edna St. Vincent Millay's *Renascence*); *A Net to Snare the Moonlight* in the *American; The City That Did Not Repent* in the *Forum;* and *The Trap* in *Current Opinion.*

In the fall the publisher Mitchell Kennerley brought out Lindsay's first book, *General William Booth Enters into Heaven and Other Poems.* His own story of his hike through the wheat country and adventures while harvesting opened in the first of six articles in the *Forum.* On September 6 appeared in *Collier's* a lively, laudatory write-up by Peter MacFarlane, presenting Lindsay as a coming literary personage, which more than anything he had written himself made the whole family connection change its opinion of "that son of Kate Frazee's."

"It's nice to have *them* a-asking *him* rather than him begging them," said his sister Joy, after the *Yale Review* had requested to see Vachel's work, the *Metropolitan* offered him $50 for a new poem, *The Congo,* and Jessie Rittenhouse, formerly on his mailing list for *The Village Magazine,* selected three of his poems for another anthology.

Earlier this year he had written *The Kallyope Yell,* celebrating the calliope—or "kallyope," as men not proud call it—whose whooping, joyous greeting he heard out at the Springfield fair ground on circus days and in State Fair week.

The time had come for a poet to conquer and assimilate, instead of running away from, a side of America that for years had filled Lindsay, as a follower of Ruskin, with fury at its brashness. Partly in irony, partly in admiration of so much vitality he picked the kallyope as a symbol of everything blatant in modern American life: staring billboards, screaming tabloids, movies, burlesque shows, winking electric light signs:

Music of the mob am I,
Circus day's tremendous cry:—
I am the Kallyope, Kallyope, Kallyope!
Hoot toot, hoot toot, hoot toot, hoot toot,
Willy willy willy wah HOO!

Yet the kallyope stood also for things deeper and finer. Though it might split the ears and set the teeth on edge, it was prophetic, the voice of the democracy:

Listen to my golden dream,
Listen to my G-O-L-D-E-N D-R-E-A-M!
Whoop whoop whoop whoop WHOOP!
I will blow the proud folk low,
Humanize the dour and slow . . .

I am the Kallyope, Kallyope, Kallyope,
Tooting hope, tooting hope, tooting hope,
   tooting hope,
Willy willy willy wah HOO!

In November 1913 *Poetry* awarded Lindsay a prize of $100 for *General Booth*. An annual guarantors' award of $250, which had been announced in the first issue, went to Yeats for his poem *The Grey Rock*. Behind the scenes it was Ezra Pound, *Poetry's* foreign correspondent, who pushed the Yeats decision, whereupon Harriet Monroe, dissatisfied that *General Booth* should be passed over, cleverly talked one of her guarantors into putting up cash for a second prize.

Lindsay gave all the money to his mother. He was delighted and yet he hoped the Kallyope would soon outshine, or rather outshout, old General Booth. He was tired of the General, having "recited him till my jaws ache—4444 times," as he wrote to Arthur Ficke on November 11. In the same letter he described a poem in progress: "A Congo piece that will make the Kallyope look like thirty cents. Every kind of a war-drum ever heard. Then a Minstrel's Heaven, then a glorified Camp Meeting. Boomlay Boomlay Boomlay Boom!"

This noisy stuff was a new departure. He was discovering

a lot of it in him, though doubtful sometimes if it was poetry. "One composes it not by listening to the inner voice and following the gleam—but by pounding the table with a ruler and looking out the window at the electric signs. Also by going to vaudeville, which I have all my life abhorred. I at last grasp what those painted folks are up to."

What they were up to was to compel attention. Lindsay was weary of having his early, delicately imaginative poems ignored. It occurred to him that his friends, or many of them, considered *General Booth* his best poem simply because the bold rhythm and trick devices—instructions in the margin and naming of a tune—*forced* their notice.

In the same way, when he bawled the *Kallyope* or parts of the unfinished *Congo* at them, though they mostly overlooked the message, they were terrifically excited by the "Whoops" and "Boomlays," and they swore to him these new poems were fine and much easier on the understanding than the little filigree pieces, moon verses and the like, that he used to bring around.

Thus casually was evolved Lindsay's theory of what he called the "higher vaudeville." Without fully approving of vaudeville, he felt in sympathy with its talky, cheeky, point blank style as a way "to get the public." He began to see that poetic superstructures could be raised on this primitive foundation. From his room upstairs his family heard him through the register humming and beating time, for he found his head jigging with ragtime hits like *My Castle on the Nile* as rendered in blackface by the minstrel Bert Williams, who cakewalked across the stages of the nation and warbled huskily of

Inlaid diamonds on de flo',
A baboon butler at mah do'.

In a letter to Jessie Rittenhouse, Lindsay explained that because Americans "hate and abhor poetry," he was inventing a ragtime manner that would fool them into thinking they were at a vaudeville show. "And yet I try to keep it to a real art."

Someday, he promised her, he would go back to Olympus, to the classical gods and the muses and the eternal standard in which he and she both believed. But just at first he must find outlet for his "sinful self," as he called the creature inside him that bucked with energy and yelled "Boomlay" and "Wah Hoo!"

His immediate inspiration for *The Congo* had been a sermon preached one Sunday in October 1913 at the First Christian Church. The minister, Brother Burnham, spoke sadly from the pulpit of the death by drowning in the River Congo of his old college friend, Brother Ray Eldred, a missionary.

Lindsay was sitting with his parents in their pew in the third row when suddenly all the panorama of the Negro race flashed into his mind. He remembered from his childhood the pious ecstasies of black Lucy, their cook. He remembered the waiters around the woodpile at the Leland rocked by laughter as by a force outside themselves. He remembered Charlie Gibbs, Springfield's gigantic Negro lawyer, who was surely born to prance on the riverbank with a coffin-headed shield and a shovel spear.

He remembered his father under the lamp reading *Uncle Remus*, and the Hampton singers in *Swing Low, Sweet Chariot* and the cackling thigh-slapping *Juba*, and the dancers of Dahomey at the Chicago World's Fair, and Stanley's tales of pygmies, fever, voodoo and the Mountains of the Moon, and—much later—the cry of the lynch mob outside the dining-room window during the race riot.

According to legend, Lindsay went home after church and dashed off *The Congo*, his most famous poem, before Sunday dinner. Actually the writing took him about two months and he did more polishing than on any poem before.

If he owed most to one source, it was to the passage in Conrad's *Heart of Darkness* describing the fascination of the map of Africa—of "one river especially, a mighty big river . . . resembling an immense snake uncoiled"—and in his ear there had long sounded also one of Carlyle's rolls of rhetoric from

The French Revolution: "Does not the Black African take of Sticks and Old Clothes what will suffice and of these, cunningly combining them, fabricate for himself an Eidolon (Idol, or *Thing Seen*), and name it *Mumbo-Jumbo?*"

The poem owed something of its metric origin to a remembered snatch of schoolboy ribaldry:

Boom found a rat trap   ‖   bigger than a cat trap

and, conforming to his idea of choosing hymns for patterns, six lines in the last stanza were set to the tune of "Hark, Ten Thousand Harps and Voices."

37

Through Judge Humphrey, Mary's father, Lindsay was asked to recite *The Congo* at Springfield's Lincoln Day banquet on February 12, 1914. The enormous affair, sponsored annually by the Lincoln Centennial Association, was held at the State Armory. Bronx cocktails beforehand and champagne with the dinner were served. Among the speakers was Rabbi Stephen S. Wise, of New York, and Lindsay sat at the speakers' table next to Monsignor Hickey, Vicar General of the Alton diocese; they were the only two heard from who turned their glasses down.

His intention in writing *The Congo* was to portray the concern of a savage, childlike race with religion, a concern that in the end will redeem the soul of the race. The Mumbo-Jumbo refrain is a symbol of "the ill fate and sinister power of Africa from the beginning," yet this fatality, which enters the Negro's history at all points, is eased by his high spirits, his incomparable gift of expressing joy, and is finally overcome by his religious faith, shown most of all in his capacity for emotion and vision.

"Thinking of this gives us too a vision, a picture of that race redeemed through the inner impulse developed in its highest form."

So Lindsay conscientiously explained his poem the day after the banquet, writing in the *State Register*. But the banquet was the first occasion on which he publicly recited it. To the rows of white shirt-bosoms that filled the Armory floor he offered no explanation: the men downstairs, the ladies in the balcony, had not a notion of what was coming when, after a word of

214

introduction from the Judge, he got to his feet, bowed humbly, breathed deeply, then pitched into his opening lines, telling of "a drunken revel of big Negroes" in a barrel house, or low drinking dive:

> Fat black bucks in a wine-barrel room,
> Barrel-house kings, with feet unstable . . .
> Beat an empty barrel with the handle of a broom,
> Hard as they were able,
> Boom, boom, BOOM,
> With a silk umbrella and the handle of a broom,
> Boomlay, boomlay, boomlay, BOOM!

Practicing the poem on his friends beforehand, he had introduced into some passages a nasal but musical chanting like the Gregorian chant he used to hear at the Paulist fathers' church, and the startling alternation of his unearthly singsong with bursts of speed and noise eventually made *The Congo* his greatest hit. But that was later.

At the Lincoln Day banquet he was still the local doctor's son. He was a poet in his own country. When the citizens saw him stand up and throw back his head and heard him emit his barbaric "Boomlays" ("Simply bellowing," remarked one of them), when they saw his eyes begin to roll like a man's in a fit and his hands shoot from the cuffs of his dress suit and jab the air and his body rock and shoulders weave to the tom-tom beat of

> Mumbo-Jumbo, God of the Congo,

they sat at first stunned.

The performance took seven minutes. As it went on and on, a few people turned away their heads to hide their embarrassment but many more let out snorts and giggles that swelled a rising wave of laughter. "What the hell was Vachel Lindsay talking about?" a number of the men asked Arthur Fitzgerald.

"It was all most uncomfortable," recalls Mary Humphrey, who felt for her father as well as for Vachel.

Lindsay wrote to tell Harriet Monroe: "I have just recited *The Congo* for the big fat-sides Lincoln Banquet here."

On March 1 he did *The Congo* at a second, smaller banquet, this one in Chicago, where Yeats, a visitor to the city, was being honored by Miss Monroe. All the rich prominent guarantors of *Poetry* were in attendance, virtually every other member of Chicago society having any claim to be in on the arts, and many of the midwestern poets, among them Arthur Ficke, nervous and elegant—on whom Lindsay now first laid eyes—and the slow-talking, dark-banged Carl Sandburg, whose controversial "Chicago Poems" were appearing in *Poetry's* current issue.

Lindsay was longing to meet Yeats, who, he realized, was undoubtedly much pursued by callow youths like him. He had had to ask Harriet for an advance on some of his contributions to pay his fare. She sent him $10 and an invitation to stay at her brother's house. The dinner was at the Cliff Dwellers' in the Fine Arts Building. In 1911 he had met many of the same men in these same rooms, but Hamlin Garland—his distinguished sponsor then—was out of town this evening, and as he passed down the reception line not a soul remembered him.

Harriet had invited Mr. Yeats to be her house guest. Without saying anything, she put the issue of *Poetry* with *General William Booth Enters into Heaven* on his bedside table. So it was that, after the preliminary speeches were over and the guest of honor, who had sat hunched in owlish abstraction, at length arose, he turned directly to Lindsay farther down at the main table, caught the young man's eager eye and, announcing that he would address his remarks "especially to a fellow craftsman," spoke first of all in praise of *General Booth*.

He had read it not once but several times.

"This poem is stripped bare of ornament," said Yeats. "It has an earnest simplicity, a strange beauty, and you know Bacon said, 'There is no excellent beauty without strangeness.' "

He sat down and the younger poet rose in his turn. For

weeks Lindsay had been counting—though trying not to count—on this evening as it might affect his future. Even without the words of Yeats to give him courage, he knew his power, knew it in spite of Springfield. "You will think lots more of me after I recite *The Congo*," he had promised Harriet.

It was the end of an overlong program. The weary listeners had had enough and some were on their feet ready to go home, But Lindsay's beginning lines, droned and pulselike, arrested them:

> Fat black bucks in a wine-barrel room,
> Barrel-house kings, with feet unstable . . .
> Beat an empty barrel with the handle of a broom,
> Hard as they were able,
> Boom, boom, BOOM!

"That 'BOOM'," says an ear-witness, "shook the room, but Mr. Lindsay chanted on."

> THEN I had religion, THEN I had a vision.
> I could not turn from their revel in derision.
> THEN I SAW THE CONGO, CREEPING THROUGH THE BLACK,
> CUTTING THROUGH THE FOREST WITH A GOLDEN TRACK.

This was an audience of Lindsay's peers, one prepared by Yeats' tribute to receive the strangeness with the beauty. It began to sway in sympathy as he chanted the next lines:

> Then along that river bank
> A thousand miles
> Tattooed cannibals danced in files;
> Then I heard the boom of the blood-lust song
> And a thigh-bone beating on a tin-pan gong.

And then, transported, and those in front transported with him, as he rocked on the balls of his feet—his eyes blazing, his arms pumping like pistons—he sang of skull-faced witchmen:

"BLOOD" screamed the skull-faced, lean witch-doctors . . .

of Death, the torch-eyed elephant:

Foam-flanked and terrible . . .

finally, with high and jubilant voice, which he dropped to a marveling whisper on the last line, of the redemption of the dark race through faith:

And the gray sky opened like a new-rent veil
And showed the Apostles with their coats of mail . . .

'Twas a land transfigured, 'twas a new creation.
Oh, a singing wind swept the Negro nation . . .

Redeemed were the forests, the beasts and the men,
And only the vulture dared again
By the far, lone mountains of the moon
To cry, in the silence, the Congo tune:—

"Mumbo . . . Jumbo . . . will . . . hoo-doo . . . you."

The audience burst into applause. The Negro waiters against the walls applauded. The guest of honor, jerked from the misty kingdom of his Celtic imaginings, must have felt like one who pats a kitten and sees it turn into a lion, and there were bravos from Lindsay's fellow midwesterners, persuading him into reciting *General Booth*.

It was his first overwhelming public experience, the end of the lonely struggle of years to communicate. Though he knew it not, but stood rejoicing in the hope of a vision shared, it was the beginning of yesterday.

38

When Octavia Roberts told Lindsay "No" for the last time in September 1913—soon afterward destroying his letters to her—he made up his mind to avoid future love affairs. But by February he had met Sara Teasdale and by April fallen head first in love again.

He was to say bitterly in retrospect that the "cruel" lady who preceded Sara in his heart and in the end chose "the security of another suitor's bank account" had been "the wicked daughter of Babylon." But a scarlet haze obscured his memories, distorting them. At the time that he loved her and laid his poems at her feet and they walked together in the mountains, she had been to him Babylon's "darling daughter."

Sara Teasdale was twenty-nine. She was a poet. Though she hovered on the verge of spinsterhood, her special gift in her art was for brief, exquisite love poems. She wrote of Helen of Troy, Dante's Beatrice, Sappho and Queen Guenevere. Her theme was woman's love in joy and in grief, and if her way of life was less emancipated and her statement less defiant than that of Edna St. Vincent Millay, her poetic note was as true.

By 1914 she had written two volumes of verse. Four of her cameolike lyrics were appearing in the March issue of *Poetry*. Harriet Monroe, outwardly the archetype of old maid, who yet well understood the fires that smolder below a maiden surface, has said of Sara Teasdale that, "delicate as a lily," she had underneath an "impassioned intensity of feeling."

Sara's parents were wealthy and elderly. She was the un-married daughter in their substantial St. Louis house, a house full of careful hush, solidly closed doors and scheduled nap-takings. Like the fragile princess in the fairy tale who couldn't sleep on a pea without becoming bruised, she had grown to consider herself as having—having literally—one layer of skin less than other people. Not only her flair for the pic-turesque but her dread of drafts induced her to wear Spanish shawls, bodices edged enchantingly at the neck with bands of fur and (this is Louis Untermeyer's revelation) chiffon evening gowns whose flowing sleeves concealed, sometimes unsuccessfully, her Jaeger underwear.

Though she had not Octavia's beauty, her charm was as perceptible in a room as the scent rising from a flower. Her eyes, wide-set, were brown, her aureole of hair was tawny and Lindsay, dreaming of Milton's Eve, was soon to celebrate them both as golden. Sara is the Gloriana of his love poems, his "Girl with the burning golden eyes" and "hair of gold."

It was Harriet who gave Vachel and Sara their spiritual introduction. Without ever having met, they exchanged letters that were almost intimate and then in February 1914, finding himself "all crowded up with things to say," Lindsay went to St. Louis.

Sara had too much humor not to feel like laughing when in the close confines of her tiny study he boomed *The Congo* at her and whooped the *Kallyope*. She had too much insight not to be impressed. Her ears ached, so did her nerves; yet his eager terrible vitality filled her with excitement and, though she had a racy tongue, never did she speak of him as she heard others do "with cruel words and gay."

"He has clean hands and a pure heart. He is a real man . . . aggressively himself," she wrote in enthusiastic report to Louis Untermeyer, who was her confidant, while Lindsay, awed and touched, told Harriet that Sara "lived in a lovely house" and was "certainly a lovely lady, a chick in a gilded cage."

She was only the third "poet-lady" he had met—the others were Harriet and Alice Corbin Henderson, *Poetry's* assistant editor—and something about her brought back to him his

New York days, a long time off now, when he dwelt as a chaste and teetotaling art student among "the most decorous and high-minded of the Bohemians."

Their first meeting, though, was rather strained. Anxious to correct the impression, he asked Harriet in April to help him make another visit. He was in special straits because Mitchell Kennerley owed him nearly $300 and refused to answer his respectful letters. In payment for a criticism of Ficke's poetry, Harriet sent him $5.oo, on which he went again to St. Louis.

For the rest of the spring he made the trip as often as he could raise the money. He and Sara sat side by side in Forest Park and drank in the performance, in which seven thousand citizens participated, of a pageant and masque full of civic vision by the poet Percy Mackaye.

Alone with Sara in her quiet study, Lindsay read her a poem he was just finishing, *The Santa Fé Trail*, which had a chorus of auto horns, and thus in his fashion he wooed her and she listened to him—she whose slight songs equally with his tremendous chants were cries for life and communication. "Come," she wrote,

> Come, for life is a frail moth flying
> Caught in the web of the years that pass,
> And soon we two, so warm and eager
> Will be as the gray stones in the grass.

The Santa Fé Trail, which Lindsay hoped would be better than *The Congo*, was another piece of higher vaudeville, with snapping rhythms and alternation of loud and soft pedal. In writing it he recalled the hours when, a tramp by the trail's border, he used to watch the traffic stream west. He meant it to express his wrath, his aversion to the honk of the auto in the twittering countryside as "the most obscene and unclean sound on the face of the earth."

Originally the poem started out with three pages of unrelieved horn sounds, which were all "*hog*-horn," all equally loud. He had been halfway through when he met Yeats, who remarked to him that he wished somebody would restore to

poetry its natural artless music, its "primitive singing"—
and back at his desk Lindsay began an attempt to put something *beneath* the cacophony: to give this latest poem distin-
guishing overtones and minor strains and whispers that would
dwell in the memory after the noise was gone by.

He added at the beginning and the end a "twilight zone,"
describing how in the hour of dawn the first faint notes of the
approaching horns sound sweet and silvery,

> Hark to the *faint*-horn, *quaint*-horn, *saint*-horn,

how, after they have swelled and multiplied, their dominion
makes the noon hideous,

> Listen to the *wise*-horn, desperate-to-*advise* horn . . .
> Listen to the *fast*-horn, *kill*-horn, *blast*-horn,

and how they again, with evening, grow musical as they fade
into the distance:

> Hark to the *calm*-horn, *balm*-horn, *psalm*-horn.

But when he recited the poem to Sara he could tell from
her face it was still much too raucous, so he increased and
prolonged the softening elements of dawn and evening and
as his very last inspired afterthought added the flute notes of
the Rachel Jane.

In the thorn hedge, imperturbable and undefeated, Nature
sits and sings of

> Love and life,
> Eternal youth . . .
>
> Dew and glory,
> Love and truth,

even while the mad machine age

> Screaming to the west coast, screaming to the East,

races by, fiend-goaded, on highroad and railroad.

The Macmillan Company had acquired the rights to Lindsay's forthcoming second book, *The Congo and Other Poems.* He owed the connection to Harriet Monroe; hearing of his difficulty with Kennerley, Harriet had brought him to the notice of Macmillan, her own publisher. And to Sara, whose poetic ear was as sensitive as her suggestions were searching and her manner of making them surprisingly blunt, he owed the thorough overhauling of all the poems for this book.

She gave much time to the work. Lindsay later put down Sara and Susan Wilcox—with Susan first—ahead even of Harriet as the two who did most for his poetic style.

Having finished *The Santa Fé Trail,* he was caught up almost immediately in the throes of new creation. As once the Congo drums had drowned out of his imagination the whoop of the kallyope, so in its turn the soft magical note of the nightingale, the "deathless bird," was supplanting tom-toms and motor klaxons.

In April 1914 his sister Joy was married, his parents borrowing to pay for the home wedding. They borrowed again a month later when, impatient of such deterrents as scanty funds and the doctor's age and failing health—he was over seventy and half-blind—they sailed for China to visit Olive and Paul. It was the longest voyage of their lives and the most adventurous, the more so in that the bandit "White Wolf" was then on the rampage near enough to the Wakefields', in Luchow fu, for some of his mutilated victims to be carried into Paul's hospital.

Vachel put his parents, with all their baskets and traps, on the train for Seattle just before midnight on May 11. As he walked back by himself from the station he felt already lonesome for them.

It was Paul's and Olive's going, in 1905, that had first turned his thoughts toward China. From then on he had looked with curiosity at Springfield's Chinese laundries and chop suey restaurants. He read Confucius. Olive sent home books on Chinese art and microcosmic treasures of jade and porcelain. In New York he haunted the Metropolitan Museum's Oriental collection; in San Francisco he explored Chinatown, a city within a city.

This was enough. Out of these bits and pieces, he had been inspired in the spring of 1914 to begin fashioning a fantastic poem, *The Chinese Nightingale*. There was one source more, the story by Hans Christian Andersen of the faithful small gray bird whose lovely singing calls back from death the forsaken emperor in the court of a fairy-tale China.

In June he left off work on the new poem to go to Chicago, where at the invitation of a group known as "Friends of our Native Landscape" he recited *The Santa Fé Trail* outdoors. *The Santa Fé Trail* and *The Firemen's Ball*, written just before it, were both to come out in *Poetry* for July. Harriet had paid him $100 for the two contributions, and when Sara opportunely turned up in Chicago on her way to New York he pleaded hard to buy her an engagement ring.

She was moved. But if there was passion under her delicate surface, there was caution, too. Hers was to be a life that dwindled and darkened for long years before its sudden close; perhaps it was then, when her memory of Vachel was like the recall of sunlit hours, that she loved him most. At the time he proposed to her—the many times this spring and summer—she saw with clearer eyes than he what life on nothing a year would offer.

"Would there be any excuse for my marrying him?" she appealed to Louis Untermeyer.

Lindsay told his parents in a letter that he was trying every way he knew to coax Sara to say "Yes." "And she will if I get the money quick. But she much prefers I stay poet than turn money-maker, so we face a paradox."

Also, though this he did not mention, she had another suitor who was a money-maker.

He bought a thirty-day excursion ticket and followed Sara to New York. He admitted the unwisdom of the pursuit: he promised to be "extra wise some other time."

39

In Chicago Lindsay now met for the first time Mrs. William Vaughn Moody, widow of the poet, who at fifty-seven was a tall, imposing, massive figure. She moved slowly, being very lame, and her handsome eyes showed the knowledge of suffering.

Harriet Moody's charm lay in her conversation. A first-rate repartee could transform her, lighting her somber face and infusing her voice with gaiety and challenge. She had a woman's gift for assembling around her—the word "collected" would be invidious—men of creative genius and in her drawing room would slight a scholar for an artist any day—also, it must be confessed, a woman for a man. Between her and Harriet Monroe, of the wrenlike plumage and eagle heart, there was little love lost.

In 1914 Mrs. Moody's old-fashioned, well-staffed and hospitable red-brick house on Groveland Avenue (later Ellis Avenue) near the University was the home for the internationally famous Tagore whenever he was in Chicago, and in years to come for Robert Frost, John Masefield, Padraic Colum, James Stephens, Edwin Arlington Robinson, Walter Hampden, Glenway Wescott, and many artists more, to all of whom she was more than a purveyor of comfortable beds and delectable dinners; she was an ear in which to confide, a shoulder on which to lean—or weep. She was mother, sister and guardian angel.

"Dear Harriet Cordelia," Lindsay often called her, because Cordelia means warm-hearted. After reading *General Booth* she had sent him a line with an overture of friendship, and when he impetuously followed Sara to New York, it was Mrs. Moody who broke the ground for him, writing to everyone she knew with literary influence and lending him her unoccupied apartment off Washington Square.

Percy Mackaye, one of the friends approached by her, tells of answering a ring at his door to find on the threshold "a country boy." "And in those days," says Mr. Mackaye, "there were country boys as distinct from city boys."

This one, bowing low from the hips, held out a small bouquet of flowers. "For Miss Arvia," he murmured. Arvia was the twelve-year-old daughter of the Mackayes.

It took Lindsay a little time to realize that almost overnight he had become somebody in New York and that the gates, which once stayed shut for all his hammering, were ready to swing open. Mackaye, very handsome, courtly and seasoned in city ways, took him to luncheon at The Players in Gramercy Park. He gave him a guest card to the club, where at first hesitantly but then with increasing expansiveness Lindsay began to eat on his own hook.

Most of the eminent men he was meeting ate there. "It is astonishing," he wonderingly reported to Mrs. Moody, "how compact is the heart of 'our' New York once we are inside!"

Edward Marsh, of Macmillan, entertained him. *The Congo and Other Poems* was to be published by Macmillan in the early fall, and Marsh, who was Lindsay's special sponsor in the office, already had plans to promote him as a poet who *recited* his work. He made clear that the first step was for Lindsay to come back to New York after publication day and help launch his book by reciting from it to audiences picked for the amount of talking they would do. Marsh intended to get all the newspaper and magazine people available to go and write up the new poet as a modern troubadour and his poems as chants, after which it would be the thing for private groups to engage him to recite.

His whole publicity policy under Macmillan was committed to reciting, Lindsay explained in a letter to his parents sent from Mrs. Moody's apartment, where proofs of *The Congo* were strewn before him on the table, along with more mail from all parts of the country than he had ever yet received. "Letters keep coming in, and it looks as though my Macmillan book will be talked about. . . ."

Taking along a lawyer, he called on Mitchell Kennerley, from whom he extracted about half the money owed him. Socially, he was going it every day, for inside "our" New York his fame was spreading. He recited in the Macmillan office to the assembled editors, salesmen and secretaries. A group of conceivably predatory editors from Doubleday, Page gave him a luncheon out in Garden City; then Christopher Morley, a member of the staff, organized a recital for the five hundred Doubleday employees. At the Liberal Club down in Greenwich Village he performed before an overflow audience. He had not come East for any of these things, yet so many of them were happening that his coming was three times justified from a business point of view.

"This has been a great month for yours truly," he exulted to Harriet Monroe, and to Mrs. Moody, who with her rival Harriet now shared his confidences—"Macmillan's are very friendly and insist in their present enthusiasm on printing everything I write."

Also, the literary people on the inside were on *his* side; they were all *for* him. They were "fine folks." With wonder and joy he met and lunched with his longtime correspondent, Witter Bynner. He lunched with William Rose Benét, whose poem *Merchants from Cathay* he knew by heart. He had cemented his friendships with Floyd Dell and Arthur Ficke. Edward J. Wheeler, the editor, had given a party for him and Sara at which Joyce Kilmer, John Hall Wheelock and Louis Untermeyer, Sara's friend and now Lindsay's champion (who publicly called *General Booth* "sheer genius"), were among the guests.

Dugald Walker, a well-known illustrator, gave a party for Lindsay, Sara and the black-haired poetess Anna Hempstead Branch. Vachel and Sara alone took the ferry out to Staten Island to sit at the feet of Edwin Markham, dean of American poets. At a literary gathering Lindsay came up against the burly Hoosier Theodore Dreiser and fairly danced around him as he tried to urge the brooding Dreiser into writing "a novel on Altgeld" that rumor had it he was considering. This was *The Titan*, which had a character based on Altgeld.

Upton Sinclair, much aroused by *General Booth* and *The Congo*, telegraphed an invitation to his country house, but Lindsay was too busy to leave town, so another luncheon was arranged at which Sinclair talked about causes till Lindsay, bursting with himself, cried across the table: "Oh, you are disappointed in me!"

Again, as it had been before to him, New York was an enchanted city. The gay and sociable days ran together, but the evenings were another kingdom. They were suffused with a romantic beauty, and even as he lived them Lindsay felt nostalgia for them.

Sara had been waiting for him when he reached New York. Four times in the past four years she had come from St. Louis to read her poems in the earnest conclaves of the Poetry Society of America and make the heady literary circuit. Now she turned over her friends to Vachel, so that he and she were moving in the same orbit. "We were handed around on black velvet," he marveled afterward, "and fed from cloth of gold."

When they could, they spent their evenings alone in each other's company, riding up and down Fifth Avenue in all weathers on the tops of buses, exploring between the clifflike buildings of lower Manhattan, threading their way dreamily through the haggard, jostling crowds of Times Square. The places where he had once been solitary, Lindsay visited again with Sara at his side. It was a time for the making of new memories.

"For over us the olden magic stirs," wrote Sara in her brief poem *Broadway*:

> Beneath the liquid splendor of the lights
>   We live a little ere the charm is spent;
> This night is ours, of all the golden nights.

The message, meant for him alone, came home to Lindsay when he read the printed lines a year later.

At the time, his excitement and joy insulated him from worry over the future. He was too entranced by the spell of Sara's presence to be anxious about losing her. He and she were no longer very young, but to them both this month of almost perfect happiness was ever afterward to stand for their youth: it was a refuge of memory that time could not touch.

In Europe war was brewing, but war was far from the lovers' thoughts.

Hand in hand they wandered down the dark, sparkling avenues—the world they were born to own—and Lindsay in creative surges improvised and he and Sara sang aloud winged stanzas that he later wove into *The Chinese Nightingale*, which is the tale of Chang, poet and poor laundryman of San Francisco from around whom, as he irons the night away, the walls of his shop fall back. He sees a vision of the ancient days of China's glory when he was king and of a Chinese lady of high degree, a princess, rosy-red:

> And thus she sang to the busy man Chang:
> "Have you forgotten . . .
> Deep in the ages, long, long ago,
> I was your sweetheart?"

40

Lindsay was back in Springfield in August. It was "hot as the nethermost abyss," but he was glad to be there. He brought with him the notes for dozens of poems and while he would be perfectly willing when the time came to boost his books by reciting, writing was his first business.

He was so full of poetic possibilities that when he sat down to develop one, ten more popped into his head. Six times in one night he got out of bed to set certain lines on paper; it was easier to rough out any number than to bring one to a final polish. His chief anxiety was *The Chinese Nightingale*, which he was copying over about twice daily, and next in importance was a shorter poem, *The Ghosts of the Buffaloes*.

His parents were still far away in the real China of railroad strikes, republicans and Dr. Sun-Yat-Sen. The house was rented for the summer, with Vachel retaining his own room and eating out. He did chores for the tenants, who in return listened patiently to his readings of the *Nightingale*.

So he labored at his desk, with the shades drawn against the sunlight and the sweat sliding down his forehead. Then war broke out in Europe and in a flash, like artists the world over, Lindsay saw his work in new perspective. Though the disturbance promised to be self-contained, it made his own aims seem trivial and he immediately sent word to Macmillan, asking if he might add some verses on the war to his prospective book. On being told he might, if he hurried, he worked "like fits" through the next twenty-four hours, turning out drafts of six poems of which the theme was opposition to war.

In *Abraham Lincoln Walks at Midnight*, the finest of the six, he pictured the lonely and paternal spirit of Lincoln, too perturbed by the news of bloodshed to rest, rising from his grave in Oak Ridge and pacing at midnight the streets of the town where he had lived:

It breaks his heart that kings must murder still.

Next day at the broiling hour of noon Lindsay rushed over with his poem to the Humphreys'. The family was at luncheon, but Mary came to the door and, without asking him in, stayed to hear him read the beginning verses.

He didn't know how to dress Lincoln, he told her, except for a top hat and black suit. Did Lincoln have a cane? No. A long coat? No, what Mr. Lincoln wore, said Mary, was what her father the Judge remembered older men of the period as wearing—a shawl or small afghan around his shoulders, and she waited long enough to see Vachel sit on the porch railing and write the shawl in:

His suit of ancient black,
A famous high top-hat and plain worn shawl . . .

It was on this same day that Lindsay had a letter from Sara telling him of her decision, finally reached, to marry her rich St. Louis suitor, who was Ernst Filsinger, a shoe manufacturer. His Lincoln poem, Lindsay used to say, never reminded him of the war or of Lincoln but of that fateful letter.

All at once he felt a longing to see Paul Wakefield, his best friend among men—to talk and thrash the whole thing out with Paul. Yet because Sara, though seeking for months to know her own mind, had been from their first meeting strictly kind and fair with him, he had known, or almost known, when they said goodby in New York that it was forever, and he felt toward her no bitterness.

"She has kept my deep respect and love," he wrote to Harriet Monroe. "Certainly the God that made her sent me an authentic message about ladyhood through her I cannot forget."

He included then in his sheaf of war poems ready to be sent off another poem, in the same meter but only indirectly related to the fighting. *Under the Blessing of Your Psyche Wings*, written a few weeks before, was to Sara. From their relationship the best remained to him: her tender, unbelittling spirit, which even now, like Lincoln's great spirit, was in time of trouble a consolation.

His literary fortunes were steadily advancing. He was contributing poems and an occasional editorial to the Chicago *Herald*. In October, carrying with him Sara's picture, he returned to New York, where this time, if the enchantment was missing, there was yet more excitement.

He went to a session made solemn by the war of the Poetry Society at the National Arts Club. He went to a meeting in Greenwich Village of the youthful editorial board of *The Masses*, the socialist paper, whose editor-in-chief was Max Eastman. Though still a good deal of a Debsite, Lindsay was no longer the "red-eyed socialist" he once considered himself. He told the editors to read Jefferson and discover how well Jefferson agreed with them. "I told them to join and capture the Democratic party, but they were poisoned by Manhattanism and patronized us green boys from the West."

On a Sunday morning he spoke in Carnegie Hall and that night recited his quieter poems at the Church of the Messiah, where he was followed as speaker by the Reverend John Haynes Holmes. Falling in with Macmillan's strategy, he gave a number of full-scale recitals. The reviewers rose to the bait. He who had been for years ignored was now hailed by the press as a "concentrated American," as "surely the most curious literary figure in America . . ." was badgered and cornered for interviews till he had to instruct the hotel desk to deny him to reporters, was hotly sought after, lionized, written up by practiced pens, gossiped about by shrewd tongues, and in a few instances even read by the solitary reader.

Most people, however, preferred to go and listen to him. "You must hear Mr. Lindsay recite his *Congo*," urged the literary critic of the *New Republic*. "You must hear this your-self, and learn what an arresting, exciting person this new indigenous Illinois poet is!"

The Congo and Other Poems, published in September 1914 was several times reviewed jointly with *Adventures While Preaching the Gospel of Beauty*, which was brought out by Kennerley almost simultaneously and contained, along with Lindsay's lively account of his third hike, first printed in the *Forum*, a number of western poems—notably one on harvest-ing in Kansas—that conjured up broad vistas in the minds of men who had never crossed the Alleghenies.

Inevitably, there were readers whom his theory of the "higher vaudeville," as faithfully quoted by Harriet Monroe in her Introduction to the *Congo* book, and his directions printed in the margin for reading aloud his longer poems irri-tated rather than impressed. "I confess to some misgiving," observed the critic for the *Nation*, "when I am invited by the margin to make 'the *o* sounds very golden,' to employ a 'lan-guorous' or a 'terrified' whisper, or to speak 'like a train-caller in a Union Depot.'"

Yet there were others—the *New Republic*'s critic among them—whom Lindsay's invitation actually encouraged to try out their powers by chanting loudly and uninhibitedly as they sat safe in their office cubbyholes:

> Fat black bucks in a wine-barrel room,

or:

> I am the Kallyope, Kallyope, Kallyope!

The two books, appearing together and combined with the new poet's unexcelled power to put over his poems to an audience, now first created the picture of him that caught the public imagination—that of a vagabond, an American minstrel, whose great lines came to him in sweeps and were shouted to the clouds and stars as he strode across the plains of the Mid-west.

In November Lindsay's parents arrived home from China. They were quite set up, said Vachel, who was in Springfield before them, by the veneration with which the Chinese treated them because of their advanced age—"and there wasn't anything in China to be readily got at, that escaped them in this six months, you bet."

Among their trophies was a banner presented to Dr. Lindsay by the Chinese students of a mission college where he lectured on medicine. "The lofty mountain is crowned with snow," was the meaning of the characters on the banner, referring to the doctor's whitening hair. Mrs. Lindsay, hopeful that her only son would soon be married, had brought home a magnificent Manchu coat of blue and rose satin as her present for Sara.

Sure enough, there was to be a wedding. In his press scrapbook Lindsay pasted a clipping from the Chicago *Tribune* with a picture, very charming, of the bride-to-be and a headline that told all: POETESS TO WED MAKER OF SHOES.

"Little Saraphin St. Louis Teasdale" had been one of his adoring names for Sara. Above all he wanted to be true to the self she had given him—"that fine 'myself' I find in me when I look at her picture."

Now she was another man's; he could no longer think of her as his. He was trying to forget her, yet *not* to forget her, and as the December wedding day drew near he confided, in a letter to Mrs. Moody, that Sara had been hard, hard to give up and there were still times when he thought of her as Dante of Beatrice.

"Then other times I think of my North Star and reflect how thoroughly consistent my artist-author life has been, and what a wavering scrappy fragmentary destiny I have from the heart angle."

He was writing from his bedroom, which had seen the labor of his best songs. It was rather grubby and mussy because he refused to let anyone else take care of it. In this little room with the door shut, or away on the highroad, he was himself. "Anywhere else," he confessed to Mrs. Moody, "I am in deadly danger of believing in that new dramatic caricature of myself the reviewers depict."

"A people's poet . . . a man with vision close to the heart of the American people," the excited eastern press had called him, and his hometown papers took up the cry, naming him "the Bard of the Sangamon."

Since New York and Boston had been heard from, there was a change in the attitude toward him of Springfield's first families. But when folk who for many years had despised him as the town freak "try to assume a simple cordiality, heart-felt and intimate—it don't quite work," said Lindsay.

Sometimes he thought he must issue another War Bulletin full of bitter truth about his town to set his townsmen against him as in days of old; it seemed to him his soul was more in harness then, when he walked alone, than now when his path was rose-strewn and those who loved him least spoke with flattering tongues.

His work was his North Star. His work, he knew, required the ascetic and the celibate. It went on within him ceaselessly, like the illumination of a manuscript in a monk's cell. He knew he should renounce money more strongly and cleave to poverty.

Yet, having still the spiritual hungers of a Franciscan monk, "I am suddenly," he cried to Mrs. Moody, "loaded with a flowering outer self and a blood-beat more like twenty than thirty-five. Flatteries and publicity and the intoxication of the crowd threaten to drag me away from the missal."

The road stood to him for asceticism, not of the monastic kind but in effect the same. As some men fly with joy to a monastery, so he when spring came would return to the road. To undertake poetry seriously is to undertake beggary religiously. "You have no idea how when I am out of this room I reach back to my former ascetic self, through today's roses, with the fear that I am losing it."

41

His brave resolution to the contrary, Lindsay never returned to the free road of the vagabond but only to the circuit of the entertainer. By 1915 he was well into the campaign to bring his poems directly to his audience that for the rest of his life earned him his living and in the next five years made him his unique name.

If this was no more than his old notion of "meeting the people" and sharing his dreams with them, it was a notion now smiled on by his publisher's publicity department and put on a paying basis. Macmillan's, boasted Lindsay, was about to "steam-roller" him, to lend him "the whole weight of their advertising and punch and prestige. You will see me rolling across the literary asphalt. . . ."

In February 1915 he appeared in Washington, reciting before half of President Wilson's Cabinet, including William Jennings Bryan, the Secretary of State. "America's coming poet!" So Secretary Lane of the Interior, considered the scholar of the Cabinet, introduced him.

This spring not only were the critics discovering in him (said one) a lion who could roar, so were the women's clubs of eastern cities and the English departments of ivy-clad colleges. He recited at Yale and Princeton and Dartmouth and the University of Pennsylvania and Haverford and Wellesley —first of all, at Olympian Harvard, where he turned up unexpectedly before Bliss Perry's English class.

Carl Carmer was one of the students who came straggling in to hear a lecture on Tennyson and heard instead Professor Perry announce the presence beside him of "a living poet," at which Lindsay started up out of his chair and stepped to the very verge of the academic dais, where he swelled his chest, tipped his head back and then let go, sock, bang, with *General Booth*.

"Tennyson," Carl Carmer writes, "was a pale wraith within us as Lindsay's bold accents beat the living daylights out of our polite concepts of poetry!"

So Lindsay came into his inheritance. He, his mother, and Olive, all had the will and power to carry audiences. They loved the limelight. Whenever she mounted a platform, said Mrs. Lindsay (whose speeches, recalled her son, were "real rousers"), she "passed from one personality into another" and was "taken hold of by a power outside herself."

Said Olive, who studied elocution at Hiram: "It sort of thrills and inspires me to stand before an audience and feel I can make them listen."

"As Vachel Lindsay came forward on a stage," one critic was to write, "the force of his personality brought an immediate sense of expectancy in his audience." Another spoke of his "electric presence. . . . He set the throng on fire."

Vachel put it simply that "each time he got up there he spread himself like battercake on a griddle."

Writes John Dos Passos, who like the young Carmer was a student at Harvard when he first heard Lindsay: "We went to kid, but were very much impressed in spite of ourselves."

Carmer, Dos Passos, Stephen Vincent Benét, Theodore Roethke—these were but a few out of the hundreds of writers of the generations to follow Lindsay who listened to him and were moved. Of his own generation in American letters, there were not many who failed to hear him, and so great became his reputation that one day on the New York streets Sherwood Anderson exclaimed to a friend that "that man there *must* be Vachel Lindsay, because he looks like someone who could be

both a Baptist—or a Methodist—and at the same time a poet!"
And Anderson was right.

This was to come. In the spring of 1915 Lindsay was being
managed for a few big appearances by Pond's Lecture Bureau,
a New York agency, but most of his engagements were still
secured, after zealous effort, by some personal enthusiast surrounded by a coterie of keen readers. He was charging the
colleges $50 and the women's clubs $100, though his free
shows in parlors for any friend who asked brought the average
down.

Also his impromptu visits, like the one to Professor Perry's
class, he threw in gratis. He did so at Dartmouth, and at Yale
under the aegis of William Lyon Phelps, and at Wellesley,
where before his scheduled appearance he recited off the record and talked and joked to the tittering girls in Katharine Lee
Bates' English class.

He was neither engaged nor married, he told them. He liked
young ladies best "when they wear their hair down their backs
in curls, Mary Pickford style."

Afterward he wrote apologetically to Miss Bates that too
often when away from home he sadly needed a monitor; the
Springfield girls, after thirty years, were used to him.

In January he had been invited by Jessie Rittenhouse to her
"Poets' Party" in New York; he had been asked by Edward
Wheeler to speak at the banquet of the Poetry Society. It was
a whirl. Yet, while he delighted in the new faces and the talk
he heard brought him up with a start—he hadn't known so
many points of view existed—still there was a thing he missed,
his inner conversation. He was imagining a new poem every
day but failing to get most of them written down. The reciting
state of mind was utterly different from that of writing and
so much gadding was like opium; the more he had, the more
he craved.

"I always am greedy, I always want each day to be grist to
my spiritual mill," he confessed to Mrs. Moody.

He wished everybody who wanted to hear him recite for
the next year would combine in one big joyous crowd and he
could do them up at once. His mother was going about to

missionary conventions, reporting on what she had seen in China; a hundred years hence women like her would be President, said Vachel. Meantime, he wished she could fill his speaking dates and eat all the little cakes and drink up all the tea, and he go home to his room and write—"write till my grey beard hangs out the window like Spanish moss, write what boileth within me."

At the end of 1915 Macmillan brought out his prose book *The Art of the Moving Picture*. This was a pioneer work. Ever since the one-reelers and nickelodeons, Lindsay—an artist rushing in where intellectuals still feared to tread—had seen the possibilities of the movie as an art form, "a giant avenue toward the soul of our democracy." In his lonely Springfield evenings he had observed the mass of the people seated in the picture theaters as if in church, and the faces the dim light revealed to him were not lumpish but tender, vulnerable and full of spiritual hungers peculiarly American.

"Edison is the new Gutenberg," he wrote in *The Art of the Moving Picture*. "Not yet has the producer learned that the feeling of the crowd is patriarchal, splendid. He imagines the people want nothing but a silly lark. . . . But now a light is blazing. We can build the American soul broad-based from the foundations. We can begin with dreams the veriest stone-club warrior can understand and lead him in fancy through every phase of life to the apocalyptic splendors."

He was writing in the era of the gold-rush West of film-makers—producers like Loew and Zukor, directors like Mack Sennett, king of slapstick, and D. W. Griffith, whose epic, *The Birth of a Nation*, had established his genius—and he pleaded with the movie men, moguls and magnates of this generation and others to come after to be delivered by their own effort from "the temptation to cynicism and the timidities of orthodoxy," to be clean minded and beauty loving, and to dare to lose money for the next hundred years till they had evolved something worthy.

In a day when the advice was new he urged them not to

photograph plays in the old style of the stage but to exploit every cinematic trick, to make artistic capital of the silence imposed by their medium and to heighten dramatic effects by symbolism like the Egyptians, the great picture-writers of the past.

As an Egyptian hieroglyph represents not only the object but also the larger idea behind it, so the image of a throne cast on the screen might stand for royalty or power, a ticking clock for a guilty conscience, a watching eye for retribution or justice.

In November 1915 *The Chinese Nightingale*, which had appeared in *Poetry* in February, was awarded the magazine's Levinson Prize of $250. This was Lindsay's first poem to be signed simply "Vachel Lindsay"; on his publisher's recommendation, he had dropped the "Nicholas."

He received and declined a telegraphed invitation from Henry Ford to join the party on Ford's Peace Ship. Jane Addams of Chicago's Hull House wrote thrice inviting him to visit her. Gordon Craig, having read his movie book, wrote from Rome asking to start a film studio with him (Craig seemed to think he could just dash over and do it), and D. W. Griffith offered to pay his expenses to New York so he could attend the premiere of Griffith's new superfilm, *Intolerance*.

In January 1916 John Masefield, on a tour of the United States, was in Indianapolis, where Lindsay and Frederic Melcher, the bookseller, went together to hear him read his poems.

The Englishman read beautifully, his contained manner the antithesis of Lindsay's. "Masefield stood in one place," says Mr. Melcher, who after the program took Vachel by the arm and introduced him (since his work hadn't yet been published in England) as "our local poet"—at which, to Melcher's surprise, the visitor's sensitive face lighted.

If there was one man in America he wanted to meet, Masefield murmured, it was Vachel Lindsay, whose poem *General Booth* was the talk of London.

atherine Frazee Lindsay, with
Vachel, Olive, and Joy, 1894.

Dr. Vachel Thomas Lindsay,
about 1910.

Vachel Lindsay at 16.

Olive Lindsay.

On the steps of Miller Hall at Hiram College. Vachel Lindsay at upper left, Ruth Wheeler next to him, and Olive Lindsay at end of row upper right.

Vachel Lindsay with his little niece Mary Wakefield, on the porch at 603 South Fifth Street in the summer of 1910.

Vachel Lindsay in 1913.

Vachel and Elizabeth Lindsay a few weeks after their marriage in 1925.

achel Lindsay, Troubadour. This photograph, taken about 1926, appeared on
Lindsay's recital programs.

Vachel Lindsay, from the bust by Adrian Voisin.

Vachel Lindsay and Stephen Graham in Springfield, 1921.

Vachel Lindsay with baby Susan, aged eight weeks, July 1926.

A MAP OF THE UNIVERSE ISSUED IN 1909.
THIS MAP IS ONE BEGINNING OF THE
GOLDEN BOOK OF SPRINGFIELD.

"The Map of the Universe," drawn by Vachel Lindsay in the summer
of 1904.

Page of a letter from Vachel Lindsay to Paul Wakefield, May 2, 1928.

The Lindsay house at 603 South Fifth Street, Springfield, Illinois, from a print by Virginia Stuart Brown. Vachel Lindsay was born in the downstairs corner bedroom at the right and died in the upstairs bedroom just above.

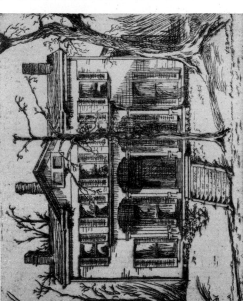

"The Tree of Laughing Bells," painted by Vachel Lindsay in July 1908.

Macmillan had purchased Lindsay's copyrights from Kennerley and this year brought out, under the title *A Handy Guide for Beggars*, a collection of his sketches written long before about his first two hikes; a number of them had appeared in *The Outlook* and *Twentieth Century*.

When he had facts to tie down his ballooning imagination, Lindsay's prose was less like Poe; it was more like Mark Twain. He told of strolling north from Jacksonville, then of beating his way from New York to Ohio, of humble true Americans along his road like the Florida cracker who gave him food and a pillow on the floor when not a soul else would.

"Democracy is not with him a phrase," wrote Francis Hackett, reviewing the book in the *New Republic*. "It is that faith in the excellence of human beings that makes life worth living. It finds that excellence by inclusiveness. . . . It is the thing Lincoln had. It is the thing Whitman had. It is the thing Emerson partly had. It is the thing that the West has, and not the East so much."

Admittedly, this Illinois poet had crude gestures. He had intonations of the preacher. He was sometimes a show-off.

"But to say these things," continued Hackett, "is not to reach the core of the matter. . . . Genius is a large word and to be used warily. It is enough perhaps to say that here is an emerging figure, a figure youthful and powerful."

And he asked in conclusion: "Where else in this country of emergence is there in combination nationalism so free and swinging, religion so vigorous, human contact so delicate, beauty so adored?"

42

Amy Lowell, of the Boston Lowells, wended her way to Chicago and delivered there in 1916 a witty, pontifical lecture on what had begun to be described, however imperfectly, as the "New Poetry." From the first issue of Harriet Monroe's magazine in October 1912 Miss Lowell traced the rise of younger poets who, in contrast to their immediate predecessors, wrote with exactness but simply, with desperate earnestness yet often colloquially, and whose rhythms were powerful and free.

Some she could conveniently classify: Frost and Robinson as "evolutionists," Sandburg and Masters as "revolutionists"— and there were the "imagists," herself among them. But Lindsay was a non-conformist in a group that broke with conformity. While his democratic spirit, sincerity, humor and the swinging rhythms of his "higher vaudeville" assured him of a place in the new movement, precisely what that place was even the Delphic Amy found hard to fix.

Lindsay had resolved that in his next book the higher vaudeville should not predominate. He did not want to be known for any one mannerism. There was no denying, though, that with his audiences the broad vaudeville technique was a hit. In 1916, notwithstanding his reiterated desire to stay home and write, he was reciting harder than ever and traveling greater distances, appearing in places he had been before, like Yale and Wellesley, and in new ones like New York's Colony Club—to excite and inspire the young folk and startle and baffle the old.

Vachel Lindsay the poet, was a holy wonder,
His eyes were shut and his voice was thunder!

runs the parody on his performance by Austin Bothwell.
But Lindsay's voice was not always thunder. He recited
General Booth and in the hush engendered by the last reverent
lines there were some who wept. He recited *The Santa Fé
Trail*—whose pastoral passages Sinclair Lewis later compared
with Gray's *Elegy*—and not only the hog-horn but the bird-
notes of the Rachel Jane and the sighing of wind over prairie
grass were in his voice. His gestures, too, were eloquent: the
clasped, supplicating hands of the revivalist, the prophet's arm
upraised in admonition, the easy backward thumbpoint of the
hiker on the highroad, the farmer at his roadside gate.

To make communication complete, he had begun to call on
audiences to join in certain poems. They were to strike the
palms together, nod or shake the head, exclaim "No!" "Yes!"
"We will!"

"Every day a circus da-ay!" he would cry like a carnival
barker halfway through *The Kallyope Yell*, then, breaking
his strut across the stage to cock his head and cup his ear, ask
"What?" and answer himself, "Well, al-most every day!"

Eight lines farther on it was the turn of his friends out front.
"Bands a-play-ing every da-ay," shouted the poet.

"What?" roared his hundreds, sometimes thousands, of new
friends.

"Well, al-most every day."

The communion was intoxicating. Those who never saw
him in his handling of an audience never knew the whole man;
he worked them up, led them row against row, aisle against
aisle, the floor against the balcony. It was self-intoxicating.
"Mohammedan dervishes howl and whirl till they find God,"
said Lindsay once, "and I am a kind of dervish in temperament."

To Olive this year he wrote that "reciting is to me a kind
of love-making, a religious service." Yet just for that reason
it could not be forced. While one month of it was a spontane-

ous and human joy, after two months he became a grinning actor.

He had a notion to carry his recitals a step forward by accompanying his reading with simple dances and pantomime—as in the old English folk games that survive in the Tennessee mountains and in children's games like London Bridge is Falling Down. What Yeats once said about "restoring the primitive singing of poetry" had sowed the seed in his mind; he first experimented with the idea in the Wellesley kindergarten, the infants toddling and capering while he chanted his sprightly *The Potatoes' Dance*.

Anna Pavlova, the great Russian ballerina, was in America and he urged Mrs. Moody through her web of connections to get hold of Pavlova for him. He had twice seen her on the stage. He wanted her to dance some of his poems—"get hold of her for me and tell her I am a wonder!"

Mrs. Moody knew a dancer who was not Pavlova but Eleanor Dougherty, a lithe, beautiful girl, the younger sister of the actor Walter Hampden. Eleanor, too, had ideas about dancing to poetry.

"Why I know someone who talks just the way you do!" said Mrs. Moody, and in the summer of 1916 she arranged a meeting at which the two enthusiasts without ado rolled up the rugs and there in her Chicago living room began to practice the first of what Lindsay called his "poem games."

He hoped to find in them, he told Eleanor, a deliverance from the perfunctory, the familiar and the routine in reciting. They were fun, of course, but to him much more. He longed to make of them a Jacob's ladder, a public prayer for the refreshment of his soul, an appeal straight up to God.

For her preparation he advised her to study high-priced vaudeville stars like George M. Cohan and the dance teams at the New York Hippodrome, whose rowdy evolutions generally got nowhere, yet—just as the same font of type can print a book or a newspaper—could have cosmic meaning if set in order and crowned with more delicate surprise.

He and Eleanor gave their first performances in November 1916 in Maurice Browne's Little Theater, which seated ninety-nine, then in Mandel Hall at the University of Chicago. They did two of his verses for children, *The Potatoes' Dance* and *The King of Yellow Butterflies*. Moving as if to music but matching her steps with the syllables, Eleanor danced the lines that Lindsay sonorously recited. The reception by the audience was speculative, part defiant, part friendly.

They did *The Tree of Laughing Bells, The Wedding of the Rose and the Lotus, Aladdin and the Jinn* and *King Solomon and the Queen of Sheba*. Eleanor, with the chiseled features of her famous brother and a mass of chestnut-colored hair, was in costume and she looked a picture. Lindsay was also in costume.

His *King Solomon* belonged to a trilogy of new poems of which the other two were *Simon Legree* and *John Brown*. They were based on all the pious, hilarious Negro sermons he had ever listened to—and he had heard many—and they were dedicated to the memory of the educator of his race Booker T. Washington.

King Solomon was the wild, gay and innocent vision of a Negro Utopia, built on Bible legend. The graceful Eleanor in yellow satin trousers played the Queen of Sheba, Lindsay in a purple robe, sandals and tall gilt crown, the King. In this poem he danced, too. For those in front who could cast out self-consciousness and enter into the childlike symbolism the performance was not without charm.

Advancing with ritual precision, Vachel and Eleanor swayed on the stage like yoked oxen, then together chanted:

King Solomon he had four hundred oxen,

at which the audience, as previously instructed, returned:

We were the oxen!

The two performers pawed the air like ponies:

He gave each son four hundred prancing ponies,

and the audience came back:

We were the ponies!

So through celebration of four hundred sweethearts, swans, sailors, chieftains and shepherds, till at the end the pair on stage stood regally erect behind the footlights:

King Solomon he kept the Sabbath holy.
And spoke with tongues in prophet words so mighty,

then began to stamp and whirl in widening circles with intense solemnity, while the spectators rose from their seats, crying

... "Glory!"
We were his people.

King Solomon stayed permanently in Lindsay's repertory. It could be presented without the dancing, even without a partner, and he needed only a moment to teach his audience the responses. Frederic Melcher tells of hearing him do the poem in the Central Christian Church of Indianapolis before a large assembly of church women whom the poet led off masterfully with

King Solomon he had four hundred sweethearts.

"I never thought I would hear it," says Mr. Melcher, "but it happened—to a woman, those good ladies sang back:

We were the sweethearts!"

43

On April 2, 1917, President Woodrow Wilson asked Congress for authority to declare war against Germany. Lindsay had been reciting in the East through most of the suspenseful period that began early in February when hostilities first threatened, but he was at home in Springfield during the three days of waiting—a hush between thunderclaps—from the President's request till April 6, when war was declared.

He wrote on April 4 to Eleanor Dougherty, who even this early had sailed as a volunteer nurse for France, where thousands were soon to follow her. Young and fair and far away, she had become to him for a time his woman who stood for all women; in imagination he gazed straight across to her, across to France.

"You are a reality to me," he wrote. "A man should turn to the best he knows. I want to write to you tonight, even if there is little chance of your getting the letter or of your reading it (if it gets to you) with any great interest. My heart is very sad tonight about the war."

No momentary enthusiasm lifted him. He had no sense of adventure in this terrible undertaking, but saw only that the thing begun would end no man knew where. While he could not find it in his heart to challenge President Wilson's decision or regret having voted for Wilson, it was the brave continuing fight for peace of Jane Addams that went home to his soul.

"I feel with her, and with him, and am all torn inside," he confessed, "and certainly I have no sympathy with the fire-eaters. It is so easy to get killed for a cause, but it is a bitter thing to think of killing other people."

"The real war begins," said Lindsay, "after the fire-eaters have had their fill."

A decision of his own faced him. When he made his first hike north from Florida, he had had talks with old Confederate soldiers who had been through all this; he supposed men had gone through it in King David's time.

"Ought I to enlist?" he asked in a letter to Mrs. Moody. He was writing to her one minute after midnight on Easter morning, April 8. "It is an Easter in which to hold one's breath. I cannot think of the resurrection but of the cannon fodder—that is and may be."

Among the poets, Carl Sandburg had come out strongly for Wilson, and Lindsay was glad; he needed Sandburg to brace him. According to the President, this war was different from all wars past: it was a war to crush German autocracy and abolish war everywhere in the future, yet Lindsay's difficulty was that when he should be called to take arms he could not be "so very certain that he was abolishing anything."

He was a pacifist in the face of the universe. Yet there were times when earth was larger than the universe. Ought he then, without waiting to be called, go to Belgium with Roosevelt's volunteers? He had lived long enough and had more than his share.

"Tell me that," he begged Mrs. Moody, "ought I to enlist?"

Though he spoke of himself as "the last Tolstoyan non-resistant," he knew that when the government summons came for him to fight, he would go. Would he be right? He could not answer.

"Where is the real non-resistant?" he asked at this time; the words are the title of one of his loveliest and least-known poems. Who can surrender to Him who bids us to resist not evil but to love our enemies?

> Who can surrender to Christ? Where is the
> man so transcendent,

So heated with love of his kind, so filled
     with the spirit resplendent
That all of the hours of his day his song
     is thrilling and tender,
And all of his thoughts to our white cause
     of peace
          Surrender, surrender, surrender?

In May Lindsay, who was thirty-seven, settled down at home to what he had accepted in three weeks of searching his soul as his own present counter to the fighting.

He began to write *The Golden Book of Springfield*, which had been glowing and growing in his imagination ever since *The Village Magazine*. It was to be a mystical portrait of his city one hundred years hence, in the year 2018, when little Springfield through the dreaming of her citizens has become a symbol and model of the world federation in which all nations, great and small, are linked; when her men and women, no better or more pious than before, have yet caught the spirit of democracy and, though still torn by factions, strive to order their lives in terms of one world.

He had been gathering notes for the book over so many years the earliest ones were dog-eared. From behind this frail barricade of dusty papers he proposed in his own way "to fight 'these times,' " he told Mrs. Moody, writing to her on May 11, and five months later—writing in October, when the first contingent of the American Expeditionary Force under General Pershing in France was training for its entry into battle—"You haven't the least notion of the heart's blood I am putting into *The Golden Book*. I would certainly die for the book, if it would do the work I want it to do."

And six months after that, in April 1918, during the darkest days of Allied reverses—"This book," he acknowledged to her, "seems to me to be the one thing that justifies my life."

Those who remember Lindsay in Springfield during the war years say that he was more than ever lonely. In June 1917 he spent an evening at the George Lees' in a living room full of

Springfield's liberals, who had once been pacifists but were ex-pacifists now. Very different in thought and method from others in town who continuously put pressure on him— unspoken from young men in uniform, openly demonstrated from the women and girls—they nevertheless, with high-mindedness and earnestness, and even with wit, tried their best, though unavailingly, to persuade him that *this* war was a good thing.

"Let me tell you of a virtuous act of mine," he wrote in self-justification to Mrs. Moody, describing the difficult evening to her.

When not long before a Negro had been burned alive in Memphis on hearsay evidence, he, Lindsay—even though no hand at skinning the Kaiser—had protested the burning in the Springfield papers, then sent printed copies of his protest to newspapers all over the South, inspiring at least five anti-lynching editorials.

And if one day he should of his own will mount a blazing pyre and die by the side or in place of some black who had not trial by jury—as he could conceive of doing—every bit of the sacrifice would be strategic and the cause worth dying for. It was egotism in him, but he valued his carcass; he would wish to die for love, not hate. If in the meantime he had to put his bones and body into a cause, he would rather put them into his book than the trenches.

At the end of June he harvested clover for four days to help out a farmer on the edge of town. In July, after his parents had gone to Colorado, he was left alone in the house.

One of his Frazee cousins, just out of Columbia, was soon to sail for France; another, still at Purdue, was a reserve lieutenant and wore his sword to class. When he thought of what lay ahead of those two boys, something in Lindsay threatened to give way. He had to harden his heart and remind himself that his book, which would have "as much sword" as his cousin in class was wearing, came first with him and the war next. His book was his work: if it turned out the way he wanted, he could look any soldier in the eye.

Yet when America first went in he had felt as guilty—he told Eleanor then—as though he were to blame. He would like to strike a bargain with the devil and be crucified for a hundred years and thus abolish war.

Now he was writing all day. Summer was always his hard-working time, and the chatter of his typewriter was loud in the empty house. But in the evenings, when he came home after prowling the streets, the loneliness was excruciating and by August even the days were lonely.

Besides trying to pin down the beginning chapters of *The Golden Book*, he was finishing some verses for a new book of poems, one of which, *The Bankrupt Peace Maker*, was a weird, self-castigating allegory, the expression of his lurking guilt and of another side of his nature from the sane, tender side.

Out of his inkwell, writes Lindsay in this poem, a cloud of smoke gushed, forming before his eyes the eternal devil, who looked like Apollo grown old.

The devil stares through the poet's heart to the mud at its bottom. He taunts him for prattling night and day of peace while he does nothing. To prove his good faith, the poet stretches out his arms and lets himself be crucified, there on the bookcase in his bedroom. He hangs for three years, then gives in. The devil returns, burns with hot irons on his breast the words "The Quitter Sublime," tears out the nails and introduces him to a "lady of sin," who takes his pierced hand in hers and bids him forget the bloody battles.

It is summer. They walk to the river. The poet becomes a serpent, the lady his serpent mate; they gambol serpentinely in the swamp and then, says the poet:

> I forgot in the marsh, as I tumbled about,
> That trial in my room, where I did not hold out.

As in a nightmare, he is back in his room, scene of his failure and lack of fortitude. The woman has turned into a diseased, ravening creature who crouches on the table where his poems were written and snatches them up—his weak, silly rhymes—and tears them into shreds and sneers at him and hisses:

I am your own cheap bankrupt soul.
Will you die for the nations, making them whole?

44

At thirty-seven, Lindsay was
not backward in proclaiming that he was still a virgin, but
he was uncomfortably aware that that part of him he called
his "Siamese twin with the hot blood" was giving more trouble
than ever. This fellow hung around the neck of the Franciscan
monk, the guardian of his literary side, and buzzed in the
monk's ear. While the monk thought clearly, the foolish twin
never had his wits.

A measure of the change in him was that in 1917 Lindsay
fell in love with Isadora Bennett, twenty years younger than
he. Both Isadora's parents were actors; she had been raised by
her aunt in Springfield, where she was the heroine and orator
of the High School, being slender, dark-haired, full of bird-
like gyrations and dramatic fire. Now a freshman at the University of Chicago, she recited Lindsay's poems better than
he did and looked up at him with the fearless eyes of the
future.

It was in this year that Sara, who was still never long out
of his thoughts and to whom he had dedicated *The Chinese
Nightingale* with its refrain of memories shared—of "sorrow
and love, glory and love"—became yesterday to him.

Isadora was tomorrow. In her youth as well as her woman-
hood lay a part of her magic. She was his model for the Lady
Avanel, heroine of *The Golden Book*, the soul of Springfield
and of America, the gallant young horsewoman who stands in
her stirrups and rides down the future: "I note her chin quite
high in the air, her spirited profile set straight forward, and

her cheeks, with color that goes like a blown-out flame and then comes again like a heart-beat."

Yet on Isadora's other side, her harum-scarum freshman side—"she is as inconsequent as a robin," he told Harriet Monroe, whom he begged to keep an eye on her in Chicago. "Robins do not always have an easy time. I do *not* want her to learn to smoke cigarettes, drink or admire rank conversation in the name of Art."

She was profoundly stage-struck. If in the end she went on the stage, he must bid her goodby, for should he ever marry, he meant to turn over to the girl of his choice the entire burden of his life's practical side, his friends and letter-writing and arrangements for recitals—"that is the housekeeping my housekeeper must needs do, even if we live on nothing but toast."

And he would want her to see this so plainly that his work would be her real drama. He would want her to be a priestess of all the arts, yet never a fanatic follower of any one. He would want her, dwelling with him in Springfield, to influence for good and beauty all Springfield's architects and city planners, but not to accept a job in any of their shops.

"This child who has conquered me," he called Isadora. Taking her hand with chivalrous gesture, he told her how in his desire for her he "beat his head nights against the wall."

In Springfield his mother invited her to dinner. Mrs. Lindsay was kindness itself, but so oppressively meaning was her manner ("Mama is at me to get hitched," said Vachel) that the nervous young girl was made more nervous and before the evening ended was obliged to flee to the bathroom, where she lost the whole elaborate meal. At the mother's right hand at table sat Dr. Lindsay, whose ulcerated eye had almost failed him and who was in body much worn down. And yet, says Isadora, had the valiant old doctor been his son's age and asked her the question his son was asking, she might have said "Yes."

Dr. Lindsay had spent so much money on the trip to China that in the summer of 1915 he took no vacation, and from that long summer of unrelieved work in the unremitting heat of Springfield his health never recovered.

In August that year he began to be subject to rhythmic fainting spells and dizzy fits. He had always been moody; now for weeks his mind was dazed and, when the daze cleared, a morbid depression set in, out of which at last by sheer grit he hoisted himself. But by 1917 only courage kept him going physically as he went out on his calls through pitch-black nights and over country roads in his horse-drawn buggy, almost the last one in town, which, half-blind though he was, he still drove himself, sitting very erect, with his hands out straight before him holding the reins up.

And Mrs. Lindsay, who still spoke in public at every chance that offered, had, like her husband, in all except her indomitable courage grown old. Myriad fine wrinkles, a source of wonder to her visiting grandchildren, made a network in her small fighting face with its imperious mouth and vividly shining eyes.

His father, his mother and he were "a triumvirate," Vachel lovingly insisted, though for the most part he was upstairs, confessedly sleeping a good deal ("Oh I am a worm, a disgrace, I am old Mr. Turtle and Mr. Snail") but sometimes writing, and the house downstairs was full as ever of people whose eyes would pop if they could see him in the world beyond, yet who here in Springfield "take little Vachel very casually."

What the three shared together no outsider quite realized. Jessie Rittenhouse had a glimpse when in 1917 she spent a night with the Lindsays and after breakfast saw the family Bible brought out and heard a chapter read by the doctor. Then father, mother, son and maidservant got down on their knees facing their chairs, while Mrs. Lindsay prayed.

Miss Rittenhouse and Vachel, whom she had known only in New York, knelt side by side. "It was a revelation to me of what lay behind his work," she later wrote.

His parents' attitude toward that work, said Vachel, was as though their son had through the years slowly built up a greenhouse in the north end of the city, "where they go once a month to view the flowers. But the rest of the time they see me at home, where we spend our time in family gossip. While they have read all my reviews, clippings and criticisms devoutly and in a great glow, they do not know Harriet Monroe from Alice Corbin Henderson, nor Francis Hackett from William Marion Reedy, though they know every second-rate preacher and third-rate missionary president for miles."

Here at home, though, he had peace in a most troubled world and for the first time he was making his keep and a little over, enough to pay the small bills that caused the biggest worries. It was he who bought the new screen door and paid for chicken wire to fence the geranium beds—"an immense satisfaction," he wrote to Olive, "after having been obliged to 'ask' for money through so many excruciating years."

Lindsay's new collection, *The Chinese Nightingale and Other Poems*, was published in September 1917. It contained *The Broncho That Would Not Be Broken*, a poem of heartbreak, and *Our Mother Pocahontas*, written when people were battering at him for something patriotic. He had been doing movie criticisms for the *New Republic*, and his *The Art of the Moving Picture* was in use at Columbia in the scenario-writing class of the School of Journalism.

Reciting, however, was still his main source of income. He left home at intervals. Out at the University of Wisconsin he recited twelve times in three days—each time for an hour and on one day five times—all most strenuously, all for one fee, till Witter Bynner, who recited for a fee himself and was in Madison, asked him in amazement where he got his strength.

"Vachel answered with a swaying shrug of the shoulders," Bynner writes, "and a characteristic wave of the hand, as if to say, 'Ask a river about its strength.'"

This was in the spring of 1918. Recruiting posters showed American fighting men brandishing the Stars and Stripes and exhorting civilians to "Follow the Flag!" Yet in the city of Lindsay's prophetic vision, the Springfield of *The Golden Book*, three flags would fly above all roofs—the flags of

Springfield, of America and of a United World, and to all three would the citizens of 2018 pledge allegiance.

"Those that can unite under the flag of Springfield with joy," he prophesied, "can some day unite the world over, under the flag of mankind."

When he was at home, he was so deep in his book that he was actually living one hundred years ahead; often the battles on the fields of France looked as far back to him as those of the Civil War.

A year earlier his hopes had soared at the hurling out of the Russian Czar and the establishment of the moderate Kerensky government. Comrade Kerensky had since fallen, but there would be others coming after him led on toward freedom by the great spirit of Tolstoy who, high in the sky above the battle-smoke, in his peasant dress, his head bent low, "is plowing yet," wrote Lindsay, is following his spirit-horses across

a field as wide as the world.

"This is the war to establish the World Union," he wrote in August 1918 to Katharine Lee Bates. "I see the international government as a thing inevitable as the sunrise, the *middle class international* that will pull down the emperors and millionaires and police the earth. I see the international army as busy all over the earth as the armies of America have been on American soil for the last hundred and more years. Federation is going to be as hard for the world as it was for America."

The present war would last anyway till 1920. Since going to war was like voting—one man, one vote—he had plenty of time yet to cast his ballot. But that his was not a popular position—neither that of fighter nor outright pacifist—was brought home to him many times. "Condemn if you must, but be friends," he pleaded with Mary Humphrey, whose brother was in the army and who was herself in France.

Joyce Kilmer, younger than he, had enlisted and died in the field. Eugene Debs, far older, was risking jail by preaching pacifism. Lindsay's age had so far spared him from being put to the test, but "I have been lambasted," he told Katharine

Bates, "by a good many people like Hermann Hagedorn for not writing rip-snorting Rooseveltian war poetry for the Vigilantes. Then Miss Jane Addams, whom I very much admire, says of me rather sadly, 'Mr. Lindsay is no longer one of us.'"

Ex-President Theodore Roosevelt, who felt intensely in the present moment, spoke out in 1918 reminding Americans that they who gave their service and stood ready to sacrifice their lives were the torchbearers. Cried Roosevelt: "We run with the torches until we fall. The torches whose flame is brightest are borne by the gallant men at the front!"

And Lindsay's mother wrote to him this summer from Colorado in the spirit and almost the words of Roosevelt's challenge, though to a different purpose. She urged him to go abroad as an entertainer and recite to the troops—to go, indeed, but not to fight. "Any man will make a private soldier," said the daughter of the Frazees. "You have a unique talent that no *one else* has, one that the entire American army needs.

"Let me entreat you not to bury your light. It is my great longing that each of my children take up the torch lighted by the prophets and Christ, carried by Grandfather Austen and Grandmother Frazee, and *run* with it, *from mountain top to mountain top.*

"My precious, only boy, think and pray, and do not let any narrow Lindsay prejudices hold you back from your best possibilities, nor lead you into a place where your life is unnecessarily exposed to danger. You have the torch already in your hand."

At the camp in Colorado Mrs. Lindsay and her husband were spending a more than usually happy summer. Dr. Lindsay needed two canes to walk by now, yet he and his wife, wobbly but game, left camp each morning to take long hikes into the hills. Afterward their son reflected that this was how a marriage should be—and how it should end. For at noon on September 11, Dr. Lindsay, while stooping over the home-made rack for milk and butter, lodged nearby in the whirling stream of Mad Creek, slipped and fell in.

The icy water was only waist-deep but it took some minutes to get him out. His wife at once lighted a fire and put him to bed with hot rocks around him, but the next morning he seemed unlike himself; he walked uncertainly, articulated clumsily, was slow in his responses and at times even, as she wrote in great anxiety to Vachel, "a little off."

Yet the next day, Friday, it was the father who wrote, in letters that staggered on the page: "Dear son, we have decided to start home Monday night, September 16, owing to the condition of my health. I fell into the creek and got very wet and cold—ordinarily it would not have given me trouble."

Vachel met the train in Springfield at three in the morning with an ambulance and saw his father, unconscious since before leaving camp, lifted out through the car window in the ambulance basket and carried to the Springfield hospital. On September 20, with his wife and son beside him, "he went away," said Vachel. "It was hard to see him go."

At the funeral in the First Christian Church a woman soloist, who had known the doctor well, sang "In the Sweet Bye and Bye"—a song Vachel was familiar with before he could read. It was the song he would remember their father by, he wrote to Olive. Strangely, he had had at this time, almost on the day of his father's death, another loss whose roots reached deep into the past. Ruth Wheeler, to whom he was once engaged and who had never married, died after a long hopeless illness.

45

Two months after Lindsay registered for the draft, the Armistice was signed. Even while the war was raging he had believed that all its sorrow might be but the birthpangs of internationalism, and now—he wrote to Eleanor Dougherty—he foresaw the secession of states from an international constitution and a future war, diminishing the memory of all past conflicts, waged in its defense.

But this, the first foundation of world order, of which Wilson surely would be president, "will be worth all our blood."

To die for anything less than the cause of human progress was like dying an infidel or a blasphemer. Death, like life, should count for something. There would be other crusades, less popular but equal in danger and superior in moral challenge to the war just ended, in which a man might use his dead body as a vote on the side he chose. Long before the fighting, Lindsay had been haunted by the presentiment that he would some day have the opportunity to die for his most personal dreams, to suffer the limit of agony—it might be with thousands, it might be in cold loneliness.

However it was, whenever it came—"I want a clean Christian death."

If the war hadn't made him a soldier, it had certainly made him a citizen, he told Harriet Monroe. He no longer considered himself the prairie poet. Carl Sandburg could take over that role. He, Lindsay, felt himself unfolding and moving on toward something that was neither poetry nor reciting but might be called "aesthetic-political citizenship."

He would just as soon shut himself away and be forgotten by his friends and the literary crowd till he had finished *The Golden Book of Springfield*, when he would come back to them all in such a different character that he could hand over his mantle to Sandburg most cheerfully, to the guitar-toting Sandburg who was plainly becoming the kind of brave and civic-hearted bard *The Golden Book* called for. Lindsay had long wanted to say to him how much he admired the "wonderful 'Chicago Poems.' "

"I don't in the least approve of free verse, but I cannot help but approve of Sandburg and Masters. I am certainly glad they are alive," he told Harriet.

Edgar Lee Masters had stirred up a storm by the frankness of his *Spoon River Anthology*, published in 1915, which was a series of poetic monologues by the dead inhabitants of a prairie town, men and women who, as they lie under the headstones of a country cemetery, speak from the grave to reveal deeds of frailty in their past lives.

Yet below the surface of the book's sordid revelations, the spare poetic style and often sardonic tone, ran an acceptance of humanity and sense of beauty and cosmic design that to Lindsay made it one of the truest and most beautiful books ever written. Always parts of it made him cry, especially the verses on Lucinda Matlock and Hannah Armstrong—"God, but they're beautiful!"

He came from the same daguerreotype world as Masters. *Spoon River* was the sort of thing he had tried to do in *The Village Magazine*, only "wasn't man enough or artist enough."

As for the picture drawn of human nature, "I am not discouraged by it," he wrote to Eleanor, herself a dreamer. "I cannot understand the people who are discouraged by it. It is the tragedy of mankind not that there are Spoon Rivers, but that there are not enough dreamers sent to them with dreaming powers and fighting powers.

"Humanity is like the ragged barefoot armies of France that won out against the world in the first days of the Revolution.

Reread that book, and say, 'This is what I have to work with, this humanity. I shall infect them with my dreams and they shall never infect me with their sickness.' Arm yourself against the worst so that disappointment in humanity is impossible. We shall teach these cripples to fight for our fancies, fight with their crutches."

When Lindsay first began to complain that the reciting undertaken originally to launch his books was in danger of running away with him, he at the same time expressed in his diary—this was in 1916—his wish for a big Chautauqua circuit. In 1919 the inner conflict still existed. If he needed solitude to write, he needed an audience to live. It was not just the money. What he said of his mother was true of himself: that she drank in nerve-force from her audiences and even if she had to crawl to the platform, her speaking was the last thing she would ever give up.

Thus in spite of insisting to Harriet that he no longer saw himself as an entertainer, and to Eleanor that his public life was becoming stale and needed poem games to save it, he plunged now willingly into a spring recital tour, between January and the beginning of April 1919 traveling to the Atlantic coast, back west through Ohio and Indiana, then—breakneck—south to Texas, into Louisiana, Mississippi and home through Kentucky.

He was offering his audiences their choice of four programs. The first, on The Gospel of Beauty, took in many of his poems about Springfield, strung together with talk of democracy and art. The second was a discourse on The Art of the Moving Picture. The third, for "tired business men" ("who have not yet bought their paintings, built their great houses, taken their stand on municipal betterment . . . these are the men I want to influence"), was An Evening of Higher Vaudeville, with *General Booth, The Congo, The Kallyope Yell* and *The Santa Fé Trail*.

The fourth included poem games and one long solo, *The Chinese Nightingale*, this last a poem that the Irish poet James

Stephens, visiting the United States, declared "the greatest written since the Pilgrims came over on the one subject that poetry has any true concern with, the soul of man and its meaning and destiny."

Literary New York was the same gorgeous drama it had been to Lindsay ever since 1914. "Everybody seems to just love to see me!" he wrote joyfully home, and to Eleanor: "I have been very very happy, and people have been amazingly good."

In Cleveland he stayed with Joy and her husband Ben Blair, who went to his recital. Joy, an active clubwoman, contrasted in a letter to her mother Vachel's friendliness and way of shaking hands with the indifferent manner of other celebrities. Vachel always gave more than he needed to, and people seemed to appreciate it. She had heard some call him conceited, "but whenever you compare him with someone else who has had the *same attentions*, you find him very democratic and childlike."

It was his biggest reciting season so far. In Texas he sensed an exhilarating difference between the Southwest and the Old South still hoodooed by Mumbo Jumbo. On his first hike in 1906 when he tramped the red roads of Georgia, it had appeared impossible for anyone not a sworn Negro baiter to mention the race. Even the Florida cracker who had been so gentle toward him, when pressed into discussion had only grudgingly conceded that the "nigger" did have a soul but "a mighty small one."

("Here," said Lindsay, "we have the whole terrible race question in one torturing line.")

Since then his Kentucky cousins, his own age, had scolded him for *The Congo* and *King Solomon*, and for *John Brown*, his tribute to the Yankee saint. Yet when he sang *John Brown* in the high schools and colleges of Texas, the boys and girls of the new generation gave not a whimper of protest but roared with him lustily in the responses.

His introduction to the great state of Texas he owed to A. Joseph Armstrong, a young member of the English department at Baylor University. In exchange for his coming all the way to Waco, Armstrong had assured Lindsay of other recitals in the Southwest, then made good his assurance. Lindsay was fed up with commercial lecture bureaus and the stagnant audiences they provided. Responding with delight to the fresh quality of these southwestern groups—mostly bright-eyed students and their English teachers, who listened for his serious ideas and put no cheap personal questions—he asked Armstrong to be his regular manager and to organize his entire tour for the next year.

He was giving of his strength and spirits at three or four recitals a day, half of them not paid for; they included classroom visits, with spontaneous readings. Again his path crossed that of Witter Bynner, who, filled with real foreboding, implored him not to squander his energy. One day, Bynner warned, the fount would run dry and leave him helpless to create.

Back from his travels and just as the white buds tipped with green were swelling into view in the Governor's yard outside his window, Lindsay finished a poem for Isadora, *My Lady Is Compared to a Young Tree.*

It was this summer—the summer of 1919—that he wrote his poem on Bryan and the tumultuous presidential campaign of 1896. He felt an awareness tinged with envy of youth—as it had fought the war, or heroically dead like Joyce Kilmer, or merely tripping down the streets—and he wrote nostalgically of Vachel at sixteen and of Boy Bryan, then thirty-six. Bryan still lived, but his frame was flaccid, his oratory out-of-date. That heaven-born boy had "gone to join the shadows," said Lindsay, whose own face at thirty-nine showed some down-dragging lines.

When he wrote the Bryan poem he was at the camp in Colorado, alone with his mother in their first summer after his father's death. He was still at the camp when a letter reached him from Isadora bringing the news that he had lost her to another man, a younger man—a man who had worn uniform.

"The better man," Lindsay at once acknowledged.

But later that evening, trying to read aloud from his manuscript of *The Golden Book,* "he choked and lapsed into silence," writes a young woman from the ranch house below, who had climbed the mountain slope to be with him. "I have never seen anyone suffer more than Vachel did that night."

Though his heart was mad for Isadora, though in the magic of her girlhood she had ruled his very blood and bones, yet his blood and bones were things she least desired. Always, ever since Hiram, it seemed to him, his luck in love had been a sort of intermittent farce—"a joke that was all on me, if I forget the mere agonies." Writing from Springfield in October, he avowed to Mrs. Moody that he was through with every idea of marriage "for a long long time."

To Eleanor, who was still in France after becoming engaged to a French officer, he wrote to say that, whether through too much baffled loving or another cause, his imagination was burnt to ashes. His life had lost its iridescence. Reciting on tour looked as much a machine to him as a roller-top desk in an insurance office. "It is no longer an adventure. It is simply an unutterable bore. So is my life in Springfield.

"I want the new special adventure that is mine alone, that is destined to get me, at least for the time, nearer to Heaven. I am almost forty, and in danger of being choked by my own machinery. I think the first thing is to set myself free, and find God, find God more intimately. If I get tired enough in body my troubles are killed, and I find Him. I am trying to clear the decks to get time to take the road, afoot. But the trouble is I will be so unutterably lonesome I have scarcely faith I will stick to it.

"If I do not walk, I explode and I am so dog lonely I cannot bear to go by myself any more. . . ."

Few of his men friends were willing to walk with him— the boy in them was all gone. Nor had he of old depended so much on real intimacy.

There came to his rescue this fall John Snigg, a young lawyer, the son of old inhabitants and the kind of youth Lindsay had been looking for, the kind Abe Lincoln was when he first came to Springfield. Every Saturday they had lunch together. Then they walked down the main street onto the prairie and far out into Sangamon County, stopping at farmhouses belonging to friends of Snigg's, with whom they ate supper, and afterward sweeping back under moon and stars to the lights of their home town.

46

Indoors at this time Lindsay was spurring and lashing himself on to complete *The Golden Book of Springfield*, the end of which seemed always just in sight. Three times at least in the past three years he had changed the form of the book. In its vague imaginative beginnings, he had conceived of it as a glorified *Village Magazine*. In the writing, it had been started as a sequence of poems on his town, something like *Spoon River Anthology;* then it became a collection of related essays, and finally, after furious rewriting, turned into a novel with himself as the hero, reborn a hundred years hence.

"Carrying on as of old, in the same conceited philandering way," one of his characters, born again along with him, describes the Vachel Lindsay of 2018.

Lindsay, the author, let the ironic self-description stand, but his latest major revision had been to cut out the romantic passages. Since losing Isadora, he was quite sure romance was a subject of which he knew nothing. He could hardly endure the thought of romance.

In January 1920, after a spurt during which he pledged himself neither to eat, drink nor kiss (keeping only the third pledge), he finished *The Golden Book*. This month his new book of verse, *The Golden Whales of California and Other Rhymes in the American Language*, was published. "Golden" was a favorite and fertilizing word with Lindsay. Whereas the gold of *The Golden Book* is the pale hue of moonlight, symbol of unrealizable Utopia, the gold of California is the color of sun and money.

Oh the flashing cornucopia of haughty California
Is *gold, gold, gold.*
Their brittle speech and their clutching reach
Is *gold, gold, gold.*

Yet under the lights of the city named for him,

St. Francis shades his face in his cowl
And stands in the street like a lost gray owl . . .

He sees on far redwoods
Dewfall and dawning:
Deep in Yosemite
Shadows and shrines.

Besides the title piece, the new collection had verses inspired by Lindsay's spiritual ancestor Alexander Campbell ("My fathers came from Kentucky" was the first of these), his poem on Bryan and one on another of his political heroes, Andrew Jackson, of whom it was the American people's beloved myth and not the historical figure that he sought to praise. These latest poems, like the earlier *Our Mother Pocahontas*, were an expression of the same need that drove him physically out of his room into the open air.

He was seeking for spiritual balance, striving to renew his hold on what was most true and steady within him. He recalled his American heritage. Boy Bryan stood to him for the idealism of youth, the legendary Andrew Jackson for cool democratic courage, Alexander Campbell for brotherhood in religious faith.

Even before America entered the war, it had seemed to him that a taint of rottenness blew over the water from Europe with its tarnished dynasties. Pocahontas, singing in her maidenhood in the green solitudes of Virginia in spring, was his symbol of his own land's untamedness, unweariedness and innocence.

From early March into June 1920, Lindsay made the first of three tremendous tours across the nation—each one increasing in scope and pace—under the management of Professor Armstrong of Baylor. Like his poem games, they were a part of his attempt to earn his living and at the same time to escape the stereotype being forced on him by undreaming organizations. There was slow death to his creative soul in casting his poems before Rotary and Kiwanis, who were alarmed lest he be not amusing, and women's clubs, whose chairmen had names like Yvetta.

Such groups invested in him on hearsay as a show; they never asked him to return. It was a yelling among strangers. Yet, as he told Armstrong, if he couldn't have "close and long-continued and sound personal relations with human creatures," he wanted none.

He wanted audiences whose minds were alive and who would *read his books*. He wanted young hearts and new territory and to feel himself "growing with the country." He had asked Armstrong to route him through to the Pacific coast and allow him time enough at every stop to cease being the mysterious stranger and get to know folks.

Witter Bynner had seen nothing yet: even this great tour of 1920, which took in mostly schools and colleges and rambled from Illinois to California, was only the start of the cross-country campaigning—first under Armstrong's, later under other management—from east to west and west to east, reciting and lecturing, year after year that, with one interval when his health broke down, Lindsay kept up almost till the last day of his life.

"With the possible exception of Mark Twain," said Hazelton Spencer in 1932, "no American writer of importance ever geographically experienced the United States so thoroughly as Lindsay did."

For if he hated the machine of touring, he still loved travel; he loved America. "I want a deeper picture of the whole United States, a balanced picture," he had written, to Armstrong, and in his diary, as he sat in the Pullman car on the first stage of the new adventure:

> I dream of flying from state to state
> Without the railroad train,
> Head foremost, sleeping on my arm—

Yet stars sweep slowly by above
And swiftly underneath go by
The trees and farms I love.

A new long poem, *In Praise of Johnny Appleseed*, was stirring in him. In 1800 or thereabouts a young man named John Chapman, a devoted Swedenborgian, had turned his back on his native New England, crossed the Appalachians and from western Pennsylvania wandered on into Ohio, carrying over his shoulder a sack of appleseeds. Till his death almost fifty years later he planted his seeds in lonely places, and in the fullness of the generations orchards came into being that blossomed and bore fruit and marked his path through the wilderness.

He was the begetter, who sows the seed and passes on— "the nearest to Buddha and St. Francis and Tolstoy of all West-going pioneers," continued Lindsay in his diary. "He is the West-going heart, never returning, yet with civilization always near enough to keep his heart tender for mankind. My God is the God of Johnny Appleseed, and some day I shall find Him."

47

Westward then Lindsay took
his way. In August 1920 he temporarily reversed his direction
and sailed for England with his mother.

After two good cups of coffee each morning, Mrs. Lindsay
felt herself full of steam till about noon. She had been set on
going back to China to see Olive, but her son switched her
to England, where the year before *General Booth and Other
Poems* had been published. All spring he had done his best to
prepare her for the celebrated writers she could expect to
meet, but her general contempt for literature as an end in
itself beat Carlyle's and the anticipation of watching her
"slay" literary Englishmen with her adroit finalities and dis-
missing wave of the hand made him snort like a rhinoceros.

"Believe me, dear Mama can lay them out," he promised
Mrs. Moody. "She will take out her revenge on them for
being obliged to play second fiddle to little Vachel."

On her side, Mrs. Lindsay confided in a letter to Olive that
Vachel had been telling her all about "Drinkwater, Masefield, Yeats and others. They call him 'the only live American
poet,' and such expressions—very extravagant."

And when they reached London—"Mrs. Lindsay told me
of her daughter in China," wrote one journalist, come to interview Vachel. "It is easy to see, in talking to this upright, determined, forcible little lady from Lincoln's city, from whom
Vachel Lindsay derives his crusading quality."

Lindsay was known to the English poets ahead of his coming. He had grown somewhat sore at Yeats for having made

no effort to keep up their one night's friendship. Yet, returning from America in 1914, Yeats had been the first to cry, abroad that Lindsay had genius. When in 1919 the much younger poet Robert Nichols went home after a visit to the United States, he cried the same thing.

It was the writers from England whom Lindsay had met in New York over the years—some of them, like John Drinkwater, author of the play *Abraham Lincoln*, having penetrated as far as Springfield—who casually invited him to their country and they and their friends who welcomed him. He had few public engagements in England and almost no fees, but his name and picture were in the papers and the comment on the small parties and private recitals arranged for him was mistakenly caught up by the American press as referring to advertised public appearances.

EVERYBODY'S "VACHING" IN LONDON! ran the complacent headline in little old Springfield.

Wherever he went, his mother went with him—"looking old, but trying my best," she told Olive. They were guests of honor at a very swell housewarming given by the Drinkwaters and there they met Ralph Hodgson, Edmund Blunden, Wilfrid Wilson Gibson, Lord Charnwood, John St. Loe Strachey, Walter De La Mare, and the American poet John Gould Fletcher. All were in evening dress except Vachel.

"Quite somebodies," allowed Mrs. Lindsay, writing to Olive. "I have no embarrassment in talking to the wives of these distinguished men. *You* and *I* know a lot more than they do."

Said Vachel: "The twelve apostles might impress her, but they are all dead."

Ezra Pound (Idaho-born, after all) brought Mrs. Lindsay the first American coffee she had tasted in London, and him she did not slay. Yet to have Pound, Fletcher, and for three years the quiet-spoken Robert Frost reside among them had done nothing to prepare the English for Lindsay. "Mr. Vachel Lindsay of the shattering voice and milk diet!" a reporter called him, after he and his mother had been dined, though conspicuously not wined, at a smart London restaurant.

Most of his London reciting was before picked groups like the Poets' Club, the Women's University Club and the English Speaking Union. He recited, too, under the auspices of the Poetry Bookshop, managed by Harold Munro, a gathering place for the very young English poets, pink of cheek and classically trained, and for the older intellectuals, who listened gravely, then applauded madly.

"An extraordinary thing, this Congo poem," muttered Arnold Bennett.

On September 20 George Bell and Son brought out *The Daniel Jazz*, a selection from Lindsay's poems already published in America. According to Lindsay, it was the publisher who, while he was on the ocean, gave this title to his English volume, which led some English critics to label him right away as "the jazz poet."

They could hardly have read his poems, said Lindsay.

In the past couple of years "jazz" had become the rage on both sides of the Atlantic. Jazz rhythms sprang from the barrelhouses and honkytonks of the New Orleans Negro district; they stood for the frenetic rhythm of the loins. Actually, Lindsay loathed jazz as something "diseased," something "absolutely smelling of the hospital," and recent poems of his like the title poem *The Daniel Jazz* (later called *Daniel*) and the syncopated, sentimental *Apple Blossom Snow Blues* were written in fun; they were ironical.

On October 15 he recited at Oxford, where he and his mother met Robert Bridges, venerable laureate and defender of the tongue, and John Masefield, always Vachel's admirer, came in from Boar's Hill to pay his respects.

"The prince of English poets," Mrs. Lindsay, impressed at last, called Masefield, and she wrote to Olive: "He has a peculiar face, is tall, slender, drooping, rather bald—gray hair, sad, thoughtful eyes. We had lunch in Oxford with him and his wife. Tea I've forgotten with whom, but Robert Graves and Robert Nichols were on hand, both *young* poets, forceful, *very kind,* appreciative, and almost reverential toward Vachel. They call me 'Mother Lindsay,' as if it were a reality."

The importation of Vachel Lindsay into the tradition-hallowed and still rural Oxford of 1920 had been engineered by Robert Graves, who meant, he acknowledged afterward, to deal the old place "a pretty heavy blow," though he hadn't expected to "inflict a knockout, as occurred."

All students in the Literature Department were invited to the evening recital and Graves had done well to round up at short notice more than a thousand. Presiding was Sir Walter Raleigh, Professor of English Literature. The dons, with the poet's mother in their midst, filled the front rows and the undergraduates—including women, recently admitted—wearing black gowns and mortar boards, the rest of the large college hall.

"Sir Walter Raleigh sat alone, front seat," wrote Mrs. Lindsay, *"very tall, very* dignified. Vachel, very much at home, removed table and chairs from the platform, to give himself plenty of room. Then Sir Walter arose, smiling, and introduced him in two or three sentences as 'the most virile poet, representing the most virile nation,' or about such words. The audience raised a shout, and nearly lifted the old valted roof (I can't spell, I'm tired, and have no dictionary here).

"Vachel gave an 'All-American program,' explaining each number very lucidly before reciting. He began with the pioneer *The Proud Farmer*, then, as nearly as I can remember, *The Building of Springfield, Ghosts of the Buffaloes, Kansas, Santa Fé Trail, Lincoln Walks at Midnight*. Sir Walter led the cheers after each recitation, and I never saw such an ovation! Nor did I ever hear Vachel do so well. Enthusiasm went wild in staid old Oxford, the heart of all educational interests in the English-speaking world!"

"Lindsay was a most staggering success!" recalls Robert Graves. "By two minutes he had the respectable and intellectual and cynical audience listening. By ten, intensely excited; by twenty, elated and losing self-control; by half an hour completely under his influence; by forty minutes roaring like a bonfire. At the end of the hour they lifted off the roof and refused to disperse, and Raleigh in returning thanks said he had never been so moved by a recitation in his life—quite like the pictures."

And Mrs. Lindsay to Olive continued: "I felt quite moved in spirit when Vachel introduced my grand old father, not naming him, as a representative leader in new American pioneer life. I hope my father and grandfather knew. Perhaps they were present, with your own father who saw the *outside* of Oxford University."

Vachel believed it was in this moment and not before—not till she saw him with Oxford at his feet—that his mother, accustomed to being first in her own world, realized his accomplishment. He was to look back on the occasion with mixed emotions, now crying out—this was after her death—that on at last perceiving he had done something worth while she immediately took credit for it, and again expressing his happiness at her share in his triumph as "the sort of thing few men can bring to their mothers."

When just before sailing for home he recited at Cambridge, he again (in the American language) struck ten. His farewell London appearance was on October 29 in Westminster Central Hall. St. John Irvine introduced him and he did three of his Negro "sermons," including *Daniel*, to which the Bloomsbury crowd surrendered absolutely:

> King Darius said to the lions:—
> "Bite Daniel. Bite Daniel.
> Bite him. Bite him. Bite him!"

Here literary London joined in, rocking, stamping and roaring at the word of command—

> THUS roared the lions:—
> "We want Daniel, Daniel, Daniel,
> We want Daniel, Daniel, Daniel!
> Grrrrrrrrrrrrrrrrrrrrrrrrrrrrrrrrrrrrrrrrrrr
> Grrrrrrrrrrrrrrrrrrrrrrrrrrrrrrrrrrrrrrrrrrrrr."

Vachel Lindsay on the platform was how the English like their Americans. While his Negro poems had for them a curious fascination, it was his poems of the American West that won their critical acclaim, especially *Bryan*, with its stirring panorama and elegiac finale. "He is easily the most important living American poet," was the opinion of a writer for the *Observer*, who added that "America can never be regarded as submerged by mere commercialism so long as Mr. Lindsay sings his songs from New York to New Mexico."

"Come soon again," Masefield urged him, in a telegram to Liverpool as the Lindsays' ship was about to sail.

But Lindsay, then and always, would far rather have the English poets cross to his side of the water. "Let me get all England to Texas," he wrote in his diary. He had noticed that for educated Americans to cast even two glances too many at the British Empire made them just a little cock-eyed and catty.

To the interviewer from the *Observer*, who called to see him before he left London, he explained his allegiance as they sat in his room at the White Hall Hotel, with his mother making a third. "I find here," began Lindsay, "that English people when they speak of America generally mean just New England. Look here."

He pulled out of his pocket a map of the United States, which was an ordinary scale map, but he had obliterated the state boundaries with heavy pen strokes, then painted in, in black ink, his own new names. Away in the west he boldly defined, with California at its heart, the New Italy; in the east the little kingdom that is New England; then the Old South, whose spiritual center is Virginia; and above, the Midwest.

But his most striking definition was of the immense tract renamed New Arabia, which ran sheer down from the border of Canada to Mexico, with Santa Fé its symbol and capital.

"That is the future of America," he told his English interviewer. "I call it 'the Desert.' It is not desert, but those illimitable plains and mountains, with oases of towns and tilled fields, are more like Arabia than anything else. I have walked across it from end to end, when the horizon seemed to me farther off than when I crossed the Atlantic. That desert is vast. It can never be subjected to the industrial civilization that has caught the East or the near West. I often call it 'the American splendor.' "

48

England had been to Lindsay merely a place to wait till *The Golden Book of Springfield* was published. In the interminable course of that book's desperate revisions, it had almost become his Old Man of the Sea. He expected that when once he held a copy in his hands he could be shot next minute and die happy!

Really, everything he had written before was but an early draft of *The Golden Book*. He had said in it everything he had to say about the unfolding of his democratic dream. Yet what emerged, when *The Golden Book* finally went on sale in Coe's book store in Springfield and elsewhere over the nation, in November 1920, was a work provoking and baffling—diffuse, sometimes hopelessly tedious and on the whole nearly unreadable.

Had he stuck to his original intention of a series of poems, or to a book of essays, he might have done better, but Marsh, his editor, had insisted on a plot and on that plot he foundered.

He began his story with the "Prognosticators' Club." In 1920 a dozen Springfield men and women (among them a Campbellite minister, a Christian Scientist, a Jew, and a Negro) meet in the sun parlor of the Leland Hotel and exchange their prophecies and visions of the mystic year of 2018, when they will all be reincarnated and witness the coming to their city of the Golden Book, a winged book of air that "gleams with spiritual gold" and lies open as it soars.

278

On its rippling pages in fiery letters are addresses from the
Bible, the writings of Swedenborg, Adam Smith, Karl Marx,
Henry George, and from the conversation of two citizens and
sages of the future Springfield—one of them the patriarch of
the tribe of the Michaels, a high-strung hardy people (akin
to the Frazees), workers with their hands, descendants of the
pioneers and thus belonging to what Lindsay calls America's
"blacksmith aristocracy"; the other, the passionate, terrible-
tempered Black Hawk Boone, who bears a likeness to Doctor
Mohawk, for he boasts an aborigine among his ancestors and
is "a short man with a curly big black beard such as Ashurbanipal and Nimrod must have shaken at their foes."

Then is Lindsay himself reborn. Like Lincoln before him
in his poem, he rises from his grave in Oak Ridge, up through
the deep darkness.

He is endowed with new powers and wears by turns vari-
ous bodies, though stepping back into his yokel self whenever
with Avanel Boone, the daughter of Black Hawk and leader
of Springfield's band of girl warriors, he explores the town,
finding it dramatically changed, yet in some ways unchanged,
for Stuart's ice-cream parlor survives, and the morning paper,
which is still the *State Journal,* runs the same old advertisements of dry cleaners and dealers in grain and feed, and both
the jail and the stairs of City Hall have "the same old skunk
smell."

But now from many a flagstaff flutter the flags of Springfield, the United States and the International Government.
Overtopping the old ones, are new buildings—permanent ex-
hibits in a great World's Fair—designed in a curving, complex
rhythm and lighted through the wild hours of darkness by
jewel-colored searchlights.

They are the dreams of men of dreams, built into visible
forms: the ninety-nine slender Sunset Towers, of the hues of
sunset, and in their midst the white Truth Tower, set in the
center of a star-plan system of avenues; and the gaudy, gorgeous, jungle houses of the Negro district, conceived by a
young Negro architect; and the splendid cathedral from whose
high pulpit the priest called St. Friend—his face "the face of

Lincoln, with a touch of St. Francis"—champions freedom of prayer without the fences of orthodox creed.

There are parks that were not in the old town, named after remembered poet-statesmen like Carl Sandburg, Edgar Lee Masters, Joyce Kilmer and Louis Untermeyer, while in the groves, orchards and aviation fields that surround the city rise on trellises the titan vines of the Apple Amaranth.

In the Springfield of 2018 there is forever carnival. Passers-by are decked with ribbons, the beautiful avenues swarm with popcorn vans; at twilight, chimes from the campaniles ring out. The ideal of citizenship is internationalism and of religion brotherhood. Yet the flavor of the old town is strong; tribal traditions are jealously fostered. Protestant, Catholic and Jew, black man and yellow man, are not lost in a melting pot, only their rich inheritance flows unobstructed.

The saloon is extinct. There is no more hard drinking, but human nature is inveterate, and Lindsay and Avanel meet corruption personified in "Slick-Slack" Kopensky, mayor of the city, who looks like portraits of President McKinley, and in "Coffee" Kosuko with his chain of evil yellow dance halls.

Outside Springfield, a mystic diabolism emanates over the earth from the cult of the great Cocaine Buddha of Singapore. It is the virgin Avanel who, as a new Joan of Arc on horseback—but with her left hand dyed crimson in token of her Red Indian ancestry—at the last leads her city's people against the armies of Singapore, the lawless imperialist state that has declared war on the world flag.

(In 1917 Lindsay had written to Eleanor Dougherty that the approaching victory of woman's suffrage already put glory in his soul, for it would be "an enormous liberalizing and civilizing force." He truly began to see the woman soldier, absurd as that might seem—"as fast as intelligence counts above brute force in war, so fast the woman will count. . . .")

And as Joan of Arc was the soul of France, so is Avanel of Springfield. At the end of Lindsay's story, she and he together "sweep up and up" through the air with the speed of light in a flying boat to follow the Amaranth vine, tracing its greatleaved, heavy-fruited stem through the spectral wasteland of the Jungles of Heaven till they discover the abandoned empty leathern sack of Johnny Appleseed, from which came the first sowing of the Amaranth.

Abruptly the vision fades, the hundred years are as naught. Lindsay hears the newsboys bawling the evening edition, and he buys a paper and—behold—its date is March 1, 1920. Avanel is a century away.

This bewildering, ridiculous narrative is redeemed by passages when the dazzling beauty of Lindsay's language lights up the labyrinth of his thought, as in his apocalyptic descriptions of the coming of the Golden Book, and of the soaring ascent with Avanel to the star-lit jungles of ancient heaven— passages that, as one reviewer suggested, need only to be put into meter to become poems—and in his scattered aphorisms, full of truth and salt.

But for the general reader flashes of poetry and wit were not enough. Like most utopian novels, this one had too little novel and too much utopia. "Utopia of Katzenjammer," sneered a critic, breaking the silence of the torturing weeks after publication when no reviews appeared at all and sickness spread in Lindsay's heart.

"The book has not even been mentioned or roasted. It has been *absolutely ignored,*" he wailed to Harriet Monroe.

On December 18, a thoughtful and sympathetic criticism did appear, in the New York *Post*. It was by William Rose Benét, who pointed out that while Sinclair Lewis' already famous novel, *Main Street*, published this fall, was an indictment of provincial dullness and commercialism by a realist, *The Golden Book*—"pervaded by spiritual conviction and an indubitable fantastic genius"—was that of a poet, "of the most intensely individual and blazingly romantic poet of this generation."

"Any one," Benét went on, "who remembers the closed eyes of Lindsay as with head thrown back he sways to the rendition of his own chants, any one who has realized the deep religious emotion and fervor underlying all his poetry, will not be at all surprised. 'Then I had religion, then I had a vision,' is literally true of him and permanently true."

Other reviews that straggled in were by no means unfavorable. The book was noticed in the London *Times*, whose critic spoke of its dreamlike quality, of how "the unconscious has vent and scope" and the writing illustrates for an English reader the American mind. But his publishers, Lindsay lamented, considered the book an "utter failure." In the market place it was a dud. To Lindsay himself, wrought up through the years of effort to a hardly endurable pitch of expectancy, the lack of public response was almost annihilating. Not since *War Bulletin Number Three* had he felt so let down.

"It is a sort of apple seed, festering in my heart," he cried of *The Golden Book*.

In spite of its popular failure, it must yet be vindicated by what he wrote, and the hint of his new direction lay between its lines, he promised Harriet Monroe. She heard him with regret. For to Harriet—who toward the end of her editor's career was to name Lindsay as "perhaps the most gifted and original poet" her magazine ever printed—it was a lasting disappointment that he had devoted to an unworkable dream years in which his creative powers were at their zenith and that might have seen the writing of great poems.

49

In 1920 he who only seven years before had been an obscure aspirant was on his way to being the most famous singer in the land. All over America dancers experimented with his poems and composers asked leave to set them to music. As a performer and lecturer, Lindsay was in huge demand.

Yet the summit is a slippery place. Already a new generation of poets pressed hard on his heels and the critics, many of them younger than he, were pointing out signs that he and his work were mortal.

In the year of Lindsay's trip to England, T. S. Eliot's first volume of poems was published. Quite suddenly it was becoming the fashion at the beginning of this postwar decade —the decade of *Prufrock*, *The Waste Land* and *The Hollow Men*—to feel a little ashamed of Lindsay, a number of whose fellow Americans were irritated by the high English estimate of his rank.

Praise of his work by one English critic drew a retort from John Gould Fletcher—a leader, with Pound and Amy Lowell, of the imagists—who not only denied genius to Lindsay but in sovereign contempt compared him with Kipling, saying that he had the "same free-and-easy facility, preference for ragtime rhythms, tone of vulgar optimism and desire to preach as the author of *Mandalay*."

Lindsay had long ago foreseen that a critical set at him was bound to be made. It would be a natural resistance to his success, the inevitable counterpoise to it, and he had begged Harriet Monroe to help him take his "skinning" like a man. Sure enough, in 1917, when *The Chinese Nightingale and Other Poems* appeared, it was skinned mercilessly in the Chicago *Daily News* by Conrad Aiken, aged twenty-eight and "one of the few American poets who does not like me much," said Lindsay.

By 1920, *The Golden Whales of California* was being on the whole disparaged as showing a decline from his previous work. He admitted that while he was writing the minor verse in that collection, it was *The Golden Book of Springfield* that took the best part of his mind; even the ambitious title poem he had kept by him as a diversion, jotting it down while on the road, in Pullman cars and hotel rooms.

"A disappointment," was the *Yale Review's* considered verdict.

Louis Untermeyer in the *Dial* called attention to the curious split, jarring to mind and ear, between Lindsay's almost opposed tendencies in this book of "the Jerusalem theme" and "the jazz orchestration."

Most wounding of all was a long thoughtful article by Amy Lowell on the front page of the New York *Times* book section, in which Miss Lowell, not without sorrow, pronounced the new collection "by and large a parody on all the Mr. Lindsays."

What Lindsay had now to do was what from his youth he had exhorted himself to do. "God help us to be brave," was the title and anxious refrain of his early poem. On his first hike, exhausted and depressed on the highway outside Asheville, he had whipped himself forward, writing in his diary: "Spirit! Spirit! Courage!"

In the face of present discouragement he must keep his nerve. While not unheedful of what the critics said, he must be undismayed. He must continue faithful to his creative purpose.

Here, though, he ran up against an adversary. In his rise to fame a certain public self had been forced on him by his audiences: the entertainer with a bawl like Billy Sunday's, the antic performer of higher vaudeville who seven years back had romped out of obscurity, bursting with bottled-up songs and ready to crack at the seams with an energy that had never found outlet. By 1920 he had outgrown that Vachel. He would as soon be encased in medieval armor or a plaster cast all over, and yet his living self went on at every public appearance aping the dead one.

He had gone to England prancing and shouting. It was not his poems, it was the caricature of a personality his whole heart was set on shucking off that had made the hit over there, he now believed.

He underestimated in his self-revulsion the critical acumen of Englishmen like Edward Davison, his host at Cambridge, who wrote of his poetry, "Lindsay has felt the pulse of the American heart, identified himself with its beat . . ." and of Masefield who, having read *General Booth and Other Poems,* said of him quite simply: "He is the best American poet."

Conscious of his need for change, Lindsay had tried to think of his trip to England as the wind-up of his reciting life. Then it would be home to Springfield forever, and those who still wanted to hear him could come to Springfield. He had fixed in his mind January 1, 1921, as the date when he would quit the road.

But he could not quit, he discovered on his arrival home. Quitting was out of the question till he had paid his debts. In the past twelve months all his books together had brought him $500, which was their best income yet, but he couldn't live on it.

In January 1920 he had given his mother $400 toward keeping up the property. In June he had privately reissued *The Village Magazine* in a second edition, enlarged by much new material. As a means of getting square again with his essential aims, the gesture was immensely satisfying, but there was only one way he knew to meet the heavy printing bill. Finally, he had paid his mother's fare to England and back, and that little excursion had turned out to be all honors and $1500 in the hole.

He went East this spring and by May 1921 was in New York, appearing publicly just often enough to keep afloat. Looking back, he was to remember 1919 as the year that had been his peak in public recognition. The honors accorded him in that year "were really," said Lindsay, "astronomical," and the glory carried over into 1920. This spring of 1921 he noticed just a little let-down, a recession of the bustle and attention that used to greet him in New York from its high-water mark. Yet those friends and editors in the literary world who understood him were every one good and loyal, he reported to Harriet Monroe. He "had no enemies."

His struggle was entirely inside himself. There was a struggle going on, though. Ever since returning from England he had felt in an oddly low state of vitality, crying easily and getting silly and excited over nothing much. While he assured Harriet that this spring he was taking things casually and not "being on the make," in his diary (as once before, in 1909) he noted just the opposite: that it was personal ambition that was turning his life barren and that he detected a sharpening of his appetite for worldly success, an eagerness pointing to degeneration of soul for "the mere checker-game of literary prominence."

"I suppose there is no living human being who more hates the formula of his yesterday," he complained to Harriet, reminding her how when they first met, in 1913, he had finished his last water-color designs and decorative fantasies in gold, silver and silk; they lay stuffed in great packages behind the bookcase in his bedroom.

If he had had to exhibit and explain them, outgrown and dusty as they were, once a week from then till now, he would feel about them as he did about reciting. Except when immediately under the intense excitement generated by facing an extraordinarily concentrated group of listeners, he had grown to dislike the very name of every poem he had recited much.

"One gets into rhyme only a self that is long dead. I do not like that Vachel very well. What then am I?"

It began to seem to him that he had missed his way. He could see where the road branched and he had taken the unlucky turning. As twenty years earlier he had written home from Hiram his revolutionary letter, explaining how it was a necessity of his very soul to be free of the formal education meant to mould scholars ("I do not care to be such a one, I cannot be such a one"), so now to Harriet he wrote passionately: "I do not want to be the slave of past performances or habits, I cannot endure to be such a slave, *I care not what the apparent praise or reward.* I am a dead man in my own eyes, and the only resurrection is in the new vista."

There was a point in his life to which he must return and the return would be a going forward. Again his soul was in revolt, his creative impulse struggled for freedom. He must go back to the time of dedication. He must join hands with the Vachel of the years before 1913: the young prophet who stood at night on the great bridge, the tramp by the long trail's border, the preacher of the gospel of beauty.

It was the past seven years that were yesterday. Out of his visions from the days when visions came to him he would build the new dream and write the new song.

PART FIVE

SORROW AND LOVE

50

One region of his country Lindsay did not yet know, a region of pine trees, purple lakes, and snow-capped mountains: the massive, magnificent Northwest. In the summer of 1921 he tramped for six weeks through the northwestern wilds, in Glacier National Park in Montana, then crossing the Canadian border in Waterton Lakes Park. With him went Stephen Graham, the English writer and world traveler.

He had first asked John Masefield to come hiking with him. Masefield was famous for having shipped aboard a tramp steamer and written up the exploit in *Dauber*. He had been one and twenty then. He was five and forty now, and at Lindsay's proposal seemed to turn pale.

"That's all behind me," he murmured.

Privately, Lindsay was afraid his own endurance was not what it used to be. No sooner were he and Graham out in the open, away from the crowds in the tourist-filled lodges and chalets of Glacier Park, than he was suffused with the old vagabond happiness: his step bounded and he exulted that he had never felt so free. Before the day was over, though, he realized that he, Vachel, the ambler across prairies, was simply not in the same class with Graham, who was thirty-five, had legs long as a grenadier guard's—he towered over Lindsay—absolute courage and infinite stamina. It was Graham who took the lead, with Lindsay scrambling a quarter of a mile behind, looking like a bright-eyed, red-faced gnome and when the breath was in him calling plaintively, across rock slides and precipices: "Stee-ven, wait for little Vachel!"

Only when they stopped to rest beside the thundering waterfalls did he have the advantage. He had had hog-calling ancestors. Graham, a gentle-voiced giant, could no more than listen while Lindsay, whose stentorian tones topped the roar of the falls, shouted poetry and cried excitedly—though, as Graham reminded him, they two and God were the only ones present—how strong was his belief in national parks and forest reserves as the natural cathedrals of America, and in the power of the wilderness to restore the soul.

They climbed to the Great Divide, where, according to Lindsay, every raindrop split asunder, spurting half east, half west. High in the mountains he drew whimsical world maps and hid them in hollow trees; he hid impromptu verses. But as they began in earnest to ascend the sheer peaks with Indian names, like Rising Wolf and Red Eagle, though outwardly gay and intrepid, he was sometimes inwardly quaking with fatigue and fear to a degree not distantly suspected by Graham.

On a bare ledge swept by icy winds at the summit of Red Eagle, while Graham beside him slumbered imperturbably, Lindsay sat awake and bolt upright the whole night, and when next morning they clambered down hand over hand, clinging to the rock-wall of a dizzy drop of water, grasping at projecting branches, touching the stones below with groping foot, reaching out to clutch a lower branch and thus terrifyingly swinging themselves forward, Lindsay—so much he admitted later, though never to Graham—felt himself "nearly *gone*."

Toward the end of his life, doing what he called "chasing Mister Dollar," he often reflected when things got hardest that one pursuit had been harder still, and that was chasing Stephen Graham up and down the Rockies—"Stephen hadn't the remotest notion how desperate I was."

Had Masefield then been in the right with his prudent refusal, his decision to hug middle age and stay below?

Not so; as the two adventurers approached at sunset the crest of their next mountain, which the Indians call "Going-to-the-Sun," while the explorer climbed onward toward the height, the poet stood where he was for a breathing space, looking out on the wide, flaming sky, and it seemed to him that beyond the heaven-touching crags and among the molten, glowing cloud shapes he saw the shadowy form of Johnny Appleseed, reading in his inspired book and praying over the western wilderness.

The sun dropped down, and it was as if the hoops of a great cask burst and a storm of crimson fruit rolled toward him. His eyes were opened as of old to the perception of splendor:

> to clouds of glory and strange homes
> Above the mountain tops for cloud-born souls:—
> Reproofs for men who build the world like moles,
> Models for men, if they would build the world
> As Johnny Appleseed would have it done—
> Praying, and reading the books of Swedenborg
> On the mountain top called "Going-To-the-Sun."

Vachel's mother had wondered where he would get the money for the railroad tickets to Glacier Park and the equipment for his climb, confiding in her letters to Olive that "Vachel does not like me to mention 'money' in his presence, he thinks it sordid."

In the spring, while away on tour, he had sent her more than $800 to help with taxes on the property. Always he helped when he could. But his boast this year to Olive that "since about 1913 I have paid all my expenses, at home and away from home, have bought for *Mama everything* she wanted Papa would not buy" is belied by his mother's words. Repeatedly she complained of his carefree borrowing. And after his return from the park in September, bringing Graham to Springfield with him, he had again to borrow money from her who had small means to lend.

"He asks for it with as little concern as a child for its dinner," she wrote.

Yet he was tender, "very tender," to her and in fairness she added that "if his mind were not entirely filled with his own work, I suppose he would not succeed as he does. You know, he is a genius, but—he needs me all the time. By careful mental suggestion I can check his erratic schemes to some extent."

Olive and Joy had protested that she was too lenient. But they both, she pointed out, had their own homes and interests. *"I am all Vachel has as his own*, and this is his *home.*"

Lindsay unwrapped for Graham his dusty packages of old drawings, mosaics of colored cloth and paper, and "Map of the Universe," and spread them on the living-room floor. His mother, entering unexpectedly, inadvertently trod on some of the precious things—*"deliberately,"* exclaimed her son long afterward in one of his spasms of savage reminiscence.

The house was a colder place since his father had died, and in November he left again on tour. Knowing Graham had deepened his ideas of travel. The Englishman, whose splendid nerves were never jaded, eagerly looked out for and philosophically related to one another, wherever he went, the *souls* of regions and races. He had evolved what the impressionable Lindsay, with suddenly recovered fervor for touring, began to interpret as "a wonderful doctrine of world and spiritual geography, representing in many ways my new start in life."

He now decided to take a holiday from writing for an entire year and to pour his creative energy into a reciting tour that should range over America and into Canada and be a spiritual search for the *"national* and *Anglo-Saxon* picture."

So he excitedly put it to Armstrong, into whose lap he dropped the tedious details.

Yet the climb with Graham had exhausted him. All fall he had felt tired. In several letters sent back from the road his handwriting showed an ominous, if temporary, alteration; it was sprawling and uncontrolled. His tone also was changing. Since the war there had been a wave of immigrants and he, who once preached that the first requisite for Americans is to "have a big heart for alien men," at this time set it down in his diary that his very first act in applying his doctrine of geography to America would be to "send back to Europe the dregs of Europe, the weak, the unabsorbed, the disloyal," and the next best step would be to "build a fence against all comers."

By New Year's he had reached the west coast, having recited all along his way to audiences that almost swamped him (2500 at the University of Colorado, and elsewhere from 1400 to 1700). At Mills College in Oakland, he gave a recital preceded by dinner in his honor in the college dining room. Seated at the right hand of the president, he had on his own right a little blonde girl, a junior, who had been selected as his dinner partner because of her high marks in English. Their halting conversation strayed to the subject of honeymoons, Lindsay's young neighbor shyly mentioning a bridal couple she once read about who went far into the desert. A strange place to choose, agreed the poet, with a blandness of manner that made her feel snubbed; she could not know it was protective armor.

"Wherever I go," he had written in his diary only a few weeks before, "they bring forth their beautiful girl as their sign and symbol and I look in her face an instant and then am gone. But I kiss one face in my dreams as the years go by. Forever a person—she is never a vision—but a girl alone on the earth, and the crowd and its hum are gone. Oh when will I speak to her?"

He was in Seattle when he had a telegram from Joy, who had rushed down to Springfield from Cleveland, saying their mother was dangerously ill. Mrs. Lindsay had caught a chill, which turned to pneumonia. She died that same day, February 1, 1922, though her son did not know of her death when, after notifying Armstrong to cancel his next engagements, he left Seattle to hurry home.

But the moment he heard she was ill, terror entered his heart. His hostility against her whom of all he loved most ("This creature known as my mother," he called her once) dissolved into shame and sorrow. In his diary that day he wrote:

For with bitter pride my heart is aching,
Pride has undone me,
Pride overwhelms me,
Pride is a sea that would utterly drown me.

Not till he reached Chicago did he learn his mother was gone, but all the way east on the train he racked his memory and imagination for what he could set down of the young woman who had been still painting when he first knew her, and meant her son to be an artist and protected him in her arms from Doctor Mohawk.

He had been seven when she lost his three small sisters.

She was never afterward the same, and the years that counted most in his affection for her were the first six of his life. But almost he could remember the young girl she had been before he was born, "raised on a farm but a real lady," who always and only was the one he looked for.

51

Even while he clung to the vivid memories of his mother, soon to fade, for all that love could do to hold them, there came to him a mortal loneliness. "It seems utterly impossible to go on without her," he wrote to Olive.

Only a week after his wild dash home, he resumed his interrupted tour. Yet if for a time his courage held, so that to Armstrong he continued to propose great and daring plans, the infection of Graham's enthusiasm was no longer in him.

"My life is most desolate without Mama, and nothing seems worth doing without her to report to. Joy is quite determined I shall marry and live in the old house," he went on to Olive, "but I have no girl and no income to take care of such a place. The only way I can live and keep ahead is to travel."

Everywhere this spring his halls were packed, absorbing the limit of his strength, with often the very platform crowded. The newspapers, especially west of the Mississippi, gave him acres of space. But too often it was not the best space, he noted critically. Write-ups of his show and interviews with him were shoved off on the society page with the lounge lizards and cake-eaters. After he had recited at almost any businessmen's luncheon to an audience intolerant of anything serious, the editor of the local sheet, if present, always said the same thing: "Mr. Lindsay, *I* didn't understand a word, but MY WIFE is president of the women's club and she likes to pet the poets. We he-men are all in politics."

"The issues of poetry *are* political *issues!*" Lindsay pointed out.

He was writing to Armstrong, and he proposed a new method of campaigning by which Armstrong would enlist, weeks ahead of Lindsay's arrival in a town, the real, meditative interest of that local editor who, in the sense that he ran the newspaper, owned the mind of the place and who, if he hadn't read a book since college, must somehow be induced to read all eight of Lindsay's.

He would find they had in them as much and lively politics as the Democratic and Republican national platforms.

He, Lindsay, had things just as vital to say to Americans as Bryan or Hughes or Hoover.

But though he was willing to go first, his dream was for others to come after him, for an army of poets—trained to win audiences as the doughboys in France to fight—to take to the lecture-road, preaching the gospel of beauty, teaching through their poems the love of God and, because the issues of poetry are root issues, being campaigned for in every city by civic-minded people as hard and spectacularly as any candidate for mayor or senator.

His dream went further: Roosevelt, for example, under his boyish disguise of a Rough Rider, was "first, last and always," said Lindsay, "a 'literary' statesman, as much a scholar as Confucius, making the scholar and student in politics possible."

And if Lindsay and Armstrong could make the American public see poets as wise and virile men, their emergence as statesmen and governors of the land would follow.

"We are planning not an economic, but an Art Revolution. We must make this a *Republic of Letters!* It is far more important that artists and poets should be in power and displace the present business caste than that their particular views should be right.

"The unwritten law should be 'only artists should hold high office.' "

In his Uncle Johnson's house in Los Angeles in 1912, alternating between despair of himself and hope for the universe, Lindsay had set down in one mighty outflow his noble "Proclamations" about the Church of Beauty in America, prophesying that one day the nation's hurrying crowds would become audiences and her restless mobs assemblies "delicate of spirit," and that this would come to pass through three kinds of inspired citizens acting in wise cooperation: spiritual leaders like England's General Booth; devoted statesmen in the tradition of Washington, Jefferson and Lincoln; and lastly the artists, of whom—"they shall fuse the work of these other workers," Lindsay cried. "We shall have Shelleys with a heart for religion, Ruskins with a comprehension of equality.

"*Religion, equality* and *beauty*! By these America shall come into a glory that shall justify the yearning of the sages for her perfection and the prophecies of the poets, when she was born in the throes of Valley Forge."

For ten years he had been waiting for the man who would make his proclamations into more than mere trumpet blasts. That he was not that man he knew. He was a monk, he was a dreamer. "Mine," he told Armstrong, "is another star."

But the direction America had followed lately was not that of which he dreamed and sang. America's entry into the League of Nations, the nearest approach yet to Lindsay's world government, had been scotched at the outset. By 1922, with Harding elected President on the slogan "Back to Normalcy," the country, having thankfully slipped the restraints and let slide the idealism of war, had embarked on the tremendous, spiraling spree of prosperity that characterized the twenties, the decade that brought forth in literature Lewis' *Babbitt* and Mencken's *homo boobiens*—a time of downgrading and debunking, of tycoons and bootleggers, jazz-babies and expatriates, an era of gaiety, fever and doom, among whose inspired spokesmen were young F. Scott Fitzgerald, John Dos Passos, Ernest Hemingway and T. S. Eliot.

It was definitely not the era of Vachel Lindsay.

"I am a 100 per cent American in deadly opposition to George Horace Lorimer and H. L. Mencken," he wrote in his diary this year. "The magazines *Saturday Evening Post* and *Smart Set* represent the most distinctive forces against which I am most definitely and clearly in opposition and whose opposition makes my own position clearer. I am for Santa Fé, and the saints, and romantic love."

Primarily it seemed to him, this first sad spring after his mother's death, that it was his home town in which he was now wholly out of place. He had never found his "set" in Springfield; his invisible companions there were the dead (like those farm boys killed in the Civil War, his girl-mother's earliest sweethearts) or perhaps the unborn.

Nearly all his living intimates had left and absolutely no new ones appeared. "The only way to find my real and private self, and my Springfield, seems to be to hunt them to the ends of the earth. I am subject to the persecution of dowagers and rank plutocrats if I return. Any effort to get intimate only gets one cheap enemies. . . ."

Again this was in his diary. But only the year before he had had "no enemies," he told Harriet Monroe.

While at home for his mother's funeral, he had caught a racking cough and on his travels ever since—hurried from train to hotel room, from town to city and city to state—felt more and more ill. At the end of March his memory failed him completely in the middle of a recital, the first time such a thing had happened. In May, reciting down at Baylor, he was a guest in the house of the Armstrongs but was so harassed and unsettled that he was not himself and his behavior called for an apology, or he thought it did.

Afterward he sent a line penitently begging Mrs. Armstrong's pardon for his burst of rudeness "about Harvard and so forth, and about ladies."

He was just on his way to Harvard to read the Phi Beta Kappa poem at the Commencement Exercises, having written for the occasion *Bob Taylor's Birthday*, which celebrated the late whimsical governor of Tennessee at the end of the last century.

Robert Love Taylor, the "Tennessee Orpheus," used in that simpler, sweeter day to rock in a rocking chair in his office in the State House, play "Old Hundred" and "Money Musk" on his fiddle on the campaign platform, and make wonderfully florid Chautauqua speeches. Lindsay describes him as fiddling and rocking eternally in a great blue rocking chair in the heavens, a symbol to practical-minded America of the poet and artist in a high seat of government.

But both the poem and Lindsay's recital of it, delivered with an epic earnestness, with much booming, striding and gesticulating, which like Taylor's sky-painting oratory would have soared under Chautauqua canvas, sank in the Harvard Yard.

Even so had Springfield received *The Congo*, but Springfield was his own.

In his diary, in words that bit the page, he wrote: "I was born with a snobbery that would make a Harvard professor turn pale with anguish and envy! My people since Noah were not only important but self-important. I do not need to have my pure scorn diluted by the more mongrel scorn of Harvard. Ha!"

No, never, he would never understand New England, said Lindsay. Boston especially remained an enigma; since 1916 he had breezed into that gray city annually to have descend on him in every school and drawing room "the Boston snub"—to have Amy Lowell out in Brookline "give me a dinner, call me a 'middle westerner' and look me over for a fresh attack. . . . My hair is not yet grown in again from her reiterated scalpings."

It was after his visit to Harvard that he finished his sardonic poem *So Much the Worse for Boston*, telling of a gentleman from the Hub who, imprudently adventuring in the mountains of far Colorado—site of the Lindsay camp—meets the tigerish talking cat of the Rockies, a beast that shuts one humorous eye and confides that it has often dreamed of old Boston—that eastern city wild and free, where eagles soar above Copley Square, young Salem witches ride the plains and the forest ranger, a reader of Thoreau by the waves of Walden, shoots cattle thieves, lumber thieves and train robbers.

"And then," says Lindsay's Bostonian,

I contradicted him, in a manner firm
and flat.
"I have never heard, in the cultured Hub, of
rowdy men like that."
"So much the worse for Boston," said the Rocky
Mountain cat.

All spring Lindsay had been troubled not only by his cough,
but by what he called "fly-wheels" whirring in his head
and by the violent jumps his heart gave after a recital.
He spent the late summer in New York, holed up through
August and part of September at the Hotel Commodore, where
isolation and cold showers soon stopped the wheels and slowed
his pulse.

But it was now that he became aware unmistakably of what
had not been noticeable on the road: that as a literary figure
he was no longer fashionable and as a public figure no longer
news. There was a cooling off in the quality of attention
shown him in Manhattan newspaper offices and editors' waiting rooms. He was forty-two and famous, and yet the current
of affairs in the world of letters, which in 1914 had caught
him up and whose crest he had ridden ever since, was sweeping
by without him.

Later he was to set 1922 as the year when almighty New
York first "slapped his face," lifted to it with his old confiding-
ness. "All I ever wanted was to be friends," he wrote sadly
then.

In the chill galleries of the Metropolitan Museum he renewed his study of Egypt. Once the great doors swung to
behind him, the bright hot pavements, swarming motor cars
and hard foreign-looking faces of the postwar city were left
behind, while the ancient past endured, balm for hurt vanity.
But in the streets the gold of modern Babylon that glittered
when he was young seemed tarnished. He went by himself
to the Ziegfeld Follies, the Follies of 1922, a brummagem
spectacle, of which, as he wrote in his diary, "the only finally
thrilling things were Will Rogers—and he looked like a kept
cowboy, *once* glorious—and the girl dressed as an idealized

Indian for the Hiawatha song. These seemed reminiscent of better days."

He was writing in his hotel room. Alone between prowlings he locked himself in, surrounded by books on Egyptology, which he had almost gone broke buying, and his letters were cheerful.

"I am exercising the egotism of the polar bear who bit a nick in the North Pole with no one there to notice it," he jauntily assured Mrs. Moody. "The bear says 'To Gehenna with those circus bears! I am just as well off right here!'"

Yet his diary this lonely summer tells a different tale. In his room in the great hotel in the unheeding city there broke over him wave after wave of a loneliness under which his spirit cringed.

> Though fallen on evil days,
> On evil days though fallen, and evil tongues,
> In darkness, and with dangers compassed round
> And solitude—

In his diary he transcribed the lines, a crash of somber chords, and a few pages farther on other lines, elfin, wistful,

> Sing me the song I delighted to hear,
> Long long ago, long long ago.

"Homer, blind and old, sang of Troy," Lindsay continued, "but the real battle was not between Greeks and Trojans. The battle was between the sweet memories of youth and the weariness of age. And so the war in heaven of Milton was the war between youth and old age in him. Satan was old age and fear and weariness."

And of himself he wrote: "The mantles of verse and speaking that have been wished upon me have become an intolerable burden and have hardened around me like plaster of Paris cast around a broken skeleton."

52

Lindsay liked to quote the limerick about the old monk of Siberia who

Sprang from his cell
With a hell of a yell,

which was what he did himself after a period of being alone, so that his friends would almost never credit him with any real desire for solitude.

With a hell of a yell he sprang from his room at the Commodore. In October 1922 he was back on the road, superficially so buoyant and refreshed that at the end of November he reported glowingly to Armstrong of his triumphal tour of Canada, just completed, of the excitement and the brand-new friends ("I dearly love the Canadian people!"), and he urged that he and Armstrong make their grand assault next on Australia, New Zealand and South Africa.

Only three weeks later the glow had departed, the refreshment worn off, the buoyancy gone flat. From Oklahoma City, where he was exhaustedly finding refuge in a hotel room with his telephone off the hook and his door barred, he wrote to Mrs. Moody to tell her that his autumn tour, though completely successful, had been *grueling*. "I here complain that Armstrong undertakes too much and drives me too hard."

So much travel had become a blur, and his audiences had grown to demand of him just two poems, *General Booth* and *The Congo*, that stood for one year of his life, his thirty-fourth, and he was forty-three this last month and had it in

304

him to write a new poem every day, if let alone. "As it is nine
years of my life are gone—my best writing years—simply
used up in shouting."

For when he had a respite, it was impossible to start his
engines of creating the very first moment. Sometimes the
process took weeks, months, during which he needed to sit
in his room with his jaw tied—"my work is *based* on privacy,
on long lonely studies."

Instead, he must be always on the move, must cart about
with him a suitcase crammed with notes, never developed and
yet to which, as the United States went by outside his train
window, he was constantly adding. There were notes for
"a big *detailed* meditative song—Lindsay's 'American Commonwealth'—about every state."

There were notes "on the odor of coffee in New Orleans,
sweeping up from the alleys," and "on eating breakfast on the
roofs of the Texas hotels, the cool breeze in a hot country and
the magnificent view."

"I hear them all calling," he declared in his diary. " 'Write
me a song,' calls the river—the headlight—the steam boat—
the little girl, the little boy. But I am whirling on, though my
heart aches with unwritten song and the Pullman rolls on."

Pictures, too, were kicking to come out of him. He felt
within him, ready to emerge, his "Congo among pictures."
He had signed with Appleton, who was Graham's publisher,
for the spring publication of some poems based on his climb
with Graham, which he had illustrated with pen-and-ink designs. Also in the spring his *Collected Poems*, with an autobio-
graphical preface, was to be published by Macmillan. His hope
was that the two new books would turn the flank of recent
criticism by acquainting the public with the person he really
was, the Vachel fond of Milton and George Washington.

He reminded himself that "every human shout has along
with it an unheard whisper for the inner ear," and what he
longed to do in his poems was "to give the shout *and* the
whisper, with the whisper remaining after the shout is gone."

The current illusory jazzy notion of him derived from his eagerness in his first year of reciting, after he had for so long faced contempt. Yet it was as hard to endure as the contempt. The very word "jazz" meant leer to him. It meant "midnight dirt and a sad morning after," and "if the rhythms and songs I teach people," Lindsay exclaimed, "do not build up toward the sky and stars, the sun and the moon, they are surely vain."

Especially he deplored being stamped a jazz poet in England, where reviewers used the term as "something synonymous with hysteria, shrieking and fidgets." He had been positively caricatured in some English papers as "in a state of jazz epilepsy or apoplexy."

"Now there must be something in my work that I do not myself understand," he somberly admitted, "that provokes this kind of extreme treatment of me."

So much he acknowledged to Harriet Monroe, in a letter of December 3, though to his other Harriet, writing on December 22, he made no such concession. Rather he raged, to Mrs. Moody: "I am nobody's pink-toed Cupid and nobody's yokel, however I may appear that way, and nobody's busy little jazzer."

"What then do I call myself?" he asked, this time in his diary, and he answered: "I call myself, in my private sanctum, alone in my room in the strange hotel almost anywhere in the United States—I call myself a student of United States and Egyptian hieroglyphics, and there I sit drawing them."

He had never called himself a poet. Sandburg was the poet. Frost was the poet. Masefield was the poet. It was his *adventures* that he loved.

"The world has not yet broken me," he reflected, then, doubling on his thought, added: "Certainly it may break me tomorrow, or my own soul, for a man's own soul becomes his final prison."

It was in January 1923 that the tide of Lindsay's fortunes, which for ten years had seemed a rising tide, turned. His tour was cut short as his health gave way under the combined strains of hard travel, of what had become to him the falseness of the personality he carried on his back, and of a disability as yet undiagnosed.

For weeks he had had the sensation of being pursued—like a mouse by a cat, up, up to the top of a high tower. Yet each time the moment came to step off into air—to walk out on the platform—all his courage instantly revived. Every new audience worked on him like alcohol; he met it in a wave of love and pleasure. Every friend he had seemed a conspirator to whip him into one more performance. But what none realized who heard him recite was that he paid for every ounce of steam expended with fits of vertigo, black depression and then such dazed dullness that he could hardly catch his train.

He spent Christmas Day in Waco, again as a guest of the Armstrongs. Afterward he considered it was on that fatal day that he caught the flu, which was ripening in him forty-eight hours later when to Armstrong, writing from the train on his way to El Paso, he had again to apologize for being rude, for having "shouted" at his host and hostess, this time some rough remarks about his family, notably his mother. "I only want to say that I enormously respect and revere my mother's memory but she was never the mushy mellow and rabbitlike mother that appears in all movies."

In El Paso, barely an hour after reciting, he suddenly collapsed and stayed in bed for the next three weeks—either in a hotel bed or his Pullman berth, for he continued to travel— every moment when he was not actually on the stage.

It was not just the flu. "Touring is killing me," he protested to Armstrong. "I am getting old and burnt out, body, mind and imagination. This treadmill is simply wrecking me."

Yet because even now when he faced an audience he still joyfully lavished his last inch of strength, he was his own betrayer and must put himself beyond temptation.

"Help me in this, my dear friend," he appealed.

Since El Paso, where, ironically, everyone congratulated him on his health and show of spirits, he had had "some very serious danger signals." "If I am to live, I *must go slow*. There is a hereditary curse knocking mighty hard at the door, and knocking with an increasing frequency, I assure you."

His lungs were sore. He had earache, toothache, but this was not all; this was "not half," he told Armstrong.

He was not more specific, but in view of later medical findings, it is probable his most serious symptoms were nervous ones. Now he suggested that his engagements after March 2, 1923, be postponed for a year and his price for each future appearance on a less grilling schedule be raised to $250.

To this Armstrong in his turn suggested, not without sarcasm, that if a poet who often before had complained of weariness and then recovered, could somehow "live through" his March commitments—as was only fair to the organizations—it might certainly be as well for him to finish his season at the end of March. It might then be as well for him to seek another manager. His present manager was sure he couldn't place him at $250 an appearance.

"Just as soon kill me as not," Lindsay scrawled in the margin of Armstrong's letter.

On January 29 he recited near Gulfport, Mississippi, at Gulf Park Junior College for girls, whose president, Dr. Richard Cox, had been at Hiram with him. Lively and antic in the girls' eyes, he showed himself behind the scenes to be feverish, distraught and so near a complete breakdown that Dr. Cox insisted he cancel by telegram his remaining engagements (some twenty, for which Lindsay would have received $4000) and then put him to bed in his own quarters, where Mrs. Cox nursed him.

53

It was a relief unutterable to let go. When his old friend invited him to stay on for a time at Gulf Park, teaching a small class in poetry, Lindsay was near crying with gratitude.

"Here I am more dead than alive," he wrote on February 1 to Witter Bynner, who once had warned him he was courting just such disaster. "I am almost a waif on this beach, wondering if I will ever be well and rested again.

"I have had a perfectly enormous education in the map of the United States, and for this knowledge I have certainly traded the two best years of my life and perhaps most of my brains forever.

"As long as my strength held out, Armstrong was the ideal *driver*. I must not censure him now, for *I* trained him. And I dimly remember I expected him to drive me till I broke. I wanted to break like a wave on the rock of the United States!

"I have given my heart to thousands and thousands and thousands of beautiful people, and I have certainly parted with many a town where I wanted to kiss them all goodby they were so good to me and parting was so hard. But in the end, such tears wash body and soul and brain to nothingness—like loving the sea too long."

At the college doorstep lay the Gulf of Mexico and he spent hours sitting on the sand, turning to the actual sea for strength. He was dangerously depressed this spring, and it was now that there rose to the surface of his behavior ominous signs of a change that had been taking place in him ever since his mother's death, and perhaps even before, the change from loving to hating.

As a boy, Lindsay called all men his friends. "Vachel," said his mother, "is never jealous of anyone, always sees the good in everyone."

As a rising poet, he remained outside the literary factions "that try to get me by two legs and one arm and pull me into bleeding pieces." The success of a fellow poet gave him only joy. "Carl is getting to be one of our pillars of state and I am *for* him," he told Mrs. Moody in 1917, when Sandburg seemed likely to outstrip him as the singer of the Midwest.

Though Conrad Aiken's scarifying review of *The Chinese Nightingale* had wounded him deeply, a few years from its appearance he sent Aiken a letter so genial, generous and unresentful that the younger poet was astounded.

And after the death in 1919 of Theodore Roosevelt, in whose later actions, he, Lindsay, had been disappointed— "Come now," he wrote in his diary,

> let us forgive the dead
> As we expect to be forgiven
> When we are in that ditch,
> After long sickness, hid away.

This was the true Vachel. But few who knew him were aware of the seriousness, or even the existence, of the disorder with which he struggled in his last years. Events contributed to undermine him, as when the challenge of the war shook his faith in himself and the disparagement of his work that began to be widespread shook his courage.

Then had come his mother's death, and with it a terrible uprooting. He had no longer his special place but was cast forth into a world that loved him with no personal love.

By 1923 it began to seem to him that, where once he had no enemies, there existed now a snide clique ("fanatical exponents of Balkan and Eastern European ideals") in whose eyes it was enough to damn him that he loved the United States at all. Writing to Harriet Monroe from Gulf Park on March 28, he told her that "those who hate 'Americanism' rejoice exceedingly and say I have written myself out."

Granted that his programs were made up principally of things written from seven to ten years ago, it was seven to ten years ago that his touring began and increased in momentum almost in spite of him. Already, after a few weeks' rest, he had begun to consider the travel and reciting, which no longer ago than January he complained were killing him, a magnificent justification of his life. In sensitive denial of what was in truth his fear—that his great deeds were behind him—he recalled to Harriet how he had chanted his poems in every state in the Union, how the major American universities had asked him back two to four times and how he had appeared in western Canada and at Oxford, Cambridge and the University of London, in spite of which—he furiously charged—"those who wish me ill anyway say I am '*written out.*' People who have not been on a college campus for years say I have disappeared, say I am 'written out.'

"I am 'written out' in the eyes of those who . . . are still inhabiting in imagination some small Balkan state and hating and slandering us all like poison when we admit we love our own.

"Well, I have met young America and am willing to meet the depreciation of my enemies with this boast. I have *met* the United States and they have *not.*

"In the last seven years I have recited for hundreds of high-school assemblies. They are nearly all two thousand strong and as hard to control as Texas cattle. I have met and addressed hundreds of thousands of dazzlingly beautiful boys and girls, from fourteen to twenty years old, and I am not ashamed to say the experience was profoundly intoxicating, they roared like a sea in heaven every time I addressed them.

"Everywhere there was beauty and glory and the blazing heart of Young America. Everywhere there was love and kindness, and not one word of poison insinuation, of literary spite or silly rivalry, or technical chatter, or social snobbery, or cheap race-hate. They were all young!

"Now that I come to land, after crossing this great sea, I am supposed to give an account of myself. I find all sorts of spite among the beachcombers.

"Well, here is the account. Let them make the most of it. I am in fighting trim. Let them look to themselves!"

54

When Lindsay cut short his tour, he owed no man a cent but nearly everything he earned had gone right back into train fare and hotel bills. He had $2500 in the bank and hoped to hang onto it till he could get out in book form a real "thousand-page successor" to *The Village Magazine.*

"It is better to go broke," he wrote in his diary this year, "than to 'make' money. It is better to sell one's patrimony than plan large schemes with money the goal. The best way is to live hand-to-mouth, *never quite* broke."

Early in April 1923 he went to the Gulfport hospital for a sinus operation, after which his mind, though fagged, grew clearer, his rage subsided, his spirits were brighter than in many a day and the writing of poems, which for months had been beyond his strength, especially of that master poem about America, his "American Commonwealth," seemed possible again.

He bought himself some white linen suits and in these, not without self-consciousness, appeared on the jasmine-scented campus of Gulf Park, where the girls from Mississippi, Tennessee and Alabama, who had been quite excited by his coming and were full of talk at his staying on, sat at his feet demurely. If they were not very strong in the literary line, they made up for it by the glitter of their eyes and unfailing coquetry of their manners. To Lindsay they were all "girls of steel and fire,"

Steel virtue,
Hollywood desire,

and of his little class of seniors, which met four times a week,
he wrote:

I read St. John's Revelation
While you made your revelations
Of garters in set stations
With glances that would paralyze the nations.

The average age of Gulf Park students was seventeen. Their
voices stroked his midwestern ear. They spoke that "slow,
elaborate Southern tongue," he declared. They pronounced
roller "rolah." They thought that Ostermoor rhymed with
Omaha. Outdoors they did graceful archery, swam off the
college pier jutting far out into the Gulf, and on the strip of
white beach joined hands and danced in a circle under the
moon.

Young things whose every motion is a rhyme,

wrote the poet among them.

In fine weather Lindsay's classes were held on a railed
wooden platform, with stairs going up to it, which was built
into the lower limbs of one of the spreading campus live oaks.
Here, in the last period of the afternoon, he discussed with
his small group of picked students the poems of Milton, Poe,
Lanier, Whitman and Masefield, read aloud the Book of Revelation—his voice thundering through the leafy branches—read
Fitzgerald's *Omar Khayyam* (one baby Venus asked if he
wrote it) and told the epic story of the rise of the New Poetry
in remote Chicago, which to these girls was like the Wars of
Troy.

He had intended to stay at Gulf Park only a few weeks. In
the end, he taught there for more than a year. It was after his
first four months that, in a letter of June 1 to Frederic Melcher,

he paid fervent tribute to "Zimmie" Cox as "the man who saved my life," and added, "I am completely well and have begun to write again."

The concentration was the thing. Since writing the poems that made him famous, he had become such a glittering generality he was like a box of last year's Christmas tree baubles. Yet sometimes now in his quiet room, from where, after seven in the evening, not even a street car was to be heard, he worked all night till the cool of dawn.

It was here that he wrote *Doctor Mohawk*, his fierce memorial to his father. He was having frequent physical examinations. "I should know the doctors better," he noted in his diary, "for they are in touch with the bleeding side of life. I remember the blood on my father's cuffs."

A year earlier Tut-ankh-amen's tomb had been discovered, so that Egypt, long his private passion, was currently the rage —college girls wore scarab bracelets and hats with bands of hieroglyphics—and it was at Gulf Park that he began his poem *The Trial of the Dead Cleopatra in Her Beautiful and Wonderful Tomb*.

Just before his breakdown it had seemed to him his salvation would be to go back to all he once preached in *A Handy Guide for Beggars*; it was only when living the beggar's life that he could write at all. Yet when at Gulf Park he reread that little book, he found it hard to believe he had ever written it, his background had become so unspeakably different. "Now the eternal sound in my ears is of cheering audiences, the clatter of banquet tables, the eternal rattle of flat-wheeled Pullman cars, Rotary Clubs in endless rotation, and my vanity fed on wind."

He was writing on March 21, in his weariest hour.

"I have at least found out about myself that I am unutterably arrogant, that what in me is not silly pride is unutterable personal vanity, that there is not one inch of the democrat in my natural instincts."

Truly, the pride of race, clan and opinion, and the game of playing for position were far deeper in him than he ever guessed when he composed that artless work. He had been humble then because his pride was hurt.

Royal Cleopatra, of whose trial by the Egyptian gods of death he had begun to write, stood for precisely the opposite of the ideals in *A Handy Guide*. "Because she is proud to the last beat of her heart, the gods recognize the unkillable principle and give her immortality. By the imaginary and successful pomps of this queen I cure my own vanity and ease my heart of its megalomaniac ambition. Thus I have done penance for all the profession of humility and overstrain at humility which is the key to *A Handy Guide*. . . .

"The whole key to the *Litany of the Heroes*, which is the key to me, is—not 'God help us to be brave,' but literally—'God help us to be proud and vain,' with the pride and vanity of the saint, the peasant or the Caesar."

And at the very climax of his Cleopatra poem he was showing how Set, the eternal accuser, going forth to tempt Christ on a high mountain, discovers Him proof against all temptation because He is

> A son of Amon-Ra, prouder than Caesar,
> And lovelier than the young Caesarion.

"So," said Lindsay, "we go full circle, and find the saint's pride, which millions of people have mistaken for humility."

The inspiration for another new poem, *Billboards and Galleons*, came to him late one night as he walked alone below the sea boulevard: on his left stretched a bulwark of advertising hoardings and on his right the great Gulf. It was a walk that released his thoughts, especially at near midnight with the stars out and the road almost empty of automobiles.

He had been striding on the edge of the beach, wading in the edge of the waves, when a storm blew up. The storm was real enough and with it came visions: the clifflike billboards—with their Arrow collar heroes and movie queens, dazzling in the lightning flashes and washed by sea-born rain—stood for the soul of modern America that looks and longs for ideal love.

Then he saw that the storm-rocked waters on his other hand were filled with the spars and masts of wrecked Spanish galleons, that the ever-advancing waves were sculptured in the forms of drowned pirates and Spanish beauties. He heard love calls, death cries, and through them a bell tolling. Up from deep-sea regions rolled the dead Spanish legions, the ghosts of ancient Spain, of fair lost Spain, land of his ancestor Don Iphan and symbol of romantic love.

Between the opposing visions he had plunged on—"burning the world like a bridge, behind me," he wrote,

> . . . walking in water so no one could find me.

Where his refrain in *The Chinese Nightingale* had been "Sorrow and love, glory and love," now it was "Courage and sleep, sleep and courage."

"These are the principal things," said the poet.

> March, while the sad heart breaks,
> Whirl on, like a leaf, then fight again—
> Sleep and courage! Sleep and courage! The
> fate of men!

In his diary he set down the same reminder: "Courage and sleep—sleep and courage—courage and sleep."

Even as the direction of his life was changing, his heart and thought changed and in the next diary-line below he wrote: "For years and for years I could walk on alone. But now I cannot do it."

The Gulf Park maidens were "sizzling," they were "Olympian," said Lindsay. He confessed that the older he grew, the younger he liked them; when he remembered Isadora, it appeared that any girl much over sixteen always got ahead of him. On Sundays, the day that cadets from the nearby military academy called at the college in their grand uniforms, he was merely a dusty faculty member. But on other days, his pretty students "impatient for cadets and seeing Sunday far away," as he explained, "shoot arrows at me."

They begged him for the history of all his loves. Taking a girl at random on his arm he would stroll to the end of the long pier with her. But the gulf dividing them was wider than the Gulf of Mexico, till out of the mass emerged one to whom his attachment began to show a special nature. She had a slender form, small lovely hands, and immense violet eyes into which one day he chanced to look—across the whole length of the college dining room—for "one moment far too long."

More shy and more reserved than any of the others, she became of them his "tall queen," his "Queen Venus," his "eternal May Queen" whose very shadow he bent to kiss. "Sassy, proud and sweet," he called her, "provoking, proud and dear." She was his "unwritten song," his "dear poem," his "psyche-butterfly."

"Once a rhinoceros went quite wild," Lindsay wrote,

> He mixed his metaphors all day long,
> He was deeply in love with a butterfly-child.

55

Long ago on his hike to California, Lindsay had called himself Ulysses and Octavia his Penelope, being pleased to imagine that she awaited him, rejecting all others. The name of his Gulf Park love was Elizabeth Wills, but he often thought of her as Dulcinea and of himself, at forty-three, as Don Quixote. It was of her youth and springtime grace that he sang in his poem *How Dulcinea Del Toboso Is Like the Left Wing of a Bird.*

He sought her out and every day her college mailbox held a message from him, if only a flower, and he wrote to her many poems—songs, he declared ardently, to "turn her blood to glory" and from which she "would not turn away."

She did not turn away, exactly; for all her youth, she was wise and tender. But outside class, as they sat *tête-à-tête* in doubtful privacy, in a double-seated wooden swing in a far corner of the campus, Elizabeth, who was eighteen, in her senior year and from a small Tennessee town, soberly consulted Mr. Lindsay on a future independent of him: whether after she graduated she had better teach, write novels, sew clothes for the poor, be an actress, or do some one other of the great things girls of talent do.

Alone, Lindsay would seek the beach in the moonlight and stride unsteadily by the edge of the waves. More than ever before, he was obsessed with physical longing. He was tormented by the need somewhere to lay his head down, perhaps on the moon's breast ("the red moon's," he cried) if not on this girl's breast.

"He who is generally sick and then too well," he addressed

Elizabeth, writing on the flyleaf of Palgrave's *Golden Treasury*, one of his gifts to her, "he who is a changeling from the cradle, hates age and loves youth, hates haste and loves meditation, always loves beauty and hates deformity, declares himself in earnest courtship of your beauty, youth and meditative mind.

"He is famed for mere racket (yet he loves above all quietness such as yours). He loves the whole United States with desperate passion, yet he is so lost and exhausted in it the hollow of your hand is dearer."

And when they parted after Commencement Day, in June 1923, Don Quixote sent Dulcinea full year's subscriptions not only to *Life, Living Age*, the New York *Post, Punch* and the London *Mercury*, but also to one of his three press clipping bureaus. Long after their separation, fat envelopes stuffed with clippings, reports of his doings in the world, overflowed her letterbox in little Brownsville.

Lindsay spent much of this summer as he had done the last—in a hotel room, this time in Cleveland, buried in his Egyptian studies. He was occupied, too, with the writing of a preface for the second edition of his *Collected Poems*. "Adventures While Singing These Songs," he had called his witty and informative preface to the first edition, written before his breakdown. "Adventures While Preaching Hieroglyphic Sermons" was the new preface, which was eccentrically diffuse and disorganized.

In the fall he took a room in Gulfport, about a mile from the college. He had resumed his teaching and in December went north to spend the Christmas holidays in Springfield with the Wakefields, who were back from China with their children on a twelve-month furlough and were occupying the old house, which ever since his mother's death Vachel had dreaded to re-enter.

Once there, he had moments of happiness. On the bookcase in his former bedroom he displayed his photographs of Dulcinea and every night his homing thoughts, no longer held by

home, flew south, as he visualized her far away, caught up in
maiden preparations, settling her ball dress before the glass,
swaying, preening,

Flixing your feathers like a swan,
Fixing your silver slippers on.

But again, after the summer's respite, distraction and despair
were building in him. Passing through Chicago on his way to
Springfield, he had talked with alarming gloom to the ever-
valiant Mrs. Moody, who had her own troubles. To Olive
and Paul, the change in him since their last trip home, in 1918,
was simply bewildering: the desperate creature within that
now often broke forth to storm at them—in "mad rages of
temper from misunderstanding," said Olive—was another self
from the merry, gentle boy they had known under this roof
and from the dreamer who wrote the great poems.

And when in January, Lindsay went back to Gulf Park, his
outlook was altered, darkened, till it began to seem to him
as if a shadow cast by a black wing lay over the fair campus,
where seven months earlier all had smiled.

It was not only that his love had been rejected; he had
lived all his life on love rejected. It was also that he had had
great dreams for this little college, and that every one of them
in his year of residence had been knocked dully on the head.

Not a girl among his nubile students, though they were all
movie crazy, had ever read his book on the movies, much less
applied it to a single film. On May Day the college held a
charming festival at which the girls danced barefoot on the
green, but nobody listened to his proposals for poem games.
When he sent to Macmillan's for a hundred copies of *Adventures While Preaching the Gospel of Beauty* and handed
them out, everybody thanked him sweetly, but of understanding of what he had to say in that book there was not a particle.

Instead, protested Lindsay, he was "jammed into tutoring in
poetry, like any fifth-rate hack." He was without an active
ally on campus in any of his projects of the seven arts. He was
becoming as much of an Ishmaelite as ever in Springfield.

After the publicity had been skimmed off his name and the credentials won in the eastern universities were exhausted, all ten of his books, representing years of struggle, were left unopened. Indeed, the very policy of the board of trustees at Gulf Park "is to have as few books around as possible. Obviously, indifference to the one maker of books present is as natural as breathing. . . ."

So he raged, and not unfoundedly. In spite of Dr. Cox's kindness, little Gulf Park ("that glorified finishing school," he ended by calling it) was no place for a midwestern messiah.

But this winter and spring his disappointment, which was natural, swelled into a resentment that was monstrous. Resentment in its turn became delusion, till he complained wildly of "keyhole peepers," of a faculty disapproval of him that did not exist and of a watch exerted over his movements and speech with his students, though no such watch was ever kept, and finally conceived of himself as hounded on campus by "persecutors."

"These," writes Dr. Wakefield, who in response to an explosion of letters and telegrams from Vachel hurried down to him in Gulfport at the end of January, "were his best friends there."

In February Elizabeth Wills came back to college for a visit, causing a flutter among Lindsay's student partisans, who were ready to be bridesmaids if a campus wedding could be arranged.

Paul Wakefield was on the station platform with Vachel to meet her. When Paul, setting aside all other business, made haste down to Gulfport he had discovered his brother-in-law— as Dr. Wakefield put it afterward—"a wreck nervously and physically . . . utterly beside himself with all kinds of hallucinations." Even in the weeks since Christmas the change in Lindsay was appalling. "His attitude towards life, his sense of responsibility, his attitude towards his friends—everything I found changed."

Paul spoke sternly to him, took him by the arm, walked

with him on the beach for hours on end ("We slept when we could") and Vachel whispered, muttered, shouted that here at Gulf Park his closest friends were conspirators against him, that he was being "persecuted."

Later he was to recall that only his plunges into the Gulf waters brought him relief, for his blood was "hot as Dante's hell."

Now to the horrified Paul he displayed a new arrogant attitude and the conviction, utterly unLindsaylike, that the world and his nation owed him a living. And there was the development of what Dr. Wakefield called "smutty stories"—the first such talk ever on Lindsay's tongue. Paul could remember how at Hiram when one boy, a hulking football player, spoke disrespectfully of a girl they knew, Vachel, flaming with anger, had knocked him down.

Dr. Wakefield wrote back guardedly to his wife: "I hope to save a tragedy." And Lindsay to his sister wrote, without guard: "Dearest Olive, I have been about half-sick, but Paul has pulled me through and has been closer than a brother."

The temporary return of Elizabeth sent his hopes soaring, yet "whether I marry her or not, for my soul's sake, make her your sister," he besought Olive. "She is the ultimate symbol of pure and honest youth and prayer to me, a symbol of the innocent Olive and Vachel on their first day at Hiram, with everything before them."

To Paul, closer than a brother, he turned with the plea to speak on his behalf to Elizabeth, to act John Alden to his Miles Standish. But their fearful hours spent together had opened Dr. Wakefield's eyes. At the end of June 1924, at his insistence, he and Vachel went north to the Mayo Foundation in Rochester, Minnesota, and there Lindsay's nervous disorder, whose nature till now had escaped general detection, was diagnosed.

This disorder, with its eventual terrible and fatal consequence, Dr. Wakefield attributed to the formation of scar tissue in Lindsay's brain after the operation on his sinuses in 1923. Lindsay, however, later told his wife that from his youth he had occasionally awakened at night to find himself on the floor, having bitten his tongue part way through, though of these seizures he never spoke to friends. His sisters knew nothing of them, and whether his mother and doctor-father were totally unaware of them is impossible to say.

To the mature Vachel, who loved beauty and loathed deformity, the medical pronouncement on his condition—to which the name epilepsy was never given publicly, even after his death—came as a staggering shock and became a burden almost too heavy to bear. He never forgave Paul for the discovery and himself would never acknowledge its truth, even though it brought him into company with many of his heroes, among them Julius Caesar and Napoleon and those visionaries who like him saw "pictures in the air"—the prophet Ezekiel, sword-wielding Mohammed, and William Blake, before whose eyes the sun rose in the heavens as a host of angels.

56

This summer a measure of calm
returned to Lindsay and the autumn found him far from the
bright waters and soft airs of Gulfport. It was in a land of
forests and meditation that he next sought sanctuary. Yet when
he left the college for the vacation he intended to go back in
September. Another year's teaching lay ahead, only he meant
during the summer months to change his center and accomplish a great curve in space—without losing touch with the
South or with Springfield to move his foothold, physical and
spiritual, to the Pacific Northwest.

Already in this decade of the exodus of Americans to Europe, he had seen a number of his friends in art and letters ("just
too elegant for their own country") drift abroad to settle in
Rome and Paris. "If in America," said Lindsay, "one does not
have the west-going heart, the thousand little nations that are
the counties of Europe pull him away from our great National
Parks."

With him the pull was in the other direction. In July 1924
he had had all his hundreds of books, notebooks, scrapbooks
and manuscripts shipped from Gulfport and Springfield to the
Davenport Hotel in Spokane, Washington, and with the ship-
ment went his portfolios of drawings, his "Map of the Universe" and his startling, great painting "The Tree of Laughing
Bells."

One of his reasons for choosing Spokane was its nearness to
Glacier Park. Another was the Davenport Hotel itself. Besides combining every modern convenience with the candlelit
atmosphere of an old Virginia tavern, the Davenport had

offered him exceptional terms, making it seem that Spokane
was his destiny. He never fully realized how much his move
thither and royal welcome owed not to the order of the stars
but to the intervention of one man.

Benjamin H. Kizer, a leading lawyer of the city, had been
one of the pioneer subscribers to Harriet Monroe's *Poetry*.
He had not only read but also bought Lindsay's first two books
of verse. *Adventures While Preaching the Gospel of Beauty*
had strengthened his feeling that here was a modern Saint
Francis, and he wrote then to Lindsay. For years they cor-
responded desultorily. It was Kizer and his handsome and
intellectual wife who induced Lindsay to stop in Spokane
on one of his past tours.

At once he was romantically attracted by the little city,
which unlike Springfield is a city of hills, pines, waterfalls,
cliffs and deep ravines. It has snow-topped Mount Spokane
in the distance; Indians, descendants of the Nez Percé warrior
Chief Joseph, stalking its main street in full regalia; coursing
through it the Spokane River—whose waters flow clear, in
contrast to the yellow Sangamon—and all but encircling it a
high basaltic wall, the Rim Rock.

From Gulfport, deep in the South, Lindsay had written to
the Kizers that he would like to make the Davenport his residence, if he could afford it, and Spokane his headquarters.
One of his latest enthusiasms was the architect and medievalist
Ralph Adams Cram, who wrote wistfully of the creating of
what he called "walled towns"—utopian communities harking
back to the Middle Ages, whose gray guarding walls, whether
real or symbolic, would shut out commercialism.

Something like this Lindsay had prophesied for Springfield,
a city of the open plain, but Spokane's rocky barrier gave
her the psychological advantage. If she could be got at from
within and made to think in terms of beauty, she would be a
perfect "walled town."

Ben Kizer, who lived there, had no such illusions. Aware,
though, that Lindsay's presence would be a boon to spiritually

aspiring residents, he went around to Louis Davenport, owner of the hotel, and made a proposal to which the materially aspiring Davenport agreed: he was to rent the celebrated poet (some of whose press clippings Mr. Kizer took along) one of his best rooms on the top floor, which customarily brought in about $125 a month, for $35. Lindsay was not to know that to this nominal figure Ben Kizer would contribute, out of his own pocket, $40 more.

Such was the arrangement behind the Davenport welcome— a welcome that made Lindsay feel, he exclaimed after his move, that he was "marvellously established . . . in perfect health again . . . in the most *wonderful* hotel in the world, and the most *home-like*, the most beautiful and the most unique."

In the Davenport restaurant the artful proprietor ("in his way," says Mr. Kizer, "as much of a genius as Vachel") had hung cages with singing canaries and erected glass columns filled with water and live goldfish. By his order, all coins used on the premises were washed till they glittered. In every bedroom he had placed ready a basket of fruit for the incoming guest. Downstairs in the lobby he kept a fire lighted in the great fireplace, the year around.

Now he caused to be displayed on his elegant mezzanine, as a sure conversation piece, an immense, strange painting, "The Tree of Laughing Bells."

Twice this summer, after settling in at the Davenport, Room 1129, Lindsay returned alone to Glacier Park, where he had gone first with Graham. He also visited in Hollywood and was entertained at regal Pickfair by Hollywood's king and queen, Doug and Mary. At the Pacific Palisades Association outside Santa Monica he lectured on the art of the films, with special reference to Douglas Fairbanks' *The Thief of Bagdad*. At the Los Angeles Chautauqua no less than twenty-three professional elocutionists told him they were earning a good part of their living reciting his poems.

Encouraged, he reminded himself that almost every year *The Chinese Nightingale* was mimed by students at Chicago and Northwestern Universities; that the glorious Ruth St. Denis, to whom he had read the poem all one afternoon, was interested in dancing *The Trial of the Dead Cleopatra;* that he had had a cable from Nigel Playfair, manager of the Lyric Theater in London, asking to do his farcical verse *The Black-smith's Serenade* in vaudeville and on the radio.

In Spokane he had already been consulted on the organizing of regional pageants. He had been introduced to local dancers who might dance his work and actors who might act it. He was getting letters from Seattle, Olympia and Portland.

All this carried him forward. He set down in his diary his nation-wide contacts in the realms of art, the dance and music, then, in connection with his pending return to Gulf Park, where he was to resume teaching, he wrote: "Why should I be assumed as a person with nothing to say in the faculty whenever my work touches at any of these points?"

Though as recently as the end of August, Lindsay had claimed that he produced "more verse the last year and a half in Gulfport than for seven years before," by October he had veered round to cry that the atmosphere of the college and of the Gulf coast turned his gifts "sterile" and that Spokane and the Northwest were making it possible for him to create again "as I was not able to create at Gulf Park."

It was shortly before he was due to go south that the accumulated, dammed-up mass of despondency over what he considered his lack of accomplishment and recognition on the southern campus and of resentment at the gadfly stings received there, or that he thought he had received, came out in a rush. He wrote sharply to President Cox to say that he would not return, would never return, to Gulf Park—"one year and a half of isolation and insulation is enough!"

Dr. Cox was understandably upset. Lindsay's vision soon cleared, however, and when he wrote to his old friend again on October 14, while reaffirming his decision, he softened his accusation of a set made against him on campus, writing— this time temperately: "My dear Zim, let me acknowledge that I may have seen an intentional thwarting of plans in many cases where there was merely a lack of interest, or a disposition to put off or postpone.

"It is not necessary that we place blame. The important point is that I must, in a large degree, live upon the response that I am able to evoke from human beings in the arts in general (of which the greatest is the art of living) and in poetry in particular."

Three years later, in 1927, Lindsay was to complain of how he *still* suffered from the inferiority complex given him at "that glorified finishing school—they did it with dresses, fans, high-heeled slippers, bathing suits, Southern dialect, formal balls, informal balls, dowagers. . . ."

Five years later he was to rave against Zimmie Cox and the kindly Mrs. Cox, his rescuers from the road, to whom he once gave credit for saving his life: "How they love me *now!* And did their *best* to break me, in Gulf Park!"

This is a charge not to be taken seriously but made when the veil of delusion wrapped his eyes. At the time, in 1924, he could conclude the exchange of letters by declaring to Cox his generous, reasoned hope that "if on the basis that we are two erring human beings, unexplained and unexplainable, we can continue to be friends, I shall be heartily glad of it."

These early days in Spokane, Lindsay joined Ben Kizer in Sunday walks along the river bank. It was through the Kizers that he met Stoddard King, witty columnist of the *Spokesman-Review*, and George Greenwood, a banker of the city and musical amateur. The Australian-born composer Percy Grainger came to Spokane, where he stayed with the Greenwoods. A specialist in folk music, he listened enthralled to Lindsay chant *The Congo*, hearing beyond the drumbeats and the jokes to the elaborate musical composition.

Other new friends were J. H. McKechnie of the editorial staff of the *Spokesman-Review* and his wife, Mary, a gifted painter; Hannah Hinsdale and Russell Davenport, both well-known newspaper writers; Lenore Glen, Spokane's young dancer; Leonardo Brill, conductor of the Davenport Hotel's string orchestra; and Anita Pettibone, an alert young woman who was writing her first novel.

Shaking off despondency, gathering energy, Lindsay predicted in a letter to Mrs. Moody that "the new life now begins with the fairest auspices and the finest friends imaginable!"

This fall and early winter he recited at a tea at the Davenport bookshop, lectured to the American Association of University Women, told tramping tales out of *A Handy Guide for Beggars* to the University Club and, assisted by two girls in costume, put on a program of his poem games for the city's Drama League that was praised by the press of the Inland Empire as "exquisite," "artistic" and "one of the most beautiful things Spokane has seen in years."

Stoddard King, in his column in the *Spokesman-Review*, printed two new poems by Lindsay, *Butterfly Hieroglyphics* ("written," said the poet, "for Ruth St. Denis to dance on the top of a watch crystal") and *The Voyage*, inscribed to Ted Shawn. If these were trifles, on Christmas Day 1924 his long poem *Virginia* appeared in the same paper and, in January, *Nancy Hanks*.

While still in Gulfport, he had noted in his diary not only that he had overwritten all his poetry for the past five years but that he felt a more controlled poetic manner forming in him. "Coming for certain," he wrote, "a new classic manner."

In Spokane, nevertheless, he drafted this winter on Davenport stationery which bore the legend "See America First," one of the finest of his chanting poems, *Andrew Jackson*, or—to give it its full rolling title—*Old, Old, Old, Old Andrew Jackson*.

57

Lindsay was invited to one of the Chamber of Commerce luncheons held in Spokane every week. This particular luncheon marked the opening of the annual Potato Show—the lowly spud was a million-dollar industry in Spokane—and the guest of honor was not the poet but this year's "Potato Princess," a young and blooming girl from Idaho.

It was here that the clever, intuitive Anita Pettibone had her first glimpse of Lindsay, as he sat at the main table, flanked by potato kings and agricultural emperors, his head cast back wearily, his eyes almost closed. Occasionally the lids lifted and the glinting whites sidled—he looked "near death," Miss Pettibone recalls. She was struck also by how Indian he looked, his features "thick and Indian," his broad, high cheeks "like pale leather."

After the luncheon, on an impulse of rescue, she went up to speak to him. She reminded him, he told her later, of portraits of Harriet Beecher Stowe.

His "splendid Egeria, newly found," he called Anita, who listened to him as no Gulf Park belle had ever listened, while he proposed fervently that they write together a long poem or series of poems with Spokane for a background, which would be "a new Milton," and yet "if possible, more epic than Milton, with the lines longer and grander."

"And Eden, only," cried Lindsay, "*not* the Fall."

But it was not in him to let the past go altogether. Though he had discovered an Egeria, he continued to write from Spokane to Dulcinea and, more fraternally, to other Gulf Park graduates, his former students—now dancing hard over the South and getting married as fast as possible—to whom he sent his snapshot taken in a cowboy suit and who returned him, some of them, "lots and lots and *heaps* of love."

"The pictures you sent, à la cowboy, were dollin," one wrote. "You are so athletic looking."

"His virginity was giving him trouble," says Mabel Kizer of Lindsay this winter. Lindsay ascribed the trouble to the human race, which "is naturally and constitutionally Mohammedan," he wrote in his diary, "and it tries to be Christian and gets mixed up."

Then he made his next entry in verse:

> I think I'll marry a cutey,
> Said young Noah Webster,
> I'm tired of these damphull highbrows all the time.
> Every girl my sister recommends
> Talks like a dictionary
> And looks like a great big barrel of lime.

He had come down in his desires. He was no longer the splendid puritan who in the passionate poems of his chaste youth besought Mother Eve to send him a divine bride—

> Make her of bread from out of your hand,
> Make her of honey from your board,
> Make her kiss like the lightning brand
> That shall pierce my soul as a sword.

So he had written then, but now "I want a little sweetey," he wrote,

> To talk baby-slang to me,
> A regular Orleans molasses honey bunch,

Real easy on the eyes,
Not so Goddam wise ..

The profanity, too, was unlike him. But what he wanted
these days, he allowed, was

a dam little canary ...
Face tilted like a fairy,
Light of thigh and airy,
Round-breasted, quick and wary!

The first crack in his contentment with Spokane showed
in March 1925 when he complained in a letter to Mrs. Moody
that he was being "speeded up" by his new active northern
life beyond all human strength, so that he actually yearned
again for the Orleans molasses and magnolias of the South,
while to Anita he darkly and untruly intimated that he had
been kicked out, fired, forced into resigning, from Gulf Park.

Sometimes, when the need for solitude overwhelmed him,
he walked far out of town to the summit of the windswept
Rim Rock, and there on the pure heights his spirits cleared.
The red cloud of anger and desire lifted. There, it seemed to
him, the soul of his father returned to walk with him and they
paced together, to the piping music of a lost Kentucky tune,
the battlements of this northwestern city. It was in the aftermath of such exaltation, such wholeness of vision, that he
promised Anita there were two things he would never do: the
first, to deny God, the second, to take his own life.

Below in the streets people stared, turning to look after him.
His swinging, ungainly gait was more marked than ever. He
carried a cane, wore his cowboy hat and often dancing
pumps—for he liked to press the earth close under his feet—
and he lifted his face as though to taste the universe, then
lowered it to note with shrewd eye some sign of the times,
like the one in a shop window on Sprague Avenue that read:
ENSEMBLE HAS INVADED PAJAMADOM.

He was also to be seen in the lobby of the Davenport, a
famous meeting place but one where Lindsay most often sat

alone, sunk in a deep chair beside the monumental and flaming hearth, his head resting against the chair back, a heavy ulster wrapped around him. Even in his corner, remote from the ballroom, the air pulsed with the cacophony of the music with which he disavowed all affinity and whose strains he cursed in his poem *The Jazz of This Hotel.*

When he went to watch the dancing, fox trot and tango, performed suggestively to the whimper, bleat and squeal of the saxophone, the sight filled him with the rage of Moses. "I want every Irishman in America," he cried, "to learn to play the harp like King David and drive out this obscene Amalekite, Perizzite and Jebusite!"

And he meditated a poem on Rapunzel to celebrate the crowning glory of woman, now shorn.

Since his examination at Mayo he had been taking luminal sodium, a sedative prescribed by the neurologist who had him in charge, in doses up to two and a quarter grains daily. In spite of it, he could hardly sleep and got through the nights, he told Anita, only with the help of scalding-hot baths.

Yet in compensation, "if I stay up late enough the Davenport fireplace is my fireplace, if I walk late enough the roof is *my* roof," he declared in his diary, in which his random notes continue: "There is something in the very ceiling of the Davenport that suggests ambition. I would like so much to consider how we can make Spokane the very top of the world, so far as imagination is concerned, and accomplish here everything that *can* be accomplished by the imagination."

He was thinking of writing *The Golden Book of Spokane* (to contain "everything left out of *The Golden Book of Springfield*"), and his diary this year has the draft of a dedication to Sara Teasdale of his latest poems, many of them first inscribed to Dulcinea, but "I will not forget," he promised,

> that golden queen
> For whom I wrote the best song of my days.

Earlier this spring, on Lincoln's Birthday, the Kizers had invited Lindsay to meet at dinner six students from the Lewis and Clark High School, competitors for a poetry prize offered by the civic-minded Ben Kizer. Almost all the contenders were girls, and when he read their entries Mr. Kizer had been dismayed by the apparent futility of making any award. But the six invited to the house were so pretty they redeemed their verse, and with them as chaperone came their English teacher, who looked almost their age and whom Lindsay, surprisingly, had met before.

In January 1922 Miss Elizabeth Conner had sat next to him at another dinner, given in his honor at Mills College. In February 1925 she was twenty-three, living with her parents in Spokane, a teacher of English and Latin at the High School. Lindsay hadn't the faintest recollection of their earlier meeting, but Miss Conner, though she did not remind him of it, recalled it well.

In the Kizers' living room—aroused by the company of so much youth to an excitement simulating inspiration and a gaiety that was almost febrile—Lindsay recited torrentially, dashed off drawings and improvised verses that he fairly begged all present to praise. From little Miss Conner, especially, he was aware of an ardor toward poetry and poets amounting to a positive emanation. Opinion differed concerning this young woman's looks. Ben Kizer found her "not particularly pretty and yet with possibilities of distinction."

She was badly dressed. Her intensity made her seem gauche. But her face, though demure, was strong and rapt, her mouth full and passionate. On her lips and in her blue eyes lingered a half-smile and her hair, bobbed in the fashion of the twenties, was of the gold of Milton's Eve.

On March 15 the *Spokesman-Review* printed an interview with Lindsay by Hannah Hinsdale. SPOKANE SUITS THIS POET'S DREAM, ran the headline, and there was a picture of him taken in his Davenport room.

"How long do you plan to stay at the Davenport?" Miss Hinsdale asked.

"Till the ants carry me out grain by grain through the keyhole," was his answer.

Yet how far he was from having found his dream the photograph betrayed: it showed the face of a man puzzled, haunted, hurt. How far he was from having put down roots he revealed when on March 31 he wrote despairingly to Mrs. Moody that since his father's and mother's deaths he could give himself no reason for going on. He was just an isolated man in a hotel bedroom and now not only the reciting but even the writing of poetry, and above all the life expected of the writer, had become harrowingly artificial to him.

"People thought I fought for fame," he told her, "but I only fought my way through from being the town fool and the family idiot."

Always there had been "just one call deep and strong," an inexpressible yearning, and that was for the open road and for peace. There was just one thing that had never failed him, and that was the highroad. "Three times I turned to it, not in vain, each time dreaming I would some day make it permanent. I really believe I will make it permanent before the year is over. My whole heart is turning to this dream, dear Harriet Cordelia. . . .

"I will change my name, write no letters and go on and on. I have not the least intention of coming back when I start. It was 1912 I was last a beggar, and it is *everything since 1912* I want to walk away from."

So much for dreams. On April 10 Lindsay, with his usual apparent enthusiasm, gave a large and successful recital at the Davenport. In the same month he lectured on some paintings (not his own) exhibited at the Art Museum. He had not felt well before the lecture. As he talked, he noticed in his audience the youthful, glowing face of Elizabeth Conner, and when he had done he went straight over to her and asked her to have tea.

"How sweet and restoring you were," he was to tell her later, "and how tired and desperately dizzy I had been."

Yet their acquaintance continued casual. On April 22 he called on the Kizers bearing an enormous florist's box, which contained two dozen rosebuds, a dozen delphiniums and a dozen pink snapdragons, all with stems nearly three feet long, and this he presented to Mabel, who wrote down the date as worth recording, for, having bought himself an audience, he stayed on and on to talk to her about three women and their effect on his life: Octavia, Sara and Dulcinea.

58

The Reverend Franklin Conner, Elizabeth's father, was a Presbyterian clergyman, unworldly, ardent and mercurial. Elizabeth had inherited his Celtic temperament but she was a child of the unsettled twenties, in whom her father's evangelical intensity of conviction sought another channel than that of a fundamentalist faith. She had also her mother's charm, which overlay immense fortitude: Claribel Sims Conner, a beguiling and very gallant woman, was from the South.

Theirs was a family that scraped and sacrificed; the father sought to save the world, the mother took in boarders. Elizabeth, eldest of four daughters, as a brilliant classical student at Mills had been offered more scholarships than she could use and from her schooldays had been pointed out as a woman with a career. She might be a poet, or a college president, or an archaeologist in Italy. Teaching prosaically at the Spokane High School, she was helping two younger sisters through college, but she dreamed of a very different life. Like Lindsay, she had a sense of destiny.

She met him on the street soon after the art show. She was with a group of younger girls and Lindsay made as if to kiss them all, but they demurred and drew back, for which afterward she blazingly rebuked them. The honor, she assured them, would have been theirs. Yet for all her hero worship, she had a wild Irish humor. "The flower-fed buffalo," after his new poem, she called Mr. Lindsay to her chum Portia, and she gave her pealing, musical laugh.

338

He came to call. Then he came to dinner. They went for walks and once, chaperoned by Judy, her youngest sister, she dined with him in his Davenport room. Having been refused by many women, Lindsay was humbler than he used to be, but there came a day when he let fall to her that "after they were married" she would be able to deal with people for him and handle all his correspondence.

She was only a little surprised. Since he made no proposal, she gave no answer, but she did not contradict him; she had a profound need to serve.

"I remember," he wrote to her, long after they had become man and wife, "the precise way you looked one day just before our marriage when you met me in the afternoon by the candy counter in the Davenport. I can still remember your lifted desperate consecrated tragic womanly exquisite face. And your step was more military than ever before or since.

"As though you were saying, 'I am going to march straight through this phantom called a man, whoever he is! I am going to accept my woman's fate and get the best of it.'"

Lindsay's actual decision to be married was made at the last moment. Early in May he wrote to Miss Sarah K. Smith, one of his staunch supporters on the faculty at Gulf Park, to repeat what he had already said to Mrs. Moody—that he had in mind soon to seek the vagabond's road and disappear, to drop out of sight completely, for truly they did not understand him in Spokane.

Between his two outcries, he had written to Elizabeth Wills—his Dulcinea—once again and for the last time proposing marriage and this time enclosing his mother's wedding ring, a broad band of heavy gold, which he begged her to wear. But when she refused his offer with a clearer "No" than ever and asked if she should return the ring, he told her to send it back immediately.

Thus was the end precipitated.

On May 15, his thoughts drifting once more to Sara ("a glory of a memory"), he described to Mabel Kizer that earlier rejection on the day when Sara's letter came telling of her acceptance of another suitor. "It was a hot August day. I was all alone."

On May 16, a Saturday, his Spokane Elizabeth went without him to a fashionable concert at which Frieda Hempel sang, and when she got home late that evening found to her surprise, for their meeting was not planned, that Vachel was waiting for her.

Hand in hand—as long ago he walked with Sara through the canyons of Babylon—they left the house and sauntered through the spring night up into the rocky heights of Cliff Park, which overlook the city. It was raining gently. Elizabeth was still in the dress she had worn to the concert. Vachel had brought with him a long strip of green linen and this he spread with ritual care on the damp ground. His thought was of the verse from the Song of Solomon: "Behold, thou art fair, my beloved, yea, pleasant: also our bed is green."

There they remained, talking and not talking, sometimes locked in each other's arms, but always quite innocently, the whole night through. They were there at dawn. Just before the rain stopped falling, Vachel knelt and kissed Elizabeth's bare wet feet; then the darkness stole away, and in the early light they saw below them the roof of the Spokane hospital, which had a golden cross.

"There's crucifixion at the heart of the universe," said Vachel softly.

At home Elizabeth soothed her bewildered mother, at whom she looked with clear eyes, saying simply that all was well: she had had a delightful evening and there had been much for her and Vachel to talk about.

On this remarkable Sunday morning, she accepted that they were really at last engaged. Tuesday morning, May 19, she was in her classroom at the High School when, unexpectedly, Dr. Charles Pease, the Unitarian minister, arrived and beckoned her outside. He had just come from Lindsay at the Davenport.

Two things the torn and transported poet had suddenly resolved: that his need for love brooked no postponement, and that his characteristic tendency to brood, overelaborate and lay too-long plans was his snare and destruction. The astonished clergyman, having gone unsuspectingly to pay an ordinary call, had discovered Lindsay in a state approaching trance, which at first alarmed and then puzzled him. Between disbelief and wonder, he understood the poet to say that he had just become engaged and that, if it were humanly possible, he desired to be married to his true and only love this very day.

At first, Dr. Pease thought the whole story of the cyclonic courtship might be a dream of Lindsay's, but a few words with Elizabeth made him sure that, though more composed and better able to speak rationally than her lover, she was in her own way quite as much aflame.

Pale, trembling, stunned by the prospect of marriage before the day was over and doubtful also how a cynical world would interpret such haste, she nevertheless quietly replied, after learning how much Vachel's heart was set on it, that if that was what was required to make him content, he should be content.

Arrangements were completed that afternoon. Elizabeth would have preferred to be married in her parents' house. Lindsay, however, insisted that the wedding be held in his room, and on this too she yielded. Besides the bride and groom and Dr. Pease, who performed the ceremony, eight persons were present: Elizabeth's mother and sister Judy; Lindsay's cousin by marriage, Lucy Robinson, and her young daughter, who lived in Spokane; George Greenwood and his wife, and Ben and Mabel Kizer.

One of Ben Kizer's last services, just before the arrival of the bride, was to hustle out of sight into Vachel's bureau drawer a perfect galaxy of photographs of Dulcinea. Someone else arranged sprays of bridal wreath around the pictures on the wall and between the leaves of books—Elizabeth was shaking them out six years later.

The hour had been set for nine because Elizabeth was first expected at a meeting of the AAUW to read a review of Michael Arlen's new novel, *The Green Hat*. The meeting was downstairs in the hotel. She finished her reading, excused herself to the others—all of them ignorant of what was about to happen—and joined her mother and sister on the edge of the crowd. Upstairs, in a brief quarter of an hour, she was metamorphosed into Mrs. Vachel Lindsay.

She wore a simple print dress of yellow silk and carried red roses. Lindsay, by her side, was in a black suit, black sateen shirt and black tie. Dr. Pease gave a quiet little talk, saying that Vachel and Elizabeth had already pledged their vows to each other. In the presence of the moved and reverent onlookers they rose, he joined their hands and pronounced them man and wife. Not a word was spoken by anyone else.

Then followed the festivities, and when by ten o'clock the guests were gone and the door closed, Lindsay turned to face his bride. "How sweet and shy and strange she was," he remembered. "How she touched me!"

"Dewy as Milton's Eden dawn," he called their bridal hour, and he later reminded her: "Dear, we were married first and got acquainted afterward. All I can remember is leaping into each other's arms. And it was all so sweet and clean as a white waterfall."

59

"The Spokane Apple Fairy," Lindsay called his bride,

> Her hair like curly sunbeams,
> Her voice a bell.

And he called her "Elizabeth Locust Blossom," for it was locust blossom time in the Northwest and every sidewalk was white with petals.

Over the dates May 19-21, 1925, he wrote in his diary in capital letters and in serious mood the words LIFE CLASS.

His mother's wedding ring, returned to him by Dulcinea, had not yet had time to reach him when he sent Elizabeth Wills the newspaper announcement of his marriage to Elizabeth Conner, over which the Spokane papers had burst into headlines:

VACHEL LINDSAY JOINS BENEDICKS
BRIDE IS BUT 23

"Tell the cock-eyed world!" he wrote exultantly to Sarah K. Smith, to whom he had but lately dropped gloomy hints of his impending disappearance, and to Mrs. Moody he wrote on May 22: "Dear Cordelia, the world has begun anew for me and all disasters have fled away. Of course, my letters about the road came from a desperate heart. They were written 1000000 years ago."

Though, astonishingly, to his sisters he did not write at all— Joy read of his wedding in the Cleveland paper—those friends

343

to whom he did write hailed the news of his marriage with cheers. Harriet Monroe, as his editor, suggested that it would bring forth new love songs, to which the bride herself made answer that she thought Vachel's most beautiful love songs had been given to the world long since.

"I aspire to be, if anything," said Elizabeth, "the background of an epic, or whatever will make him happy."

Only for a moment had a shadow crossed her own happiness. On the morning after the wedding, in their room at the Davenport, her husband told her for the first time, in a low voice and with something of shame in his manner, that he was subject to occasional nocturnal seizures—he gave them no precise name—and he showed her his bottle of luminal sodium.

But the shadow had since slipped away. Even though at the end of the first week the school board dismissed her from her post as teacher because of her marriage, Elizabeth's happiness remained undimmed.

"Life with Vachel is a poem and an unceasing adventure," she wrote buoyantly to Paul Wakefield, her new brother-in-law, "and surely more of beauty and of joy than I ever thought this tired old star, the earth, could hold for me. Twenty-three is painfully cynical, and I had thought the Galahad species extinct. Then I discovered myself married to a husband who is worthy of the old Siege Perilous, every way.

"I want so much to be good for Vachel—everyone advises me as to the responsibility which devolves on the helpmeet of Genius."

In the Davenport lobby, through which he and she strode as conquerors, and in the dining room where their self-absorption raised a barrier around their table for two, residents smiled and strangers stared at the quaint couple—the bridegroom still in unrelieved black, his face showing his forty-five years but blissful and infatuated, and the golden-haired, radiant bride, girlish in her straight-cut silk dress with a broad sash and a floppy leghorn hat.

Once on Spokane's main thoroughfare, directly in front of the hotel, they clung together and passionately embraced.

"Gosh, we gave that town a treat!" Lindsay remembered.

In July they spent two weeks in Los Angeles, where he had a series of lectures at the university, and there each day they stole into one of the empty classrooms and kissed themselves giddy for five minutes before his talk began. In August they left Spokane again, this time for their real honeymoon in Glacier Park, taking with them, besides a granite coffee pot and cans of beef and beans, an Egyptian hieroglyphic grammar and the *Spoon River Anthology*.

Scarcely an hour after setting out from the tourist lodge, their packs on their backs, they found themselves in the deep stillness of the mountains.

By day his bride in hiking clothes reminded Lindsay of Rosalind. By night she was Juliet, tender and absolute in her devotion. She was Pocahontas in her vernal innocence. To the mountain-flowers in the path he gave the names of Juliet's Bed and The Breasts of Pocahontas. And when—as on their afternoon beside the sequestered glittering lake they called The City of Glass, which is known to tourists as Waterton Lake—the sun shone on her golden hair and white body, she was Milton's Eve to him, the Eve who walked with Adam.

Lindsay wore a hat with two feathers, a redbird's and a bluebird's, and a quarter-breed Indian girl they met on the trail told him that thus to wear two feathers was a sign of loyalty and devotion. Here among the Indian-named mountains he felt himself a member of the tribes forever, and the Mohawk Medicine Man, his father, spoke to him thunderously, as in his childhood, bidding him:

> When you take your bride
> Be a bull of power!
> Be an eagle
> Flying over Red-Eagle,
> A whirlwind
> Going up a flower!

Roaming through the park, they came on five log cabins. One cabin, unfinished, built of logs still in the round, was partly open to the sky and set in a grove of birch and aspen shut in by towering cliffs. That night it rained and inside the little shelter, far from the world and its wrongs, far from the saxophone, Lindsay took a candle out of his pack and lighted it, to him a ceremony symbolic of the act of love.

Often they slept outdoors, with the spangled sky immense above them, sharing one blanket on a bed of fir boughs by the campfire, unfrightened at the mysterious rustlings nearby in the bush and the faraway yowl of the mountain lion. A year before Lindsay had lain alone in these mountains. The trees had been friends to heal his loneliness, the rolling mists had brought him peace of heart, and the blazing campfire had been a chariot for his "Elijah soul" to ride.

All this was changed by the presence of the girl beside him. "Oh, once alone in the wilderness," he wrote,

> I built myself a fire . . .
> How the mariposa lilies in the dim light gleamed,
> The stately dress of the wilderness
> Where I lay and dreamed . . .
>
> Now, my love and I, this night, build again a fire,
> And the strange God-breath of the wilderness
> Turns to desire.

It was on such a night that Elizabeth woke suddenly to see her husband a few feet away struggling on the ground in terrible convulsions. Frozen with terror, she watched him to the end. Later she considered it was the exertion of their climb to this remote plateau that had brought on the seizure; never afterward, so far as she knew, did he have another so severe.

By dawn he was fully recovered. But when that same day the suspicion, truly founded, crossed her mind that she was pregnant, all the panic she had felt on the morning after her wedding returned; for a few desperate hours it seemed to her that she was trapped.

Then the ardor of her nature came to her rescue. She renewed her hold on her chosen cause, the career of a great man, and her world steadied again. Over the panic uncertainty within her she drew the veil of love and courage, and when she and Vachel arrived home in September her beaming face announced her expectations before she put them into words.

Lindsay's own testament to the valor, ecstasy and springing hope of these weeks is in his poems. His diary has drafts of many poems that appear, with scarcely the change of a word, in his book *The Candle in the Cabin.*

> Oh, the tremendous leaping of ambition
> When new strength came with the wind,
>   and the high climb.
> How we planned and plotted against gloom,
> Against the sorrows of the world and time,
> The gray hairs of the years,
> The sod of the grave.
> How we planned and plotted against tears.

The lines are from *The Hour of Fate,* which, with his poem *The Writhing, Imperfect Earth,* is dated in his notebook as of August 31. To his honeymoon also belongs the muted, flawless lyric *I Saw a Rose in Egypt.*

In the mysterious land of Egypt, symbolic kingdom of his imagination, a place of dark magic and the exotic lotus, he saw—says the poet—one rose

> Alone there in the sand,
> The glory of the world.

This was his western love, his young brave dreamer.

PART SIX

THE HOME-GOING
HEART

60

When Lindsay and Elizabeth went east in October 1925 and arrived in New York, it seemed to him that the landmarks of his youth shone again in their original glory, only he had never valued them so deeply before. With Elizabeth beside him, gone was the loneliness in which he last had walked these streets.

Taking a horse-drawn cab, they drove to the middle of Brooklyn Bridge, there to watch the lights of the skyscrapers flash on through the brown autumn dusk. They knelt together during Mass in the Church of the Paulist Fathers and Elizabeth sobbed at the beauty of the ritual. She was near to tears when at a concert in Carnegie Hall Louise Homer, the great contralto, sang to a vast audience an arrangement of *General William Booth Enters into Heaven.*

Before her marriage, Ben Kizer had doubted whether she could really be called pretty. Now success lighted her face till her blue eyes beamed, her lurking smile grew full and dazzling, and literary New York thought her a tearing beauty, sent her roses, gave a dinner in her honor and congratulated her burstingly proud husband with a warmth he hadn't felt in years.

Sara Teasdale Filsinger, who now lived in New York, received the pair with a quiet kindness of which the true extent conceivably was lost on the radiant Elizabeth. Sara's own marriage was near the breaking point. And in the formidable office of Macmillan's, where, since the departure of Edward Marsh, Lindsay had had no special sponsor, his bride was the talisman that ensured a welcome, bringing good humor even to the face of "Ivan the Terrible," as he called President Brett.

He had accepted a few engagements, to increase their budget. In Chicago, Carl Sandburg came to a tea given for him and Elizabeth by Harriet Monroe. Elizabeth thought Carl "a dear," and "How much she thought of you! How much she envies just the sort of thing you have done," Vachel wrote in thanks to Harriet.

In Washington, in the dining room of the Wardman Park Hotel, a brown-skinned bus boy in a white jacket ignored senators and oil magnates, sidled shyly up to the wall table at which the only poet in the crowded room sat opposite his wife and laid a slim manuscript by Lindsay's plate. That evening Lindsay opened his recital in the little theater of the hotel by reading the poems the boy had given him. It was the beginning of fame for the young Negro poet Langston Hughes.

Washington was still buzzing with the Teapot Dome oil scandal. Lindsay and Elizabeth were in the city on Thanksgiving Day—"our first," as he noted, writing on the back of the hotel dinner menu, which featured on its fair side the Roast Turkey special at $1.75, and, improvising, he continued:

> Here, as it were, in the heart of roaring Rome,
> Here as far as men may get from the soil,
> Here where political lords are proud of oil,
> Oil in their skins and oil in their robber-wells,
> Where money and stone and orations are combined,
> Here where sins are refined and over refined,
> Here where they ape the very walls of Rome,
> The temples and pillars of Imperial Rome—
>
> We think of when the wild-cats kept awake
> Our little camp, and filled our hearts with fright,
> When the porcupine and bear-cub stirred the brake
> And the friendliest wind seemed cold and impolite.

It was in another hotel in another city, on this trip with Elizabeth, that he improvised on the back of still another menu the lines about his father during the Cotton Hill years. But most of the slight verses scribbled while they waited to dine were love poems addressed to her and almost all expressed his

longing to escape, to begin anew, to go—somehow—somewhere else.

They would pass together, magically, through the flower-
papered wall of their Davenport room, or through the doorway
of an old haunted house he remembered on the edge of Springfield. Their honeymoon dwelt in his memory as an idyll, and
yet at the time he had taken it for granted that of course they
would *always* live like that: they would be adventure seekers
all their days. Meeting her eyes across the table, he wrote

> Oh beautiful adventure
> Called Elizabeth,
> Glory comes from you
> With every breath.
> So, with song I conquer,
> I live, and by God's help
> I will conquer yet
> The world with all its weariness
> Its fever and its fret.

They were at Wellesley College when Helen McMillin of
the *Transcript* came out from Boston for an interview. "Yes,
Mr. Lindsay is married," she told her readers, "much married,
happily married."

Yet his contentment with his new state served strangely to
accent another difference in him, one that Miss McMillin
found puzzling and saddening. She hadn't seen him for eight
years and she remembered a "boyish poet who pranced across
the stage, whose contagious enthusiasm swept his audiences."

"Such a change those years have wrought!" she exclaimed
now. "Compared with that buoyant young man, Mr. Lindsay
today is weary, worn and inexpressibly sad. His smile is the
same—that big wrinkled smile that literally wreathes his face
and sends his eyes completely out of sight. But his face in
repose has lines of suffering. Instead of roving the platform,
he stands almost still behind the reading desk, kept there, one
feels, by rigid determination. And most strikingly sad of all
the changes—the old spirit of comradeship between poet and

audience has given place to restraint, distrust, something that at times borders on definite antagonism."

In Springfield over Christmas, Vachel and Elizabeth stayed at a hotel, but on the holiday they walked together, heads bent against wind and snow, past the Lindsay house, which had been rented and was occupied by members of the Business and Professional Women's Club.

It was three days later—three days after that mournful glimpse—that Vachel, speaking before the Midday Luncheon Club of Springfield, a business men's organization, suddenly let go with an angry tirade against all the women's clubs of America, exclaiming that he had sworn off reciting to them because he preferred hostesses "who do their own work and who also read."

Cried Lindsay: "Almost any college professor's wife is this sort, but the women's clubs hate such people with a deadly hatred. They thrust me among hostesses where there is much tea, a smothering of servants, and if there are husbands present, they are the kind of business men who find their chief nourishment in the full-page advertisements of office supplies in the back of the *Literary Digest* and *Saturday Evening Post*."

Thus began the great Women's Club Controversy. The Associated Press picked up his diatribe, spreading it in headlines through the forty-eight states

VACHEL REVOLTS
LINDSAY HITS TEA-SIPPING WOMEN
"HOBO POET" SNEERS AT FORMER HOSTESSES

and the retaliatory comments continued almost into the spring.

"If Mr. Lindsay does not like tea, he can stay home," was the editorial decision of the Miami *Herald*, though the more friendly Chicago *News* allowed that "Vachel has our sympathy."

"He may not like us," blandly admitted a number of spokeswomen for the offended groups, "but for that matter, we do not like his poems."

"Is the man an American?" a lady president in Berkeley, California, demanded.

And on the other side of the country—"Vagabond poet of Springfield, Illinois, stands snubbed by clubwomen of Boston," revealed the *Evening Traveler* of that city. "When informed of Lindsay's attitude toward the modern women's club, they said it really does not matter what he thinks for it is not important."

Hardly were the Lindsays back in Spokane and settled, when Vachel left again. But Elizabeth, who expected her baby at the end of May, could not go with him on his new, hard-driving tour, which by the spring of 1926 was a financial necessity and for which she had made all the arrangements.

On the first morning after their marriage her husband had dumped thankfully into her hands his enormous personal and business correspondence. She had been his secretary and manager ever since, and never were his affairs so vigorously administered. She was his "young ruler," his "young governor," for lack of whom, he confessed, he had been "going all to pieces" in those last frantic days of bachelorhood.

To Elizabeth it was axiomatic that a poet who has written great poems at thirty, writes greater ones at fifty. As his achievement is progressive with age, so are the world's rewards, of which he is increasingly deserving. On her campaign for the first of her husband's tours under her management she brought to bear all the imperious expectations of her nature, which her demure front concealed, boldly setting his fee for a recital at $250 (the figure that Armstrong considered too high) and sending out five thousand circulars, which proclaimed "Vachel Lindsay, Troubadour, in Chanted Recitals of his Poems to his Own Tunes."

To organizations that had engaged him she despatched a list of General Suggestions.

"Make sure of a packed house," was one. Also, "See to it,"

she directed crisply, "that competent literary and musical critics are in charge of the reporting of Mr. Lindsay's recital, and not ordinary reporters."

Thus heralded with loving arrogance, the American troubadour again turned east. He did so with infinite reluctance. He was facing his first major tour since the failure of his health and his first separation from his bride since their wedding day. Yet this was adventure, too.

"I will be good," he vowed to her, "and keep my promises and try to earn some money for our baby."

On the day they parted, March 9, he wrote four times to her from the train, writing first, "I can think of nothing else except I want to make you happy," and again, "Parting with you is too hard, my darling. I love you and will do my best for you," and the third time, after reassuring her that he had taken his dose of quieting medicine, "I am still in a daze from saying good-by to you."

His fourth note a few minutes later, written just beyond Bozeman, Montana, contained a poem:

Now it is twilight. Farewell to the sunset.
The blue-gold river sweeps on past the train . . .

61

Vachel Troubadour, as Elizabeth called him, must sing for his supper again but with the difference that Vachel Troubadour was no longer his own man. He was a family man.

Before his marriage he had issued a third, and soon after his marriage a fourth, edition of *The Village Magazine*. The cost of the two ran to several thousand dollars, and as recently as February 1926, with his funds at a warning ebb and Elizabeth's confinement in the offing, he had had printed on huge sheets of expensive paper two thousand fresh copies of his "Map of the Universe."

By March there was almost no money left. FUNDS NEEDED THIS WEEK, he telegraphed to Harold Latham, his present editor at Macmillan's. PLEASE WIRE CHECK TO OLD NATIONAL BANK SPOKANE MANY THANKS.

Five days later he departed on tour, but because he loathed the prospect, Elizabeth, to whom nothing was impossible, undertook while he was gone to find him a job, preferably a contributing editorship to some magazine of national circulation that would allow him in future to sit at home and dictate.

Then from Philadelphia on March 15 he wrote back to her the "absolutely resurrection news" that it looked as if he had landed the job himself. He had asked for and been given interviews with Barton Currie, editor of the *Ladies' Home Journal*, and Thomas Costain, assistant to the editor of the *Saturday Evening Post*, both of whom had almost promised to accept from him not only big full-page poems but also peppy well-paid articles on "How It Seems to Speak to One Million

People" and "How It Feels to Be an American Poet in 1926."

"It's a *wonderful* opening, dear," and he bade her get off "Maps of the Universe" and *Village Magazines* right away to the entire staff in the Curtis Publishing Building. "I want that skyscraper honeycombed with Lindsay ideas!"

Next he had an hour's red-hot talk with George Horace Lorimer, editor-in-chief of the *Saturday Evening Post*. This was the same Lorimer to whose principles he once maintained he stood in deadly opposition, having planned, though never executed, a poem on the *Post* that would hit that organ without mercy. "Picture Andrew Jackson," he had written then, "tearing the *Saturday Evening Post* into shreds and shoving it into the open fire with his cane!"

Yet now he cautioned Elizabeth that, since he had a prospect of getting the whole Curtis combination under his hand inside a year or two, they ought to pick up everything they could about the policy of all Curtis papers.

Between Vachel and those merchant-kings who sat in the chairs of editors, it was a contest of wits and wills, just as it had always been in his own family. "The *Saturday Evening Post* is Uncle Lucius incarnate and the *Ladies' Home Journal* Aunt Fannie incarnate, and believe me I know how to please such people year after year and have my own way besides. I howled at Lorimer like a Dutch Uncle. Believe me, I talked up to him, little lady."

In New York, Lindsay was engaged for only one recital, a big one at the Art Center. He had not wanted to go to New York at all, and Elizabeth had moments of self-reproach for having sent him there.

She enclosed in a letter her ribboned garter and a baby sock. She was his "utter slave," she told him, and in return he sent her one of the printed forms provided for each room by the Hotel Commodore, which said: GUESTS EXPECTING VISITORS KINDLY SIGN THIS CARD. *Mr. . . . .* (here Lindsay filled in) *and Mrs. Vachel Lindsay are expecting a large bundle wrapped in red flannel they call he-she.*

From Spokane, Elizabeth had been following his recitals eastward by the clock, counting the difference in hours. They were both dreading the New York appearance.

"Dear and faithful heart," he wrote to her just after midnight on March 23, "tomorrow—that is, today, this afternoon at 3:30—I do my best for you. And whether I do well or ill I am this moment at peace. If I do well and am strong, I will *brag* to you. If I do poorly and am weak, I will turn to your sweet breasts for refuge and be as sure as life itself you will hold me close and comfort me."

That afternoon kind Frederic Melcher sent Elizabeth a telegram to let her know that Vachel had done nobly. Melcher particularly admired the new poem *Virginia*, which Lindsay about a fortnight later recited again, with several of his old ones, including *The Congo*, to a circle of distinguished men in armchairs in the library of The Players.

For years he had been inordinately eager to join The Players and on this visit to New York Edgar Lee Masters proposed him for membership. But his reading of *The Congo* so shattered the after-dinner peace of several members in rooms nearby that at least one of them tried to bar his admission on the ground that it would be intolerable to have "that fellow" around all the time. An awkward delay followed, during which Masters, who had obtained a guest card for Lindsay, endeavored, in the end successfully, to convince the directors they could not afford to blackball so important a figure in American letters.

Lindsay never dreamed his welcome was not with open arms.

"Believe me, if I have a card at The Players I am *nobody's* lost darling," he assured Elizabeth. For not till The Players gave him one did he feel this spring that he had a local habitation and a name in New York, though five months earlier the presence of his bride had given him both.

And it had been otherwise at the outset of his career, he recalled to Masters, as they sat reminiscing in the club library. In 1914 the city loved him. He had had to put the chain up on the door of his hotel room and hire a secretary to answer

the telephone and turn away reporters. Now he came and
went without notice, almost, except that now when Prohibition was the law and it had become fashionable to eulogize the
ancient days of the barroom, the critics, having discovered that
he had been a temperance worker in his time, were rediscovering and holding up to ridicule his rather poor Anti-Saloon
League verses.

Masters reminded him that this was natural. New York
notoriously turned to rising personalities. "My friend," said
Masters, "you have written immortal poems, and what more is
there to do?"

Masters was a philosopher. But when the two parted and
Lindsay rose, smiled, raised his hand in jaunty salute and then
took his way alone toward Fourth Avenue, rolling on his feet
and casting his head up at the tall Babylonian buildings, his
very back betrayed his state of mind. "I saw," writes Masters,
who had lingered in the doorway to gaze after him, "that he
was an unhappy man."

In his hotel room, writing, writing in his diary, Lindsay
acknowledged in somber and unsparing self-analysis: "Ambition and spread-eagle vanity devour me, like a lion and eagle
devouring a living bull of the herd. I always had a-plenty, but
the really international flatteries of the last ten years have
increased them beyond all reason."

He was especially sure of this in New York. Yet as his
dreams grew greater, his strength diminished. Since the genie
of his ambition would never again return to the bottle, his only
hope to satisfy it was in showing more courage than other men.
"It is the only thing I have endlessly, and which seems to fail
all other men soon."

He went alone ("utterly alone") to see Walter Hampden in
Cyrano de Bergerac, a study in courage, and he thought of
his father, the Mohawk, whose courage was as simple as an
arrow. "Dearest dearest," he wrote to Elizabeth from down-

stairs in the Commodore lobby, which was darkened and full
of scrubwomen and vacuum cleaners at 1:30 in the morning,
"I *know* ambition just *eats me up* but New York did not seem
to wake the crowing rooster in me before, say, 1920."

In his room he had placed her picture next to the Gideon
Bible. He considered the garter a promissory note. At night
he called his pillow Elizabeth.

He had been at the Commodore ten days when the desk
clerk telephoned up to say that the management liked its bills
settled weekly. This was something new. Astounded but peni-
tent, he wired home for $100, which Elizabeth somehow wired
back. Then taking a bus on Fifth Avenue, he called at the
office of *Vanity Fair*, where he hoped to sell some drawings,
but both Frank Crowninshield and Condé Nast were away,
"and there was not ready money there."

To save what he had, he ate stand-up meals in Grand Central station at the buttermilk bar. He did not this time attempt
to call at the Macmillan office, and "how happy I am that I do
not need to," he confessed.

But he saw his old fellow art student George Mather Richards, who was doing illustrations for Macmillan's ("and who
does not chafe as I do under their squelching tactics"), and he
had been to see Sara, who informed him plaintively that in
New York ever since the war the New Poetry movement had
lapsed completely in the sight of the "avaricious" publishers.

And since the war, Lindsay continued violently, "I think
there are far more middle-class hard-boiled Russian Jews—the
toughest God makes—now than of old. This is *my* city, where
I was a student, not theirs, and I want to push them off the
walk!"

Again it was locust blossom time when he returned to Spokane, and as he drew westward his heart opened to the scenes
he loved. Babylon was not America. "In spite of all the struggle of this tour," he wrote to Elizabeth from the train, "I love
the land I have passed over, and the land I have looked upon."

Singlehanded during his absence, Elizabeth had moved their

things out of the Davenport. The tiny apartment she rented was on a pine-covered hill behind Cliff Park. It was from there that she and Vachel drove in a taxi to the hospital in the early evening of May 28, 1926. Elizabeth, very gay and talkative, carried a single American Beauty rose, which her husband placed in her hand. When next morning he came trembling to her bedside, her smile was grave and sweet as she told him: "Little Susan Doniphan was born last night."

They had chosen the name after that great-grandmother of Lindsay's in whose veins flowed the blood of Don Iphan. "Because I am a blond, people do not even suspect I am an Indian and Spaniard inside," he wrote to Harriet Monroe three weeks after his daughter's birth.

Elizabeth was back at home; their little household was settling down. Yet his letter concerned itself less with Susan and the happily expanding future than with long-accumulating resentments. On the subject of ancestry and inheritance he went on to rage to Harriet that the late Amy Lowell once took two pages of the New York *Times* book section expressly to write him down as "a crude middle westerner of the middle class."

In her article, which was her critical, yet thoughtful review of *The Golden Whales of California*, Miss Lowell had commented that "in the case of Mr. Lindsay a hen has hatched a song-sparrow who yet retains a love of the barnyard," and by "hen" she meant the nonconformist American middle class.

Try as she would to keep it otherwise, her tone was condescending. In other moods, Lindsay could admit that his middleclassness was one of the ideas behind his religious poems; it had been dingdonged into him by his mother before he was six. Yet now to Harriet, he charged angrily that in all his years of knowing Amy, whenever he had dinner at her big house near Boston, she had "with incessant persecution" thus *insulted* him.

"I ventured in the midst of a conversation when she suddenly and irrelevantly insisted once more that I was a 'middle westerner' (she did not say 'middle class' to my face), I ventured to say I was a Virginian!"

As "Virginians"—a word he was making his own—he had

begun to characterize all Americans, wherever born, who value leisure and spaciousness, are gallant, chivalrous and cut a dash. They are the opposite of Babbitt. An example was Bryan, born in Illinois, and later Lindsay was to call Helen Wills, the tennis champion, and the great aviator Charles Lindbergh "Virginians."

His romantic definition cut no ice with Harriet Monroe, who retorted that "all we Illinois suckers came from somewhere, but the Middle West is good enough for me. Why bother and brood about what Amy said, or what Mrs. Toplofty of Springfield thinks of us? Ancestry—bah! You had too many ancestors flung at you in your childhood—I hope your daughter will have better luck. You ought to heave them overboard for good and all—you who can say, like Napoleon, *'Je suis ancêtre!'* "

In an essay on Lindsay, written two years earlier, Harriet had praised in him the genial American humor that rollicked in many of his poems. "The law of perspective, which ensures sanity," she called it then. "It is in such laughter that hate dies among us—" and lest this saving grace fail him now, she urged him in her reply to "laugh—laugh at the silly world!

"Get small grudges out of your mind—get yourself out of your mind. You should be thinking of more important things —'man's origin and destiny,' as James Stephens put it."

62

On the day of his daughter's birth, Lindsay's book *Going-to-the-Stars* came out under Appleton's imprint.

Like its predecessor, *Going-to-the-Sun*, the new collection, which again made a feature of his pen-and-ink drawings and embellishments, was more a notebook of jotted-down suggestions than a finished volume. It had such robust pieces as *Virginia* and *Old, Old, Old, Old Andrew Jackson*, and also—written in what Lindsay thought of as his new, quieter style—*The Flower-fed Buffaloes*, muted and lovely evocation of the pioneer twilight; *These Are the Young*; *The Jazz of This Hotel*; *Three Hours*, and the soaring love song *The Angel Sons*.

But the few fine poems were outweighed by trivial epigrams and half-worked fantasies. "Let it be said of *Going-to-the-Stars* that it is very bad," declared Genevieve Taggard in the New York *Herald Tribune*, while a critic in the *Literary Review* of the New York *Evening Post* pronounced the book "a gross travesty of Lindsay's genius, an empty, often insane, echo of the kind of thing we have learned gratefully to expect from him."

In general the press reception was scathing. It was now that Edgar Lee Masters, who despised pretentiousness, was cynical toward the hucksters and full of spleen for his enemies, went out of his way to write warmly to Lindsay, his friend, whose poetry, he believed, had at its best an "unparalleled originality," which neither the critics nor the poet's own diligence

could bestow but which could be dimmed—dimmed fatally—
by criticism and self-consciousness.

"Don't give the miserable squeaks of this New York crowd
a thought," Masters advised. "Don't read what they write.
Don't let anybody tell you about it."

In October 1926, Masters reviewed at length in *The Bookman* not only *Going-to-the-Stars* but also the *Collected Poems*,
the offering and record of a lifetime.

With the best and generous side of himself that association
with Lindsay always brought to the fore, Masters did his
utmost to redress what he considered a foolish wrong by contemporary poetasters, writing of Lindsay that "nothing like
him has ever been, he derives from no one. The passing of
time cannot detract from his originality. . . . I can see the
probability of his becoming the most magical figure of this
day to the Americans of one hundred years from now, when
the rising generation will dwell upon his quests and his wanderings, his faiths and his passions, his tramps preaching the gospel
of beauty, his devotion to Lincoln, to Jackson, the unsullied
goodness of his heart, the element of divinity in him. . . .

"I can overlook the daisies, the hieroglyphs, the Egyptian
symbols of fertility and immortality with which he decorates
his pages. . . . He is not to be judged by his prefaces, his works
on the movie art, in which his Egyptian and Swedenborgian
conceptions furnish the basis for aesthetic argumentations. He
is to be judged by his best poems."

And the best poems of Lindsay, said Masters, "move me
profoundly because they give me the feeling of America.
Always there is back of what he says the energy and the
abounding faith of the sound and devoted American that he is."

Then Masters, who had not forgotten his friend's discouragement in New York and who especially admired the great
chanting portrait of Andrew Jackson, before which some
critics hesitated, ended in words that more than any others
were calculated to give present help: "Lindsay's visions have
not ceased to flit palpably before him; his gusto and his rever-
berating music are still with him. As lives go in America he is
at the apex of his power, and *Going-to-the-Stars* shows no
abatement of his genius."

63

Only once during this last and most difficult tour had Lindsay's health threatened to betray him. Toward the end of April he had overdone. He had given too much of himself one morning in a poetry class at Syracuse University and again at his evening recital before the college, with the result that he felt dizzy and ill and, in defiance of his resolve to keep his courage up, terror swept through him.

As instructed, he took notes on his condition to send the neurologist at Mayo under whose special care he was. But the violent convulsions that terrified Elizabeth alone with him in the remote heights of Glacier Park had not recurred. "Leyden jar explosions," he privately called his rare spasms, which with that single long-past exception were relatively mild, and in his diary in this connection he drew a skull and crossbones.

On his way back to Spokane he had stopped at Mayo for a personal report to his physician, who then suggested to him that " 'over-thwarting and strain in his art' " might be a possible aggravation of his trouble.

But his artist's ambition, Lindsay protested—again in his diary—was "like his very life blood." "Asking me to make it second-rate is just awful. It is *killing* advice. What is good in my doctor's advice is to be thus translated: go slow—pick out the *principal things* and do them more thoroughly than ever."

The doctor had remarked encouragingly that there are a thousand different kinds of "spasm," all of which run to periodicity—the general term means nothing—and in his diary Lindsay avoided the use of a specific term, setting down another consoling dictum of the doctor's, that " 'any hereditary trait, unless both have it, will be submerged.' "

"I am sure," he added on his own, "the family inheritance is a highly specialized, slowly maturing nervous system, not a diseased one. . . . This is the substance of my case—I have cut my nerves into three pieces trying to win first honors in creative work in speaking, writing and drawing. Hence rhythmic exhaustion."

Since he had been on tour, sticking tight to luminal sodium, the constant small "nag" of his nerves had disappeared and his only really remaining symptoms were the inability to recite more than once a day and a whirling sensation in the midst of reciting unless he had a whole pot of strong coffee beforehand.

The prognosis of his condition was not hopeful, but this he did not know. He did not know he fought a losing battle, only that he faced a further challenge. Granted that he had, in the fight to control his nerves, his share of the human curse. But all, all have their stigmata, and "the *great people*," as he had once written to Olive, the nearest to him now of his blood, "can rise above these things, and balance them."

Yet he felt a panic fear of nervous collapse he had never known before his breakdown three years earlier. When in August 1926 he and Elizabeth went again to Glacier Park for a holiday, he was aware of a certain risk. He put his faith in luminal sodium and courage.

This time their expenses were being paid by the Northern Pacific Railroad in return for their consent to plenty of publicity. They took with them Susan, eleven weeks old, on a papoose-board strapped to her father's back, and Elizabeth's younger sister, Claribel, to look after Susan.

All went well till one afternoon when, leaving the baby with Claribel in their cabin near the main chalet and accompanied by ranger guides, Lindsay and Elizabeth rode on horseback up one of the thickly wooded mountain trails. They were on their way back down when Lindsay decided to finish on foot and, disregarding the guides' protests, their warning against the danger of losing his path, of the deadly cold that strikes after sunset and the possible attack of fierce bears, he dismounted.

Elizabeth begged him in vain to come with the others, then, bound by a nursing schedule, she reluctantly went on ahead. When he had not arrived at the cabin by dark she and Claribel put lighted candles in the window. When he was not back by dawn, Elizabeth, after a night of apprehension past the power of words to communicate, during which her hopes rose at every snapping twig, called out the rangers and sent them up into the mountain.

They returned unsuccessfully that afternoon and almost at once set out again, taking with them an Indian boy who knew every trail. It was the boy who discovered Lindsay in the gray dawn of the second morning. He was not far from the spot where he had been left. For a day and two nights he had gone without his medicine and the beast of panic had sprung.

When they came on him he was utterly lost, traveling in a circle, chilled to the bone, ragged, dirty, stumbling through the rocks, falling and staggering up with outstretched arms, pursuing a phantom wife and crying, "Elizabeth! Elizabeth!" He gave no answer to the rangers' halloos and calling of his name, or to their final glad shouts on his discovery, nor did he seem at first to be aware of them as they lifted him on horseback and led him down.

After a day in bed he was physically himself. He crouched by a fire in the cabin, wrapped in blankets, while Elizabeth washed and dried his clothes. But the joy of adventure was gone from both their hearts and the delusion, which later became Lindsay's firm conviction of what had taken place, was already forming in his mind—that the ranger guides had deliberately abandoned him.

Only Elizabeth's sister and her mother knew why she and Vachel cut their trip short and came home earlier than expected. Neither the railroad company nor the press ever knew.

64

Later this autumn the Lindsays moved from their pine-covered hilltop to the city below.

In a new apartment at 2318 West Pacific Avenue they entertained, and nothing in Spokane was like their large bare living room, where high around the walls ran a frieze of the Egyptian Book of the Dead and lower down hung "The Tree of Laughing Bells." Elsewhere were Vachel's swirling pen-and-ink sketches; there was a mosaic by him in colored paper and transparent mending tape illustrating Coleridge's Xanadu and the pleasure dome of the great Kubla, before which, wearing a black Chinese robe embroidered with gold dragons (his gift to Elizabeth), he loved to stand and strike an attitude and recite the poem.

But the entertainment that made the room rock was the revived poem games, whose present stars were Lenore Glen and Stoddard King.

On their carpetless floor the Lindsays had painted a red disc representing the sun, with rays shooting out from it, and surrounding it a huge red circle. While people on the sidewalk peered in through the window curtains, and the Methodist family in the flat upstairs was driven half crazy, Vachel, Elizabeth, Stoddard and Lenore and a few picked participants, wearing bathing suits and floating scarves, danced down these paths chanting Vachel's poems. Sometimes Vachel stood on the painted sun and chanted solo, occasionally whirling where he stood like a teetotum—the others around him moving rhythmically and posing statuesquely to a tin-pan tomtom (all Elizabeth's saucepans were beaten out of shape).

Roland Hayes, the great Negro tenor, who was in Spokane for a concert, came to dinner with the Lindsays. Harriet Monroe came from Chicago; from New York, Frederic Melcher, who sportingly took part in a poem game in his honor; then John Erskine, the novelist; Percy Grainger, and Gene Tunney, the young heavyweight champion who had knocked out Dempsey and read Shakespeare.

The new apartment was close to Indian Canyon and there Vachel and Elizabeth strolled and picnicked. It was close also to the center of town, where they went to the movies. On winter evenings they read aloud—poetry and American history and Emerson—and on fresh April mornings, when rain threatened and the birds sang outside, Elizabeth sang inside—the liquid duet reminding her husband of Swinburne's lines

> With kisses glad as birds are
> That get sweet rain at noon.

This was in the spring of 1927. Determined to tour no more, Lindsay had re-engaged his room at the Davenport as a studio, paying the whole rent himself. He went there each morning to write all day—on the surface a simple program. The first of his articles for the Curtis Publishing Company, an essay on Douglas Fairbanks, had appeared in the *Ladies' Home Journal* for August 1926, and in November that year an article by him on "What It Means To Be a Poet in America" was published in the *Saturday Evening Post*.

On the one hand, he longed for access to a tremendous audience. He wanted a magazine for which he could produce steadily, he told Tom Costain of the *Post*. Not the most ample book publication could furnish the "close-to-the-people sway" he desired.

On the other hand, he privately complained that to keep up this fearsome production without ruining his style, wrecking his disposition and selling his democratic soul was nearly impossible, that a man must have "running off at the ink bottle" to fill the demands of office spiders whose general assumption seemed to be that he would bring forth articles for them one after another till he dropped in his tracks.

Yet it was a trial that must be made. "I must pay the stork for Susan Doniphan—" and not only this, but his little family was soon to be increased a second time.

In his diary he noted that, as well as writing lots of articles, he ought to "pour out the books," letting Elizabeth hold them for insurance. Less than three months after the appearance of *Going-to-the-Stars*, another book of his poems and drawings, *The Candle in the Cabin*, was published. At the turn of the year he had offered Appleton three more books: a collection of his impromptu "menu poems"; his autobiography, so far unwritten, and finally a book to contain 300 drawings and no verse at all. Since 1920, when he began to draw again and with longer, bolder strokes than of old, he had been confident that he had it in him to produce pictures with lines as buoyant and fluid as *The Congo* was in verse, once he got the swing.

John Williams, his editor at Appleton's, rejected outright only the third offer, but he forwarded to Lindsay a bundle of unfavorable reviews of *The Candle in the Cabin* with the advice to think them over—"mighty carefully," said Williams. Lindsay also had a letter from Masters, who warned him that he was writing too fast, that he should rather let what he had written enter thoroughly into the memory of the country while he matured ("very carefully," said Masters) what he had yet to write.

"It comes only to this," Masters went on, "that I'd love to see you brood on your American interpretations. Carry them with you. Write them slowly. Believe that they will find their true way, after the hurrah and the envy of the day have died down like the weeds, leaving the oaks unhurt by the frosts."

"Truly your friend," Masters signed himself, and Lindsay took the warning in good part.

But to Fred Melcher, whom he was pushing hard to find an opening in New York for his book of drawings rejected by Appleton, he now railed against those editors of publishing houses ("discreet embalmers") who tried to jam his future work into a pigeonhole, laid funeral wreaths on his hopes of ever doing something different, and sent him instructions that lopped off every single unexpected blossom or bloom and read like "the mimeographed orders of The Standard Oil Company to a branch filling station."

They could not realize, he protested to Melcher, that since his marriage he was a new man. He was desirous of experiment; he was capable of fresh achievement. At forty-seven, he was not much older in heart than Susan. His happy life with Susan and Elizabeth was a *new* life! Though inconceivable to New York that he should be married to "the Lady California" and have a roaring year-old daughter, so it was and he must proclaim these splendors.

Yet his spirit was not at rest. There were days when he hated and was homeless. At this time, writing to Masters, he charged that after his mother's death he had been "banished" from his town and "lost" the home that was his by right owing to the machinations of those whom he called, on a rising note of fury, "the fat rich illiterate climacteric women of Springfield."

"My father, my mother, my ancestral home and my city, the very city of my special choice and illimitable dreams—all lost at one fell swoop . . . because a few fat illiterate rich women hated the whole New Poetry movement *and all it implied with a deadly hatred*."

He was writing on June 28, 1927. Eighteen months earlier, he had hurled his tirade against the clubwomen of America soon after he and Elizabeth walked by, almost like strangers, the house of his boyhood. Again it was in the recollection of that unspeakably dispiriting glimpse that he now told Masters: "The whole house looks like the wrath of God."

He seriously declared to Masters that it was the Springfield bankers' wives, his lifelong enemies, an "absolutely close corporation," who in 1922 had run him out.

"Lustful of useless power . . . those fat females," cried Lindsay, had deliberately fomented a disagreement among him and his sisters about the handling of the property—"the whole thing was to give the local trust companies fat pickings on a hundred thousand dollar estate *entirely out of debt*. . . ."

Since 1921 the management of Dr. Lindsay's estate, a part of which was mortgaged, had been in the hands of a Springfield bank. The officer directly responsible for the administering was an old family friend; he had reported to Mrs. Lindsay and after her death to her three children. Then for a year the house was rented to a private family—though Vachel, before his move to Spokane, still kept his books and papers there—after which the Wakefields occupied it on their furlough home in 1923. When Olive and Paul returned to China, it was Joy, the youngest but most practical of the heirs, who with the consent of the others made the decision to rent the house furnished to the Business and Professional Women's Club.

All this Lindsay ignored in his letter to Masters, which, written in a blinding nervous rage, was yet the source of the account of his leaving Springfield later given by Masters in his biography of Lindsay.

Masters had his own grudge against the Philistine small cities of the Midwest. He swallowed his friend's extravagant accusations greedily and entire, making no allowance for a state of mind indicated even by the deteriorating handwriting, and replying, "I never have read of anything more infamous except in books of history. . . . Be sure history will want the story."

Lindsay had forgotten that only in January he had been anxious to part with the very house from which, by June, he claimed to be debarred.

On January 16, 1927, Joy wrote worriedly to George Greenwood, her brother's banker in Spokane, to say that at the present moment Vachel seemed bent on selling the old house. Yet five months earlier she had had a thirty-five-page letter from him protesting excitedly that the place belonged in spirit more to him than to anyone, that he cared *deeply* for it, which made her think then that they ought never to sell.

His feeling for the house varied with his mood. In just which of several moods he would be a year from now she could not prophesy. Her own judgment was that Elizabeth and Susan would be better protected if at least a part of the property remained unsold. An empty lot and several little houses built as investments by Dr. Lindsay had been sold some years before, but rents still came in from a small apartment building; the proceeds were divided into three shares. One of the largest lump sums to go to Vachel was $5,000 after his mother's death. What had he done with it, Joy wondered.

Much of it had been sunk in *Village Magazines*. This Joy did not know, but she recalled the summer Vachel had spent at the Hotel Commodore in 1922 and the next, when he lived in costly solitude at a hotel in Cleveland, though her own house was open to him. When he finally met and married the lady of his heart, little, if anything, was left to finance the marriage. Then in December 1926 he had received a payment amounting to more than $5,000 from a further sale of property belonging to the estate, with the present result that he was encouraging Elizabeth to buy a grand piano and had resumed his "study" at the Davenport.

Here Joy—her father's daughter, in whose veins the Mohawk blood boiled—could not forbear asking *why*, when so much high art had its birth in attics, her brother's took on increased value for being born in expensive hotels. It seemed especially inconsistent in a poet who advocated democracy and fulminated against "Babylon, Babylon, Babylon."

65

The happiest moment of their life together, exclaimed Lindsay, was when he and Elizabeth arrived at that Franciscan point where you have no money and owe no money.

"Divinely poor—" he called their condition, writing to Olive and Paul in June 1927. "We never have any money, and that keeps off bloodsuckers, bootlickers and the like, and we never owe any money and that keeps away every form of outside bully, and that's the way to live!"

He was writing to them on a special expensive heavy paper ornamented with his printed designs. "This paper, one more example of my howling extravagance and non-Spokane asininity, is the basis of a new book of my drawings."

Though only the day before he had received a further dividend of nearly $300 from his father's estate, the next day after writing to the Wakefields he was obliged to ask Latham at Macmillan's that whatever royalties were outstanding might, as a favor, be paid him immediately instead of in November, when they were legally due.

Macmillan prepared a statement, sent on June 27, with a check for $836.48.

"We have achieved *complete* financial independence of the *book publishers* and the *recital platform*," Lindsay assured Mrs. Moody a few weeks later, blissfully unconscious of any inconsistency.

His Curtis articles and two or three others, including one on Gene Tunney accepted by *Vanity Fair*, indicated to him that he, like other men, could fight his way through the world

375

for his wife and child. On the strength of them, he told Elizabeth this summer to cancel eight hundred dollars' worth of recitals already scheduled for October and November—this though on September 16, 1927, their second child was born, a son whom they named, for his father's family, Nicholas Cave.

But Elizabeth from her hospital bed, where she remained longer than the statutory two weeks, for she was exhausted, confided in a letter to Harriet Monroe that she felt as uneasy at their continually mounting expenses as though a taxi meter were clicking. She felt guilty, too, guilty that a genius should be burdened with a family and that since his poems for *The Candle in the Cabin*—most of them written on his honeymoon —Vachel had produced almost no real poems.

Instead, as the alternative to travel and reciting, he was forced to brood over, tediously revise and attempt to market unending magazine articles, and while for the past twelve months he and she had "gambled on" through a giddy series of inflations and deflations, the showdown was near.

Harriet was still weighing Elizabeth's communication when she had one from Vachel that made her doubly anxious. The Macmillan office had passed on to him an inquiry from a Mr. Augustus Smith, of the School of Religious Education and Social Service at Boston University, who innocently asked permission to have Lindsay's poem *Foreign Missions in Battle Array* set to music.

In the past Lindsay had said "Yes" to similar suggestions, as when John Alden Carpenter asked to compose a light opera based on *The Congo* and the musical accompaniment was written for Louise Homer's singing of *General Booth*; he had been eager to find some young woman, as gifted in music as Eleanor Dougherty in the dance, to sing *The Chinese Nightingale*. But into the present harmless request he read the threat of hostile domination, of an attempt by outsiders to run his show for him. Though in the end he merely returned a blunt negative ("Dear Sir, No, no, no, NEVER!"), before doing so he worked himself up in the drafting of a raving reply, which he enclosed in his letter to Harriet.

He was the composer of his own music and no one else was the composer of his music! Every poem he had ever written was set to his own tune or to a tune of his choosing! "You are just one more fresh fakir, wanting to steal my work under a religious cloak—" ran his original multi-page answer to Mr. Smith, scrawled in an enormous hand and snagged with misspelled and oddly aborted words.

That the approach to him had been made through his publisher he interpreted as a club held over his head.

"If the threat is to throw my books into the street if I will not submit to fresh men like you, the Macmillan Company can throw them into the street. . . . No gentleman, no artist, no Christian, would write such a letter to a harried man who sees a lifetime work as a troubadour torn to shreds before his eyes by such parasites as yourself. . . .

"You think because I write religious poetry that any sneaking Annas or Caiphas who rubs his oily hands and acts pious can steal and steal and steal my song. . . . If there is hell, men like you will fry on the first griddle, and I hope you are fried on both sides. . . .

"Thou shalt not steal. Moses said that and he was a Jew. He knew that much. . . . Mind your own business, you dirty Boston sneak, and beware of a law suit. . . .

"So much the worse for Boston. May the ghost of Amy Lowell dance on your grave. Woe unto you scribes and Phrisees hypocrits. You are inwardly full of dead men's bones and all uncleanliness. You are just a plain dirty thief. . . ."

Acknowledging the disordered diatribe, the reading of which turned her cold, Harriet wrote to Lindsay, on November 8: "I thank the kind fates that you didn't send it. There are libel laws." Then she begged him, as she had done before, to take the larger view. "Why waste your time and nerves over such futile controversies?"

Like his emphasis on his "Virginianism" and overpreoccupation with his drawings, these verbal explosions seemed to her a sapping of his vital force and cluttering up of the free pathway of his genius. When she reviewed in *Poetry* for January 1927 his two most recent books of verse she had expressed regret that he ever discovered the "new and madly absorbing toy" of illustration, which was playing ducks and drakes with his writing of poems worthy of his fame, declaring then that Mr. Lindsay seemed to be reversing the usual process of growth and living his childhood *last*.

This was deplorable in a poet who, for all the current belittling of his work, had in his early and great poems "planted a flower of pride in the rich but dry soil of America."

Now she concluded her direct appeal: "Remind yourself, day by day and every day, that poetry is your art, your true and only grand art, that whatever power of imagination you have belongs by divine right to poetry."

When Elizabeth, with Nicky in her arms, came home from the hospital in October, there was $5.00 in the apartment. She used it to pay the little nurse who had been helping with Susan, and from then till February the four Lindsays lived on credit.

She could see afterward that the trouble of this never-to-be-forgotten winter began when Vachel, revolted and bored by the business of reciting and its effect on his art, had canceled his fall tour; it increased when not one but several articles on whose acceptance he counted were returned to him, and it reached a crisis in January and February 1928, when he grew panicky and paralyzed. Yet up to Christmas the grimmer realities were spared him, for most of his waking hours he spent immured in his room at the Davenport, where the management allowed him to charge everything, including cash for tips.

It was Elizabeth, half a mile away, who stalled the grocer and cajoled the landlord and went to the back door in the dark at five in the morning to tell the milkman softly they would pay him when they could but they just couldn't now and the babies did need milk.

"That's all right," said the milkman (Elizabeth never forgot his words). "It'll come out of my salary, but I understand. It must be tough to be a poet."

Nor did Lindsay, in his eleventh-floor eyrie, ever know that of those friends and sponsors in Spokane whose practical advice since his marriage he violently resented, at least two came forward in this all too obvious emergency. Ben Kizer, meeting Elizabeth out wheeling Nicky, urged her to let him know if she needed money. George Greenwood called her into his office at the bank to tell her she could have what she required, just to write a check.

From Chicago, Harriet Monroe proposed tentatively that Elizabeth might do something at home to help—perhaps sell corsets by telephone, then she withdrew the suggestion for fear it would be laughed at. "Indeed I do *not* laugh," Elizabeth answered. "I'm past that. It's simply a question of what can be done—and if it's corsets, then corsets it is."

What she most wanted to do, she went on, was "to get behind Vachel and push. If he will just be sensible—even half-way—write prose articles for a month or so every year, speak for a month or so, compile a book or two from his articles, and cut down a *few* extravagances (par exemple—a bill at the Davenport for $600—tea, room, barber, etc.—and giving away $850 worth of books this Christmas, without telling me) we should make it."

More than a year earlier Mabel Kizer had called on the Lindsays and happened to find Elizabeth alone in the rueful aftermath of what she admitted was her first tiff with Vachel, who had rushed out and down into the city—they were living then in the apartment behind Cliff Park. At that moment the doorbell rang and a special messenger handed in Vachel's peace offering, sent from below: four dozen roses, six pairs of silk garters and three sets of appliquéd lace-trimmed silk underwear from Haddad's, one of the most expensive specialty shops in the West.

Did she mean to keep the gifts, asked Mabel.

Certainly, answered Elizabeth, smiling. Vachel could spend his money in any way he pleased.

But time had passed. Nicky had been born, and she could smile no longer. She was writing to Harriet in February 1928, when they were still bleeding from the wounds of Christmas, at which season, with nothing coming in, Vachel had ordered from Macmillan six boxes of his books to give as presents. The copies were charged to his royalty account and the total cost, though under her frantic estimate, was $552.72. Since Christmas he had given up his room at the Davenport but the financial advantage was offset by his perpetual presence at home, where he simply sat all day long and brooded, she told Harriet—"stunned by worry, absolutely *clammy* and cold with misery. . . ."

Harriet's next step was, with utmost delicacy, to send Elizabeth a check for $100—a tribute, she truthfully explained, from an admirer personally unknown to Lindsay but "who would like to help out, just a little, a distinguished poet in a time of financial stringency. . . ." and on her own she continued: "Are things any better? Would a loan help?"

Elizabeth could only answer: "God bless you! We say it with all our hearts."

The $100 would pay the rent, the milkman, the iceman, the laundryman; it would pay for the mending of Susan's shoes and the cleaning and pressing of Vachel's suit. There would be even a little left for the four-month-old grocery bill.

On the wall of Harriet's office in Chicago had hung for many years, much treasured by her, a framed page from Lindsay's original *Village Magazine*, which bore his texts "Where there is loveliness there is God," and "Seek ye first the kingdom of beauty."

Later this spring she came to his rescue a second time, accepting for *Poetry* his single new long poem, *Every Soul Is a Circus*. She hesitated to do so; an earlier version had already been published in the Kansas City *Star* and *Poetry* never used anything that first appeared elsewhere. But it was that or nothing for the present, he told her. She was the only human being on the face of the earth who wanted him to write more poems and, confidentially, he hoped she would take this one; once more their landlord was glaring at him for back rent.

Breaking her precedent, Harriet accepted the poem and sent her personal check for $50.

Lindsay's letter of thanks was quiet. Little need be said by him and nothing emphasized to this friend whose loyalty, good faith and earnest championship were an asset in his soul's life "never to be forgotten, always a well-spring. I feel so sure you are doing for the boys and girls what you once did for me when a boy, that I almost feel like an intruder . . . in this sense, that if I cannot make my way in the big world now, *after all you have done for me,* I am not much of a singer, not much of a leader."

He knew that in his work he must go forward. Old Milton, who being blind could concentrate, was one of the few poets who ever built a second story on his poetry. But he, Lindsay, was overstimulated for his strength; he was made drunk by his love of the Democracy and though he had lately given up his drawing, Egyptology, movie criticism, parlor tricks and hiking, he still got "ten too many ideas every day."

"Downtown I get 100 too many ideas, they rush by like a movie newsreel" (he was writing now in his diary). "Let me always say to myself, I will act upon the one best and swiftest idea, born in the deep silence of my own study. . . ."

But he had no longer his study at the Davenport and concentration came harder at home, where Susan yelled, the landlord and grocer were restive, his young wife wore old women's hand-me-downs, and the four of them lived on their prospects like the Micawber family.

66

In 1922, alone in New York after his mother's death, Lindsay had written with sadness in his diary that it seemed to him he was always "passing through," a citizen of a city of the future, and that as long as he passed through he prospered. "It is when I endeavor to *sit down*, someone puts a tack in the chair."

Five years later, on March 3, 1928, during what started as a friendly talk (at $20) before the Spokane branch of the AAUW, he flew suddenly into a frightful rage, crying out to the embarrassed members that never, never in all his nearly four years' residence had he been made to feel at home in Spokane. There were "ten business men" in the city who had tried to drive him out and were determined to "crucify" him.

They were against him, he charged.

He remembered afterward that before he rose to speak he had felt a strange sweating, precursor of loss of control. His outburst was almost like a physical attack, recalls Mary McKechnie, and those in the audience who were his friends could scarcely bear to look or hear.

A few days later he began to write under his byline in the Spokane *Daily Chronicle* a weekly column, "Home Town Topics." His still hopeful theme was the building of Spokane, as under other skies it had been the building of Springfield. Taking as his starting point the Rim Rock, with the ideas of eternity and destiny there inscribed, he wrote that from the encircling rampart he saw the brilliant little city as a nest of singing birds. "It does not look like a prison or a place where people's tongues are cut out or their feet are hobbled."

But the hopes that would build a singing city were dimmed of late by the anger that recurred in blinding, smothering waves. This same month, in letters to friends, he called himself and Elizabeth "two bronchos who would not be broken" as they two alone bucked the prosperous local gentry, who considered Eddie Guest a bookworm, and the "ten or twenty Poloniuses," multi-millionaires who ruled the city of Spokane —ruled it "like doges behind closed doors, behind the arras . . . senile pests . . . whispering, paddling carpet-slippered old idiots. They envy me my beautiful wife and babies!"

And he had been "thoroughly skinned" by that "marvelous Lorenzo" who was one of his first inviters to Spokane. "This town invited me here as its guest," cried Lindsay. "Its hospitality was bunco from first to last."

Two months later, on May 2, he wrote in the same vein to Paul Wakefield. Like other missionaries, Dr. Wakefield had been forced by the civil unrest in China to flee the country with his wife and children and, back in America, was appointed to a state medical project in Massachusetts. Though every dollar counted with him, he managed at this time to send Vachel and Elizabeth, whom he knew to be in straits, $100.

Lindsay wrote to express his thanks and then, with no apparent connection, moved on in his letter to complain to Paul of how, behind the policies of the admirable but overly executive friends of himself and Elizabeth, who had declared war on them the instant they were married because of their *daring* to take such a step, were the "secret rulers of Spokane": the Jesuits, occupying a monastery on the hill, and the newly rich Irish Catholics, arrogant, ignorant and dominating every avenue of the town, and the ten or twenty business men who were the real rulers and played the Masons against the Jesuits, and behind these the absentee landlords, who owned the city from Boston, Chicago and New York.

"What is our crime?" asked Lindsay. "*Disobedience.* . . . When I came, I was ordered not to write my poem on Andrew Jackson. Read it and read between the lines. I was ordered to write a poem in praise of the man who produced the Astor

millions. The week after we were married Elizabeth was
thrown out of her High School position as a punishment for
marrying me."

Most of his account was morbid fancy. But it was true
that in the last four years he had been harried with advice
about his life, his marriage and his writing of poems that flicked
him like the lash on the back of the broncho long ago. Now his
whole desire, he told Paul, was to get quit of Spokane. "I want
to go *home!*"

His aim was to get back to Springfield, to get free, to be
a real Midwesterner, a singer of the Midwest, and to carry
Elizabeth "away from the Jesuit lawyers who break anyone—
man or woman—who does not OBEY."

Yet, strangely, in this too he was thwarted. Unbelievably,
he found himself blocked even in Springfield—by individuals
like the woman who was pumping Olive full of stories about
him, and the one who was pumping Joy; like the hell-cat
bankers' wives who strove to keep the family scattered, to
keep Nicky, "the only son of the only son, out of his natural
home," and Nicky's father "out of his only natural refuge";
like the bank executive and supposed good friend who was
handling the estate and who "*does not want me in Springfield
in that house.* He has always considered it sheer impudence
for me to write books. . . ."

Thus Lindsay to his brother-in-law.

And when in June his half-grown nieces, Catharine and
Martha Wakefield, on their way east to join their parents,
stopped in Spokane, he spoke tragically of his "persecutors"
to the puzzled Catharine, who was fourteen and in earlier,
happier glimpses of him had been on a child's footing with her
"Uncle Boy."

67

In October 1928, Lindsay, conquering his revulsion for the road and acting against his previous resolution and against the advice of his physician at Mayo, who urged a simple life outdoors, left his fireside to tour the Midwest and East. Four months later he had done what no person in Spokane believed possible—wiped out his last debt.

Again he had sung his way across the country.

"A giant who is storming along toward heaven and trying to drag the whole boiling world behind him," said the Providence *Journal*, after an evening recital at Brown University for which Lindsay had spent the whole day nerving himself. "He startled his inquiring audience wide awake! Storming across the stage, striding to martial rhythms, cake-walking through the jungles, whispering, roaring, laughing, mocking. . . ."

This was in October. But when by February he had won his battle, it was time; what the victory cost him not even Elizabeth could know.

"My bed has not been soaked with blood from child-bearing," he wrote to her on February 14 (Valentine's Day), "and I have *not* endured for you what you have for me. Nevertheless, the score is a little evener."

With two children to care for, she could no longer direct his campaigns and he had signed with William B. Feakins, a lecture agent in the New York *Times* Building, who looked like a much tougher boss. Arrived in New York in November, he called first on Feakins, then at the Macmillan office, where he was sent up to interview "Ivan the Terrible"—otherwise, President Brett—who beamed at the photographs of Susan and Nicky, about a score of which Lindsay carried with him.

When the errant poet assured his publisher that he had no notion of straying from the fold again—as once to Appleton's—Brett "licked his lips," Lindsay told Elizabeth, "like the cat that ate the unfortunate canary. 'Papa' has seen my little hostages and thinks he's got me and is satisfied."

On his way east, Lindsay's earnings had been wonderfully augmented by a windfall of $500 from *Poetry* magazine. "The only prize of that size we were ever able to give," said Harriet Monroe, who editorially announced the award as made "to Mr. Lindsay not for any recent poem or work, but for the high distinction of his best work."

Adding this sum to what he sent her, Elizabeth was able to pay their long overdue bill at the Davenport just before Thanksgiving. The manager then presented her with a turkey. But Lindsay on Thanksgiving was in Baltimore, where he ate a late dinner by himself in the almost empty dining room of his hotel—"lonely enough to die," he confided to his wife. He had now to make five important professional appearances: at a luncheon of the National Council of English Teachers; the Council's evening banquet, for which several prominent speakers were assembled; the Poetry Society of Maryland; a private club; and a large Baltimore bookstore.

What these things had to do with poetry he knew not, only that if he stubbed his toe *once*, New York would know it. "So Mister toe, I address you—Please Mister toe, do not stub! Oh Elizabeth—Darling I will quit depending on you the minute I am strong enough. But I can't quit tonight. . . ."

In the next few days his fellow entertainers heard him talk enthusiastically, saw him pass around his pocketful of snapshots, and they heard him laugh tremendously—"disconcerting and appalling and unexpected laughter," was his own comment, in his diary. "Yes, and I don't know what about— never at a joke."

One night he stayed up till two, swapping jocular arguments about Prohibition with "the sassy and dirty-tongued" H. L. Mencken, whose "main trouble," said Lindsay, "is he has never met the American people."

At the English teachers' banquet he could hardly sit still, but drummed with his feet below the table, tapped his fingers, intoned and vocalized under his breath, finally rose and brought down the house with an electrifying performance of his new poem *The Virginians Are Coming Again*, quite stealing the thunder from Robert Frost, who followed him on the program with a quiet reading of *Birches*.

Then at the meeting of the Poetry Society he stubbed his toe after all. It had been a fight against exhaustion to recite ("I never tried so hard in my life"), and afterward he lost himself in a bog of garrulousness and as in a nightmare heard himself speak indiscreetly of his private affairs to the audience.

This was what happened when he was tired, when Elizabeth—who before he left home had warned him always to keep a public front of self-control, dignity and authority, never to "explain" his poems or "jabber or spill over"—was not with him to put him on his guard.

And as he had prophesied, New York knew it.

He was quoted by Harry Hansen in the *World* and rebuked by Feakins, who wrote after him to Chicago on December 13: "I think you are making a mistake to give the impression that your moving from Spokane to Springfield and your family's ability to get enough food on which to live is dependent entirely on whether you get enough engagements to speak or read. Your bookings will actually be lessened and the fees secured for them much reduced if you continue to do it."

While it was cheaper for Lindsay to stop with friends along his route and sing for his supper, it was too much of a strain to do often. Yet in hotels his money melted away in food and tips and telephone calls; besides, in hotels he got lonely. In Chicago he stayed once again with Harriet Moody in her large old-fashioned red-brick house, whose hospitality could not be beat for saltiness and general human kindness—stayed in the same dowdy guest room hung with her dead husband's paintings to which he had been welcomed breathlessly as the newest lion in 1914.

Now his welcome was a bread-and-butter one, yet underneath it, as ever, "something mighty honest."

Mrs. Moody was ill in bed. Her fortunes, like his own, had dwindled. He sat beside her; they talked of old times, he of his new ties—then with the desolate realization that he could not get home for Christmas, even for a day, but must head east again instead of west, he broke down in her presence and cried.

He had sent all his money home. He borrowed $5.00 from his straitened hostess to take him to Cleveland, where he was to spend Christmas with Joy and Ben Blair. Then after Christmas it was another agony to leave the Blairs' house. Never had he felt so much like a soldier at the front, in a panic lest he be not fresh and strong for the next drive over the top, nor so much like a tired business man, concerned with nothing but money—with money that "I must earn away from home," he reminded Elizabeth, "*plenty of it*, and the minute I lose glory and power in your eyes I must go out into the world again."

Beyond the settling of his debts, there was money to save for the move to Springfield, on which he was determined. In his letters to his wife he began to rail against his loving sister Olive, because—though Joy, when he stayed with her, had agreed to let him rent the old house—Olive had not by mid-January been heard from on the subject, and her slowness to reply gave rise in him to new delusion: "I will tour till I *drop* to get the money, rather than argue for my *own house*, especially with the woman who deliberately drove me out. . . ."

Something else that put him in a stew was the fear that he might not do well for Feakins, who was nice, humanly speaking, and on the square, and gave him a big welcome at the New York office and landed him excellent fees, but whose management was wholly cut and dried. The courage, the dash, the creative force, he must supply himself—not easy when one was contracted for, labeled and shipped like canned goods:

```
NAME. . .          Mr. Vachell Lindsay
AUSPICES. . .      Book and Play Club
HOUR. . .          7:00 p.m.
                   Dinner (Dress, Tuxedo)
AUDITORIUM
LOCATION. . .      At the residence of Mrs. U.S. Schwartz
SUBJECT. . .       Recital of his Poems
FEE. . .           $250
REMARKS. . .       Mrs. Schwartz asks that you include in
                   your program "The Chinese Nightingale,"
                   "The Virginians are Coming Again," and the
                   poem about Negroes whose name Mrs. Schwartz
                   does not recall.
```

Elizabeth wrote, in would-be encouragement: "I'm going to get behind you and push till you just can't bear it!"

Her words "thrilled" him, he answered soberly. She was his youth, his hope and his love. "If all is well with you, then all is well indeed. All then seems hopeful, beautiful, young, real and steady, part of a great adventure."

In spite of which, one afternoon in his room at the Commodore (for he was back in New York) he gave way again and cried. Though what he most longed for on his return was to melt like a cloud into her sweet body, instead—being terribly and constantly tired—he would go home to her stale and spent, he feared.

That same evening, January 18, 1929, he recited out at Briarcliff Manor, a finishing school in Scarborough, which, reminding him of Gulf Park, undid him with the temptation to be flip to what appeared a cocky, shallow audience (" 'Oh yes,' said the English teacher, 'we had Mr. Frost last year and Mr. Lindsay this year! The girls, being so near New York, have *every advantage* like *that*, you know!' "), and in his room again he raged: "I will NOT be run through the mill! I will NOT be sold like links of sausages! It is simply *deadly*!"

He thought by contrast of his freedom of movement in 1914—"like Susan dancing." Then every exuberant waking hour was like yeast, phosphorus, radium, whether on the platform or in his study or in casual talk. Then nothing stopped him. Then the thing that did not have to do with the artist's creative moment he would not touch with his little finger— "and *everybody knew it, too*. Well, I begin to see how machinery closes in around the very topmost-seeming Americans. And how subtle is the appeal. It's a temptation and a complex of gathering forces no European ever faces, and hysterical shrieking against it keeps you right on the level with it, like Mencken, Lewis, *The Nation, The New Republic*."

Only a few were there who were not pulled down. Robert Frost was one, and Woodrow Wilson till he took sick, and Henry Ford compared with all other automobile men, and Harriet Monroe as an editor—"compare her freedom with the slavery of George Horace Lorimer."

Gene Tunney was another free soul, "as an adventurer, not as a prize fighter," and so was Charles Lindbergh, the lone-eagle aviator—"he does as he pleases. . . .

"So how would I define supremacy in America? Here it is: *to be above every single piece of machinery without shrieking against it. And yet to be completely effective as a traditional American*."

Again he met and matched histories with George Richards, whose hack work as illustrator for Macmillan filled about the same place in his life as Lindsay's work for Feakins. Richards exhibited other pictures outside and his ambition was to paint *one* great picture.

"He keeps up his pride fairly well," said Lindsay, "as well as I do."

Going by himself to see the Coburns, Charles and Ivah, in their revival of *The Yellow Jacket*, he found the audience positively sneering because the two stars were no longer the rage.

The same thing was true of Walter Hampden, whose Cyrano was out of fashion. He and the Coburns had had their tremendous vogue ten to fifteen years ago: once venerated like Aztec deities, they were now slaughtered for the Aztec god, and Lindsay felt consolation in watching men and women outside the literary field thus struggling against public favor.

Wrestling with America was like wrestling with Proteus. Artists were doomed as public persons unless they laid hold on the *deeper wisdom* that he, when in the West, saw as the clear way out, yet here in the East lost sight of—partly through blasting loneliness, partly through something more: "I think it's my damned Doniphan pride. New York was once at my feet. I cannot now submit to New York and I cannot now conquer, and we glare at each other like two grey cats!"

This even while the Mohawk in him spat scorn in the Spaniard Don Iphan's face, saying, " 'Go away, pale face! Who are you to croak in my ear about your silly paleface victories? It is I, the Indian, who write the songs and sing them! No Doniphan ever did a creative thing.' "

His New York friends were disappointed that he was not the dynamite they once predicted. It was true he was no skyrocket this winter. "But I *can* prove myself a bull-dog," he promised Elizabeth, "it's just hang on hang on hang on hang on. . . ."

The sweet in the bitterness of staying away was that he actually served her more the longer he stayed away. "It is infinitely dearer to me and more precious to know you are wearing beautiful shoes, with me away from home, than that you are down at the heel and me at home."

Thus he was determined to stick with Feakins, repellent though the routine was, so the office would think him a first-class attraction and book him for a bigger run next fall. While in New York, he took the snappiest moment of every day to visit Feakins and pay him his commission, then often spent the rest of his time in bed till the hour to catch the train out of town for his recital.

He was reading Strachey's *Elizabeth and Essex,* a book that for all its brilliancy depressed him with its "foxiness." He was reading Emerson and wishing he could be so steady; he needed not Elizabeth's disdain to tell him how unEmersonian his squalling letters were.

He read his own poems, and half of them sounded foreign in his ears, because when he wrote them he had not heard Susan's chirp or Nicky's crow, nor met the fair lover who had led him into paths alien to his Gothic mind, from whose hand he had drunk the cup of Faust, whose boiling beauty in his veins had either destroyed him or recreated him.

Though he could not publicly repudiate his gospels—before God, he would burn all his books for one true-love kiss from her, like their brief first kiss "on your Mama's front porch, oh what a *girlish* girl . . ." and the long kisses of their honeymoon with "the flowers coming up through the melting snow, I can *see* the flowers, and hear your voice—the only 'lady's' voice I have ever heard—and hear the melted snow-water running between patches of sod . . . and I see you naked before me with hair spread out from your head like a fire-queen. . . .

"Oh for even *one day* of all that again."

Meanwhile, calling on no one in New York outside the Feakins office, nor wanting to, he waited for her letters, which contained his courage, then waited for his train and that was all, except that each day had its one dark hour of noon or midnight when he was desperate enough to make an end of life. It was then that he put up her picture and prayed before it till despair went from him.

68

Lindsay came back to Spokane in March 1929 and in April he departed for Springfield, with his family and for good. His heart was in the town of which he was a citizen and the house where he was born.

"*Get me home,* and I will do whatever else you say the rest of my life," he had besought Elizabeth from the road during those whirling days and aching nights when to write to her brought him his only steadiness.

On January 30 he had ended a second series of articles for the Spokane *Daily Chronicle,* which were written before he left on tour but had been appearing once a week since August. "Vachel Lindsay, Citizen of Springfield, Illinois—Guest of Spokane," he signed them, and in his final columns he had begun wistfully to compare his native city at many points with his more brilliant and enterprising adopted one.

Springfield, little farmyard capital, cannot touch the city of the Rim Rock for dramatic scenery or civic get-up-and-go. Yet something Springfield has that Spokane has not. "Springfield has a dream," he declared, "as do the old towns of Ireland and Scotland, and over the dream hovers the vision of Abraham Lincoln, the lumber jack, the rail splitter."

More strongly even than the association that gave her her place in history, his own remembered loves were drawing him back to her, associations of home and youth. "Mohammed went away to Medina," Lindsay cried, "but oh—he returned to Mecca," and to Elizabeth: "Get me home, darling, get me home, where I can work without *insult* and *molestation*! And sing my *own song* again!"

393

The house of his boyhood was his ink bottle: he could not write well anywhere else. That funny little town was like a scratched violin but *his* Stradivarius, on which he could play immortal music.

In the farewell weeks before his home-going, he posed for a bust to Adrian Voisin, a gifted sculptor who was briefly in Spokane. These days when he was off the platform, there was a downward-sagging tendency to Lindsay in the flesh. His shoulders drooped, his face hung in lines like a discouraged business man's as he sat to Voisin, who notwithstanding perceived the dreamer and conqueror.

At one of the sittings Voisin seized a bunch of eagle feathers that lay on his studio table and held it upright behind the half-finished clay head. The effect was startling, for Lindsay's Indian look leaped forth.

When it became known that he was leaving the western city, a number of his close friends, among whom the condition of his health as well as of his finances was an open secret, presented him with several hundred dollars. Thus was he sped on his way and mourned in his absence (he left Spokane "poetless," said Stoddard King), while back in his home town "Cousin" Vachel and his bright-haired trio, including even the shy toddler Nicky, were entertained by the Midday Luncheon Club, which rose on his entrance, then voted unanimously to ask the state legislature to name him poet laureate of Illinois.

It had been suggested that a delegation of Vachel's one-time "inspiration girls" should be on hand to greet his wife. This was not done, but there was handshaking and backslapping and shoulder-circling—he was with them to stay "till the cows came home," he promised the reporters. The Midwest *was* a different land. Every time he entered it his very voice and manner changed; his audiences understood his smiles better and the jokes made by committee members were genial as pumpkin pie.

The agreement within the family was that he and Elizabeth would occupy the house at an annual rent of $500, assuming the costs of repair and upkeep, while the estate paid the taxes. Joy had warned them that "the cellar was the principal problem." All the pipes had burst and the cellar was flooded with icy water. A sewer pipe had broken, too, so there was danger that the drinking supply might be contaminated.

"But I see more poem games in the parlor than struggles in the cellar," Joy's brother blithely prophesied.

His own "hereditary castle," he called the house. While the plumbers worked day and night, the masons laid a cement floor in the basement—uncovering a nest of pots and pans that went back to the time of the C. M. Smiths. The painters swarmed over the outside, and Nicky promptly fell the whole length of the precipitous stairs. Vachel roamed from room to room in a daze of reminiscence.

On May 10 an elaborate banquet, sponsored ostensibly by *Poetry* magazine, was given for him in Chicago. Its moving spirit was Fred Melcher, who having seen Lindsay in New York in February had divined his crying inner need and could not bear that his return to the Midwest should pass unnoticed.

Lindsay himself had written to Harriet Monroe to ask about his old Chicago friends: "Are they all gone? Are they all tired of me? Do any of them want me to turn up, and if so who?"

It seemed at first that less than one hundred could be prevailed on to attend the dinner in his welcome, but in the end there were some three hundred and the affair was moved from a private dining room of the Sherman Hotel into the main ballroom. The guest of honor, his hair now gray and his dress suit shabby after many wearings, looked "somewhat frayed," noted one of the lesser guests, but he smiled beatifically all through and when during the speeches Eunice Tietjens mentioned the ages of his children, he put in quickly that his wife's age was that of Helen of Troy, at which all cheered.

And though on rising he declared that he returned to them at forty-nine an "old and broken man," his leonine vigor in the next moment as he recited *The Virginians Are Coming Again* seemed to belie his words.

He returned this spring to the First Christian Church and on Sundays he and Elizabeth were to be seen in his parents' pew, the Presbyterian Elizabeth having been newly baptized in a ceremony of total immersion. "I saw Vachel Lindsay Sunday morning walking home," cozily reported a local columnist. "His wife was with him. I knew Vachel's father (I can see him now with his gray-streaked beard). I also remember very well Mrs. Lindsay."

But if Vachel's parents, resurrected from the plot in Oak Ridge, had revisited the old house later this summer they would scarcely have recognized it. Outside the clapboards were dazzling with white paint, and inside their dimmed eyes would have been startled, first, by the circus gaiety of a curtain of scarlet oilcloth looped with gold braid across the entrance to the dining room.

In the long dining room, where Mrs. Lindsay once presided over her legions of church workers, hung inescapably "The Tree of Laughing Bells" and on the wall opposite two Chinese scrolls. In the parlor was Vachel's mosaic of *Kubla Khan*. In his parents' downstairs bedroom, which he and Elizabeth had made their library, they had set up their bookshelves filled with bright-jacketed books and had pulled a couch before the fireplace and over the couch thrown the Manchu woman's satin coat of blue and rose, once intended for Sara.

Only in the southwest room, the original library, would the shades of the old couple have felt at home, for here the well-worn, dark-brown look of their own occupancy still prevailed. Here were preserved the family editions of the classics, prints of the old masters, photographs and mementoes. But even here, when a breeze drifted through open windows on the floor above, the exotic tinkle of Chinese windbells, hung by Elizabeth in the narrow upstairs hall, could be heard.

69

The painting and necessary repairs to the house cost over $3,000, with the consequence that Lindsay, in debt again, had to telegraph to Macmillan to pay his agent Feakins $250 in back commissions. This left his royalty account virtually without a balance.

In August 1929 he lectured in a summer course for English teachers at State College, Pennsylvania, though teaching tired him more than anything these days. In October he toured Texas and California, writing to Elizabeth from Los Angeles: "God, how eager I am to do well by you, and how willingly I would die for you, if that would settle anything."

He was at home for a few days in November. On November 10, his fiftieth birthday, at a ceremony to dedicate two sculptured panels of "Health" and "Happiness" placed on either side of the city's Water Purification Building, every speaker quoted from *On the Building of Springfield*. Eight days later, he gave a recital of his poems at the First Christian Church, which was packed to the doors.

SPRINGFIELD'S OWN, read the legend over a picture of him in that day's *State Journal*.

It was with the plaudits of his town ringing in his ears that he set out again. In one of his turnabouts from despair to elation, he wrote back to Elizabeth on November 24 that that loyal reception ("the *first time* my town has shown loyalty") was continuing in audiences all along his eastward route. Already this fall he had recited to 50,000 or 60,000 people, including wild fourteen-year-olds whose fathers had heard him in college.

Each time the tension of their response to him was rising. Something that far transcended an income seemed on the way and he bade Elizabeth: "Be all ready for the success when it comes, when our sudden majority arrives over the U.S.A. as it did at the Christian Church in Springfield! We are on the edge of Bryan's power. I mean it seriously. We are on the edge of Bryan's power. They are coming to *us*, dearest, for personal leadership in *citizenship* and *ideas*. They follow us as the Black-Shirts do Mussolini, with a slant almost political. . . ."

He returned home for Christmas. But though he came with his whole soul consecrated to please his wife, once there, the power went out of him and with it his dream of glory, till it seemed to him that he "loafed and grouched" about the house, growing diminished in her eyes and his own.

Back on the road, he wrote to her early in January 1930, in a mood as gray and empty as that of his November letter had been crimson and inflated: "I have not done *one thing* to set my town permanently aflame for God and Beauty and Democracy. I have merely babbled and written about these things."

Lindsay's book *The Litany of Washington Street*, a collection of discursive and imaginative essays on American themes and figures, which was brought out by Macmillan in March 1929 and which endeavored to say to the "smart boys" of the twenties that the fathers of their country had been real men and heroes, was selling badly; it lacked the vigor of his early prose, while his latest volume of verse, *Every Soul Is a Circus*, published in October, was disappointingly poor.

October 1929 was the month of the great stock market crash that signified the climax and end of the whooping decade— and of an era. November was a month of panic, and December one of melancholy adjustment, while by January the indications of a new, somber state of the economy were plain to see.

When on Sunday morning, January 26, Lindsay took a long walk through the New York streets, which in their Sunday quiet felt "like 1906 again," he told Elizabeth, he observed traces of upheaval and rout. Enormous quantities of books, many of them by men he knew and all in their proud, shining jackets—on which the critics hailed nearly every one a master-piece—were being remaindered in drug stores and in book stores, including those of the powerful Doubleday Doran chain, which were packed to the very tops of their show windows with the undignified avalanche.

"And signs like this—" he went on, " 'Publisher's Over-stocked Sale!' 'Quantities Limited.' And then the dead give-away, 'New Titles Received Daily.' I say with pride, not one of my books, prose or verse, is in any window as yet, not even *The Litany of Washington Street*."

"America's greatest poet," he had often been called on this tour, and yet the fear in his own soul was that he was becom-ing merely a legend of the past. In the current *Harper's* he had read an article by Oswald Garrison Villard, in which Villard said of Senator William E. Borah that "his inability to see things through to the bitter end has steadily handicapped his progress."

Lindsay applied this to some extent to himself, promising Elizabeth that when he had his own bitter-end disposition screwed up to its very height, he was going to go the rounds and call on every professional acquaintance in New York— "such a silly procedure would work wonders in the tone of the reviews. I am going to call at 50 offices! I am a bitter-ender!"

With hat in hand, he began his campaign by stopping at the cynically spoken headquarters of *Liberty* to see if they would take an article, or, anyway, see what he could do there. "If we get anything into that paper, we will earn the money."

At the *Saturday Review of Literature* his interviewer was his old friend William Rose Benét, who regretfully turned down, as being "somehow out of step," every poem that Lind-say tried to sell.

On January 30 he called at the Macmillan office.

"My first call for a year," he reminded Elizabeth. "Young Brett phoned for me 'to autograph a book.' But he sent the book out by his stenographer in the hall for me to write in it, when I arrived at the skyscraper. Nice cheery welcome! But they said Mr. Tidbit or whatever his name was had taken Latham's place while Latham was in Europe, and 'did I want to talk to Mr. Tidbit?' I wasn't urged, you know. I was just asked! So I went in and had a jolly old ten minutes with Tidbit. Nothing special happened except that he says 2000 copies of *Washington Street* have been sold."

Next, having long harbored hopes of persuading one of the large talking-machine companies to record his recital of his poems, Lindsay went over to Victor, and there—his tale, set down at midnight, continues—they "sent out the office boy (Mr. Kuhl, secretary to Cairns, the biggest man in the company) to jolly me, and he said in substance that even John Barrymore's soliloquies had no sale, that until I could get front page stuff in the newspapers like Marion Talley and sell records 16,000 at a clip they were in for a dead loss.

"In short I was to go out and get a reputation like Lindbergh the day he landed, or else go to the devil. Unless I could get the kind of a tie-up where I could be advertised on all the screens of the movie-houses of the United States the same day the records were released all over the U.S.A. it was no use.

"A very cocky young man, who assured me he was the only person in the office who had ever heard of me, he having heard me in a mid-west college somewhere once.

"He was like all subordinates, talking very big for the chief. I was merely amused. He said of course if there was a big news story that broke all over the U.S.A. one morning, front page stuff, they could 'sell' me for a month or so after that, but would have to work fast, for the thing would soon die down.

"Then Mr. Kuhl went on to say that: Now if I was the author of the theme-song of the 'Love-Parade' etc. or this French actor who sings it in broken English—I might be a success like he is—(it's so late I cannot remember his name, something like Chivalier).

"In short at last I have the *proof* I am not the Jazz poet.

I am to go right back and sit in the corner with Ezra Pound and Conrad Aiken! Just a dam poet.

"I see now it will be a long, long battle; and the line of jollying sounds *exactly* like the fatherly talks I heard in 1906 in New York in the magazine offices. Did I tell you the fresh youth in the Victor took down my 'name and address' as they did in every magazine office in 1906, with the promise to send for me after they had considered the matter?

"My Lord, the office mouse-traps! Utterly *hollow*, cheaper than Woolworth's.

"And what does all this have to do with United States Poetry? Not a dam thing. Not one fly-speck. To have people demand I go forth and swell up my self-importance even more, and then bring it back for them to gaze upon is indeed ironical."

The outcome of Lindsay's call at *Liberty* was a request for a one-page poem on the "jazz age" ("Problem: 'How to write a one-page poem the cigar stands will read?' Still I shall try"), and he had an encouraging interview with young Lorimer, heir presumptive at the *Ladies' Home Journal*, and another and "pleasanter" talk with Lewis Titterton, the editor he had seen at Macmillan's.

Yet even those he encountered who were of good intent, like Titterton and his agent Feakins, stood to him for half-measures, dilutions of his natural creative force, and for so long as he sat on their doorsteps, for so long would he do "second-rate, tributary, Babbitt-flavored work."

"Feakins dodges the Universities and thinks the *Ladies' Home Journal* is a 'great opportunity.' Titterton thinks the *Ladies' Home Journal* is a 'great opportunity' and thinks 'maybe' he can improve the printing of my books 'a little bit,' cautiously of course. . . ."

This getting down to particular maneuvers simply bewildered one in whom something demanded the farthermost horizon around every object and idea he dealt with. He had been to see the statues by Rodin at the Metropolitan and once again his imagination swelled with the portent of things tremendous, Rodinesque.

"I *know* that sometime, with the right concentration I can do them. I would love to alternate Glacier Park and Rodin both in drawing and in song. And I want all to be gigantic units of things above and under the earth. The thwarting of gigantic units in my mind is a thing I have allowed to go on too long:

"Springfield as a world-pilgrim place.

"Spokane as a new Nuremberg for a thousand years.

"The 48 States of the Union, clothed in light.

"The Metropolitan Museum—stretched from the beginning to the end of time.

"The publishing game as a vast literary venture, not a box of office tricks.

"The reciting game, as a vast singing adventure, not as a set of trick entrances and exits and the catching of trains.

"The whole picture of Christendom from A.D. 1 till now, stretching from every art and literature to the millennium. . . .

"I want action, splendor, light and human aspiration to the uttermost! And all these things now turn over in my skull like birds still in the shell."

70

For her husband's study at 603 South Fifth, Elizabeth had fixed up a onetime maid's room at the very back of the house out of earshot of doorbell and telephone. Here, when he was at home and while his little household tiptoed below, careful of his silence, Lindsay—parent and provider—spent many hours, hours that slipped past emptily even as he whipped himself to improve them.

Often he peered from the back window, welcoming distraction, his lost face visible to the neighbors. His brain was distended. His fancy blazed, as when long years ago, bowed on his knees, he had felt his oneness with an embracing force. Now, seizing a blank page, he wrote

> If this hour is not a success,
> If this day is not a success,
> Nothing will ever be a success—
> Therefore let us turn to God
> In union and communion with Him.

It was the power to produce that failed him. In his old bedroom were steel filing cabinets, repositories of former abundance. Sometimes he wandered down the hall to draw out one of the tiny well-thumbed diaries of his student days or of his three great hikes and, turning its pages, breathed in again the young manhood preserved there, strong and fresh. It was there that his youth lay.

"Thank God the core of our life is youth! Susan and Nicky singing in the nursery, and Mama combing her hair at her mirror. Youth, youth, youth, the only brave enemy of death!"

So he cried to Elizabeth when on his travels, far away from her. Yet it seemed now as if each moment he was at home and in his young wife's presence, weakness, uncertainty, heartache, dependence and petition returned to him, till she had someone as childlike and sensitive as Nicky on her hands.

He had had photographs of himself and Elizabeth—who at his request had let her shining, fair hair grow long—and Nicky and Susan, seated all on the library sofa, taken by Springfield's best photographer. And he had discarded the upright piano in the front parlor and bought a beautiful new grand, on which Elizabeth played hymns while he and the children sang. In the past year he had abandoned his teetotalism, the prop of a lifetime, and he drank wine—one glass to Elizabeth's two—and smoked heavily.

"It was surprising," recalls Stephen Graham, who visited them in Springfield, "to sit with Vachel in his home, drinking red wine and smoking cigarettes. He adored his wife to a point that was almost embarrassing to a guest. . . ."

Indeed, an extravagant, unreasoning jealousy had begun to worm in Lindsay. He ordered from the house in a burst of fury a young man of Elizabeth's age, a neighbor, who had dropped in innocently. Setting out on one of his enforced departures, he wrote back to her: "Be as dangerous as you please while I am away, for what I do not see or know won't hurt me."

"I am yours ever and every way," Elizabeth told him, and again to her he poured his soul out, writing: "Beloved . . . all I gamble on is your heart, your heart, your firey youthful heart, that *struggles so hard to behave* (if you think I have no sympathy with your struggle, you do not know me). But darling I am always begging for one more chance to be a man in your eyes and my own. I know now that when I am with you, I know my love is too relentless."

When he looked back past his children to his own childhood, it seemed to him a remote and gentle kingdom; he had not needed then to turn a flinty face to the world.

He was traveling most of the spring of 1930. Hotel clerks recognized him, having "studied" him in school. College instructors introduced him to their classes like Lazarus. A table of his books for sale and autograph was on hand at his recitals, but few sold. Certain organizations were slow in paying (the chairman would be hurt when he asked for his check the same evening) and to save hotel bills he hung for long hours about the railroad stations and in the free museums.

Yet the coin in his pocket melted like snow, he knew not how, nor did Elizabeth, who prepared his income tax return, listing his occupation as "Artist, Writer, Poet, Lecturer." For 1929 his gross income had been $11,628, of which $1,022 was from royalties on his books and rent on property owned by the Lindsay estate. The remainder came from his recitals. He had paid $2,387 to his agent as commission. Yet Elizabeth was baffled by the resulting net income, after legitimate deductions were made, of only $3,293, for it seemed impossible that so much had been swallowed up by "travel expenses," even including first-class hotels, Pullman berths and dining cars.

But it had gone for $2.00 breakfasts and $1.00 tips ("to make people good to me"), for hundreds of solitary and solacing movies, theaters and vaudeville shows. It had gone for more books on Egyptology—Lindsay was renewing his Egyptian grammar—and for lavish gifts to friends along the way and "incendiary ornaments" for his beloved at home.

Financial intemperance was growing on him. Two years earlier he had sent home faithfully all he earned. These latter days it was not unusual for him to send back from a $250 engagement only $90, with the agent's commission still unpaid. Since their first six months in Springfield, Elizabeth had become aware of an increasing, bewildering discrepancy between the amount earned and the amount available for settlement of expenses.

Yet on her side, she—like Vachel—had the giving nature. If she had not his improvidence, no more than he had she the knack of thrift. More than once when he was at home they entertained two hundred at an evening gathering, and if it was Vachel who bought the ill-advised piano and ordered expensive photographs, it was Elizabeth who bought a victrola and sent all the curtains in the house to the laundry at a cost of $20.

This spring, while he was on the road, she delivered several lectures for good pay in towns near Springfield, and in August —the summer was the lean season—Vachel and she together, appearing at different hours, lectured before the vast Chautauqua assembly in New York State, an experience that to the naturally shy Elizabeth was like "facing death."

On October 10, 1930, Hiram College awarded Lindsay the honorary degree of Doctor of Literature, thus fulfilling his youthful prediction that his *alma mater*, from whose bosom he had torn himself prematurely, would "give him a degree yet."

But an unexpected honor was Macmillan's invitation to Elizabeth to submit a volume of her own poems—this in an awful year for publishing—and her husband ordered her to "write it *instantly*. Free me from the fear that I am thwarting you. God-in-heaven, it will be so much easier than some of the unnecessary things you fondly *imagine* I want you to do, like scrubbing the kitchen floor. Let the floor stink, and write your immortal songs—

> I want Athena in my house,
> Athena born to sing—
> I want Athena in my bed
> With wide Homeric wing."

He was addressing her late in October, again from the East (the trains that brought him here had been almost empty) and again it was the prospect of going home to her, though he had only just left, that kept him afloat at all—"You *say* you *want* me, and my silly old heart *believes* you."

Yet before leaving he had disgraced himself anew by a scene

in her presence and that of the Reverend Clark Cummings, minister of the First Christian Church. Now he wrote, on October 28, "I want to apologize to Cummings and to you for threatening Hara Kari and scaring the pee-peeeeeee out of him. It was all Doctor Mohawk's fault."

In Spokane, during the dire winter of 1927-1928, Lindsay had dwelt on the thought of suicide almost daily. "But Doctor Mohawk," his present apology continued, "must *not* break out in me except when I write *poems*. He's my whole title to glory and shame, but we must mitigate the shame. . . ."

Still he begged Elizabeth to write many of her own songs. She might have to wear the mantle of Elijah any day.

71

Lindsay's net income for 1930 had been over $6000, almost double that of the year before, and this was in spite of the stock-market crash, the panic and spreading depression. It should have been enough. Yet from the road his enclosures to his wife were sometimes lately no more than $5.00 or $10, with occasionally an especially drawn check:

> Land of Love.   Bank of Wild Time, and Kisses.
> City of the Soul.
> I promise to pay Elizabeth Darling. . . .
> $1000 - - -   (one thousand requests)
> on instant demand.
>   Signed Vachel Lindsay

In Springfield Elizabeth found it necessary to ask among friends for paid jobs of typewriting, and she had increased the number of her lectures within easy distance of town. Out of her own earnings she engaged a maid. But the house this winter had a neglected look. The snow in front lay unshoveled and a neighbor wrote to the papers to complain that if the shade of Lincoln, celebrated by Lindsay, had walked that way he would have sunk waist-deep.

In December 1930 Lindsay was in California. Though his performances were well attended, his pockets were almost empty by the time he reached New York in January, when he made his first and only recordings of some of his poems, under the auspices of Columbia University.

Early in February he was briefly at home. He was under the care of Dr. Claude V. McMeen, a Springfield physician, who now discovered him to be suffering, like his father before him, from diabetes mellitus—a mild case. But for Lindsay it was one thing more, and on this visit, one terrible night, Elizabeth, who was half beside herself with what had become the certainty of uncertainty and with a financial anxiety for which a better word was agony, which since 1927 had never really let up and which she must endure alone, cried out to her husband what she felt about life, about him, about everything, and declared that henceforth she would be his wife "in name only."

She did not keep her vow, but to Lindsay the words once spoken were confirmation of his failure as a man. He retaliated with a stream of threats to disappear, to drop out of sight, to be a beggar and vagabond.

Yet once away from her, restored to the weary circuit of his bondage, he reached toward her anew, writing from New York on February 17: "Blessed blessed passionate beautiful rebellious Elizabeth . . . you should not sleep with a mummy and I will protect you like a palace guard while you choose a fit lover."

He blamed his age for their estrangement.

He had been again to see Sara, who was separated from her husband, and come away saddened, for truly she seemed old and down; by comparison with Sara, he was surely on the fighting line. And he had read Masters' recent biography of Lincoln, finding it a twisted, unworthy book. Both little Sara, become at forty-six a fanatical hypochondriac and lonely recluse, and Masters, whose debunking biography of a spiritual giant degraded only its writer, were not only old, they were tragically sick: to grow old was not necessarily mellowing.

"*You* must be free of any such growing old in me," he told Elizabeth.

And Elizabeth to Olive wrote: "Vachel is really good. He has always meant to be an angel, and if he hasn't quite succeeded all the time, who has?"

Yet in view of his repeated threats to run away she had

begun to doubt if the fundamental lesson "that one cannot live without food, shelter and clothing, and that money must be given in exchange for the same" would ever be learned by him.

She had repented of her angry pledge. "Your sweet letters were waiting for me here," her husband wrote to her from Muskegon, Michigan, "and so cheered me and touched me and stirred me all up I cried all through dinner-time till the waitress was all fussed up."

And when that night he faced his audience, a tide of strength rose up in him from he knew not where. He felt a resurgence of confidence and joy and every rag of humiliation dropped away.

Elsewhere, it seemed to him, he was barbed and baited. At a women's club in Lake Forest, Illinois, he ran across the eldest of the Logan sisters from Springfield, who assured him that she still had in her attic a whole trunkful of his youthful drawings and his poems, some of them written to her—"your messy old junk," she called it.

On March 14, 1931 he was in Asheville, North Carolina, to recite at a preparatory school for boys. Half an hour before his program began, when he needed most to be let alone, the school principal, "accustomed," said Lindsay, "to breaking his students," tried to break the poet by the same "horrible bullying" because Lindsay refused in advance to recite *The Congo*.

Lindsay felt the familiar ominous sweating. He burst out with a torrent of abuse, though he managed to confine it to the headmaster and did not bawl out his audience. The next day he sent a telegram to Elizabeth

> THIS SCHOOL HERE PUT ON THE THUMBSCREWS TILL I WAS READY TO SCREAM BECAUSE THEY COULD NOT SWEAT THE CONGO OUT OF ME TWO MORE SUCH PERSECUTIONS AND I AM A GONER FOR SURE

and one to Feakins, demanding that Feakins tell the Asheville people what he thought of them.

But that was impossible, replied the harassed agent. "Please remember that we have to deal with these people on account of several speakers."

And there was a legal point, Feakins went on, since both *The Congo* and *General Booth* were offered by Lindsay on his circular; if he refused to recite them when called for, the organization might feel justified in paying him no fee.

Lindsay, with hands raised to heaven, had sworn not to apologize ("No one is going to bully me any more . . . my soul is my own!") but in the end he did apologize to the irate headmaster by letter, calling it "a forced apology, lest our check be stopped."

Meanwhile, Elizabeth, fighting down her horror at the new outbreak and what it might portend, sent him a wire that was "balm of Gilead," and he answered her: "I tell you darling, I *want* to get my self-control back, I *want to*, and I know I *must and I will.*"

And a day later, "I was nothing but a baby a squallor a spoiled child and a hysteric. And I did the *same thing* at Bryn Mawr, bawling out the committee. . . ."

And the next day, "I *know* you are a bit ashamed of me. I get so angry at myself for being angry."

Yet to be hectored and hectored and hectored like a small boy expelled from school because he declined to recite as a stunt two old, worn-out poems that made him seasick to think about and penned him, agonized, in his thirty-fourth year— "I simply can't bear it, Feakins," he wrote, in a second plea. "Put it on all my contracts that I refuse hereafter to recite *Booth*, *The Congo*, or any other poems I do not choose to recite."

And again to Elizabeth: "You will have to wait till you are all of 51 before you know what it means to be doomed to sit in the attic with your dustiest poetry and feel your creative force thwarted every day, and youth making its last desperate despairing cry for new children within your very marrow. It's the feeling of having the door of the artistic future slammed in my face forever, the whole creative side of my future, when I used to create *new* things daily. . . ."

"I will *not* be a *slave* to my yesterdays. I will *not*. I was born a *creator* not a parrot. . . .

"Darling I want to go on to the greatest glories of our lives. Do not abate a single creative ambition. Let us conquer no less than the Universe."

But his maledictions this spring were not confined to school principals and committees. Olive and Paul had been in Springfield; he had been shamefully rude to them and to them also he had since apologized. When his brother-in-law, who was contemplating a trip south, proposed toward the end of March to stop in Springfield on his way, Vachel at first encouraged him to come.

A few days later, he suddenly and furiously rescinded the invitation in a tortured and accusing letter written not to Paul but to Elizabeth, which spoke for itself of his deterioration. It seemed to her "quite, quite mad."

72

If the nature of Lindsay's affliction was known to a few in Spokane before he left, it remained a close secret in Springfield. Outside the four walls of the house none except his doctor knew even that he was ill; into the preserving of a public front Elizabeth threw all her energy. But during the winter just ended, of 1930-1931, she had become thin and pale, her once bright and joyful face the picture of despair.

She was the more deeply discouraged because at first, on the return to Springfield, she had hoped the dreadful happenings of Spokane might be forever behind them. Vachel was back in the precise setting he clamored for; he was among old friends who loved him and yet did not intrude; he was under the eye of the family physician and had (she thought) as good a chance to earn his living as any man.

But none of these things made any difference.

Not till after his death could she accept fully that his decline was "inevitable," and it was to seem to her then as if at least a precipitating cause of his outbreaks, which increasingly in his last years took the form of explosions of despair and rage, was the thwarting of creative energy that in former days had found a glorious release, for when his poems came—she recalled—his attacks did not come.

But now at home the empty hours he spent shut in his room—hours that he seldom any longer could fill creatively—recoiled on him till he grew maddened. Away on tour, he was so quickly exhausted that good-humored audiences calling for his famous poems became distorted in his eyes into "tyrannical, ignorant mobs." Elizabeth had been on tenterhooks ever since the affair of *The Congo*, foreseeing the smashing of business and friendly relationships essential to his career and livelihood. When his unreasoning wrath came finally to focus on herself and Paul Wakefield, in connection with Paul's proposed between-trains visit, she realized at last the extent of the crisis.

So, when he read the letter from Vachel, which she sent on to him, did Dr. Wakefield: it carried its own testimony. After writing it, Lindsay himself was afraid to come home.

His engagements were over but he remained brooding in a hotel room in Baltimore, where on April 1 Elizabeth, who throughout his last tour had let almost no day go by without sending him a loving letter and often a wire, telephoned to him with words of reassurance. He had passed the climax of the storm for the time; he broke into tears over the telephone and promised to be good and to come right along.

To Elizabeth the fear of destitution was more real than that of the physical violence with which Vachel had begun to threaten her; in his worst moments he threatened to kill. But Dr. Wakefield, now fully alarmed, believed that Lindsay should be placed in an institution. He had lately consulted other doctors, among them a well-known Boston psychiatrist, to whom he showed several of Lindsay's letters and from whom he had come away with a depressing prognosis and even a warning of danger—to the writer of the letters and those around him.

One great difficulty was Lindsay's unwillingness to submit to treatment. From the beginning he had shied away from the very mention of psychiatrists and psychologists; there had been a good neurologist in Spokane but Elizabeth was never able to get her husband across the office threshold. Now the condition first discovered in 1924 had gone on too long. The fact was hard to admit; it was terrible to apply to a man who had contributed so much to his time, but "Vachel," said Paul, "is sick—as sick as a man with pneumonia—and it should be faced."

Dr. Wakefield next wrote directly to Dr. McMeen—no specialist but the only physician in Springfield whom Vachel would readily consult—who dismissed as absurd the thought of legally committing Lindsay. He disagreed with the original diagnosis made at Mayo and with the long-distance opinion of the big man in Boston. Granting that Lindsay had a history of a few attacks, which were sometimes convulsive, sometimes emotional, Dr. McMeen protested the labeling of him with the tag of idiopathic epilepsy, implying fits and dangerous furies. Though Lindsay might threaten fatal violence and had three times laid hands on Elizabeth, none of his assaults had been serious.

Yet to the doctor in his office Lindsay showed one side, at home another. A "home-wrecker" was only one of his wild words for the devoted Paul. In the rage of his jealous delusion, he had come to hate the very qualities of warmth and manliness he once had loved in the friend of his youth and brother-in-law closer than a brother. It was seven years since Paul had come to him in Gulfport, come at his call to save him from unutterable despair.

As he told Olive at the time: "Paul was the only human being in the whole world who could do me a bit of good. It is my heart of heart's conviction that he is a very very noble man."

No one had wrecked Vachel's home but himself, and for this he was not accountable. To understand was to forgive, and Paul forgave his friend. Not without just estimate of their relation had Vachel called his poem to Paul, set down when they were boys at Hiram, *The Triumph of Friendship*. Not without premonition had he written then

> let our friendship still be trusting
> Though I seem to curse thy name.

Less forbearing was Elizabeth's father, the Reverend Franklin Conner, who was making a long visit to Springfield and had taken a room in a small hotel. Some things he could not help observing and out of a slender church pension he occasionally gave Elizabeth money and food. But though he had been witness to a few blow-ups when his son-in-law's Rasputian glares struck chills down his spine, not till March 1931, when his distracted daughter took him into her confidence, did he become aware of the real nature of the case.

Vachel was still on the road. Torn between hope and hopelessness, crying aloud to her father that she was trapped and at other moments praying to God for strength to go on—for the high courage with which she entered marriage, which was almost gone now, every bit—Elizabeth told everything.

Springfield goes early to bed. There were few abroad to see the lights of the house burn almost till dawn, as the father and daughter sat in desperate consultation.

There was not a thing in the "category of action" her husband had not accused her of, exclaimed the older man brokenly; he was writing in his turn to Dr. Wakefield, warning that some step for Elizabeth's protection must be taken. When Elizabeth, seeking not to provoke Vachel, passed over his accusations in silence, Vachel interpreted her silence as admission of guilt. Himself, as a father, Mr. Conner felt stunned and cold, scarcely crediting his daughter's predicament, yet full of dread at what worse might befall her.

Lindsay returned to Springfield on April 3, and before his next departure he slept a great deal and on waking went to the movies, which seemed to be, said Elizabeth sadly, the only thing he cared about. When she remonstrated at so much bad air and cheap sensationalism, he told her not to ruin his prospects of writing by failing to sympathize with his intellectual interests.

As much to keep up his pride as because he needed them, she went with him to buy two new suits and a dressing gown. This used up their last cent; they had to borrow from the bank for the railroad fare to Oklahoma, whither he departed on April 8, shedding tears at the station when he said goodby. Yet when she suggested that he cancel his Oklahoma recitals, he declined to do so.

In March this year Professor William Lyon Phelps of Yale had publicly named Lindsay as one of America's five great living poets, the others being Robinson, Frost, Stephen Vincent Benét and Edna St. Vincent Millay. Considerable notice had been taken of Phelps' nominations, and Elizabeth, exploring every avenue, now wrote to Harriet Monroe, who was appointed to the advisory committee for literature of the Guggenheim Foundation.

Was there any chance for a Guggenheim fellowship for Vachel, Elizabeth asked. This was notwithstanding his age and his desire to do his work in Springfield, and notwithstanding— as she admitted—that a poet so deep in debt for food, rent, taxes and repairs was rapidly approaching a state where only the Pulitzer or the Nobel Prize, notably the latter, could help much.

Harriet promised and gave her assistance, though nothing came of her pleading. She had repeatedly in the past urged Lindsay's name for the Pulitzer Prize, and he had been put forward unofficially by several newspapers as standing in line for the prize for his *Collected Poems*. The award had gone to Miss Millay, to Frost, twice to Robinson, and to the younger Benét, but not to Lindsay; by 1931 he was the only poet on Phelps' list who had never received it.

Lindsay, meanwhile, first in Stillwater, Oklahoma, and then in Tulsa, was fighting an inner battle with the demon that bewildered him. "One thing sure," he wrote to his wife, "I love you more desperately than ever, desperately, desperately, too often despairingly, but surely if love will win there *must* be some kind of a victory in sight."

On his return to her a few days later he seemed almost normal—"serene as a May morning," she reported on April 23 to Paul, whose name she refrained from mentioning to her husband. But already the cause of his last crisis was becoming blurred in Vachel's memory, and she prophesied that the next time the lightning would strike in a new place.

73

In May and early June 1931, Lindsay set down in a small red diary rough notes for a book he was considering writing on Springfield. He had not the strength, nor yet the hope, to sustain the actual writing and indeed, once finished, such a book would be soon forgotten, he wearily reminded himself. And he, the author, would be forgotten too, "forgotten like the Democratic nomination for Vice President after defeat, forgotten like an old Biograph film."

But into an article for the Illinois *State Journal* on June 17 went much of his thought for the book unwritten. PLEADS FOR UNIQUE CITY ran the headline above a picture of him by the *Journal* staff photographer, which showed the strain in his face.

Lindsay himself wrote that he was jealous for his town of all that was first-rate in America, like Washington's Freer Art Gallery, the George Pierce Baker classes in drama at Yale, the new Negro play *The Green Pastures* on Broadway, and the gigantic bell tower recently raised by Edward Bok in Florida. It was Springfield that should inevitably have attracted these institutions, these fair buildings, and others like them.

"Washington," declared Lindsay, "is merely the seat of government. Springfield, the home of Lincoln, is the romantic national capital of the United States."

This summer, his last summer, he submitted to Macmillan an unsolicited new preface for *The Litany of Washington Street*. Harold Latham acknowledged the manuscript, writing that Macmillan had already on hand a very large stock of *The Litany* and his associates in the sales department did not feel a new preface would help to move the book.

Lindsay also offered his publishers a booklet for children containing one long rhyme, *The Ting-a-Ling Jingle of Wall-paper Willy*. Nothing came of this either, but some rambling verses on the topical subject of air conditioning, which had been commissioned as a rush order by the *Ladies' Home Journal* and turned out by him in ten days, were accepted at a good price for October.

Thus he strove to boil the pot, though it was Elizabeth who kept the fire going. For the last six weeks of the school term she had taught an eight-hour day as a substitute in English at the Springfield High School.

And as summer advanced and his little city smoldered on the plain, the familiar need for heights and liberty came over Lindsay. On July 16 he wrote to President Budd of the Great Northern Railway, who had done favors for him in the past, to petition that in exchange for his train fare to Glacier Park and his board while there, he be permitted to describe that beautiful place in a new way—anything he might produce to be at the disposal of the railroad's publicity department. "You have at your command a man who can talk his old head off about anything he looks at. . . ."

"All I need," said Lindsay, "is a change and a rest, a new sight of the Park."

The invitation was not forthcoming. It was nevertheless the opinion of Dr. McMeen that some change and rest outdoors were imperative for Lindsay, and in August Elizabeth went with him to Minocqua in northern Wisconsin, where she settled him at a small hotel in a country of forests and many lakes, and left him, to return herself to Springfield.

In sylvan Minocqua the nights were cool. Lindsay stood by the shore of Lake Kewaguesaga with a bright moon behind him and saw reflected the lights of the Aurora Borealis. He sent Elizabeth a picture postcard of the hotel, which had printed on it, "Meals are just like mother's." But the best sign in town, he told her, was three boards nailed one under the other on a stump in the yard of a neat residence, reading

FISH-WORMS

NIGHT-CRAWLERS AND WORMS FOR SALE

ROOMS

Though he had come north incognito, a reporter from the Minocqua *Times* appeared at the hotel. Lindsay, all ready for a walk, was dressed in a blue work shirt, denim coat, blue corduroy trousers, workman's boots, and a slouch hat from under which he stared through half-shut eyes, his head tipped back, sometimes closing one eye and gazing at his interviewer steadily out of the other.

They strolled together down the highway.

"It seemed like one of those impossible dreams just before one awakens," wrote the young journalist, "this walking with Vachel Lindsay, the outstanding American poet, taking his arm to steer him to the side of the road as the never-ceasing cars whizzed by."

The outstanding American poet, having heard that Bernarr Macfadden had bought *Liberty* from the Chicago *Tribune*, wrote at this time to his wife that distinctly he remembered from his boyhood Macfadden's own original crude little magazine, *Physical Culture*, which "was about the size of this letter with articles on Macfadden not being constipated, Macfadden not having dioreahha however you spell it, Macfadden having a good waist line (photograph of his navel), Macfadden eating fireflies for the phosphorous so he would be prolific and male! photograph of Macfadden in a big diaper and his seventeen girls in a row, and Mrs. Macfadden not so good so you knew the picture was the real thing, articles on how many times a month etc and no photographs, lots of articles like that. . . ."

So, in vein unLindsaylike, he continued through many pages.

He spent $5.00 to make his first and only airplane flight—in a hydroplane over the lake, bidding Elizabeth *at once* to get even with him by painting the kitchen and buying new curtains, linoleum and slip covers. He himself had been "sweating his brains" over how to pay the rent. The best stunt he could think of was sometime this fall, when he had a week free, to dictate to her a pot-boiler prose book in six days.

Meanwhile, Elizabeth, who had paid the rent herself for months past—first by teaching at the High School and this summer by private tutoring—had had no chance, nor yet the heart, to put together her poems for Macmillan. One or two of her poems, however, had appeared in print. Nosing dull and solitary through the magazine rack in the Minocqua drug store, Lindsay came across one in the August *Literary Digest*, reprinted from the *American Mercury*, and instantly he bought the copy and joyfully he scrawled on the page, which he cut out to send her: "The thrill the thrill the thrill of my life! I am *so* proud—my darling—so proud."

In the quiet country evenings he was rereading *Paradise Lost*, which brought back memories of his entire life. He had read it first when he was ten and with each of many readings since made new discoveries: this time that the first two books ought to be read aloud as rapidly as the first section of *The Congo*, the scanning and blank verse ignored; the third and fourth books, like the second section of *The Congo*, in quickening speed and intenser pitch, and the descriptive passages from the fourth book in the slow, entrancing tempo of *The Chinese Nightingale*.

Thus did the tired "apt quotations" disappear, the total music emerge.

He was taking notes and in his diary drew careful diagrams of Milton's universe, showing the course of outcast Satan as he flew, batlike, hither and yon. And now—as never earlier—Lindsay understood what in the jargon of alienists was the "problem" of this Puritan poet, a virgin till his marriage to a girl years younger than he, whose beauty snapped his intellectual pride like brittle, dry twigs, leaving him in humiliation.

"Milton's whole domestic tenderness, helplessness and hopeless dogmatism," Lindsay wrote, ". . . is summed up in the early part of Book VIII, where Eve, after listening through endless cantos, takes a sneak to the flower-garden and lets the men go on chewing the rag—

Eve . . . Rose and went forth among her fruits and flowers—

"Milton, when first married, saw that beautiful wife leave the room when he would have given all his soul either to have gone with her among the flowers or turned the talk so she would have had unity with him and stayed.

"In short, to Milton as to any other man on earth his wife's beauty is worth more than all Heaven all Hell all theory all dogma—though he chokes when he tries to say it.

"God in *Paradise Lost* is merely Milton the bachelor—Adam Milton after one devoted kiss."

Lindsay's plan had been to hike from Minocqua back to Springfield, renewing his contacts with simple country folk and returning to Elizabeth's arms "the real Vachel." But the face of America had changed since he was a pilgrim; there were too many and too powerful cars on the road for a poet to go wandering. In early September he did walk a few miles south to the tiny village of Hazelhurst, putting up at the Log Cabin Inn, which was in the middle of a birch wood on the shore of Lake Katherine and had ten guest cottages around a central dining room.

Here he rented a cottage at $25 a week, to be paid for with the money his wife made by tutoring. He admitted the impulse as "wildest extravagance," and yet for this he was past caring. It was a question of survival. He no longer felt, he admitted to her, "the least *obligation*" to get to work till he began to tour. The important thing was that in Hazelhurst were no cars and no radios, and whichever window he looked out of he could see the blue, peaceful lake or birch trees.

Everybody was in old clothes like his and every face relaxed. At night he heard crickets, which was a lesson for a loud-mouthed man. He built a fire in his own cottage and sat reading desultorily some old novels he found left behind there. He was rediscovering that a vacation can be just that—a vacancy, and do one good without being an adventure. "It is like putting a large blue mat around a small picture, to rest the eye. Every benefit has been negative—a sort of vacuum cleaner run over a dingy rug, called me."

In the reciting season to come, he meant to *raise the standard* of his platform work; he meant to "burn up" his audiences as never before, he promised Elizabeth. Yet he begged her, whenever he should be at home, to play the piano for him, to play it fast so it would outrace in his mind the clickety Pullman cars and the saxophones heard in hotel lobbies and so he could forget every jazz-spewing radio he had ever listened to. "There is some classic music that goes faster than jazz. *Please* find it, darling, *please. . . .*"

But there was no vacation for his heart. "Always it will tear me cruelly for you."

His biting desire and blind jealousy, these if he could he would transform to trust and gentleness. But he had come to marriage with a dream. He had had no training in the actuality of Woman (or of Man). Every moment of his first year of marriage he had spent, as it were, "in a sculptor's studio" adoring a marble statue eternal as Athena, who had about her no human whim.

Now in one after another of the novels he was reading was presented that civilized, modern heroine whose qualities in life confused him. And yet it was to her he must be reconciled, to the real woman and the living wife. "Whatever you are," he wrote to Elizabeth, "you are noble, beautiful, faithful."

Yet still he entreated her on nights when her heart was high to lead him by moonlight to the Acropolis. He needed that marble dream, needed it insatiably. It was as true, as real, as realism.

74

The moon shone no more for Vachel and Elizabeth. The marble dream had crumbled. Almost at once on his return home, Lindsay in a renewed fit of deranged suspicion forbade Elizabeth's father ever again to enter the house (*"my* house") on the ground that Mr. Conner was his enemy and planned to murder him.

Then, having lately, to his extreme pride, been made a member of the Masonic order, Lindsay hung his Masonic insignia on the library wall at 603, with the disordered notion that his fellow Masons would somehow "get" his father-in-law; it was they, the Masons, who had heard the clergyman's plot to kill being hatched over the telephone.

His face was drawn and his eyes haunted, in spite of his weeks of holiday. On November 10, 1931, he turned fifty-two. The *State Journal* mentioned him in its regular list of "Today's Anniversaries" along with Martin Luther and Oliver Goldsmith.

He was on the road again, booked through till spring, again under contract to Feakins, at rates somewhat lower than heretofore—the times were hard—but having since he left home on November 1 earned over $600 of which he had sent not a penny back. His total debts had risen to $4,000, and all hope of restoring the family solvency rested on Elizabeth, who had obtained a position as regional director of a university extension course, a job that promised well.

"I know only two things," she wrote to Paul this month, "that every cent I have earned has gone into food, repairs, clothing, help, milk, medicine etc., that a wife is legally responsible along with her husband for family expenses, and that, even if it were not so, I should make myself responsible until the last cent was paid."

Daily she wrote to her husband. His letters to her enclosed poems and drawings, including a pencil sketch of her from memory, sent from Washington, which showed plainly the shape of her body through a thin garment. "Lady, I would draw your soul," declared the verse accompanying,

> But beauty wraps it veil on veil—
> Even to draw the outer veil
> My fumbling lines must fail.
> Vachel.

This was his last letter to his wife.

To little Susan, now five, he wrote "Dear Daughter, when Mama comes in from her work be especially kind and good to her." And to four-year-old Nicky, "Darling Nicky, as long as Papa is gone you are the man of the house, responsible for your Mama's protection and health."

In New York, on his way to Washington, Lindsay lunched with Latham of Macmillan's, who thought him in "high spirits." In Washington he gave a single recital, on November 17, in the assembly hall of a large school. The audience seemed well disposed till unaccountably, near the middle of the program, a number of people at the back and in the gallery rose and walked out. Those downstairs, sitting toward the front, at first were not aware of this but only observed that Lindsay, while he recited, kept looking up at the gallery with a puzzled and then a distressed expression.

Altogether about two hundred left. The next evening Lindsay dined with friends who had been present, and "he tried hard," writes one of them, a young woman teacher who had known him at Gulf Park, "to rouse himself from what had been a very bitter experience. None of us could understand or explain why it had happened."

Nor in the remnant of his life did Lindsay ever learn the cause of the exodus, which was that the amplifier carrying his voice beyond the first rows had broken down, and when the man, or student, in charge was unable to fix it, he had simply quit, without notifying anyone on the platform of the failure in power.

Lindsay gave another recital in Cleveland, where he spent Thanksgiving with Joy and Ben. They saw that he was weary. On his way to Springfield, he stopped for a sight of Hiram, still unspoiled and dreaming on its Hill. Meeting him at the Springfield station on November 29, Elizabeth noticed a slight thickening of his speech; he seemed dazed as he climbed down from the train and his hands were shaking.

They had supper at home. At once he told her how in Washington a part of his audience had decamped. Some unconventional things he said about George Washington might have offended them, he speculated, though in his heart he had grown convinced that it was his power to hold any audience that had failed—was failing—him. But after an evening of talk by the fire ("which was very sweet," Elizabeth remembered), he appeared soothed and gay, was very much in love with her and most passionate in his addresses.

Later that night, unable to fall asleep, she stole out of their bedroom and tiptoed downstairs to sit alone before the embers in the fireplace.

Next morning, as she was ready to leave for her work, which three times a week took her a few miles out of town, Vachel, to her horror, for he had seemed quite himself, asked: "Who was that man you met downstairs last night? Was it your father coming to blackmail me, or somebody else, or a group of people? You can't fool me, I heard you all talking. What's more, you came upstairs and dressed and painted your face, and brushed your hair three separate times. And you said,

as you went out, 'Don't tell any of them that you are my husband. If you do, they will kill you.'"

He was to recite that very evening, Monday, November 30,
at the First Christian Church. Hastening home in the early-
falling dusk, Elizabeth caught sight of him when she was still
a block away, seated in his little lighted office on the second
floor, working on his program. Cheerful when she entered, he
promised her that that night she would be proud of him.

The church was crowded, and from the pulpit Lindsay
spoke emphatically, assuring his audience that any or all might
leave at any moment it pleased them. Responsive then to the
friendliness flowing back, he recited movingly, though he
stammered a little over a few lines—something he had never
done before—attributing this afterward to the bad light, in
which indeed his face looked ghastly.

As an encore he read *The Lame Boy and the Fairy*, read it
directly to Elizabeth in the front row, his eyes seeking hers,
so that she had to fight to keep back her tears.

> We shall see silver ships.
> We shall see singing ships,
> Valleys of spray today,
> Mountains of foam.
> We have been long away,
> Far from our wonderland.
> Here come the ships of love
> Taking us home.

Lindsay, too, was on the verge of tears, which seldom if
ever happened when he recited, and he cut the poem a little
short. But, "I feel that at last I have won Springfield!" he
exclaimed happily to Dr. Cummings, the minister, after he had
stepped down from the pulpit to mingle with his friends.

Three of his oldest friends (Mary Humphrey was one),
aware of Elizabeth's struggle, had for weeks been making

efforts to find or create a permanent place for Vachel at the University of Illinois, such as a chair of poetry. They also suggested to Susan Wilcox that he might be engaged for a series of lectures at the High School. But after a moment's thoughtful hesitation, Miss Wilcox had firmly vetoed this suggestion.

In the two days that followed his recital Lindsay spent much of his time in bed, enjoying the company of the children. On Thursday morning, December 3, being up and out early, he ran into the Reverend Franklin Conner at the corner of Fifth and Jackson Streets and at the sight of him began to curse, threaten and rave, flourishing his cane and shouting, again on the ground that his father-in-law plotted to kill him.

Utterly convinced of what he had suspected before, that Vachel was both crazy and dangerous, Mr. Conner hurried to the office of Dr. McMeen. Lindsay turned back to the house alone. As Elizabeth was about to leave for the day, he threw his arms around her, kissed her frantically, wept and besought her always to remember, whatever happened, that he loved her.

75

The walls of his prison were closing on Lindsay like the collapsing room in the tale by Poe. It was not his debts—whose extent, said Elizabeth, he grasped only vaguely—nor was it the public neglect of his work, nor even the dimming of his muse that wholly undid him at the last. He was ill.

Coming home on Thursday, December 3, she had found the library desk and table covered with the pictures of her and the children that Vachel carried with him on his tours. The next morning he awoke much depressed. In the afternoon—not having to leave town that day—she put him to bed for a nap, then roused him to go with her to a small tea being given at the Abraham Lincoln Hotel for two young women friends. He got up eager and happy, and at the tea party was talkative and humorous.

Pleading a business appointment, Elizabeth left him. Her appointment, made secretly, was with Dr. McMeen, who acknowledged to her and her father, as they sat in his office, that the situation was very serious. But there was nothing to be done and no danger of violence, said the doctor, so long as Vachel relieved his emotions by talking and shouting.

Lindsay, meanwhile, once more and for the last time went home. Returning, Elizabeth found him back in bed. He came down to supper in his pajamas and dressing gown and again he wept and begged his wife, now that he was an old man, not to wean him away from his childhood memories. Then he moved from the table and lay down on a sofa in the hall and cried. Nothing she could say gave any comfort; indeed, it seemed to her that her reasonable words were not only ineffectual but rapidly becoming all wrong.

With difficulty, she coaxed him upstairs. Sometimes if she sat beside him, just so that he was not alone, it helped, but not this time. Fiercely resenting her maternal attitude, he dismissed her and she went back down, leaving him lying alone in the dark.

She, too, lay down then, on the couch in the library, and presently Lindsay appeared, more wrought up than ever. He sat down near her before the fire in the room where he was born and talked himself into a tearless fury, beginning with his childhood when the boys on the school playground refused to play with him, then on through his life, dwelling on every slight ever administered by anyone anywhere, till the night when she—Woman—took from him his virginity, which was his might. Then he spoke with rage of the years of their marriage in which, in her woman's tyranny, she had broken his man's pride.

All this was interrupted by desperate avowals to her of how hard he had tried to please her and how much he loved her.

While she lay back and closed her eyes, he taxed her anew with the hallucinations of Sunday night and in the next moment cried out that she was indeed the best, the kindest and the noblest human being he had ever known.

He began to rail against Paul, reviving the old charges, and against her father, vowing to foil the plot threatening his life. He must leave his wife and children forever, he exclaimed. He must be free to dream again the dreams of his youth and write his songs. He had often spoken of another begging trip. When Elizabeth asked now who would take care of him, adding that she would never stand in the way of what made him happy but hold herself in readiness to come to him if ever he needed her, he muttered that he would be very well taken care of by "the One who watches over the sparrows."

And he promised her: "When I leave this town you'll never see me again."

"Never, Vachel?" she asked, to which he replied very earnestly: "I'll see you again in *The Golden Book of Springfield*, not before."

The dreadful monologue wore itself out. At the end of three hours, Lindsay stalked upstairs, leaving Elizabeth with a blinding headache and foreboding thoughts. Though his raving was no worse than it had been before, it seemed to her ominous when coupled with his remoteness of the week past and her failure then to reach him. In spite of the doctor's sanguine words, she began to suspect that the break with reality, which she and Paul and her father had feared ever since the spring, might be nearer than they knew.

Yet Vachel and she together had weathered much. She roused herself and went up to their room, where he was reading in bed, looking so austere that she dared not touch or kiss or try to soothe him. He returned no answer to her soft "Goodnight," but after she was in bed he rose and noisily proceeded downstairs. Following, she found him in the dining room setting up her pictures again, and this time "he looked," she says, "calm, happy, peaceful and firm."

When she asked, "Are you all right, dear?" he gazed full in her face and answered: "Yes, dear, I'm quite all right. I'll be up in a little while."

Upstairs again, Elizabeth dropped off to sleep.

In about a quarter of an hour she was awakened by a crash below. Then she heard other noises, then rapid but extraordinarily heavy footsteps thudding along the lower hall, and then Vachel crawling up the almost perpendicular stairs on his hands and knees with unbelievable swiftness and force. Her instant thought was that he had had some hideous seizure, had reverted completely to the subhuman and was coming up to finish off her and the sleeping children.

She sprang out of bed and screamed for Irene, the colored maid. Then she rushed out to intercept Vachel before he could get to the nursery. But the moment she saw him running through the upstairs hall with his hands raised, she knew it was for him she should be afraid. His eyes were distended; his face was white, wild and terrified. She screamed a second time, wordlessly, and at the sound Lindsay fell, just outside the nursery door. He rose by himself, and with both arms around him, she got him into bed, where he asked for water and when she brought it managed to say, in reply to her anguished questioning, "I tried to kill myself by drinking Lysol."

As she was hurrying from the bedroom to call Dr. McMeen, he threw down the glass and shook his fists in the air and gasped out something to the effect that "I got them before they could get me—they can just try to explain this, if they can!"

By the time she returned, he had fallen back half-conscious on the pillows. He did not speak again. He did not groan, though the pain of the burn must have been fearful. Elizabeth and Irene, working frantically together, poured down his throat every emetic prescribed on the bottle, but it was no use. At the doctor's arrival, Lindsay was still alive, with a very faint pulse, but he had turned blue and stopped breathing. He died a few minutes later, at one in the morning of December 5, 1931.

It was the almost immediate decision of Dr. McMeen that the death should be reported as heart failure and nothing else. At his instruction, Elizabeth went down at once to put the house in order and she found that Vachel had arranged all her pictures and the children's around the centerpiece on the dining-room table and lighted two candles before them, which still were burning.

On the shelf in the downstairs bathroom was a stained and empty glass, and a large, nearly empty bottle of Lysol. Lindsay had laid a pillow from the library couch and a little blue coat of Susan's on the bathroom floor, where he planned to die, and on the coat he had propped his favorite picture of Elizabeth, a high-school graduation picture, showing her at seventeen in a dress with ruffles that she had made herself and with flowers at her breast.

In the volume of his *Collected Poems*, which lay on the library table, he had inserted two markers at two poems, *Doctor Mohawk* and *The Hearth Eternal*—his father and his mother.

76

VACHEL LINDSAY DEAD, proclaimed the Springfield paper. The headline streamed across the page.

"Suddenly this morning, from an attack of angina pectoris," began the account below, which dominated all other news. "Dining at home as usual with his family last night and concerning himself with his literary work during the evening, Mr. Lindsay retired at an early hour. At about 12:30 a.m. he complained to Mrs. Lindsay that he was suffering severe pain in the region of the heart. A severe physical collapse followed and he died in Mrs. Lindsay's arms."

The event soon became known over the country. All day the office of the *Journal* and *Register* was flooded by telephone calls from shocked acquaintances. Those whom Lindsay had hailed on the street only the afternoon before now recalled that he had not looked well, while to some it seemed that the mark of death was plain on him even then. But only to his sisters and to Paul was the truth revealed at this time by Elizabeth and the doctor: that he had taken his own life.

Elizabeth later told Masters, who was preparing his biography of Lindsay, that her husband had epilepsy, which at her request Masters did not disclose, and she told the circumstances of his death, which Masters faithfully described. But the "heart attacks," to which Masters—who knew better—declared Lindsay to have been subject, were seizures of another sort. "So far as I know," said Elizabeth then, "there was never anything wrong with Vachel's heart."

And to Harriet Monroe she wrote: "I marvel that Vachel held out as long as he did. It seems to me nothing short of a miracle that he achieved a major work so magnificently, and made anything at all of his personal life, when his burden was bitter, heavy, and much of it inevitable from the first."

Carl Sandburg, writing in the Chicago *Daily News* of December 6, was reminded by his friend's swift departure of General Booth entering into heaven. "With such a stride," wrote Sandburg, "Vachel Lindsay might cross to the afterworld. He deserves a lullaby such as he wrote to Altgeld, 'Sleep softly, eagle forgotten.' As Lindsay so surely remembered Altgeld, there will be others coming after who will remember Lindsay."

Lindsay's face, from which a cast was taken, looked calm and sublime when his body, removed from the house before dawn on the day he died, was brought home that evening. All trace of discontent, despair and the last agony that none but Elizabeth had witnessed was smoothed away.

"To gaze upon this poet's face in death was to admit his greatness," said Harriet Monroe, who had come quickly on from Chicago, and Susan Wilcox, gazing likewise, remembered Vachel at fifteen, aspiring and innocent.

His funeral at the First Christian Church was attended by every prominent person in the city, including the mayor and governor. At the same hour a service was held in all classes of the Springfield High School. On both sides of the altar the space was banked with flowers. While the organ played slow strains and the choir sang softly, Lindsay's body rested in its coffin in the shadow of a great brass altar-cross presented to the church by the *Via Christi* society in memory of his mother (whom many at her death called "the mother of Springfield"), which towered in the center of the chancel, shining and unadorned.

It was a week to the day since he had recited on this spot. Elizabeth was present now on her father's arm, swathed and veiled in black, and Dr. Cummings, who preached the funeral sermon, recalled aloud Lindsay's hopeful words to him: " 'I feel that at last I have won Springfield.' "

Then a cavalcade moved out of town, up the northwest road beside the meadows—over which so many years before the sea-mustang carried the unborn child—and on a slope of Oak Ridge, near Lincoln's tomb and beside the graves of his parents and his infant sisters, the earth closed over what was perishable of this poet.

"Whereas, Nicholas Vachel Lindsay has passed to that world of beauty of which he sang—" ran a resolution of sympathy by the House of Representatives of the State of Illinois,

> And whereas, his literary genius and ability to see beauty where the world ignored it, established him as a world famous poet, and
>
> Whereas, he won not only the affection, but that which is proverbially far more difficult, the acclamation and recognition of his own people, and was proclaimed as their first citizen; and
>
> Whereas, he was beloved by those in all walks of life of every faith and creed; now, therefore, be it
>
> Resolved, that we recognize the loss to the State and Nation and to all his fellow men, in the passing of this great man.

"In memory of Vachel Lindsay," wrote Sara Teasdale, the princess of *The Chinese Nightingale*, who little more than a year later was, like Vachel, to die by her own hand,

> "Deep in the ages," you said, "Deep in the ages,"
> And "To live in mankind is far more than to
>   live in a name"—
> You are deep in the ages now, deep in the ages,
> You whom the world could not break, nor the
>   years tame.

Elizabeth's golden hair turned white in the months that followed. She moved west with the children, and the old house stood empty. Her husband's debts had all been paid, both by her unremitting efforts and by the contributions, amounting to several thousand dollars, of his friends in Springfield and true admirers elsewhere.

Nevertheless, that "America does not deserve her great poets" was an opinion expressed directly or by implication in many of the articles inspired by Lindsay's death. The idea was revived by the appearance in 1935 of Masters' biography in which—with a bitterness born rather of his own than of Lindsay's experience—Masters described his friend's struggle with poverty, the neglect into which his work had fallen, and revealed his suicide. Springfield, too, came in for criticism, though many hands had been raised to help Lindsay in Springfield.

"They were very good to us," said Elizabeth afterward of the people of her husband's town.

In his last years, one of the long-pending civic projects with which Lindsay was in eager accord—for it fulfilled a part of his dream for Springfield—was the creation of a manmade lake south of the city. This had been accomplished, and on July 12, 1935, a beautiful bridge, built to span the new Lake Springfield, was dedicated in a public ceremony to Vachel Lindsay. Willis Spaulding had taken the initiative in purchasing through the subscription of about twenty citizens the noble bust, now cast in bronze, modeled of Lindsay by Voisin, which toward the close of the summer afternoon was unveiled by Elizabeth, who had come from far away.

It was placed at the western end of the bridge, where once the green prairie stretched unbroken, on a spot over which many and many a time Vachel's father rode on horseback when he was a young doctor in Cotton Hill.

Sources and Acknowledgments

This biography was begun with the encouragement of Elizabeth Conner Lindsay and Olive Lindsay Wakefield and could not have been written in its present form without their generous understanding and early help. The foundation of the book is the enormous collection of letters, diaries, unpublished poems and other personal papers belonging or relating to her husband that Mrs. Lindsay made available to me. And I am grateful to Susan Doniphan Lindsay and to Nicholas Cave Lindsay for the interest they have shown in the undertaking; the kindness and active co-operation of Mr. Nicholas Lindsay, his father's literary executor, have been unfailing.

My thanks go also to Mrs. Claribel Sims Conner, the poet's mother-in-law, and to Mrs. Catharine Wakefield Ward, his niece, both of whom turned over to me large collections of family material, and to Miss Eudora Lindsay South, from whose charming unpublished memoir of her cousin Vachel I have taken a number of details about his background and youth.

The book owes something of its atmosphere and many of its facts to the memoirs in manuscript lent to me by Mrs. Conner, Mrs. Octavia Roberts Corneau and Mr. Benjamin H. Kizer. Mr. and Mrs. Kizer gave me access, as well, to their private collection of Lindsay letters and documents, as also did, most generously, Mr. Witter Bynner, Mr. Edward Davison, Mrs. Mary W. Hart, Mr. Frederic G. Melcher, Dr. Leo Leonard Twinem, and Miss Elizabeth Mann Wills.

I have drawn, too, on the vivid personal recollections of Vachel Lindsay of Mrs. Corneau, Miss Wills, Mr. Davison, Mr. Melcher, and Dr. Twinem, and on the recollections of other friends of Lindsay's in Springfield, Chicago, Spokane and New York: Miss Isadora Bennett, Mr. Arthur Fitzgerald, Miss Elizabeth Graham, Mrs. Marion C. Guilbert, Mrs. C. Rudyard Hallowell, Miss Mary Humphrey, Miss Maud Humphrey, Mrs. Francis P. Ide, Mrs. Clarissa Jorgensen, Mrs. Mabel Kizer, Miss Elsie Logan, Miss Marjorie Logan, Mr. Percy Mackaye, Mrs. Mary McKechnie, Mrs. Christine Brown Penniman, Mrs. Gladys S. Puckett, Mrs. Anita Pettibone Schnebly, Miss Sarah K. Smith, Mr. Willis Spaulding, Mme. Eleanor Dougherty Trives, Dr. Elizabeth B. White, and Miss Lucy Williams.

I am indebted to Mrs. Judith S. Bond, Curator of the Harriet Monroe Modern Poetry Collection at the University of Chicago, who allowed me to read and make use of Lindsay's correspondence with Harriet Monroe; to Miss Grace Gilman, Librarian of the Lincoln Library, Springfield, Illinois, for permission to study the Library's collection of Lindsay papers; to Mr. Donald C. Gallup, Curator of the Collection of American Literature at the Yale University Library, for his prompt and courteous attention to my inquiries; and to Dr. Richard Paul Graebel, Pastor of the First Presbyterian Church, Springfield, Illinois, for his suggestions and encouragement.

Grateful acknowledgment is made also to Mrs. A. Joseph Armstrong, Director of the Armstrong Browning Library of Baylor University, for permission to quote from *The Letters of Nicholas Vachel Lindsay to A. Joseph Armstrong*, Baylor University Press, 1940; to Mr. Carl Carmer, for permission to quote in Chapters 41 and 69 from his article "Three Aprils and a Poet," *The Atlantic*, April 1956; to Mrs. Arthur Davison Ficke, for permission to quote in Chapter 26 from an unpublished letter from Arthur Davison Ficke to Vachel Lindsay; to Mr. Robert Graves, for permission to quote in Chapter 47 from an unpublished letter written by him, which describes Lindsay's recital at Oxford University; to Mrs. Edgar Lee Masters, for permission to quote in Chapters 61, 62 and 64 from three unpublished letters from Edgar Lee Masters to Vachel Lindsay, and in Chapter 62 from a review of Lindsay's poems by Mr. Masters, originally published in *The Bookman*, October 1926;

to Mr. John S. Mayfield of Bethesda, Maryland, for permission to quote from his unique collection of reminiscences of Vachel Lindsay gathered by Mr. Mayfield, as a labor of love, after the poet's death and from which come the comments on Lindsay and stories of him by Sherwood Anderson, John Dos Passos, Sinclair Lewis and Upton Sinclair that appear in Chapter 41, the Foreword, and Chapter 39, respectively.

Quotations from editorials in *Poetry, A Magazine of Verse*, June 1913, April 1914, January 1927, November 1928 and January 1932 are made with the kind permission of *Poetry* and of Mr. Henry Rago, editor.

Quotations from *The Shane Quarterly* (now called *Encounter*), April-July 1944, are made with the kind permission of Christian Theological Seminary, Indianapolis, Indiana, and of Mr. Ronald E. Osborn, editor. They are from the articles "Vachel Lindsay, Disciple," by Olive Lindsay Wakefield, and "Vachel Lindsay," by William H. Rothenburger. Mrs. Catharine Wakefield Ward has also given her permission for use of the material from her mother's article, which includes details of Vachel Lindsay's childhood—among them, the catechizing of Vachel and Olive by their teacher in Sunday School, quoted in Chapter 2—and of his years at Hiram. From Mr. Rothenburger's article comes the exchange between Vachel and another premedical student beginning, "Price, if you were sick and I were a doctor. . . ." which is quoted in Chapter 8.

Acknowledgment is made to The Macmillan Company for quotations from the following books by Vachel Lindsay: *Collected Poems*, edition of 1937; *The Chinese Nightingale and Other Poems*, 1917; *Adventures While Preaching the Gospel of Beauty*, 1914; *The Art of the Moving Picture*, 1915; *A Handy Guide for Beggars*, 1916; *The Golden Book of Springfield*, 1920.

Acknowledgment is made to Appleton-Century-Crofts, Inc., for quotations from the following books by Vachel Lindsay: *Going-to-the-Sun*, 1923; *Going-to-the-Stars*, 1926; *The Candle in the Cabin*, 1926.

Acknowledgment is made to Henry Holt & Company, Inc., for permission to quote the first three lines of "Chicago," by Carl

Sandburg, *Chicago Poems*, 1916, and the two lines beginning, "Home is the place . . ." from "The Death of the Hired Man," by Robert Frost, *North of Boston*, 1914.

Acknowledgment is made to Harcourt, Brace & Company for permission to quote two brief excerpts from the letters of Sara Teasdale to Louis Untermeyer, from the book *From Another World* by Louis Untermeyer, copyright 1939, by Harcourt, Brace & Company.

The first two lines of "Sonnet XIX" by Edna St. Vincent Millay, copyright 1921-1948 by Edna St. Vincent Millay, from *Collected Poems*, Harper & Brothers, are quoted by permission of Norma Millay Ellis.

Acknowledgment of brief quotation is made to the authors and publishers of the following sources: *Collected Poems of Sara Teasdale*, Macmillan, 1937, for lines from Miss Teasdale's poems "Come," "Broadway," and "In Memory of Vachel Lindsay," which are quoted in Chapters 38, 39 and 76; *Companions on the Trail*, by Hamlin Garland, Macmillan, 1931, for the remark by Garland to Lindsay's parents, beginning, "Your son is a genius. . . ." quoted in Chapter 29; *My House of Life, an Autobiography*, by Jessie Rittenhouse, Houghton Mifflin Company, 1934, for Miss Rittenhouse's words about Lindsay's life with his family: "It was a revelation to me of what lay behind his work," which are quoted in Chapter 44; "My Tow-Headed Pupil," by Susan Wilcox, *Elementary English Review*, May 1932, for the dialogue between Vachel and Miss Wilcox, quoted in Chapter 5; *Tramping With A Poet in the Rockies*, by Stephen Graham, Appleton, 1922, for two remarks by Lindsay to Graham, quoted in Chapters 24 and 50; *Vachel Lindsay, Adventurer*, by Albert Edmund Trombly, Lucas Brothers, 1929, for the exchange between Vachel and his father beginning, " 'Then what will you do?' asked Dr. Lindsay. . . ." quoted in Chapter 2.

Of permanent value to anyone interested in Lindsay's life and work are *Vachel Lindsay, Adventurer*, by Albert Edmund Trombly, Lucas Brothers, 1929, which is a brief biography and critical study, and *Vachel Lindsay, A Poet in America*, by Edgar Lee

Masters, Scribner's, 1935. Mr. Masters' thoughtful book was the first full-length biography of Lindsay to appear.

City of Discontent, by Mark Harris, Bobbs-Merrill, 1952, a fictionalized account of Lindsay's life, is remarkable for its sympathetic picture of the poet.

Tramping With A Poet in the Rockies, by Stephen Graham, Appleton, 1922, is a delightful description of Lindsay's and Graham's climb in Glacier Park.

From Another World, by Louis Untermeyer, Harcourt, Brace, 1939, has revealing chapters on Lindsay and Sara Teasdale by a fellow poet who was close to them both.

And of the many excellent articles on Lindsay, one recommended for its biographical interest is "Vachel Lindsay in Spokane," by Emmett L. Avery, *The Pacific Spectator*, Summer 1949.

Index

443